John Surratt

ALSO BY FREDERICK HATCH

*The Lincoln Assassination Conspiracy Trial
and Its Legacy* (McFarland, 2015)

*Protecting President Lincoln:
The Security Effort, the Thwarted Plots
and the Disaster at Ford's Theatre* (McFarland, 2011)

John Surratt
Rebel,
Lincoln Conspirator,
Fugitive

Frederick Hatch

McFarland & Company, Inc., Publishers
Jefferson, North Carolina

LIBRARY OF CONGRESS CATALOGUING-IN-PUBLICATION DATA

Names: Hatch, Frederick, 1945– author.
Title: John Surratt : rebel, Lincoln conspirator, fugitive / Frederick Hatch.
Description: Jefferson, North Carolina : McFarland & Company, Inc., Publishers, 2016. | Includes bibliographical references and index.
Identifiers: LCCN 2016024106 | ISBN 9781476665139 (softcover : acid free paper) ∞
Subjects: LCSH: Surratt, John H. (John Harrison), 1844–1916. | Lincoln, Abraham, 1809–1865—Assassination.
Classification: LCC E457.5 .H3249 2016 | DDC 973.7092 [B] —dc23
LC record available at https://lccn.loc.gov/2016024106

BRITISH LIBRARY CATALOGUING DATA ARE AVAILABLE

ISBN (softcover) 978-1-4766-6513-9
ISBN (ebook) 978-1-4766-2546-1

© 2016 Frederick Hatch. All rights reserved

No part of this book may be reproduced or transmitted in any form or by any means, electronic or mechanical, including photocopying or recording, or by any information storage and retrieval system, without permission in writing from the publisher.

Front cover: Albumen print of John Surratt taken between 1861 and 1865 (Library of Congress)

Printed in the United States of America

*McFarland & Company, Inc., Publishers
Box 611, Jefferson, North Carolina 28640
www.mcfarlandpub.com*

To the Surratt Society of Clinton, Maryland,
and especially to Laurie Verge, Joan Chaconas,
and Sandra Walia. Their dedication and
hard work helps keep history alive.

Acknowledgments

The planning and writing of this book has stretched over a period of more than thirty years. The greater part of that time consisted of the accumulating and evaluating of great masses of material in books, articles, documents, private and public papers, and conversations with others. Some travel was involved: visiting public and private sites and institutions and attending conferences. Through all of that, the assistance provided by individuals and institutions has proven to be gladly given and often invaluable. It would be impossible to list all of the individuals and institutions that have contributed information and encouragement, but certain ones do stand out and must be given my special thanks. In doing so, it is not intended that the contributions of others has not been greatly appreciated.

I want to give my special thanks to the following, listed alphabetically: David R. Barbee, John C. Brennan, Joan L. Chaconas, William C. Edwards, James O. Hall, William Hanchett, John Howard, Alfred Isacsson, Michael W. Kauffman, Steven G. Miller, Floyd E. Risvold, Richard E. Sloan, Edward Steers, Jr., Gene Thomas, Laurie Verge, Sandra Walia, and Frank J. Williams.

Institutions that were especially helpful include the following: Georgetown University, Washington, D.C.; Library of Congress, Washington, D.C.; Mariner's Museum, Newport News, Virginia; Maryland Historical Society, Baltimore, Maryland; National Archives, Washington, D.C.; Surratt Society, James O. Hall Research Center, Clinton, Maryland; U.S. Department of State, Washington, D.C.; University of Arizona, Tucson; University of California at Los Angeles; University of Texas, Austin.

Table of Contents

Acknowledgments vi
Preface 1
Introduction 3

1. Beginnings 5
2. Rebel Courier 14
3. Confederates in Canada 27
4. Conspiracy 38
5. Assassination 63
6. Hiding 85
7. Flight 98
8. Capture and Escape 113
9. In Custody 130
10. A Jury of His Peers 150
11. A Long Twilight 168

Chapter Notes 193
Bibliography 201
Index 207

The immortals know no care, yet the lot they spin for man is full of sorrow; on the floor of Jove's palace there stand two urns, the one filled with evil gifts, and the other with good ones. He for whom Jove the lord of thunder mixes the gifts he sends, will meet now with good and now with evil fortune; but he to whom Jove sends none but evil gifts will be pointed at by the finger of scorn, the hand of famine, will pursue him to the ends of the world, and he will go up and down the face of the earth, respected neither by gods nor by men.
—Homer, Iliad, Book XXIV

Preface

It was probably the most sensational crime in American history. The president of the United States was struck down in the hour of his greatest triumph—the end of the bloodiest war in American history—by a band of conspirators who became the center of the nation's attention for months, culminating in a trial, execution, and imprisonment for a relative handful of suspects and leaving behind questions and doubts that linger to this day. One of the foremost members of that conspiracy was John Harrison Surratt, Jr. The only one of the named suspects to escape swift justice became the most wanted fugitive in the world, the object of a manhunt across three continents. His story is a tangled tale of uncertainty, of twists and turns of fate, and of an unexpected outcome. It is a fascinating story, combining political intrigue, murderous conspiracy, pursuit, and legal drama to rival the best mystery and adventure stories. The elements of epic adventure are all here: crime and punishment, fearful flight and relentless pursuit, the drama of a great courtroom battle, and the efforts of an aging man to rationalize, if not to escape, the recklessness of his sensational youth.

John Surratt's story has been told before, of course, but previous accounts have left out much detail, and have often tended to accept rumor and fabrication as fact. Hard questions that should have been asked have too often been glossed over. One could argue that whenever the actual facts are unknown or unobtainable, those parts of the story should be left alone. This study, however, rejects that easy way out and delves into areas of uncertainty to a greater depth than any known previous effort. When the facts are missing and unlikely ever to be known, that must be acknowledged; but theories and speculation, even when not supported by hard facts, may still be worth exploring. In the process of such exploration, new discoveries can occasionally be made. Whenever this has been done in this telling of the story, the reader has been informed that I am probing the shadows at the edge of the stage, well beyond the glare of the spotlights.

In the course of my research for this book, there have been a few new discoveries, and it has been thought desirable to include certain details of background information to help the reader have a better understanding of the story. It is for the reader to decide upon the ultimate value of such background, but it is hoped he will accept the author's judgment that these occasional excursions away from the main pathway are worth pursuing for the goal of a broader and deeper understanding.

The moral of the story of the life of John Surratt is left to the judgment of the reader to decide. Like us, he had no choice of time, place, or circumstance into which he was born, and, as we will show in these pages, chance and accident played as great a role in shaping his life as they do for any of us. Whatever we ultimately think of the man and of the actions he took in his life, our judgment of him—whether broad or narrow—will ultimately reflect as much upon ourselves as it does on him.

Introduction

The huge and horrendous Civil War, which had raged across America for four years of bitterness and misery, anxiety and uncertainty, heroism and corruption, and blood—seemingly endless rivers of blood, staining the landscape indelibly—was finally drawing to a close. In the North, victory celebrations were already underway, and contending plans for the reconstruction of the Union as "one nation, indivisible" were being argued and considered. In the South, hopes and plans had been shattered, and there were many who could not accept an outcome that seemed to say all of their courage and sacrifice had come to nothing. In spite of the obvious defeat, some Southerners and sympathizers with their cause simply could not bring themselves to accept that all was lost. Desperate people sought ways to reduce, if not to eliminate, the painful sting of Southern defeat.

Although there were many heroes who stood out on both sides, it was beginning to be realized that one in particular had risen among them, and possibly above them too. The tall, thin, homely figure of Abraham Lincoln could smile again, could laugh and rejoice among his people, people who were at last beginning to realize how big a role he had played and how much they owed him. Many cares had weighed him down, as they had all the people of North and South alike. Many tears had run down Lincoln's sunken cheeks. Many agonized cries had escaped the mouths of these people and of the one among them who had, perhaps, borne the heaviest burden. At last, the sun was rising again, shining more brightly, it seemed, than it had for many a year.

Where the shouts of joy from the North met the bitter tears from the South, geographically and in the hearts of the people, the desperate last hopes of the Southern rebels coalesced. There had to be one last chance, one more blow to strike, a blow made more devastating by the strength of that desperation. The target of the blow was never in doubt. It fell to a small group of conspirators, young men who had not hitherto been in the forefront of the Confederate effort, to rise to the ultimate height in the minds of their people and in their own minds, searching for the stolen greatness of the destroyer, he who would achieve the loftiest position among his people—with or without their approval and consent—and in rising in the estimation of others achieve the greatest boost within themselves that could be possible. Now, at the very end, they would grasp the crown of greatness and place it upon their own heads, to shine across the ages, however awkwardly and uncertainly it fit them.

One of these young would-be heroes, John Harrison Surratt, Jr., is the principal subject of this book. We will see how, by both his own efforts and the rushing tide of history, this unlikely young man came, however briefly, to attain the center of the stage of history, to bask in the glare of its spotlight, only to be burned and nearly consumed by it.

Many biographies deal with individuals who achieve their prominence in the middle or even toward the end of their lives, as their early years often passed in relative obscurity. Surratt, however, was just the opposite. He was only 21 years old when he suddenly became famous—or infamous, depending on the reader's standards and point of view—and became, like a supernova in the heavens, a star that glows with unexpected brightness but lasts only very briefly before cooling and disappearing. Almost consumed by that explosion of notoriety, Surratt managed to survive and to achieve what most of us would call a "normal" life. It might have been normal outwardly, but, as we shall see, he was never entirely able to live down the damage done in his reckless youth. The lesson of his life is, perhaps, one we all can recognize: while "man's reach must exceed his grasp," the strain of that reaching can leave lifelong soreness and regret.

John Surratt has been described by some as the only one of the Lincoln assassination conspirators to have escaped the consequences of his act. This idea, however, expresses only a very superficial assessment. While Surratt never felt the hangman's rope around his neck and did not have as long to languish without hope in a hellish prison, it cannot be justifiably said that he escaped punishment. Punishment comes in many shapes and forms and falls upon most offenders, however unevenly.

The story of Surratt's life contains many twists and turns. Sometimes it roars along with inexorable force. Other times the stream becomes diverted, almost coming to a standstill. Many other streams run into and through it, adding their share of both strength and complexity. In the end, it runs into the great sea of common humanity, dissipating and dissolving. Surratt lived in the nineteenth century, the age of Romanticism. In some ways his story shares elements from the great romantic novels of that period. It is a cliché that reality can sometimes imitate fiction, but, like all clichés, there is to be found in it a grain or two of truth.

1

Beginnings

For centuries, the Pyrenees Mountains have formed the border between France and Spain. The saw-like ridges of these mountains are the origin of the word serre, which in modern French can mean close, compact, tight, clenched, concise, terse, or serried. Serrer can mean to press, to tighten, to squeeze, to contract, to crowd, or to grow tighter. French towns in the region bear the names Serres, Sarre, Serret, Sarrat, referring to high ground. The Latin word serra means a saw for cutting, thus having tooth-like ridges. In Spanish, the word is sierra, with diente de sierra meaning saw-toothed. The English word serried, meaning standing close together, probably derived from the French serre.[1]

It is possible that the ancestors of the Surratts in America were among the French Protestants who migrated to the New World to escape religious persecution. If they chose to settle south of the French colonies established in what is now Canada, perhaps it was because of the desire to seek a milder climate. Prince George's County, in the British colony of Maryland, was laid out in 1696 and included most of the western part of what is now the state of Maryland. The county was eventually divided into several other counties and the District of Columbia.[2]

The earliest documented resident of this area named Sarratt was Kathrine, widow of Joseph Sarratt, who was named administrator of Joseph's estate on January 18, 1715. Neighbors Samuel Weighel and Evan Jones also contributed to the cost of the bond, a formidable 60 pounds sterling. Joseph Sarratt's son, Joseph, Jr., and his wife, Mary, owned property called "Thomas' Inheritance," lying partially in Prince George's County and also Charles County to the south. Joseph Jr., and Mary gave this land to their son Alphonsis in 1767. By this time, Alphonsis and his wife, also named Mary, had moved northward to a property named Oxon Hundred, in what is now the District of Columbia. They apparently found employment on the estate of the Neale family, "Foxhall."[3]

The census of 1790 lists Francis Sarratt and two "free white males of sixteen years and upward including heads of families ... six free white males under sixteen years" and two "free white females." Francis Sarratt is probably Alphonsis. Vestry minutes of St. John's Parish at Broad Creek list Ann Saratt and her husband, Alphonsis.[4] "Heirs of Francis [or Alphonsis] and Ann conveyed their title to "Thomas's Inheritance Enlarged to Caleb Thomas" in 1810. The names of the six Surratt heirs were Josias, Dickerson, John, Nathaniel, Henry B., and Samuel: "It seems likely that one of the six heirs of Ann and Francis Surratt must have been the father of John H. Surratt" [Sr.]. "The 1790 Census lists a neighbor of Francis Surratt named John Harrison.[5] Nathaniel, John, and Samuel served in the War of 1812, Nathaniel in the 17th Regiment of Maryland Militia; John in the 34th Regiment of Maryland Militia; and Samuel in the 1st Regiment of the District of Columbia Militia."[6]

With the end of the war in 1814, members of the Surratt family began moving westward to Ohio and beyond. The Ohio River facilitated such movement, affording faster and easier travel than over land. Much of the new states and territories of Ohio, Indiana, Kentucky, Tennessee, Illinois and beyond were at that time undeveloped wilderness. By the time the census of 1820 was taken, the only Surratt remaining in Prince George's County or the District of Columbia was John Harrison Surratt [Sr.], aged about seven. He was living with the family of Richard and Sarah T. Neale.

Although young John must have been a grandson of Alphonsis and Ann Surratt, no record has been found of who his parents were or why they left him behind when they moved west. It is possible that John was illegitimate.[7]

The census of 1820 lists Richard Neale of the Spalding District, Prince George's County, Maryland, and mentions a white male under the age of ten years. It is thus accepted that John Harrison Surratt, Sr., was born around the year 1813. The census of 1830 again lists a male under the age of 20 living with the Neales. Richard Neale was born around 1770, being over 40 when he married. The large estate, called "Foxhall," he inherited occupied land today partially in the District of Columbia and overlapping into Prince George's County, Maryland. Richard Neale married Sarah Talbot on June 20, 1813. Sarah was a good deal younger than her husband, having been born in 1792.[8]

Archibald Jenkins (c. 1780–1825) married Elizabeth Ann Webster (1794–1878), daughter of James Gibbs Webster (1768–1858), and Sarah Webster, on January 4, 1821. Archibald became a prominent citizen of Prince George's County, Maryland. His father, Zadoc Jenkins (?–1811), had worked the land of the Calvert family, a parcel called "His Lordship's Kindness." Some of this property was later purchased by Archibald. Today most of this land makes up Andrews Air Force Base, where the presidential aircrafts are based. The children of Archibald and Elizabeth Jenkins were John Zadoc Jenkins (1822–1896), Mary Elizabeth Jenkins (1823–1865), and James Archibald Jenkins (1825–1903). Mary Elizabeth's exact birth date is unknown, but it is believed to have been in May or June of 1823.[9]

Archibald Jenkins died in the fall of 1825, when his daughter Mary was only two years old. Mary's mother assumed the leadership of the family, having the assistance of several slaves of varying ages. Family stories say that Mary's grandmother provided money for Mary's education and that Mary had private tutors at home and later in Washington, D.C. When she was 12 years old her mother enrolled her in a school, the "Academy for Young Ladies," run by the Sisters of Charity of St. Mary's Church in Alexandria, Virginia. Although the Jenkins family was Protestant, Mary decided while attending this school to become a Roman Catholic and remained a devout Catholic for the rest of her life. She adopted the name Eugenia, after the saint whose feast day is December 25. Church records mention Mary Eugenia Jenkins as a sponsor of Henry Randolph Webster, a distant relative, on August 26, 1838. There has been confusion over her middle name ever since, with many authors believing the middle initial, "E," stood for Eugenia, instead of her actual name, Elizabeth.

Father John Smith, S.J., had persuaded the Sisters of Charity to establish a school for girls at St. Mary's Catholic Church, Alexandria, in 1832. There exists a receipt, dated November 26, 1835, acknowledging $25 paid by Mrs. Elizabeth Jenkins for three months' board and tuition for 12-year-old Mary Elizabeth Jenkins. It is signed "Sister Bernardina," who was in charge of the school. The Daughters of Charity show a Sister Bernard Boyle (1803–1879) who was at St. Francis, Alexandria, in 1833 but who was not called "Bernardina." We cannot say whether Sister Boyle was the "Sister Bernardina" who signed the receipt for Mrs. Jenkins. There was a Sister Eugenia McGinnis (1812–1872) at the school in 1836 and 1837, and we can wonder if young Mary Jenkins became friendly with this sister and decided to adopt the name "Eugenia" as much for Sister Eugenia as for the saint. School records do not say how long Mary remained at the school, but it was closed in 1839, and it is possible she attended until that date.

The Academy for Young Ladies was located at Fairfax and Duke streets in Alexandria, which was then part of the District of Columbia but is now part of the State of Virginia. Subjects offered at this school included French, music, drawing and painting, English, orthography (spelling), grammar, composition, writing, arithmetic, geography, ancient and modern history, natural philosophy, chemistry, bookkeeping, and plain and fancy needlework. French instruction included having the students speak the language both in class and during recreation periods. Emphasis was on the "correct principles of literature and morality." The Sisters of Charity had been founded at Emitsburgh, Frederick County, Maryland, in 1809. They were incorporated by the general assembly of Maryland in 1816. Sister Bernardina headed the school throughout its existence, from 1832 to 1839.

John Surratt was deeded one-half of the land "whereon I at present reside," called "Pasture and Gleaning," by Richard Neale on March 13, 1835. Surratt paid $5 and "Love and affection," and, in addition to the land, Mr. Neale deeded John four slaves named Henry, Gurty, Alfred and Louisa, as well as one-half of all stock and monies owed to Neale as an heir to Foxhall estate. Thus, John Surratt must have felt he was in a good position to be married and start a family of his own.[10] A marriage license was issued on August 6, 1840, to John H. Surratt and M. Elizabeth Jenkins in the District of Columbia. The marriage may have been performed at St. Peter's Church, at 313 2nd Street, SE, near C Street. This is near the present-day Madison Building of the Library of Congress.

The three children of the Surratts were all baptized at St. Peter's Church. The firstborn, a son, was Isaac Douglas Surratt, born June 2, 1841, and baptized July 7, 1841. The second child was Elizabeth Susanna Surratt, born January 1, 1843, and baptized December 10, 1843. The third child was named John Harrison Surratt, Jr., the principal subject of this book, who born on April 13, 1844, and baptized on September 20, 1847.

John Jr.'s exact birth date was called into question by the records of the family doctor, John Henry Bayne (1803–1870). The doctor charged ten dollars for a night visit on April 10, 1844, with additional visits on April 14, 16, and 17, charging much less for these later visits. With no record of a visit on April 13 and such a large fee on April 10, it raises the question of whether John Jr.'s birth may have actually been on April 10. Four years later the ten dollars still had not been paid.[11]

On May 24, 1842, Richard Neale deeded to John H. Surratt, Sr., an additional 236 acres from the tract called "Foxhall." Regardless of whether John Surratt, Sr., was Neale's nephew or only his ward, the Neale family was very generous to Surratt, who now had a wife and child. The 100 acres previously given to Surratt was now expanded to 336 acres, partly in the District of Columbia and partly in Prince George's County, Maryland. John Surratt was eager to acquire more land. On October 25, 1843, he borrowed $450 from John Bayne of Washington, D.C. This loan must have been required to cover an agreement made the previous day, October 24, to pay William A. Kerby and his wife Henrietta $800 for another 119 acres of the Foxhall tract. This increased the Surratt holdings to 455 acres. Surratt was able to pay Bayne the $450 by December 1847. One dollar in 1852 would be the equivalent in buying power to about $29 in today's money.

Richard Neale was also adding to his land holdings. He bought land bordering on his own property, part of a tract called "Pasture and Gleaning," in 1837. The Neales were living on this land at the time of John Surratt's marriage to Mary Jenkins. The Surratts settled on it as well. Richard Neale died around September of 1843, and Sarah Neale remained a neighbor of the Surratts until her death, about two years after her husband's. John Surratt, always interested in acquiring more land, purchased 18 acres of the tract "Little Gleaning" on August 8, 1846, paying the owners, Henry A. and Elianor H. Callis, $100. On March 4, 1847, John acquired an additional 96 acres of "Pasture and Gleaning" from Rachal A. Jarber for $50.[12]

For a time in the late 1840s and early 1850s, the Surratts lived in a mill house, with the mill for grinding grain close by. This house burned down, and the Surratts accepted the hospitality of Mrs. Annie Hoyle, a neighbor. The mill became the property of a man named Condon, who built a new house of brick, replacing the frame house that had burned. The mill itself burned down during the Civil War. It appears that a mill was built on or near the location of the original mill, according to an 1878 atlas.

In a deed dated May 6, 1845, Sarah C. Neale signed over all property she "held in common with John H. Surratt, consisting of about ninety-six acres in Washington, D.C., the 'Pasture and Gleaning' property, and a Negro woman of about forty-five, named Patty." John Surratt's three children are mentioned in this document. Mrs. Neale left personal property consisting of three slaves as follows: One Negro named Nace, about 20 years old, who was to be freed when he was 35, and one featherbed, to Isaac D. Surratt; a Negro named George, about 21 years old, to John H. Surratt, Jr., George to be freed at age 35; and one Negro girl named Jane, about 15 years old, to Elizabeth "Anna" Surratt to be her slave for life.

The census of 1850 listed not only the Surratt family but four additional residents: William Chinn, age 28; James Barrett, age 33; Sarah Barrett, age 30; and William Barrett, age 5. The occupation of John Surratt, Sr., is given as "farmer." There were also William Chinn, "miller," and six slaves: one male, age 38, one male, age 32, one male, age 28, one male, age 26; one male, age 23; one female, age 18. Some of these slaves may have been rented from other slave owners.[13]

When the Calvert family began to sell off "His Lordship's Kindness," around 1851, John Surratt, ever acquisitive, began to purchase the land to add to his holdings inherited from the Neales, as well as what he had already purchased, mostly on credit, from others. He bought 280 acres in Prince George's County, Maryland, on January 1, 1852. This land included the area now consisting of downtown Clinton. Surratt gave Charles B. Calvert two notes, each for $398.50. The land included the intersection of the Marlboro-Piscataway road with the New Cut road, now called Highways 223 and 381. This intersection was a good place to build a tavern, which also became the Surratt family home. Jeremiah Townshend was hired to build the structure (Surratt failing to pay Townshend in full for his work). On September 23, 1852, John Surratt obtained a license for an "ordinary," or pub, and purchased wines, liquors and cigars. He was operating on credit and never paid his debts.[14]

The Maryland General Assembly created the Ninth Election District in 1854. The new district, part of Prince George's County, was bounded on the north by Centreville and Upper Marlborough, on the east by Piscataway Creek, to the south about two miles past Surratt's tavern, and on the west by the road which ran north-south through Allentown. The Surratt tavern was a little south of the center of the district. The Ninth Election District was soon called "Surratt's Election District," and the little settlement that began to grow around the tavern became known as Surrattsville. "Surratt's Hotel," as the tavern was called, was designated as the polling place for the election district. On October 6, 1854, the United States Post Office Department designated the tavern as a U.S. Post Office, with John H. Surratt, Sr., named postmaster.[15]

The two-story frame structure in Surrattsville was both a home and a business for the

Surratt Tavern, Surrattsville (now Clinton), Maryland, was the family home of the Surratts from 1852 to 1864. Author's collection.

Surratt family. Entering through the front porch, on the long side facing the road, one was in the center hall. To the left was the tavern, with a small bar, behind which were boxes for mail sorting. Across the hall was a parlor, or sitting room. Behind these two rooms was the public dining room, behind the tavern, and the family dining room, behind the parlor. The kitchen adjoined the family dining room. The upper floor was reached by a staircase at the back of the entry hall. This floor originally consisted of bedrooms, for both the family and travelers, and storage space.

It would seem that John Surratt and his family were prospering in their new tavern-hotel-home, but their property was based on borrowing. It was commonplace to borrow money in those days, and the practice was even viewed as a positive factor in creating and confirming relationships among one's neighbors. Being in debt, even deeply in debt, was not unusual and was not viewed as a social negative. Surratt gave Jeremiah Townshend a promissory note for $278.21, the balance of what he owed the builder for the tavern. Surratt performed a financial balancing act, selling one property to develop another. The 114 acres where the family had lived in the District of Columbia, "Pasture and Gleaning," was sold to Augustus A. Gibson for $500 late in 1853. Part of this deal was Surratt's acquisition of a house in Washington at 541 H Street, NW, a house that would figure prominently in the lives of John Surratt's family in years to come.[16]

Upon establishing his tavern, Surratt amply provisioned it with 77¾ gallons of whiskey, ten gallons of brandy, five gallons of wine, 21 pounds of sugar, and about 550 cigars, ordered from Jackson Brother & Company. One of the elder Surratt's problems stemmed from his practice of helping himself to his tavern's stores of drink. He also indulged his passion for hunting, keeping dogs for the hunting of foxes and deer and becoming very well known by his neighbors, whose own hunting dogs would often answer Surratt's call to his dogs.[17]

John Surratt, Sr., continued his practice of buying land, making deals involving trading, and operating on credit, Surratt also extended credit to his customers at the tavern-hotel, where a night's lodging could be had for around 25 cents. He kept the tavern open even on Sundays. In addition to room and board, Surratt expanded his operations at Surrattsville to include a blacksmith shop, built around the end of 1854, and a corn storage house, granary, and carriage house, all built by early 1857. Also completed by mid-1857 were a hog pen and a tobacco shed for drying harvested tobacco leaves. Surratt's account book lists only those to whom he extended credit, but it does tell us that most of his customers were local people. Of the 40 different surnames listed in Martenet's Map of Prince George's County, 29 of the same names are in the account book.[18]

The marriage of John Surratt to Mary Jenkins appears to have been a less-than-entirely-happy one. John indulged himself with drink and provided little help in maintaining a home for his wife and children. Mary's willingness to send her children to boarding school may indicate that she did not want them to be exposed growing up to the atmosphere at the tavern.

Two letters Mary Surratt wrote to Joseph Maria Finotti (1817–1879), a priest who oversaw the establishment of St. Ignatius Church at Oxon Hill in Prince George's County, have survived and tell of her concerns for her children, especially Isaac and John Jr. Mary had met Father Finotti between 1847 and 1852. He moved to Boston in 1852, so she could communicate with him only through letters. She obviously regarded him as a friend and sought his advice and aid in bringing up her children. The two letters are dated in early 1855, when Isaac was 13 and John, Jr., was between 10 and 11:

> I could always go to [you] in confidence in all my trubles, and so far from getting less it seams as though they come two for one evry day. Mr. Surratt has be come so that he is drunk on evry occasion and are more and more dis-agreeable evry day.... [Anna] is delighted with her teachers and improves very fast. I am trying evry day to make some arrangement for Isaac to go to [s]chool but I can not tell how it will be yet as you know how often misfortune has visit us in the last few years.... [I]t seams the whole charge of the [children has fawlen on me I must trust in God and do the best I can for them.... [I]t is time for him to leave this publick house [the Surratt tavern] as you know how many temptations thire is all ways before him ... [and] you know that I always have the burden to stand up to while my husband wollars in the mire of drunkenness.

Four months later, Mary wrote to Father Finotti in reply to a letter she received from him:

> Annah is still with the Miss Martins [school in Frederick, Maryland] and improving very fast she begins to play very well, and her teachers think her very apt she is getting along very well with French; she intends to

Mary Elizabeth Surratt, mother of John H. Surratt, Jr. (Surratt House Museum/MNCPPC, Clinton, Maryland).

write to you very soon; Isaac is at St. Thomas [s]chool it is a [s]chool that has been commenced in the last year under the direction of the Rev Father Wiggett.... [H]e is im prooving very fast I hope he may be come a Preast Johny I hope thire may be some opening that I may get him to [s]chool when the [s]chool commences after the vacation for I have found out long ago a publick house is now place for children.

There are hints in these two letters that Mary Surratt may have had strong feelings for Father Finotti. It was rumored by the Surratts' neighbors that Finotti had been transferred to Boston to avoid scandal.[19]

Anna attended St. Mary's Female Institute in Bryantown, Maryland, operated by Mary and Winfred Martin, beginning around 1854. Southern Maryland was mostly rural, and many of its inhabitants knew the Surratt family. Dr. George Dyer Mudd (1826–1899), a cousin of Dr. Samuel Alexander Mudd (1833–1883), who would later become involved with John Wilkes Booth (1838–1865), spoke of knowing John Surratt, Jr.:

> I knew him very well. He made my house ... his stopping place whenever he visited his sister, who was at the neighboring seminary. John had stopped with me many times. In those days, before the war, he was as modest and nice a young fellow as one could meet, but after the war began his tavern was made the stopping place of spies and go-betweens, and he finally mustered up courage to cross the Potomac River [into rebel territory]. After that he was a changed man. He had become self-important. He wanted to distinguish himself, to have money, to be talked about.

Dr. George Mudd was also asked about John's mother, Mary Surratt:

> Mrs. Surratt was a respectable, plain wife and widow, whose course of life would have been happy enough but for her intemperate thought and speech on questions of politics and the war. She worked herself up into a passion, hardened her nature, and so she too was ripe for Booth to come along and make prey of her, as he did of the others.[20]

The two boys, Isaac and John Jr., attended St. Thomas Manor, Chapel Point, and Bryantown, in Charles County, Maryland. Mary had taken the opportunity to speak to a visiting priest, Father Nota, who stopped at the tavern on December 30, 1854. Nota spoke to father Bernadine F. Wiget (1821–1883), Father Superior of St. Thomas Manor. Thus began a friendship between Mrs. Surratt and Father Wiget that would last the rest of her life. St. Thomas Manor had to close in 1857, and the anxious Mrs. Surratt asked Father Wiget to help her boys. John Surratt, Sr.'s drinking was a continuing and worsening problem, and Mary did not want her sons to fall under their father's influence. Father Wiget helped 16-year-old Isaac get a job in Baltimore. John Jr., had to return home, and his mother's fears seemed in danger of coming true. Finally, John Jr., was able to enter St. Charles College at Ellicott's Mill, Maryland, on September 2, 1859.

St. Charles College was founded by Charles Carroll of Carrollton (1737–1832), a signer of the Declaration of Independence who laid the cornerstone of the first building in 1831. The college was managed by the priests of the Sulpician Society, French Catholics whose interest centered in establishing schools "for the education of young men of the Roman Catholic religion, for the ministry of the gospil." The church was having difficulties attracting young men for the priesthood; not every student attending such a school would become a priest following his basic education. Carroll petitioned the Maryland legislature for a charter for the school on January 21, 1830, and the legislature passed the bill on February 3, 1830. Carroll saw to it that the college was not to stray from its original purpose as a school for students for the priesthood. Carroll's death on November 14, 1832, slowed down the process of establishing the school, and it did not open until October 31, 1848. In 1859, the year John Surratt, Jr., entered the college, there were 102 students, and work was underway on an extension. A separate chapel was under construction by 1860.

Courses offered included Latin, Greek, English, French, German, history, geography, mathematics, moral and natural philosophy, Catholic doctrine, religious ceremonies, and singing. Father Jenkins stated, as policy, "Every effort will be made to promote the happiness of those confided to the care of the institution; to maintain a spirit of piety, and that practice of those Christian virtues, which will prepare them for becoming zealous and efficient clergymen and future ornaments of the sanctuary."[21]

It was at St. Charles College that John Surratt met Louis J. Weichmann. Born in Baltimore on September 29, 1842, Weichmann had attended public school in Philadelphia, graduating in February of 1859. Although young Weichmann expressed an interest in going into the drug business, his mother, a pious Roman Catholic, insisted that Louis study for the priesthood. He entered St. Charles College on March 1, 1859. Weichmann described his studies at St. Charles as "severe, and the discipline was rigid." Students were shut off from the world except for letters they could write home and receive from there. Vacation time was allowed in the months of July and August.

Weichmann met John H. Surratt, Jr., in September of 1859. Weichmann described Surratt as "tall, erect, slender, and boyish, with a very prominent forehead and receding eyes. His nose was sharp, thin, and aquiline; his face bore an unusually keen and shrewd expression.... He was neatly dressed, and I remember he provoked the risibilities of the older students by wearing a white necktie." Weichmann and Surratt became fast friends: "[H]e was a very orderly student and one of the best young men I ever knew."

The boys at St. Charles knew very little about the momentous events affecting their country at that time. They were told of the execution of John Brown (1800–1859) in 1859 but were not informed of the motives of Brown, whose raid on the federal arsenal at Harpers Ferry, Virginia (now West Virginia), on October 16–17, 1859, had sent shock waves throughout the country. Brown had intended to take the weapons from the arsenal and arm abolitionist zealots and freed slaves to provoke a general rebellion.

The issue of slavery and its spread into the territories had been a major source of tension throughout the nation for years. In 1858, in the contest for United States senator in Illinois, slavery had been the principal issue between Democrat Stephen Arnold Douglas (1813–1861), who argued that the citizens of the new territories should settle the question of slavery in their territories locally, and Republican Abraham Lincoln (1809–1865), who opposed the spread of slavery beyond the states where it already existed. Although Douglas won the Senate election, Lincoln's prominence as a result of the debates propelled him to the Republican nomination for president of the United States, and the divisions in the Democratic Party caused by the slavery issue resulted in Lincoln's election as president in 1860.[22]

Weichmann told of an occasion in March of 1861, when one of his teachers at St. Charles College read Lincoln's inaugural address to his class. He later wrote of his friend and classmate, "John H. Surratt was a pronounced friend of the Southern cause from the start, yet I do not recollect that he ever made himself offensive to anyone by the persistency of his views." Feeling that he was not being allowed to progress in his theological studies as he desired, Weichmann left St. Charles in July of 1862.

Some doubt has been cast on whether John Surratt, and Lou Weichmann as well, were seminarians, i.e., students preparing for the priesthood, or only collegians, students receiving a general education but not as preparation for entering the church. Anna Surratt stated in her testimony at the trial of the conspiracy suspects that, "My brother [John, Jr.] was at St. Charles College, near Ellicott Mills, Maryland, in 1861; but he was not a student of divinity. He was there, I think, three scholastic years, and spent his vacations, in August, at home. During the time he was not at home for vacation he was at college." In his testimony at the same trial, Louis Weichmann stated, "John H. Surratt is a Catholic, and was a student of divinity at the same college as myself." In a statement by Weichmann to Colonel Henry Lawrence Burnett (1838–1916), one of the prosecutors, Weichmann modified his earlier testimony, quoted above.

> It has been stated that neither John Surratt nor I were "students of divinity"; that I said I was going to study law etc. was going to Hamburg etc. Very few except my parents knew that I intended to resume my studies next fall but written evidence can be adduced to show that such was the case. I may have been wrong when I said "student of divinity" it should have been "ecclesiastical students" I only used a general term. If I ever said anything about Hamburg, I did so to conceal my real intentions of going to the seminary etc.

This leaves open the question of exactly what the intentions of both Surratt and Weichmann were. We can say that it is possible that the matter may not have been decided in either of their minds at the time of Weichmann's departure from St. Charles.[23]

While John Surratt, Jr., was away at St. Charles College, all was not going so well in Surrattsville. John Sr. was increasingly in debt. The records of the Circuit Court of Prince George's County show numerous cases involving the senior Surratt. In the years between 1854 and 1871, there were 52 cases brought against Surratt and his heirs. Some of the cases were complex, with Surratt named as one of several defendants. By 1862, Surratt's indebtedness totaled around $3,500. He owed $797 to Charles B. Calvert for the land upon which his tavern-hotel stood, and he owed $278.21 to Jeremiah Townshend for his having built the tavern.

An early volunteer for the Confederacy was Mary Surratt's older son, Isaac. It appears that Isaac, who had been educated in civil engineering and was involved in railroad work in Alexandria and Baltimore, decided to head south even before hostilities commenced. He left home sometime in late March or early April 1861 bound for Texas. According to Confederate military records, he joined the Thirty-Third Texas Cavalry on May 7, 1862. In a letter dated April 23, 1861, to her friend Elizabeth Louise Stone, Anna Surratt, still a student at St. Mary's Female Institute in Bryantown, Maryland, wrote, "[T]he thoughts of war have distressed me so much today that I was unable to study—not so much as the 'Loved One' that I know is engaged [a reference to Isaac]—but I hope God will protect him."

On August 26, 1862, John H. Surratt, Sr., died. He had seemed normal the previous day, entertaining friends well into the evening. In another letter to her friend Louise Stone, Anna stated, "The evening previous to his death we did not retire until quite late and he was even more animated than usual. We hoped at first that he was paralyzed and that reason would be restored—but the Doctors knew that he was dead and were afraid to tell us.... [W]hat renders his death more painful poor John [Jr.] was not at home—I will make no allusion to Isaac for we have not heard from him since the outbreak of the terrible war." The funeral for John Surratt, Sr., cost $57, including a "mahogany coffin case." He was buried in the cemetery of St. Mary's Catholic Church in Piscataway, Maryland.

Upon the death of his father, Mary called her son John Jr. home. Louis Weichmann later wrote that John left college "with the determination to abandon a vocation [the priesthood] to which he did not feel himself called." As we have already seen, John may never have seriously considered becoming a priest. Only a little past his 18th birthday, the fun-loving boy may have already set his sights upon a more adventurous life. John left St. Charles and Weichmann continued: "Father Jenkins on that occasion said, 'Goodbye, Surratt, God bless you, you have been a good student here; we will always remember you.'"[24]

Time was to provide an entirely new reason for all who had known John H. Surratt, Jr., to remember him.

2

Rebel Courier

The widow Mary Surratt needed her son John, Jr., at home to help manage the tavern. His father's death had left a vacancy in the position of postmaster of Surrattsville. Author Kenneth Zanca states that Reverdy Johnson (1796–1876) helped John, Jr., get the appointment as Postmaster. Johnson was a famous and well-connected man, though he was not serving in the U.S. Senate in 1862. However it came about, on September 1, 1862, John Harrison Surratt, Jr., aged eighteen years, was named the new postmaster.[1]

With the beginning of the Civil War in April 1861 it soon became apparent that what we now call intelligence services were needed by both sides. Even before secession, the Virginia state government was organizing for war, including a covert war. Much of this exchanging of information was carried out through the mail, which may be how the Surratts—father and son—became involved.[2] John Surratt, Jr., later described his early involvement:

> I was ... mostly engaged in sending information regarding the movement of the United States army stationed in Washington and elsewhere, and carrying dispatches to the Confederate boats on the Potomac. We had a regular established line from Washington to the Potomac, and I being the only unmarried man on the route, I had most of the hard riding to do. I devised various ways to carry the dispatches—sometimes in the heel of my boots, sometimes between the planks of the buggy. I confess that never in my life did I come across a more stupid set of detectives than those generally employed by the U.S. Government. They seemed to have no idea whatever how to search men.... It was a fascinating life to me. It seemed as if I could not do too much or run too great a risk.[3]

Over the course of the war, the Confederates gradually created and developed a complex set of agencies which today we can describe as making up the Confederate Secret Service: State Department Secret Service, War Department Secret Service, War Department Signal Bureau and Signal Corps, Provost Marshal of Richmond, War Department Torpedo Bureau, Navy Submarine Battery Service, War Department Strategy Bureau, Greenhow Group, Cavalry Scouts, and Operations in Canada. All of these groups and agencies engaged in espionage—the gathering and passing of information—and sometimes in sabotage—damage or destruction of anything useful to the Union war effort.[4]

As early as late April 1861 Major William S. Barton from the Virginia State Militia suggested to Virginia governor John Letcher (1813–1884) that "a line of express may be established to Balta[more] from opposite Aquia Creek [Virginia]—a reliable man here will assist." This is described by the authors of *Come Retribution* as the first step in the development of the "secret line." By September of 1862 the Confederates had established contacts across Maryland and were looking at the possibility of extending their "secret line" as far as Quebec, Canada.[5] Among the contacts along the "secret line" was Thomas Austin Jones (1820–1895). A farmer in southern Maryland, Jones was recruited by Major William

Norris (1820–1896), commander of the Confederate Signal Corps. Jones later described his work:

> He [Norris] spent a night at my house, and in the morning walked out with me on the bluff that overlooks the [Potomac] river. He was struck with the extensive water view from that point, and remarked to me: "What a place this would be for a signal station!" ... Major Norris had said that it was of the utmost importance to the Confederacy that it should have communication with points north of the Potomac, and that nowhere on the river was there a better location for a signal station than the bluffs near Pope's Creek, or a more suitable place for putting the mail across the river than off my shore.
>
> I agreed that, if I was given the entire control of the ferry and all the agents in Maryland, and also allowed a voice in the management on the other side of the river, I would undertake the work.... It required great caution and unrelaxing vigilance to successfully carry on the operations in which I was now engaged. The river was filled with gunboats plying up and down, day and night. An armed patrol guarded the shore and the Federal Government had a spy upon nearly every river farm in Southern Maryland. There was a detachment of troops stationed at Pope's Creek....
>
> The pickets went off duty in the morning. Sometime during the day I would go down to the shore and get the packet left there the evening before. Letters, etc., going north, were addressed to the parties for whom they were intended. All I would have to do with them was to put them in a post office. I seldom posted them at my nearest office, which was Allen's Fresh, about three miles distant, for fear of exciting suspicion, but would send them by our trusted agents to be posted at different places some distance off.
>
> Especially important matter was never sent by the mail, but was always entrusted to our agents. Stowten [Stoughton] W. Dent, M.D. [c. 1803–1883], and my brother-in-law, Thomas H[enry] Harbin [1833–1885], were two of our most active agents.
>
> Every packet, going north or south, was conveyed to and from the boat in my own hands. I trusted no one that it was not absolutely necessary to trust. The result was that not in a single instance was I betrayed.
>
> The United States Government knew, of course, that communication was going on between the South and North of the Potomac; and it exhausted its ingenuity in vain in trying to discover how it was managed.... From the time I accepted the position of chief signal agent north of the Potomac, which was in the Spring of '62, till the close of the war, there was scarcely an evening that the boat did not make its trip across the river, and not one letter or paper was ever lost.[6]

Thomas A. Jones makes little mention of John Surratt in his book, but it is a reasonable assumption that he knew John or knew of him. John enlisted in the Confederate service around summer or fall of 1862, soon after his return home from school. Assigned to the Confederate Secret Service, he became a courier of the sort mentioned by Jones, along the "secret line" between Washington and Richmond.[7] The hotel-tavern in Surrattsville was only thirteen miles south of the capital city, making it a convenient stop along the secret line. Crossing the Potomac River at Matthias Point, John depended upon a boatman from Port Tobacco, Maryland, by the name of George A. Atzerodt (1835–1865). In time, he would have more to do with the boatman with the thick German accent. If Surratt was traveling north toward Washington, he could put stamps on the letters and packages at the post office in Surrattsville—his mother's tavern—to disguise the rebel messages as official U.S. mail.[8]

The Union government was certainly aware of the rebel activity in southern Maryland, as Thomas A. Jones mentioned. Lafayette C. Baker (1826–1868), who headed a Union intelligence service first for the State Department in early 1862 and for the War Department, described the activities of the postmasters of Southern Maryland:

> It was a surprising fact during the first six or eight months after the war began, that the result of every Cabinet meeting at Washington was reported in Richmond within twenty-four hours after it was held. The secret was, that every postmaster in lower Maryland, comprising the counties of St. [sic] Charles, St. [sic] George, and St. Mary's, with three exceptions, were disloyal. It had been taken for granted that the state [Maryland] was true to the Government, while rebel emissaries were constantly conveying information from Washington to the post offices along the Potomac, from which it was transmitted to Fredericksburg [Virginia] by blockade runners and spies, and thence telegraphed to Richmond. By this arrangement, uninterrupted and unrestrained communication was kept open between the rebels North and South.

A letter written after the Lincoln assassination mentions John Surratt and one possible source of information obtained by him for the rebel Secret Service. The letter was written by Frank Russell Reading, to Brigadier General Schoepf at Fort Delaware:

April 29, 1865

> Respected Sir,
> Since my removal from the hospital, I have heard the name of "Surratt" mentioned in connection with the attempt to take the life of Mr. Seward. [John Surratt was at first suspected of being the assailant of Secretary of State William Henry Seward (1801–1872), until the actual attacker was identified.]
> Surratt was frequently at the office of the "Constitutional Union," a newspaper published in Washington. His interviews were always with Mr. Callahan [John Callahan (1812–c.1865)], who was engaged by Col. Joe Severens to write articles denouncing Mr. Lincoln and his Cabinet. Callahan was very intimate with Surratt, who used Callahan for the purpose of obtaining information relative to any movement about to be made by the Federal army. Callahan formerly live[d] in the same town as Surratt, who always supplied him with money. Callahan lives or did live when I was in Washington, in the neighborhood of 7th and 8th Streets, near the residence of Surratt [Mrs. Surratt's boardinghouse was located at 541 H Street, NW, near 6th Street]. Surratt was a violent opponent of the government, and ready to do anything for the rebels. I have often seen them conversing together. The name of Surratt appears on the subscription book of the Constitutional Union. I think in the month of September, 1863. Callahan was the chief writer of secession articles for the paper and obtained much information from the professors at Georgetown College relative to army movements. He [Callahan] was formerly Governor Floyd's [John Buchanan Floyd (1806–1863), Governor of Virginia, 1849–1852, U.S. Secretary of War, 1857–1860. Brigadier General in the Confederate army] clerk when Floyd was the Secretary of War. I think Callahan may know something of the whereabouts of Surratt. Callahan I believe is still writing for the Constitutional Union. He was educated for the church and once editor of the Madisonian. He is somewhat intemperate in his habits. I know most of the contributors to the "Constitutional Union."

Reading asked that his "name should not be mentioned in connection with this statement" and it appears that it was not made public.

Georgetown College teachers might seem to be an unlikely source of information about military movements, but a comparison of the list of Georgetown faculty with the "Union Provost Marshal's File of Papers Relating to Two or More Civilians" produces four names: John Early, Frederick Holland, Clement S. Lancaster, and Michael McKenna. The 1850 census records show John Callahan, age 38, his occupation being "porter at College gate," and a similar listing for the census of 1860. So the provost marshal—military police—had an interest in at least some Georgetown College faculty, and John Callahan existed and was also an employee of Georgetown College [now Georgetown University]. How well Surratt knew Callahan and how often he might have been given useful information we can only guess at, but we can say that such a connection is at least a possibility.[9]

That the Surratt tavern in Surrattsville, Maryland, was officially recognized as a stop along the "secret line" cannot be doubted, for it is mentioned in the *Consolidated Report of the Signal Corps, C.S.A., East Miss for Quarter Ending March 31st, 1864*:

> Under the control of this bureau there are three lines of communication with the United States—two communicating with Washington City and one with Fortress Monroe.... [O]pen lines by which agents, scouts, etc. can forward letters, papers, and light packages to the Dept ... are as follows:
> I. Matthias Point, King George Co. Va. Liet C.H. Cawood commanding, via Allen's Fresh, Newport, Bryantown, Surratt's Tavern, & to Washington.
> II. Pope's Creek, Westmoreland Co. Va. Sergt. H.H. Brogden commanding, via Marlborough, T.B., to Washington.
> III. Burwell's Bay, Isle of Wight Co. Va. Sergt Jno. F. Moore commanding, via Williamsburg, Yorktown, Hampton to Fortress Monroe.
>
> Respectfully submitted
> (signed) Wm. N. Barker
> Capt. in Charge Signal Bureau[10]

"Surratt's Tavern," mentioned in the document and described as "under control of this bureau," is the only structure on the list specifically named rather than a town or place. The words "'under the control of this bureau" should be taken to mean that the lines are "'under control" and not the places mentioned. In other words, the tavern was a stop along the line but was owned and operated by the Surratt family, not the Confederate government or military.

One of the Confederate operatives who frequented the Surratt Tavern during the war was Thomas Nelson Conrad (1837–1905). Conrad was one of the South's best "scouts," or spies. His services were personally acknowledged by Jefferson Davis:

Richmond, VA, May 27, 1864

Mr. T.N. Conrad.

Dear Sir: Please accept my thanks for the zealous and patriotic manner in which you have lately served the Confederacy by going within the enemy's lines. If the expression of my satisfaction at the efforts made by you, for the advantage of our cause, will afford you gratification, it is a pleasing duty to me to thank you for them. With the assurance of my regard, I am,

Very respectfully yours,
Jefferson Davis

Conrad described himself as "intensely Southern in every fiber of my nature.... I loved Virginia and her traditions as I loved my life. My father was a slaveholder, and I believed slavery scriptural and God-ordained. I burned to draw the sword in its defense."[11] He wrote of his knowing the Surratts before the war and stopping at the tavern on his way to visit his sister or when hunting. During the war he "took a meal at Surratt's tavern either going or coming and sometimes both."[12] It is easy to picture young John's excitement at associating with such a dashing and important rebel spy.

Conrad, a Virginia native, was pro–South from the beginning. While working at a school in Georgetown, D.C., he was arrested by the army provost marshal, William E. Doster (1837–1919), at the beginning of August 1862. He was charged with "holding communication with the enemy and attempting to send his scholars as recruits to the rebel army." Apparently Conrad was being watched, as he was described as the "same man who was noticed ... having allowed his school to indulge in secesh [a common abbreviation for secessionist] demonstrations at an examination. The route for sending these recruits was through Marlboro and Horsehead, Md, and thence to the [Potomac] river, when they are transported across." Conrad was held in the Old Capitol Prison. He was paroled on September 3, 1862, and required to report weekly to the headquarters of Brigadier General James Samuel Wadsworth (1807–1864), the military governor of Washington, D.C.[13] Conrad knew both of John Surratt's parents, describing his father, John H. Surratt, Sr., as an "impetuous southerner, full of intense prejudice and hate toward the Yankees—as was almost everybody in lower Maryland—outspoken in his convictions and proud of every Southern victory." John Surratt, Sr.'s name was at the top of the list of "active secessionists" in the Surrattsville area. Others on the government's list were Bennett F. Gwynn (1823–1897), E. Plinney Bryan, Walter P. Griffen, Dr. Joseph Lattimer, and Thomas Henry Harbin.

John, Jr.'s mother, Mary, was described by Conrad as an "amiable, motherly woman, full of human kindness and sympathy."[14] Management of the tavern in Surrattsville after the death of John H. Surratt, Sr., fell to his widow, Mary E. Surratt. John, Jr., would combine his duty to his family with his Southern espionage service, taking vegetables grown on the Surrattsville property to Washington to sell at the markets there. On one of these excursions, John encountered his old school friend, Louis J. Weichmann (1842–1902). Weichmann had left St. Charles College in July 1862 to accept an offer from E.Q.S. Waldron to assist him in his school for boys in Pikesville, Maryland. Weichmann stayed in that position until November 1862. Answering an advertisement in the *Catholic Mirror* for a teaching assistant in Washington, Weichmann found himself principal of St. Matthew's Institute in Washington on 19th Street between G and H streets, NW, beginning on January 2, 1863. He slept nights at the institute, but had to take his meals at a nearby boardinghouse. Weichmann later wrote as follows:

> On one of these occasions, in the spring, a short time before Easter [1863], he [Surratt] invited me to accompany him on his return home. I gladly and willingly accepted the invitation.
>
> Surratt's home was located at the junction of a crossroad and the road ... leading from the Capital to Bryantown and to the Potomac River. The house was a frame structure. The entrance to it was from the main road to the center of the house. To the right, as you went in, was a parlor and a room in the rear of that. To the left was the country post office, with barroom attached, and in the rear of it the dining room. There was a large cellar beneath the house. The second story was used for bedrooms. There was also a farm and a fruit orchard where the family raised cereals, vegetables, and fruits for their own use, selling the surplus that was not needed. At the date of my visit, a half dozen or more colored people who had been Mrs. Surratt's slaves were still dwelling on the place.[15]

It may have been on the return from this visit that Surratt and Weichmann made the acquaintance of Henri Benjamin Ste. Marie (1833–1874), who was also to play a large part in John Surratt's life. Ste. Marie later described their meeting:

> I have known Weichmann at Ellen Gowan, a small village 15 miles from Baltimore, where I was a teacher. He and Surratt visited me there in the Spring of 1863. It was my first interview with both. By their conversation I understood they were strong secessionists and more particularly Weichmann. I then and there hinted of my intention of going South where I had no other intention than that of following the profession of teacher of the French language. Surratt then told me that his house was the rendezvous of all land blockade runners to Richmond—that he often went to Richmond and was in communication with prominent men there. Weichmann and Surratt were intimate friends.[16]

Weichmann and Surratt continued to be friends with Ste. Marie. On April 23, 1863, Weichmann wrote to Ste. Marie:

> I do not blame you for leaving so lonely and deserted a place as the romantic village in which your [sic] are now at present stationed. [Ste. Marie was then in Texas, Maryland]. I have made several applications by letter to some of my most influential acquaintances but up to this period I have not received any answer either favorable or unfavorable. I expect a reply in a few days. I also wrote to my friend Jno Surratt about the position of which he spoke when in Texas [Maryland]. As soon as he gives me an answer I shall inform you of the result.... Rest assured that I shall do all that is in my power. I have no doubt that if you come to Washington you will by your exertions eventually obtain some position. I am sure of it.... Let me know, if you please, whether you intend to come to Washington as soon as you leave Texas. I shall certainly be very happy to receive you. In the meantime have courage; all things will be right bye and bye.

On the following day, John Surratt wrote to Ste. Marie. If Weichmann's letter seems routine, John Surratt seems to be hinting at something, as he seems to boast about what he can do for his new friend:

> I received a letter from Mr. Weichmann yesterday, stating your intention to leave Texas [MD] by the first of May. I spoke to Mr. Hill about a teacher. He said he wanted one and was willing to have you as our teacher, but he could not build his schoolhouse for some time.
>
> If you have made up your mind to go s__ [South] I can send you all safely. Do not have the least doubt of it. Times are better than they were. All you have to do is to let me know what day you will be in Washington, and I will meet you. You can carry a hand trunk with you.
>
> There will not be the least difficulty, only perhaps you will have to remain among us some two or three weeks. Still we can easily make the time pass agreeably.... Do not fail to come to Washington.
>
> > Your friend,
> > J. Harrison Surratt[17]

It seems likely that John's reference to going S__ meant "South," suggesting that John could easily arrange such a trip through the lines, something he was doing as a courier for the rebels. Ste. Marie was doing menial work in Maryland as a result of having fled Canada, defaulting on his debts. The ship he took was stopped as a blockade runner, landing Ste. Marie in prison at Fort McHenry in Baltimore. He was released with the help of the French Consul at Baltimore and was working on a farm at the time he met Weichmann and Surratt. Although Weichmann helped Ste. Marie find work as a teacher in Washington, Ste. Marie left after a few weeks because, he said, of a disagreement with Weichmann.[18]

It appears that Louis Weichmann may have had an interest in John Surratt's sister, Anna. Years later, he described her as "a tall, well-proportioned, and fair complexioned young woman of about twenty-six years [born January 1, 1843, making her twenty years old in the summer of 1863] ... possessing many of the features and characteristics of her brother John. She had received a very good education in a Catholic seminary at Bryantown, Maryland, not many miles from Surrattsville. Besides being an accomplished pianist, she was a young woman of much culture. Staying a few days with the Surratts, Weichmann emphasized that they, and most of their neighbors, "were all bitter secessionists." John's mother, Mary, Weichmann called "a woman devoted, body and soul, to the cause of the South.... Next to her church and family, her love for the South was her meat and drink." However, Weichmann allowed, even in his later years, "Her manner was genial and social and she had the rare faculty of making a stranger feel at home at once in her company." It was on this same visit to Surrattsville, he later wrote, that Weichmann met David Edgar Herold (1842–1865), who would later become another accomplice of John Wilkes Booth in his infamous crime.[19] Weichmann made additional visits to the Surratt tavern in fall of 1863 as well as in the spring of 1864.[20]

Weichmann's friendship with Henri B. Ste. Marie continued to grow. He was impressed with Ste. Marie's fluency in French and Italian and with his musical abilities, playing the guitar and singing, as well as being an entertaining conversationalist. Weichmann secured a job for Ste. Marie in Washington, teaching at St. Matthew's Institute, where Weichmann was employed. However, less than a month later, Ste. Marie was gone. Without a word to his friend, he walked out, joining the Third Delaware Regiment; he soon deserted and was captured by the Confederates. Neither Weichmann nor Surratt would hear from Ste. Marie for another four years, by which time their relationship to each other had changed drastically.[21]

John Surratt, Jr., enjoyed his dispatch riding, later describing how he easily evaded Union forces with the help of pro–South sympathizers. He became adept at crossing the Potomac River while avoiding Union patrol boats. He weighted his secret dispatches and towed them behind the boat, to be cut loose if he was stopped. He found dark, rainy nights to be the best times to cross the river. John and his fellow couriers occasionally came under fire, John luckily avoiding being hit. Once he was in the Union states, he would travel by train, appearing to be just another passenger traveling on business or pleasure. He used disguises at times, mostly when passing through the more heavily patrolled areas, but not on the train.[22]

John continued helping his mother with the management of the tavern. Licenses for the tavern were issued in the name of John H. Surratt on May 7, 1863, and on May 21, 1864. Mrs. Surratt, not her son John, Jr., signed the receipts for whiskey and food for the tavern. The abolition of slavery in the District of Columbia on April 16, 1862, made it difficult for Mrs. Surratt to retain the slaves, who tended to leave for nearby D.C.: freedom lay only thirteen miles up the road. On November 17, 1863, John, Jr., was "removed" from his postmaster's duties for disloyalty. Andrew V. Robey became the new postmaster, although the Surratt tavern remained a post office only until May 3, 1865.[23]

With expenses for the operating of the tavern, the unpaid debts left behind by John, Sr., the loss of slaves, and the requirement for Mrs. Surratt to hire laborers, there was a chronic need for more money. John, Jr., applied to his congressman, Charles Benedict Calvert (1808–1864), for help obtaining him a job. The spoils system was then the dominant method of obtaining employment in government. This meant that public offices were appointed by those in senior positions. The modern system of civil service, with examinations to determine the abilities and suitability of applicants, did not exist until decades later.

On October 14, 1863, Congressman Calvert wrote to Secretary of War Edwin M. Stanton (1814–1869) "to recommend the bearer Mr. John Surratt to your favor for an appointment in the Paymasters Department." Calvert described Surratt as "a very worthy and energetic young man [who] desires a situation to assist him in maintaining a widowed mother." Although Calvert's letter was written on official Thirty-seventh Congress Stationery, his term had already expired by this time. Perhaps for that reason, John wrote his own letter directly to Stanton, dated October 17, 1863, requesting a position in the Paymaster General's Department. He described himself as "almost an utter stranger to you." Why he used the word "almost" is an intriguing question. Where and how John Surratt might have met Edwin Stanton is a mystery. Most probably, he was using the word in a self-serving way, in the hope that a suggested connection with Stanton might help him obtain the post. John also mentioned his widowed mother along with his college education. He stated in the letter that he included references and testimonials and signed off with the words "humbly," "very respectfully," and "your obedient servant." Apparently, there was no reply, and it was noted on the letter that it was to be filed. The name Surratt must have meant nothing to the busy secretary of war, but both John Surratt and Edwin Stanton would later come to know each other in ways neither could have imagined in 1863.[24]

John Surratt became acquainted with Dr. Samuel Alexander Mudd (1833–1883), perhaps, even before the war, but he certainly knew him during the years between 1862 and the beginning of Booth's kidnap conspiracy sometime in 1864. One of Mudd's former slaves, Mary Simms, testified at the 1865 trial:

> Q. State whether there was any man who visited his [Mudd's] house often last summer [1864].
> A. There was a man visited there last summer by the name of Surratt—John Surratt....
> Q. Who called him that?
> A. Dr. Sam Mudd, and Dr. Sam Mudd's wife, called him Mr. Surratt.
> Q. What sort of a looking man was Mr. Surratt,—young or old?
> A. He was a young-looking man.
> Q. State whether he was tall or short.
> A. He was a slim-made man, not very tall, and not very short.
> Q. What was the color of his hair?
> A. His hair was sort of light: it was not black.
> Q. State whether he came very often or not.
> A. Yes, Sir: he was there from almost every Saturday night to Monday night. When he would go to Virginia, or come back from there, he would stop.
> Q. Where did he sleep when at Dr. Mudd's?
> A. He slept out in the woods. All of them slept in the woods.
> Q. How many were with him at times in the woods?
> A. Captain White, from Tennessee (I heard them say, he was from Tennessee); then there was a Captain Perry, and Andrew Gwynn, and Ben Gwynn, and George Gwynn.
> Q. How did they get victuals, if they got any, when they were at his house?

A. When they came into his house to eat, they put us [the slaves] all out to watch.
Q. Who put you out to watch?
A. Dr. Sam Mudd, to see if anybody would come; and, when we told them anybody was coming, they would run out, and go off to the woods again; and he would make me take the victuals out to them. I would set the victuals down, and I would stand and watch; and the rebels would come out and get the victuals, while I stood behind a tree and watched them.
Q. State to the Court whether this man Surratt ever came to get victuals in that way?
A. Yes. Surratt and Andrew Gwinn were the only two I saw come for the victuals.
Q. When you were set to watch that door if anybody came while they were eating in the house, did you at any time give notice to Dr. Mudd that some person was coming to the house?
A. Yes, sir. One time I was standing at the door watching, and a gentleman came up—by the name of Mudd also,—a next door neighbor. I told them he was coming, and the men ran out....
Q. Did you ever see Surratt in the house of Dr. Mudd at any other time than when he was eating?
A. Yes, sir. I have seen him in the house, up stairs with him, and in the parlor.... They never talked very often in the presence of the family: they always went off by themselves to talk.

U.S. Secretary of War Edwin M. Stanton was the moving force behind the trial of the Booth conspirators and an advisor behind the scenes for the Surratt trial (Library of Congress).

Mary Simms stated that the men from Virginia wore uniforms and gave letters to Dr. Mudd, who would then give the men letters to take back with them. She was cross-examined by Dr. Mudd's lawyer, General Thomas Ewing, Jr. (1829–1896), who asked her,

Q. Are you sure that you saw Mr. Surratt at that house more than once?
A. Yes, sir: I saw him at that house a dozen times or more.
Q. What was the last time you saw Surratt there?
A. I do not know what the month was when I last saw him. Apples and peaches were all ripe the last time I saw him [around September]. He went away then, and said he was coming here to Washington....
Q. Did Mr. Surratt never take dinner at the house when he was there?
A. Yes, sir: he has taken dinner in the house, but never slept there.
Q. How many times did he take dinner there last summer? [1864]
A. About six or seven times. All the rest of the time, when men from here were going after them, they got scared, and ate out in the woods...
Q. You never saw him [Surratt] then, in company with any of the other neighbors?
A. No, sir: when any of them came, they would not let them see these men.
Q. What was the first time last summer you saw Surratt there? How early was it?
A. The first time he commenced coming there was in winter, and he kept coming on and off until summer was out, and after that I did not see him.
Q. About how many times did he come?
A. About a dozen times. He used to go to Virginia and come back, and go to Washington and come back; and every time he would come he would fetch the news.

Thomas Ewing, Jr., served as a defense lawyer for Mary Surratt at the conspiracy trial in 1865 (Library of Congress).

> Q. Would he be there about once a week?
> A. Some weeks he would come once a week, and then again he might not come for two weeks. Sometimes he would go to Virginia, and stay two weeks.... I reckon he was [at Dr. Mudd's house] more than a dozen times. I cannot tell you how many times, there were so many of them, and he would keep coming and coming.

Mary Simms' brother, Elzee Eglen, also testified to having seen John Surratt and other rebels at Dr. Mudd's house prior to Eglen's leaving in August 1863.[25] Other former slaves of the Mudds, Melvina Washington and Milo Simms, corroborated Mary Simms' testimony about the rebel visitors at the Mudd house, though Washington did not name John Surratt as one of them. Milo Simms did say Surratt was mentioned:

> Q. Who called him John Surratt?
> A. I heard his name called in the house. Dr. Sam Mudd's wife called him by that name.
> Q. Was Dr. Mudd present when he was called by that name or not?
> A. Yes, sir: he was there.

The description of Surratt given by Milo Simms is similar to that given by Mary Simms. Milo also testified to having seen Surratt at the home of Dr. Samuel Mudd's father, Henry Lowe Mudd (1798–1877).

> Q. Was Surratt there when Andrew Gwynn and Jerry Dyer were at Old Mr. Mudd's?
> A. Yes, sir. He came there, and has a horse taken out of a buggy.

Q. Was that before or after the war commenced?
A. That was after the war commenced...
Q. When you saw John Surratt, at old Mr. Mudd's, that was last year [1864], in the tobacco-planting season?
A. Yes, sir.[26]

Mudd's defense lawyer produced a witness in rebuttal to the testimony of Mary and Milo Simms. Jeremiah Dyer had been a resident of Charles County, Maryland, living only about four miles from Mudd's house:

Q. Did you meet ... Surratt ... at the house of Dr. Mudd's father?
A. Never. I never saw Surratt there. I have seen him; but never at Mr. Mudd's place, or anywhere in the neighborhood. The only time I ever saw him in that vicinity was when I met him coming from Bryantown: he was going towards home, and I rode up the road with him.
Q. When was that?
A. Some two or three years ago [1862 or 1863].
Q. Do you know whether or not any of Surratt's family were at Bryantown then?
A. He had a sister at school there.

Dyer stated that he and the Gwynns had received word that they were targeted in a mass arrest and that was why they hid in the woods.

Q. Do you know whether there was any warrant for your arrest, or any charges against you?
A. I do not. There was a general stampede, or a panic, in the whole community; and a good many left their homes and went to friends' houses from place to place,—the whole community, pretty much.

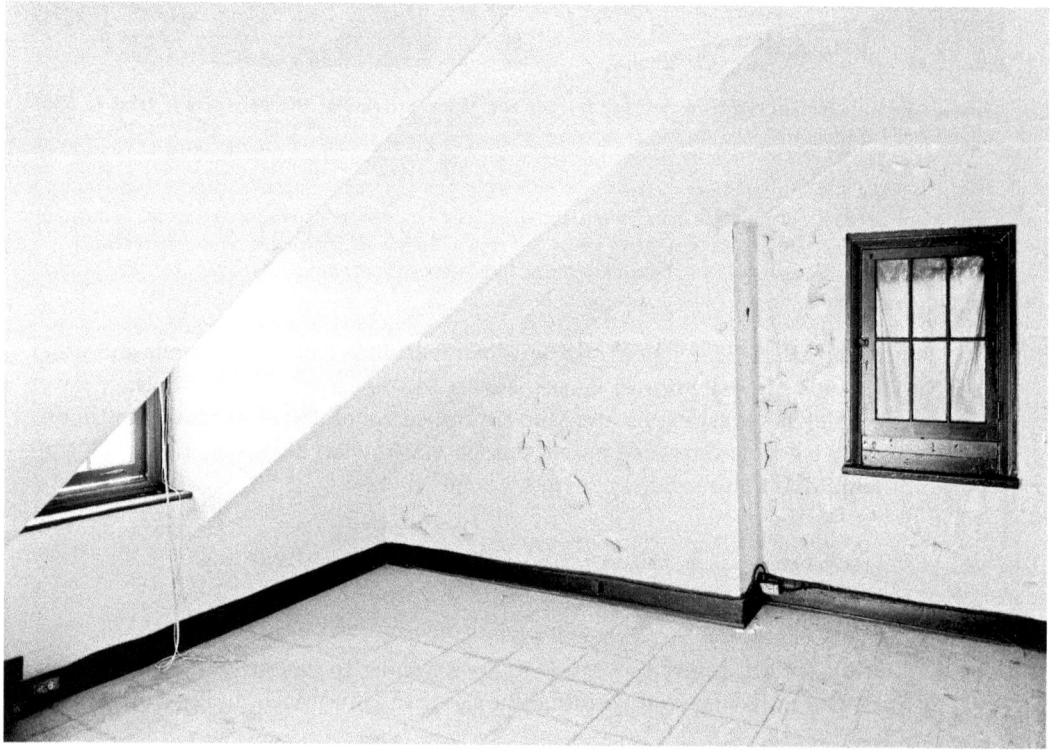

The Surratt House interior, 4th floor, a photograph taken many years after Mrs. Surratt's death (Library of Congress).

On August 8, 1862, Secretary Stanton had issued an order that read as follows:

1. That all U.S. marshals and superintendents or chiefs of police of any town, city or district be, and they are hereby, authorized and directed to arrest and imprison any person or persons who may be engaged, by act, speech, or writing, in discouraging volunteer enlistments, or in any way giving aid and comfort to the enemy, or in any other disloyal practice against the United States.
2. Such persons may be tried before a military commission.

Incredible as it may seem to us now, this order was considered to be lawful under the U.S. Constitution, which states under Article One, Section 9, that the privilege of the writ of habeas corpus shall not be suspended unless in cases of rebellion or invasion the public safety may require it.

A writ of habeas corpus is a legal order requiring the government to produce a person who has been arrested before a court, where the charges against such a person can be stated, and where the person charged shall be allowed to defend himself. Stanton's order, supported by President Lincoln and other leaders of the U.S. Government, though very controversial at the time, was not successfully overturned. The constitutional provision stated above still exists, and other incidents in American history have occurred in which basic rights have been suspended and military forces have assumed domestic police power. Under such conditions, anyone might assume that the rights the Constitution guaranteed no longer existed, and such a person might very well have taken refuge in the nearest patch of woods.[27]

Another of Dr. Mudd's former slaves was called as a witness at the 1865 trial. Julia Ann Bloyce was asked about the men hiding, including John Surratt:

Q. Did you ever know while there [at Dr. Mudd's house] of any party of men sleeping in the pines?
A. No, sir.
Q. Did you know of any Confederate officers or soldiers being about Dr. Mudd's house?
A. No, sir; I did not.
Q. Did you ever see a man they called Surratt there?
A. No, sir; I did not.
Q. [Exhibiting to the witness the photograph of John H. Surratt, marked Exhibit No. 72] Look at that likeness.
A. I have never seen it before.
Q. You never saw that man before?
A. No, sir.
Q. Did you ever hear Surratt's name mentioned?

Surratt House stairway. This photograph was taken when the house was no longer occupied. Today the home is a Chinese restaurant (Library of Congress).

A. No, sir.
Q. Do you know what the general opinion of Mary Simms among the colored people is, as to her being truthful?
A. She is not a very great truth-teller.
Q. Do you know what the colored folks around there generally think of her as a truth-teller?

Surratt House, Washington, D.C., exterior (stairs from street level) as it looked in 1865 (Library of Congress).

A. They think she is a liar.
Q. Do you know what the colored folks there think of Milo Simms as a truth-teller?
A. They thought of Milo as they did of Mary. If he would get angry with you, he would tell a lie on you to get his satisfaction.

The point of all this is not to try to decide who was telling the truth but to establish Surratt's involvement with the Confederate Secret Service and their "secret line" connecting Richmond with the North. As the majority of the people of the southern Maryland counties were pro-Southern, it is not too much of a stretch to conclude that Surratt knew Dr. Mudd or at least knew of him. A visit by Surratt and other Confederate agents and sympathizers to the doctor's house is entirely within the realm of possibility.[28]

3

Confederates in Canada

Looking for ways to create problems for the Union and further the chances of Confederate independence, the rebels began to encourage and aid the peace movement in the North. The war which began in the spring of 1861 had confounded the expectations of both sides by failing to reach an early resolution. Early Confederate victories did not bring about the weakening of the resolve of the Lincoln administration to suppress the rebellion.

It is not always noted today that the American Civil War was more than a conflict over the existence of human slavery. There was also the issue of State's Rights, with the South claiming that the existence of the states preceded the national government, and because the states had voluntarily entered into the Union they could withdraw from it if they chose to. But beyond those reasons lay another one, probably deeper and with an even stronger impact: the economic issue. Cotton was America's greatest export product. American cotton imported by the United Kingdom in 1861 amounted to 819,500,528 pounds. That number declined to 13,524,224 in 1862. In 1863, it was only 6,394,080. This was because the South was the primary cotton-growing area of the United States. Thus, the loss of the South stood to cripple the American economy. While the increase in other economic growth was accelerated by the war, the serious decline in American exports provided reason enough for the North to wage a huge and desperate war to recover their greatest export product. The South hoped that the loss of so much cotton by the European nations—especially Britain—would lead those nations to aid the Confederacy, perhaps even to military intervention. What the Southerners did not anticipate was that American cotton, though favored over other sources, could be replaced by cotton grown elsewhere. Mexican cotton exports to the United Kingdom increased from 3,131,520 pounds in 1861 to 36,664,880 pounds in 1865. Similar increases in cotton exports to Britain came from South America, Egypt, the British East Indies, and China. Then, as now, economic issues often lay at the bottom of policy and decision making.

Although the South initially did very well on the battlefield, they experienced shortages of resources almost from the start. These shortages could not be eased. The Union blockade was ineffective at first but grew stronger with time as new ships were built and acquired and manpower increased. It became clear to the Confederacy that they needed more than one way to weaken the North. Confederate diplomatic efforts to enlist Britain and France to intervene were not successful, though Confederate agents were able to acquire considerable quantities of weapons and equipment from those nations.[1]

In the early years of the war, the Confederacy sought to deal directly with Britain and France, using diplomacy as well as economic factors to encourage the Europeans to become involved. The British were particularly careful to avoid Canadian territory being used by the Southern rebels, in order to avoid a war with the United States, but it was impossible for Canadian authorities to prevent individual Southerners and rebel sympathizers from entering Canada. Once there, secret agents operating with the official backing of the Confederate government, as well as unofficial pro–Southern individuals, some of whom were British citizens, made themselves available for the Southern cause. Escaped Southern prisoners of war could cross the long border with Canada, make their way eastward to Halifax, take a boat to Nassau in the Bahamas, and from there head to Wilmington, North Carolina. Confederate agents could reverse this route to get to Canada.

The Confederates enhanced their diplomatic offensive in the fall of 1861, sending James Murray Mason (1798–1871) and John Slidell (1793–1871) to Europe—Mason to Britain, Slidell to France. Their mission was to encourage the Europeans to recognize the Southern Confederacy and to arrange to obtain weapons and other war supplies. The Union was aware of their mission, and the United States Navy sought to intercept them as they ran the blockade. The two emissaries managed to make the first part of their voyage, from Charleston, South Carolina, to Havana, Cuba, without difficulty. They boarded a British ship, the *Trent*, bound for England, but the *Trent* was stopped on the high seas by the U.S. sloop *San Jacinto*, commanded by Captain Charles Wilkes (1798–1877). Wilkes removed the two Southern commissioners under arrest. The British were indignant that this act almost accomplished what the two were sent to do—that is, provoke war between Britain and the United States. The war scare sparked an economic recession in the North. When the British sent troops to Canada and demanded that the North apologize, President Lincoln stated American policy, "one war at a time," and smoothed over the crisis diplomatically. Mason and Slidell were able to go to England and France and were well supplied with funds, but they were unable to convince the Europeans to go to war with the United States.

Canada was ruled by Britain prior to its obtaining dominion status in 1867. With the exception of the French-Canadians, most residents of Canada in the 1860s were British or descendants of British colonists. It had not been forgotten that Canada had twice been invaded by the United States, once in 1775 and again in 1812. Thousands of escaped slaves had crossed the border into Canada, where there was no slavery. Britain had also sent 2,144 soldiers to Canada in 1861 to protect its border with the United States. Editors of the *New York Herald* proposed an armistice between North and South so that the combined forces could not only invade Canada but also Russian North America—modern-day Alaska. Secretary of State William H. Seward (1801–1872) sent what the Canadians considered to be far more consular agents to Canada than necessary, leading to the suspicion that the agents were actually spies.

The *Trent* affair caused Canadians to expand militias and improve military defenses. Britain sent an additional 14,000 troops, equipped with artillery, to Canada. The Union blockade of Southern ports had its effect on Canadian maritime trade, causing further hard feelings. Neither the North nor the British could possibly patrol a border more than 3,000 miles long, so entering or exiting Canada remained easy to accomplish. Blockade runners were built in Canadian shipyards and supervised by Confederate officers in uniform. As the American Civil War reached its end, it became obvious to Canadian and European observers that a Southern victory would be impossible, and tensions along the border eased.[2]

By early 1864 the Confederates realized that by establishing an organized, well-financed operation based in Canada, serious damage might be inflicted upon the Union effort. The U.S. would then be faced with what amounted to a second front to the north. Even a small number of men crossing the border into the Northern states could surprise and terrorize the Northern population and draw the Union forces away from the battle fronts of the

South. An American consul in Quebec sent word in December 1863 calling for efforts to "prevent the consummation of contemplated deeds of reckless wickedness" by pro–Confederate raiders operating from Canada. At this time, however, there was no overall organization or centralized leadership for such operations. That was to change in the coming months.³

By early 1862 the Confederacy had an estimated twenty agents in Montreal, Canada. Though the agents were not formally organized, one of the most influential Southerners was William Lawrence McDonald (1821–1895). Another was Patrick Charles Martin (1817– 1864), a blockade runner from Baltimore. Alexander Keith, an agent of B. Weir & Co. of Halifax, proved useful to the expanding Confederate espionage activities. American consular offices reported the comings and goings of known Confederates, and by summer 1862 they noted that George Nicholas Sanders (1812–1873) met with former Kentucky governor Charles Slaughter Morehead (1802–1868) at Niagara Falls, Canada. Sanders was a longtime revolutionary and was an active business agent, diplomat, and dispatch bearer for the Confederates. Sanders had the friendship and support of no less than the Confederate president, Jefferson Davis (1808–1889). The increasing dangers of such efforts led the Confederacy to favor blockade running ships built for speed to outrun the Union blockaders.⁴

Confederate agents and pro–South sympathizers met at Montreal's St. Lawrence Hall, a large and elegant hotel at 13 Great Saint James Street, one block from the Place d'Armes Square in the heart of the city. Several banks were located within an easy walk from the hotel, most of them also on Great Saint James Street or in the Place d'Armes Square. The Confederate agents in Canada were well financed and became regular customers of Canadian banks. The St. Lawrence Hall also contained the headquarters of the British army forces stationed in Canada. Union agents kept a close watch on St. Lawrence Hall in an attempt to identify rebel sympathizers. Information about the hotel guests was sent to the U.S. State Department.⁵

President Jefferson Davis employed one of the couriers, Thomas Henry Hines (c.1840– 1898), to deliver a letter to Senator Robert Mercer Taliaferro Hunter (c.1809–1887), informing him of the efforts to set up an organization of Confederate spies in Canada:

> I have made attempts to engage for the service in Canada several gentlemen deemed competent. The subject is too delicate to permit entering into details until I have the pleasure of seeing you. I confine myself to saying that two persons specially qualified are now on their way here [Richmond], from the South, and I have reason to believe that they will depart for their duty in a few days. One of them is known to you.

The two persons referred to by Davis were Jacob Thompson (1810–1885), a former U.S. senator from Mississippi and U.S. secretary of the interior before the war, and Clement Claiborne Clay (1816–1882), a former U.S. senator from Alabama. Davis wrote to Thompson on April 27, 1864: "Sir: Confiding special trust in your zeal, discretion and patriotism, I hereby direct you to proceed at once to Canada; there to carry out the instructions you have received from me verbally, in such manner as shall seem most likely to conduce to the furtherance of the Confederate States of America which have been entrusted to you."

Thompson and Clay departed from Richmond on May 3, 1864, in company with William Walter Cleary (1831–1897), who would serve as secretary of the Canada mission. Cleary, born in Kentucky, had attended Transylvania University and graduated from Transylvania Law School in 1851. His marriage to Ann Wherritt brought him important connections with some of the more prominent Kentucky families. Cleary's pro-rebel activities drove him to avoid arrest by going to Canada in June of 1862. The Confederate army of

General Braxton Bragg (1817–1876) entered Kentucky in September, prompting Cleary to return home. When Bragg's forces retreated southward only a month later, Cleary followed them. Arriving in Richmond on January 7, 1863, he secured work as a clerk in the second auditor's office. Cleary was sounded out for a mission to Canada as early as June of 1863, but it was not until April of 1864 that he was engaged by Secretary of State Judah P. Benjamin (1811–1884) to join the Confederate mission to Canada.

Running the Federal blockade, barely escaping a Union gunboat, the new "commissioners" arrived in Montreal on May 29, 1864. Another rebel agent, James Philemon Holcomb (1820–1873), who had been in Montreal for several months, joined them there. The three men were called "commissioners" rather than ambassadors or ministers because Britain did not officially recognize the Confederacy. Their instructions were to "crystallize anti–Northern feeling in Canada and to mould it into some form of hostile expression." They were also to try to encourage anti–

Judah P. Benjamin was the Confederate secretary of state in 1865. John Surratt was sent by Benjamin with dispatches for the Confederate undercover agents in Canada (Library of Congress).

Lincoln administration sentiments in the North, looking toward the elections in the fall of 1864. Moving on from Montreal, they established their headquarters at the Queen's Hotel in Toronto.[6] There was no doubt as to the person in charge of the Confederate Canada mission, as stated in the following dispatch from the Confederate secretary of war, James Alexander Seddon (1815–1880) to Thompson: "[Hines] is to report and confer with the Hon. Jacob Thompson, Special Commissioner of the Confederate States Government in Canada, and be guided by his counsel in his proceedings and actions in his present service. He may consider his instructions from this [War] department subject to modification and change or revocation by the said Commissioner, and will take further instructions from him."[7]

The Confederate mission in Canada was very well funded. One of the few surviving documents linked to the Secret Service is a request on Department of State stationary, dated April 25, 1864, which reads as follows: "To the Secretary of the Treasury, please cause a warrant for the sum of one million dollars payable out of the Appropriation for 'Secret Service' Act of 15 Feb. 1864, to be issued in favor of Hon. J.P. Benjamin Secretary of State Payable in foreign countries £206,185. 11.4 [206,185 pounds, 11 shillings, 4 pence] Exchange on England requested. Jefferson Davis, President C.S.A."

The money referred to was not in paper—the value of which varied over the course of the war and was seldom accepted at face value—but was one million dollars in gold. This huge sum represented about 20 percent of the gold appropriated for all Confederate

Secret Service operations.[8] It can thus be seen that the South was serious about undercover operations, particularly in Canada.

An analysis of President Davis's requests for treasury warrants gives us an idea of how much money was involved, when it was requested, and for whom it was intended. Money earmarked for undercover activities was usually labeled for "Secret Service" or "Necessities and Exigencies" (NE) for the Confederate executive department—the president and his cabinet heads. The "Necessities and Exigencies" account had $840,000 as of March 15, 1861, and the "Secret Service" account, with no explanation for exactly what kind of activity the money was intended, contained a huge sum: $5,000,000. By late February 1865, the NE expenditures totaled $601,523.66 in gold. In the period between the beginning of 1864 and the end of March 1865, $1,257,666 in gold had been paid for "Secret Service." Secret Service funds were handled through the Confederate state department, with money specified in gold requiring the authorization of Jefferson Davis.

A record book kept by William J. Bromwell, a disbursing clerk in the Confederate state department, recorded accounts for Jacob Thompson, John Slidell, James M. Mason, James P. Holcombe, Colin J. McRae, and others. The sums listed are very large, demonstrating the difference in the buying power of the money of 1865 compared to today. One appropriation for "Secret Service" totaled $5,000,000. Enough documentation survived to confirm that this money was handled and approved for Secret Service operations by the highest authorities of the Confederate government.[9]

Confederate agents Clement C. Clay and James P. Holcombe became acquainted with William Cornell Jewett (1823–1893), who had been trying to promote peace between North and South through diplomatic means. Jewett contacted New York newspaper editor Horace Greeley (1811–1872) and told him "two ambassadors of Davis and Company are now in Canada, with full powers of peace." Clay and Holcombe had no such authorization from Richmond, but Greeley, a passionate advocate of peace between the sections, strongly urged President Lincoln to explore a chance for a possible end to the bloodshed in spite of his pro–Union orientation. Greeley reminded Lincoln that many Northerners felt as Greeley did about ending the war, and Lincoln might improve his reelection chances through such means. Although skeptical, Lincoln decided to authorize such a meeting to demonstrate that he was willing to consider a sincere chance for peace. He would not, however, recognize any rebels as having legitimate official diplomatic status, just as he refused to recognize the Confederacy as a sovereign nation. He agreed to allow the passage through the military lines for "any persons any where professing to have any proposition of Jefferson Davis in writing, for peace, embracing restoration of the Union and abandonment of slavery,—whatever else it embraces." Lincoln also deputized Greeley to serve as the Union's chief negotiator.[10]

Clay and Holcombe informed Greeley that they lacked the full power of the Confederacy to negotiate for peace but advised him to obtain safe passage for them—together with George Sanders—to go south, obtain the authorization from Richmond, and then come to Washington to discuss peace. John M. Hay (1838–1905), assistant to Lincoln's personal secretary, in New York City at the time, suggested he might write the safe conduct papers in the president's name and deliver them to the parties to save time. Lincoln agreed with this idea and sent this message:

Executive Mansion
Washington, D.C., July 16, 1864

The President of the United States directs that the four persons whose names follow—to wit: Hon. Clement C. Clay, Hon. Jacob Thompson, Prof. James P. Holcombe, George N. Sanders—shall have safe-conduct to the City of Washington in company with the Hon. Horace Greeley, and shall be exempt from arrest or annoyance of any kind from any officer of the United States during their journey to the said city of Washington.

By order of the President:

> John Hay
> Major and Assistant
> Adjutant-General.

Hay joined Greeley and traveled to Niagara Falls, Canada, to meet the Confederate agents. Hay gave them a letter from Lincoln, addressed "To whom it may concern," suggesting that the President did not recognize them as representing a sovereign power. The note stated, "Any proposition which embraces the restoration of peace, the integrity of the whole Union, and the abandonment of slavery, and which comes by and with an authority that can control the armies now at war against the United States, will be received and considered by the Executive government of the United States, and will be met by liberal terms on other substantial and collateral points; and the bearer, or bearers thereof shall have safe conduct both ways." Of course, the terms spelled out by Lincoln were considered by Southerners to be nothing more than demands for surrender. Consequently, they served only to be useful in rallying rebel support in the South and antiadministration sentiment in the North.[11]

Probably the best surviving document describing Confederate undercover activities in Canada is a lengthy letter in which Jacob Thompson relates the actions of his agents to the Confederate secretary of state, Judah Philip Benjamin (1811–1884). The letter was written in Toronto on December 3, 1864, and received by Benjamin on February 13, 1865. It would have been carried by couriers such as John Surratt, though we have no evidence Surratt was involved in transporting this particular document. Thompson mentions that he had sent similar letters before, "but I have no assurance that any one of them has been received." He writes, "[W]e have afforded the Northwestern States [the area known as the 'Old Northwest' because it was the northwestern part of the country before the Louisiana Purchase; it made up the area which is now the states of Indiana, Illinois, Michigan, Wisconsin, and part of Minnesota] the amplest opportunity to throw off the galling dynasty at Washington and openly to take ground in favor of states' rights and civil liberty."

Jacob Thompson, the leader of the Confederate spy mission in Canada from 1864 to 1865, might have helped Surratt escape across Europe (Library of Congress).

Thompson got in touch with anti-Union organizations such as the "Sons of Liberty" and said he was received by them "with cordiality, and the greatest confidentiality...." It was hoped that Ohio, Illinois, and Indiana could be taken out of the Union, relieving Kentucky and Missouri as well. A "general uprising" was planned to coincide with the Democratic convention in Chicago on July 4, 1864, but that was put off and eventually had to be abandoned. Thompson lamented, "A large sum of money has been expended in fostering and furthering these operations and it now seems to have been to little profit."

A scheme was then conceived to capture the Union steamer U.S.S. *Michigan*, the only Union gunboat on the Great Lakes, and make use of it to liberate Confederate prisoners of war being held at Johnson Island in Lake Erie. Union authorities were able to prevent the ship's capture, and the plan fell through. Another plan was to organize pro–Southerners in the North "to convert their paper money into gold and withdraw it from the market." This, it was hoped, would cause economic problems in the North and thereby hamper the Union war effort. Human nature helped to foil this plan: as the price of gold rose, those who had converted their money were tempted to sell the gold at a profit, thus minimizing the economic effects. Thompson enlisted a former Nashville banker, John Porterfield (1820–?), in the gold scheme, giving him $100,000. The failure of this plan did not shake Thompson's faith in the idea: "I am inclined to the opinion that this theory will work great damage and distrust to the Federal finances, if vigorously followed up, and if no untoward circumstances should interfere with the operation."

"Incendiarism," setting fires wherever and whenever possible, seemed like a good idea. Steamboats on the Mississippi River were set ablaze at St. Louis, "involving an immence loss of property to the enemy." A "Mr. Churchill" was paid to set fires in Cincinnati, but either he missed his opportunities or simply pocketed Thompson's money, as no fires resulted in that city. A serious effort was made to burn much of New York City. A group of Confederate agents planned the attack to take place in late fall of 1864 using a substance called "Greek fire," a combination of phosphorus and bisulfide of carbon, which would supposedly burst into flames upon exposure to the air. Simultaneous fires were to be started around the city. Hotels were singled out because agents could simply check into a hotel, go to their rooms, and ignite the furniture. Targets selected were the St. James Hotel, Fifth Avenue Hotel, La Farge House, Metropolitan Hotel, St. Nicholas Hotel, Tammany Hotel, Astor House, Lovejoy's Hotel, Howard Hotel, Belmont Hotel, and United States Hotel. For good measure, fires were to be started at Barnum's Museum and aboard ships docked in the Hudson River. The "Greek Fire" did not work the way intended, and the fires were extinguished before they could inflict serious damage. By coincidence, the night for the firing of New York City, November 24, 1864, was the night of a benefit performance of Shakespeare's *Julius Caesar* at the Winter Garden Theatre, with the three acting Booth brothers, Junius Brutus Booth, Jr. (1821–1883), Edwin Booth (1833–1893), and John Wilkes Booth (1838–1865), appearing together on the same stage for the one and only time. Edwin was able to calm the audience by assuring them that the theatre was not on fire.

Thompson's fellow commissioner, Clement C. Clay, parted company some time prior to the writing of the letter to Benjamin, and the two commissioners divided up the money. Thompson wrote, "As the money was all in my name, which I supposed to be controlled by us jointly, and as he [Clay] desired to have a sum placed in his hands, at all times subject to his personal control, I transferred to him $93,614, for which I hold his receipts, and for which he promises to account to the proper authorities at home. Including the money turned over to Mr. Clay, all of which he has not yet expended, the entire expenditures as yet on all accounts is about $300,000. I still hold three drafts for $100,000 each, which have not been collected."

Clement C. Clay was one of the leaders of the Confederate espionage and sabotage agents based in Canada from 1864 to 1865 (Library of Congress).

Thompson also assured Benjamin that he would remain in Canada or depart according to orders and suggested, "I had best return with the funds remaining on hand." He also noted, "I have so many papers in my possession, which in the hands of the enemy would utterly ruin and destroy very many of the prominent men in the North, that a due sense of my obligations to them will force on me the extremest caution in my movements." It is intriguing to speculate on the identities of the "prominent men in the North" who had been involved with the Confederates. In closing, Thompson stated, "This letter, though long, does not, I am aware, report many things of minor importance which have occurred during my sojourn in Canada, but I shall omit them at present." One of the "things of minor importance" he mentions only in passing, and then denies any personal involvement in, was the raid on St. Albans, Vermont.[12]

Twenty-five Confederates crossed the Canadian border and attacked the town of St. Albans on October 19, 1864. Three banks were robbed of about $150,000, buildings were set afire, and five people were shot (one fatally) before the raiders returned to Canada. Most of the raiders were arrested by Canadian authorities, and the United States began extradition proceedings. Thompson's denial of knowledge of the raid would seem to be thrown into doubt by John William Headley (1840–1930), one of the Confederate operatives in Canada, but not a participant in the raid. Headley stated in his memoir, "I soon learned that Colonel Thompson knew nothing of the expedition, but knew Lieutenant Young [Bennett H. Young, c. 1843–1917, the leader of the raid]. A few days afterwards Mr. Clay came up from Montreal to Toronto and gave us all the particulars, as reported to him by Lieutenant Young and his men. I met him [Clay] in Colonel Thompson's rooms at the Queen's Hotel. He said he had authorized the expedition."

Headley appears to be referring to Clay. We can certainly wonder why Clay would give the go-ahead for such a sensational raid without telling Thompson. Later in his account, Headley states that after Young had run the blockade to return to the South, "at Richmond the authorities cheerfully agreed to the recommendation of Mr. Clay," after which Young returned to Canada. It is not clear which recommendation was "cheerfully agreed to," but Headley tells us this in the context of relating the background to the planning for the St. Albans raid. Thompson obviously did not disapprove of the raid, even if he had not been involved in planning and authorizing it, for Headley tells us that "the friends of Lieutenant Young in Montreal at once united with the Confederate Commissioners in securing the services of all the leading lawyers of this Canadian province." During the trial of the raiders, $50,000 was transferred from St. Catherines, Canada, where Clay resided, to the Ontario Bank in Montreal. The case against the raiders was eventually dropped.[13]

The Union was very much aware of the Confederate spy mission in Canada and had their own spies keeping track of the rebels. Most of these Northern spies remain nameless, though we know something of one of them, H.H. Emmons, due to the survival of a letter of his to Secretary of State Seward. Emmons is thought to have been employed by Seward rather than any organization of Union spies. An excerpt from Emmons' letter to Seward follows: "I conversed with you at Washington in relation to the information obtained of a plot in Canada to import infected goods into the country, and to take the lives of the President and the heads of the departments." This refers to what is called the "Yellow Fever Plot," which involved the carrying of clothing and bedding used by yellow fever patients in Bermuda into the United States and distributing it among the people of the North, especially soldiers. A valise was specially made up for delivery to the White House, though it was not actually delivered. Yellow fever was a dangerous epidemic disease that had ravaged American cities in the past and for which no cure was available. However, the plot could not have worked, since yellow fever cannot be spread by "infected" clothing. It was not known until well after 1865 that the disease is spread by mosquitoes.

Emmons' letter details his contact with Colonel Lafayette Charles Baker (1826–1868), chief detective of the War Department, to find out about the plot and report on it to Secretary of War Stanton. Baker was recalled by Stanton to head the investigation of Lincoln's assassination, making him unable to go to Canada with Emmons. On his own, Emmons was able to obtain evidence of the "Yellow Fever Plot," which he gave to the judge advocate general of the army, Joseph Holt (1807–1894), who made use of the evidence at the trial in 1865. Author William A. Tidwell (1918–1999) suggested that Emmons' letter, as well as responses to it, created the suspicion that Union authorities knew in advance of the assassination plot against Lincoln involving Confederates at high levels, raising the possibility that "the government conducted a massive coverup of the facts ... so they protected the Union officials who committed gross negligence deliberately or not.... Could it not be that Emmons' knowledge and testimony

Lafayette C. Baker served as the head Department of War detective and helped in the search for Booth and Herold (Library of Congress).

would not only have condemned the Confederacy for murder but high ranking members of the Union government of abhorrent negligence."

We know that John Surratt was a courier for the rebels, and it would be logical that he might have made a trip to Canada any time after May 1864 when Thompson and Clay arrived there. There is no certain evidence that Surratt went to Canada before April 1865, although as a courier who traveled in secret, probably using assumed names, it is possible he did make one or more such trips. In the register of the St. Lawrence Hall, Montreal, we find on January 23, 1865, the name "Harrison" arriving at 11:30 a.m. from Toronto and staying in room 186. The following day we note "E.G. Lee and Lady" arriving at 11:00 a.m., room 10. General Edwin Gray Lee (1836–1870) would replace Jacob Thompson as head of Confederate operations in Canada in early April. On February 3, we find "H.H. Emmons" arriving at 9:00 a.m., room 132. As we have seen, Emmons was the U.S. district attorney in Detroit and made extensive investigations of Confederate agents in Canada. Jacob Thompson arrived at noon on February 14, apparently as part of a group, as he signed for several rooms: 144, 10, 150, and 107. The following day, "Mrs. N. Slater" signed in at 3:00 a.m., from New York, room 138. Sarah Antoinette Slater (1843–1920) was a highly capable Confederate spy and courier who often traveled to Canada. H.H. Emmons returned on February 28 at 12.30 p.m. from Detroit and booked room 2. Thus, from late January through February 1865, there were known Confederate agents coming and going from Montreal's premiere hotel; there was also one Yankee agent who may have been tracking them. We can be tempted to speculate that there was some sort of summit meeting of rebels during that time, though we cannot be sure of that. St. Lawrence Hall was well known to be a major headquarters of Confederates in Canada, and rebel agents, or suspected agents, were in and out of Montreal on a regular basis.[14] Surratt wrote to his friend Louis J. Weichmann on September 24, 1864:

> Dear Friend
>
> John Surratt is neither dead nor drafted; though he ran the gauntlet of both. I am just able to walk about a little, yet very weak. I've had the chills and fever pretty severely. In hopes I have entirely escaped. I shall be in Wash. as soon as possible; in fact I intend to stay up some few days in order to recuperate. Possible of certain events having turned up. I am quite sorry "Miss Estelle" has gone to Phila. There is no attraction there now for me. Miss Fannie and I were getting on a fair road to a flirtation, when she bundled up bag and baggage and left for Washington. She says "She is glad Mr. Surratt intends moving to town." All right we will see. Write soon and tell me all the news. Nothing would give me greater satisfaction than to a long, long letter. I am very happy to state that I escaped the draft. I sincerely hope you may do the same. Family are well and send respects to you.
>
> Yours as ever,
> Harrison Surratt[15]

In a later statement, Mary Surratt, when asked about where her son John had gone, replied, "He did not [say where he was going]. When he left he was a little vexed. The draft was being enforced in Maryland, and I told him to go to Mr. Bell and pay in the fifty dollars for exemption."

In the letter to Louis J. Weichmann quoted above, John referred to the draft. He may have escaped the draft for medical reasons. He often had bouts of ill health and may have gotten an exemption that way. He refers to his health trouble in the letter, describing conditions which resemble malaria. He may have paid for the exemption, as his mother advised him to do. Congress passed a conscription act in 1863 calling for army provost marshals to create records of all men between the ages of twenty and thirty-five. This would have included John Surratt, Jr., after his twentieth birthday on April 13, 1864. A quota of draftees was set for each district, and if the quota was not met, a lottery was held. It is possible that John's name was in the lottery and was not drawn by chance. So, there are several possible ways by which he could have avoided the draft legally. It is unlikely that he resorted to draft-dodging, as he was living at his mother's house in Washington from around November 1864 until March 1865. He was appearing on the streets and public places during that time, using his true name. We do not know who "Mr. Bell," the man referred to by Mrs. Surratt, was, but the sum of $50 would not have been enough to pay for a commutation. The full fee was $300, and that would not have applied to future draft calls.[16]

4

Conspiracy

John Surratt, Sr., had mortgaged his property in Prince George's County, Maryland, on December 6, 1853. This land, called "Pasture and Gleaning" and "Little Gleaning," was traded to army captain Augustus Abel Gibson (?–1893) for $5,000 for the 114 acres, while Surratt paid Gibson $4,000 for a property in Washington, D.C. This transaction eased, at least temporarily, Surratt's mounting load of debt. In this way, John Surratt, Sr., acquired the house at 541 H Street, North West, Square 454, Lot 20, whose street address was originally 541 H Street, NW, and was built in 1842 by Jonathan T. Walker, who sold it to Hugh B. Sweeny, a Washington money-lender and real estate-dealer, on July 1, 1843. In 1850 the lot was assessed at $864, the house at $5,000. Sweeny sold the house to Augustus Abel Gibson and Sarah Knowles Gibson on June 5, 1851. John W. Maury of the Bank of Washington provided what can be presumed to be a loan of $3,500 to the Gibsons. The price of the house was not recorded.[1]

The house—which still stands and the address of which was changed in later years to 604 H Street—was rented out by the Surratts from 1853 until 1864. Daniel J. Browne rented the house in 1855. He was an agricultural clerk at the patent office and had previously worked in the Bureau of the Census. He lived in the house until at least 1858. In 1862 Alfred L. Treadway and William H. Treadway rented the house. Alfred Treadway was a lawyer and William Treadway a clerk at the patent office. Perhaps William Treadway had heard about the Surratts' house from fellow patent clerk Daniel Browne. In 1863, the house was rented to Mrs. E. Brainard, who worked for the Michigan Soldiers Relief Association, and James F. Drake, a professor of music. We don't know how many people lived in the house before Mrs. Surratt moved into it in late 1864. It is possible that the residence of these tenants overlapped, as the house had enough rooms to accommodate multiple tenants.

In the fall of 1864, the house became empty when Mrs. Surratt's tenants moved out. Unable to deal with debts left her by her now-deceased husband and with economic problems caused by the war adding to her troubles, she decided to lease the tavern at Surrattsville and move herself, her daughter, Anna, and her son, John, Jr., to the house in Washington, D.C. She hoped to raise much-needed income by taking in boarders.[2]

Mrs. Surratt advertised for boarders in the *Washington Evening Star* beginning on November 30, 1864, with the ad appearing again on December 8 and 27. Anna was the first to move in, on October 1, 1864. Honora Fitzpatrick (1846–1896) arrived October 6 and Louis J. Weichmann (1842–1902) took up residence on November 1. Mrs. Surratt had moved in by the beginning of December, and John, Jr., came and went as it suited him. Mary Apollonia Dean (1855–1894) moved in early in 1865 and attended school nearby. The Holohan family arrived on February 7, 1865. The family consisted of John T. Holohan (1829–1877), his wife, Eliza Jane (1832–1899), their daughter, Mary C. (1851–?), and their son, Charles E. (1853–1909).

John T. Holohan, a stonecutter by trade, was working for the post office at the time he and his family moved to Mrs. Surratt's house. The Holohans' marriage was not a happy one. His wife had once had her husband arrested for assault. The *Washington Evening Star* for March 6, 1862, reported: "The Second Ward Police patrol arrested John T. Holohan for beating up his wife. He gave security to keep the peace to Justice Hazard at the station house." For a time John Holohan was able to make money arranging for substitutes for the draft, a practice that was then legal.

When the Surratt boardinghouse and its residents became suspects in the assassination, Mrs. Holohan and her two children moved to the residence of her mother. Later, the family would move to Baltimore. It has been suspected that Mrs. Surratt may have been related in some way to Mrs. Holohan, although no obvious connection can be established. Mrs. Holohan's maiden name was Smith, not Surratt or Jenkins. Mrs. Surratt and Mrs. Holohan may not have been related, but they shared their faith in Roman Catholicism. Indeed, all of Mrs. Surratt's boarders at the H. Street house were Roman Catholics.

Weichmann later wrote that he paid thirty-five dollars a month for his room, which included having to share with occasional boarders, especially John Surratt. Weichmann had secured a clerical position at the War Department with a salary of eighty dollars a month. He later wrote of his satisfaction with his new position:

> [T]he work of the office was laborious but there was rich compensation for this in the company of the gentlemanly and kind-hearted clerks who were my associates. John H. Surratt now came to see me frequently, sometimes spending a few days with me at my boardinghouse [this had been before Weichmann moved to Mrs. Surratt's house]. He was always welcome; whatever I possessed was his own, as much as mine....
>
> Surratt informed me of a purpose on the part of his mother to lease her country home [the tavern at Surrattsville] and occupy her residence in Washington City, the intention being to open a private boardinghouse. In that event I was invited to make my home with the family. Cheerfully did I consent, for I was weary of the loneliness of the large house where I resided. I was then boarding at the corner of Nineteenth Street and Pennsylvania Avenue in a house kept by a colored caterer by the name of Purnell.
>
> I was delighted with the opportunity of being with the friend of my college days, a friend whom I trusted, and honored....
>
> Mrs. Surratt ... had leased her property in the country to a man by the name of John M. Lloyd [1824–1892] at five hundred dollars per annum. I was a witness to that lease and in that way became acquainted with Lloyd, who was a very plain and unpretentious individual, but abundantly able to run the farm and sell whisky to his neighbors

Weichmann described the house as being "lead colored." The floor at street level was the basement, divided into a sitting room in front with the dining room and kitchen behind. The first floor, which at that time had a stairway and entrance outside from the street, consisted of Mrs. Surratt's private room in front, a parlor in the middle, and two small bedrooms in back, one for Mrs. Surratt herself and the other for Miss Fitzpatrick. The second floor (third level) had three rooms, the forward two rooms and foyer housing the Holohan family, the rear room being Weichmann's. In the attic were the rooms of Anna Surratt and Mrs. Surratt's niece, Olivia Jenkins (1846–1898). There was also a small attic room used by a servant. A hallway ran along the right side of each floor (as one entered from the front), with the stairway in the rear of the hall. On the left side of the front rooms on the first and second floors was a fireplace. The house measured, then as now, forty-nine feet deep by twenty-four wide.[3]

It was in the summer of 1864 that John Wilkes Booth began to recruit men to help him carry out a grand scheme to kidnap President Lincoln and ransom him for thousands of Confederate prisoners of war being held in camps around the North. Bearing a name made famous by his father, Junius Brutus Booth, Sr. (1796–1852), John Wilkes Booth (1838–1865) followed his father and older brothers, Edwin Thomas Booth (1833–1893) and Junius Brutus Booth, Jr., (1821–1883) into the acting profession. By 1864, John Wilkes was one of the major theatrical stars of America as well as a Southern patriot. Though not joining the Confederate forces, he claimed to have smuggled drugs for the Southerners. It has been suggested that Booth required—and doubtless received—the assistance of the Confederate government and military in organizing and carrying out his conspiracy. While the evidence for this assumption is not absolute, it is strong enough to overpower the argument for coincidence.

In October 1864 Booth visited Montreal, Canada. As we have seen, the Confederacy had by that time established a large and well-financed espionage operation in Canada. Arriving in Montreal, Booth registered at the St. Lawrence Hall on October 18. As previously noted, this hotel was one of the centers of the Confederate clandestine operations in Canada. There is a possibility that Booth met with Jacob Thompson, leader of the rebel spies in Canada. It is known that Booth met with George N. Sanders, Patrick C. Martin, and probably others. That the Confederacy was interested in the idea of kidnapping Lincoln cannot be disputed. Confederate officers Captain Thomas Nelson Conrad (1837–1905) and Brigadier General Bradley Tyler Johnson (1829–1894) were known to be planning, and possibly even attempting to carry out, such an action. Booth must have received money while in Canada, for he opened an account with the Ontario Bank in Montreal, depositing $455, in company with Patrick C. Martin. Martin gave Booth a letter of introduction to Dr. William Queen (1789–1868), who lived in southern Maryland.[4]

As he planned his abduction plot, Booth recruited his accomplices. Two old school friends, Samuel Bland Arnold (1834–1906) and Michael O'Laughlen (1840–1867), are the earliest we know about. Help from the Confederates put Booth in a position to gather others into his fold. Traveling to Charles County in southern Maryland, Booth looked up Dr. Queen, and Queen's son-in-law, John C. Thompson, who introduced the

John Wilkes Booth was the mastermind of the conspiracy to kidnap the president. He later changed his plans and decided to assassinate Lincoln (Library of Congress).

actor to Dr. Samuel Mudd (1833–1883). Dr. Mudd claimed that this was an entirely innocent meeting:

> I was introduced to [Booth] by Mr. J.C. Thompson ... in November or December last [1864]. Mr. Thompson resides with his father-in-law [Dr. Queen], and his place is about five miles southwesterly from Bryantown, near the lower edge of what is known as Zechiah Swamp. Mr. Thompson told me at the time that Booth was looking out for land in this neighborhood ... and Booth inquired if I knew any parties in this neighborhood who had any fine horses for sale.... The next evening he rode to my house and stayed with me that night, and the next morning he purchased a rather old horse, but a very fine mover.

Dr. Mudd originally stated that this was the only time he had met with Booth before the assassination.[5]

It appears that Booth was getting help from the southern Confederacy in organizing his kidnapping plot. It can be no surprise that the fanatically pro-rebel Booth should seek help from that quarter. Indeed, he might have joined the secret "Knights of the Golden Circle," a pro–Confederate organization, as early as 1858. He had spent much of the formative years of his acting career in Richmond and toured several Southern cities before the war. Historians Tidwell, Hall, and Gaddy speculate that Booth began an association with the Confederate Secret Service around mid–1863. It would have been natural for Booth to seek help from the rebels, and also perhaps the other way around. When Booth paid another visit to Charles County, around mid to late December 1864, Dr. Mudd introduced him to Thomas Henry Harbin (1833–1885), a local resident and member of the Confederate Secret Service. James O. Hall (1912–2007) believed that it was Harbin who probably introduced John Wilkes Booth to John H. Surratt, Jr.[6] We have evidence that Booth knew Surratt at least by January 1, 1865. At the trial of John Surratt, William E. Cleaver testified to that question:

> Q. Are you the Dr. Cleaver who kept a livery stable in 1865 on Sixth Street?
> A. Yes, Sir.
> Q. Near what place?
> A. Near the corner of Maryland Avenue; between B Street and Maryland Avenue.
> Q. When did you commence there?
> A. In January, 1865...
> Q. Did you know John Wilkes Booth?
> A. Yes, sir.
> Q. Did you know John H. Surratt?
> A. Yes, sir.
> Q. How long have you known John H. Surratt?
> A. About twelve years, I think—ten or twelve years.
> Q. Have you had a speaking acquaintance with him?
> A. Yes, sir.... He came down to hire a horse of me at the time Booth kept his horse with me.
> Q. When did Booth first bring his horse to you to keep?
> A. The 1st of January, 1865—the day we got the stable.
> Q. And to that stable on Sixth Street?
> A. Yes, sir.
> Q. State whether you saw him [Booth] and Surratt there together.
> A. Yes, sir.
> Q. What were they there together about? What did they say and do?
> A. I do not know; the first time, I hired a horse to them.... The first time I saw Surratt there with Booth, Booth came, I think, and paid one or two weeks' livery. Then, three or four days after, he came down and I hired him a horse to go into the country.
> Mr. Bradley [defense attorney]: Hired to whom?
> A. To Surratt. He came and hired a horse two or three times. The next time, Booth and Sam Arnold came there together.... The last time Surratt came there and hired a horse he came there about three or four o'clock in the afternoon.

Q. When was that?
A. That was the 25th of January, 1865.

As we shall see, there is every reason to doubt Cleaver's testimony, but regarding the simple fact of Surratt's association with Booth this testimony can be said to establish that Booth and Surratt were acquainted with each other at least by the beginning of 1865.[7]

Once Booth and Surratt got together, Booth knew he had a reliable man. Booth's presence at Mrs. Surratt's house in Washington became more and more frequent. In his lecture, John Surratt described an incident that led him to believe Booth's plan was not the only conspiracy afoot:

> I had good reason to believe that there was another conspiracy afloat in Washington. In fact we all knew it. One evening as I was partially lying down in the reading room of the Metropolitan Hotel, two or three gentlemen came in and looked around as if to make sure that no one was around. They then commenced to talk about what had been done, the best means for the expedition, etc. It being about dusk, and no gas lit, and I partially concealed behind a writing desk, I was an unwilling listener to what occurred. I told Booth of this afterward, and he said he had heard something to the same effect. It only made us all the more eager to carry out our plans at an early day for fear some one should get ahead of us. We didn't know what they were after, exactly, but we were well satisfied that their object was very much the same as ours.

The Confederacy was certainly involved in Booth's plot to kidnap Lincoln. Word went down the "secret line," which linked Richmond with points north and eventually all the way to Canada. Thomas Austin Jones (1820–1895) was the chief signal agent of the Confederate secret line where it crossed the Potomac River. Jones later described the plot:

> Sometime in December, 1864, I heard that there was "a big scheme" afoot to abduct President Lincoln....
> Briefly stated, the plan was this: The President, when he went for his customary evening drive toward the Navy Yard, was to be seized and either chloroformed or gagged, and driven quietly out of the city....
> The carriage was to be escorted out of the city by men dressed in Federal uniform. Relays of fast horses were in readiness all along the route, and a boat in which to take the captive across the Potomac was kept on the west side of Port Tobacco Creek, about three and a half miles from the town of the same name....
> There were quite a number of persons in this abduction conspiracy; prominent among whom were the actor, John Wilkes Booth, and his friend, John H. Surratt.
> The house of Mrs. Surratt,—mother of John H. Surratt,—in Washington City, was the frequent rendezvous of the daring conspirators. The arms and ammunition that would be needed in carrying out the contemplated enterprise were placed at Surratt's house, Surrattsville [the tavern], Prince George's County, Maryland, eight miles southeast of Washington.

Louis Weichmann fills us in on John Surratt's other activities during this period:

> In pursuance of his mother's wishes, one of John's first moves after his arrival in Washington was to seek employment. The Adams Express Company was then unusually rushed with business. Boxes and packages were pouring in from the North and West by the thousands for shipment to the Boys in Blue at the front. The company was in need of help and Surratt applied for work to the agent, Mr. Charles C. Dunn. In his letter of application he stated that he had "a ready hand and a willing heart," and that he would be faithful in any position given him. Mr. Dunn himself told me during Surratt's trial that he was so much pleased with the expression "ready hand and willing heart" that without hesitation he granted him the coveted position. This occurred on December 30, 1864.... [H]e did not retain his place long. Other influences were at work to drag him from his desk.

If Weichmann means the word "desk" in the sentence above to be taken literally, we have a clue that Surratt's duties at the Adams Express were along the lines of paperwork and record keeping, not in the handling or transport of packages.[8]

Louis Weichmann described at length a different story of how Booth and Surratt met, neatly including Dr. Mudd as well. He changed some details every time he told the story. At the 1865 trial of the conspiracy suspects, Weichmann said he and John Surratt were walking along Seventh Street in Washington when they heard a call: "Surratt, Surratt!" John Wilkes Booth was introduced to Weichmann and Surratt by Dr. Mudd. In the 1865 testimony, Weichmann said this happened on January 15, 1865. At the trial of Surratt in 1867, he said it was "in the winter of 1864–65." Other testimony put the date of the meeting at December 23, 1864. Booth invited them to his room, number 84, at the National Hotel. Weichmann described Booth conversing with Dr. Mudd "out into the passage," where John Surratt joined them after a few minutes. He said the three men were out in the hallway "about fifteen or twenty minutes." When they returned to the room, "Booth ... took out the back of an envelope, and made marks on it with a pencil. I should not consider it writing, but more in the direction of roads or lines. Surratt, Booth, and Dr. Mudd were at that time seated round the table,—a centre table,—in the centre of the room." At the trial of John Surratt, Weichmann added that the three men were "about eight feet from me." At the 1865 trial, Weichmann was questioned closely about this.

> Q. But you did not hear a word spoken yourself...?
> A. No, sir: I do not know the nature of the conversation they had at all.
> Q. I understand you to say you did not hear any of their private conversation?
> A. No, sir: I did not.

Is it not extremely curious that Weichmann insisted he heard nothing of the conversation when sitting only eight feet away? Weichmann at that time was only twenty-three years old, and nowhere did he mention that he had any hearing problem, not then and not later.

In the 1890s, Weichmann wrote an extensive history of the Lincoln assassination from his point of view. He was very concerned that his book be considered the definitive account by a key witness to the events. In it, as he told the story of this meeting for the third time, he introduced a new element: Booth used an alias. He quoted Dr. Mudd as saying,"[L]et me present to you my friend Mr. Boone." Relating the story of the mysterious meeting again, Weichmann referred to Booth as "Boone." After they had broken up, "on the return home that night, John Surratt remarked that the brilliant and accomplished young gentleman whom we had met was no less a personage than John Wilkes Booth, the famous actor." Weichmann writes, "When I saw Booth on Seventh Street I did not know that he was an actor nor was I aware that he was John Wilkes Booth until Surratt told me." Then he adds as a footnote: "The name Boone, first given me by Dr. Mudd, was, I believe, for the purposes of deception and to conceal Booth's identity."

In his statement of April 30, 1865, Weichmann also forgot to mention the "Boone" alias: "Dr. Mudd introduced Booth to Surratt and Weichmann." Why would Weichmann fail to reveal that Booth used an alias? Or, if he didn't, why would Weichmann make up such a detail? If the alias story was true, it might be seen as casting doubt upon the guilt of Dr. Mudd, suggesting the doctor might not have known the true identity of the actor. It also creates problems with the idea that this was the first time John Surratt met Booth, as Weichmann tells us in his later book that Surratt told him "Mr. Boone's" true identity. How did Surratt know that if he had not met Booth before? As we shall see, there are many questions raised by Weichmann's accounts and much room for reasonable doubt.[9] Another account of how Booth and Surratt met comes from Booth biographer Francis Wilson (1854–1935):

> Booth had been down into lower Maryland, where he had met Dr. Samuel Mudd, and under the pretense of buying "farming lands" and riding horses (he purchased a horse), was looking over the ground with which, for his purpose, it was necessary for him to have familiar acquaintance. Indeed, he must be able to recognize every feature of the landscape, night or day. In short, it was the route over which, if his plans carried, he intended to convey the President as a prisoner to Richmond. In southern Maryland he was

among Southern sympathizers and made it known that he needed some one who knew the territory thoroughly. On learning that Dr. Mudd knew Surratt, he solicited an introduction. Later, as Booth and Dr. Mudd were walking along Pennsylvania Avenue in Washington they met Surratt and Booth was made acquainted with him.[10]

In an 1898 article, a shadowy reporter using the name "Hanson Hiss" presented what was purported to be Surratt's own account of his involvement in the conspiracy: "Wilkes Booth was never introduced to me by Dr. Mudd on the street or anywhere else. Booth came to me with a letter of introduction from a valued and trusted friend.... Weichmann was nowhere near when Booth presented his letter." The Hiss article contains so much that is improbable, so many statements that are at best self-serving and at worst entirely false, that we cannot place any credence in it, except to say that the above quote just might contain a kernel of truth.

Surratt himself, in his lecture, provided few details of how he came to meet Booth: "In the fall of 1864 I was introduced to John Wilkes Booth, who, I was given to understand, wished to know something about the main avenues leading from Washington to the Potomac. We met several times, but as he seemed to be very reticent with regard to his purposes, and very anxious to get all the information out of me he could, I refused to tell him anything at all." He went on to say that he did not trust Booth, and doubted that his kidnap plan could be successful: "After two days' reflection I told him I was willing to try it. I believed it practicable at that time, though I now regard it as a foolhardy undertaking." We must remember that Surratt's own account of his adventures is also suspicious and obviously self-serving.[11]

Whatever the truth may be as to how Surratt met Booth, by the beginning of January 1865 John Surratt was fully involved in Booth's conspiracy to kidnap President Lincoln. John Surratt now busied himself in furthering the kidnap conspiracy plan. He transferred his interest in the family property to his mother on January 3, 1865. This was probably a way of protecting himself, for as an active courier for the Confederacy and now becoming involved in Booth's conspiracy he may have been concerned about his property holdings being seized should he be captured. The deed was recorded with the land records of Upper Marlboro on January 23, 1865. There was a fee of $1, payable to the federal government, and a fee payable to the clerk of the court, not recorded. This latter fee may have been only a "tip" for services rendered. A law passed by Congress on July 17, 1862, stated that a person guilty of treason "shall be imprisoned for not less than five years and fined not less than ten thousand dollars," further stating that "said fine shall be levied and collected on any or all of the property, real and personal, excluding slaves, of which the said person so convicted was the owner at the time of committing the said crime." Transfer of Surratt's interest to his mother would avoid the family's loss of most—if not all—of their assets should John be convicted of treason. Mrs. Surratt—tried for conspiracy in the kidnap-assassination plot—did not have her property confiscated because she was tried by a military court under military law, which did not contain such a provision. The family eventually lost their property, but it was taken to satisfy debts owed by John's father. The transfer of property to Mrs. Surratt might indicate that she was not involved in her son's schemes and commitments to the rebels and to Booth. Those who believe Mary Surratt to be guilty and an active participant in the Booth conspiracy are yet unable to establish when it was that she became involved.

M. Edward Martin, a Confederate treasury department agent, found himself in Port Tobacco, Maryland, in January of 1865. While trying to get "a man by the name of Andrew Atzerodt [George Andrew Atzerodt (1835–1865)] to take me over the river to Virginia," he was "introduced to a man called Surratt, stopping at same hotel. Surratt came to the hotel one evening after dark and remained that night. The next day at the supper table, remarked he intended to return to Washington that night. I asked him why he would return that night, and he replied he was in the employ of Adams Express Company, and had three days leave, and had to be back the next day at 9 o'clock." Asking about making the river crossing, Atzerodt told him "he had parties to carry over within a week; that they had bought two boats capable of carrying ten men. He said he bought them for Surratt. Surratt appeared to be the manager and had Atzerodt in his employ. The parties were to come from the vicinity of Washington.... Surratt was in company with a tall man about 6 feet 1 inch, well built, fine appearance, hair long of a dark brown color, florid complexion. I think he had a beard on his chin."

The tall man in company with John Surratt may have been Thomas Henry Harbin (1833–1885), another Confederate agent. Martin guessed that the party of men they were planning to get across the river was composed of escaped rebel officers, though Atzerodt probably was expecting the kidnapped President Lincoln. Regardless of that, this account establishes that Surratt was making trips into southern Maryland and that he was in touch with Booth conspirators and rebel undercover agents. This is further mentioned in a letter of Provost Marshal James L. McPhail (1816–1874), reporting to Secretary Stanton: "A man named Harbaum [Harbin] living near Piscataway, Prince George's County, Md. ... was associated with Surratt in blockade-running, and was seen with Surratt in Port Tobacco, in February or March [1865]."

John's employment with the Adams Express Company ended on January 13. When his mother learned of it, she tried to get the company to take John back; she must have been counting on John's salary to ease the family's indebtedness. Adams would not take John back nor did John want to return. He had other commitments. He didn't even go back to collect the pay due him.

Around mid-January, John Surratt accompanied Thomas H. Harbin to Port Tobacco, Maryland. They were looking for a boat large enough to serve the kidnappers' needs in crossing the Potomac River. They also needed a skilled boatman to handle their boat in crossing the river, with its tricky currents and eddies. Harbin introduced Surratt to George A. Atzerodt. A German immigrant, Atzerodt did carriage repair and other odd jobs for a living in Port Tobacco. His expertise in boating came from his helping the Confederate secret line. Atzerodt was pro-South, but his allegiance was for sale. John Surratt had money, not from the Adams Express Company but undoubtedly from Booth; Atzerodt was signed on as a member of the conspiracy, and a boat was secured from a local farmer, Richard Mitchell Smoot (1833–1906). The boat was owned jointly by Smoot and James A. Brawner (1835–1886). Smoot later described the transaction in detail.

> I owned a good large and stout boat, and fell into the way of transporting goods and passengers across the Potomac, and from that occupation to that of running the blockade was but a short step and an inviting one. [In other words, Smoot became involved with the Confederate Secret Service as part of the "secret line."]
>
> In the early part of that year [Smoot says 1864, but he must have meant 1865] I received a visit from John H. Surratt, who expressed a desire to purchase my boat. He also said that he would have use for two other boats which, however, must be capable of transporting fifteen persons each rapidly and safely across the Potomac.
>
> He was noticeably eager to secure my boat, and incidentally explained his desire to have the boat by saying that it would be needed in an emergency which might arise within a very short time. He also said that if purchased the boat would be immediately removed to a point up King's Creek, which is a branch of the Potomac about ten miles from Port Tobacco, where it was to be held in readiness for instant use. With reference to the other two boats wanted, Surratt said they were to be stationed at certain unnamed points to meet exigencies which might arise and cause well-laid plans to go astray, and which did arise. I was using my boat, and asked Surratt if he could not do without it for a while; but he declared that if he bought it he

would want possession right away, as the need of the boat would be the consequence of an event of unprecedented magnitude in the history of the country, which would startle and astound the entire world.... I was inclined to associate the coming event with a plan to abduct Lincoln, concerning which plan I had heard vague rumors.

   I went with Surratt to the office of ex-Judge Stone in Port Tobacco. There he placed in the hands of Judge Stone one hundred and twenty five dollars in trust for me, and Judge Stone became personally responsible for the payment of the balance.

The Frederick Stone (1820–1899) named in Smoot's account was undoubtedly the same man who took part in the defense of some of the conspirators at the military trial. He was a descendant of Thomas Stone, (1743–1787), a member of the Continental Congress from 1775 to 1779, and a signer of the Declaration of Independence. Frederick Stone was admitted to the bar in 1841 and was practicing in Port Tobacco, Maryland. A member of the Maryland legislature in 1865 and 1871, he served in the U.S. House of Representatives from 1869 to 1871. Historian Michael W. Kauffman speculated that Frederick Stone might have joined the conspirators' defense in order to help avoid any of the defendants identifying southern Maryland residents as members or aiders of Booth's conspiracy.[12]

John Surratt was actively helping Booth recruit additional conspirators. In addition to George Atzerodt, Surratt made a trip to Baltimore to engage another new member of the group, a large, muscular young man who went by the name of Payne but whose real name was Lewis Thornton Powell (1844–1865). Looking menacing and saying very little, Powell was exactly the sort of man Booth needed in his kidnap conspiracy. Powell had been serving in the Confederate army since the beginning of the war, first in the Second Florida Infantry. He participated in the siege of Yorktown, Virginia, in 1862 and in the battles for Williamsburg, Seven Pines, Gaines Mill, Second Bull Run, Antietam, Chancellorsville, and Fredericksburg. At Gettysburg he had been wounded and captured. He served as a hospital steward, first at Gettysburg, then at Baltimore. Escaping from the hospital, Powell joined the partisan forces of Colonel John Singleton Mosby (1833–1916) in early 1864. By the beginning of 1865 Powell was in Baltimore, living at a rooming house managed by the Branson family at 16 North Eutaw Street. Powell had previously met Margaret Branson (1832–1914), who had volunteered to work at the hospital at Gettysburg College, where he, then still a prisoner, also worked. It appears that at least one of the Bransons' friends may have had connections with the rebel Secret Service. Jacob B. Heim was a dealer in imported liquors and made trips "on business" to Richmond.

Another Baltimore businessman was David Preston Parr (1819–1900), who had a shop at 210 West Baltimore Street called "Mr. Parr's China Halls." In addition to selling china and glassware in Baltimore, Parr also traveled about looking for business, often to the South. Parr was actively involved with the Confederate Secret Service, and his shop was a rendezvous point for rebel spies.[13] A letter about Parr is among the documents gathered for the trial of the conspiracy suspects:

J.L. McPhail to Col. H.L. Burnett   May 29, 1865

   Sir, in accordance with your request, I give you my knowledge of Mr. David Preston Parr, of this city [Baltimore]. Frequent reports have come to me of his visiting Charles County, Md., Surrattsville and other places in that section of the country. Mr. T. Robey gave me the information. Mr. Parr has always accounted for his visits to this section of country as being in pursuit of business, collecting and drumming up trade. With regard to his sentiments, he is secesh. His character otherwise is without reproach and as gentle as a child and I would as soon believe an infant guilty of a criminal act as he.

Respectfully yours,
J.L. McPhail
Pro. Mar. Gen., S. Md.

The mild-mannered Mr. Parr was interrogated on April 29, 1865, as part of the assassination investigation:

> Q. When did you first become acquainted with Jno. Harrison Surratt?
> A. I suppose it was two years ago [1863]. It was in the stage from Leonardtown [Maryland] to Washington.
> Q. Where did he get in?
> A. I am not certain. The stage stops at a number of places.
> Q. Did he come a large portion of the way or only a small portion?
> A. I do not know.
> Q. Where did you get in?
> A. Leonardtown.
> Q. What kind of acquaintance did you make on the stage? ...
> A. [A] casual acquaintance with him on the stage. A question arose in regard to the passage of the pickets [guards] at the bridge. Some inquiries were made.
> Q. By him? [Surratt]
> A. I do not know whether by him or someone else, or myself. It was a general conversation. In the stage they asked where I was going and I told them. I told them what my business was. I do not remember whether I had samples with me. My samples are of no value when we are done with them, and we give them away or leave them.... Surratt I think stopped at his house [the tavern] as we passed, at Surrattsville. I do not know whether he came on to Washington or not.... He told me who he was. He seemed to be quite communicative. He was quite young. He was pleasant. He spoke of my business, etc. and of being able to send me some leads or something of that kind.
> Q. When did you next see him?
> A. It must be several months after that.
> Q. Where?
> A. He called on me at my store.
> Q. What purpose?
> A. Merely as a casual acquaintance.
> Q. No business?
> A. None, sir.
> Q. How often did he call to see you up to the 1st of January last? [1865]
> A. I am not certain.
> Q. About how often?
> A. Two or three times.... One morning ... I started to go out, and I met Mr. Surratt.... There was standing there, or there came up at the time, another person, looked like an ordinary countryman. It strikes me he named his name. He talked more to him than to me.

Parr went on vaguely for some length. He made the excuse that his epilepsy affected his memory. Obviously he would not have discussed secret espionage activities, either Surratt's or his own. What is significant is that he acknowledged knowing John Surratt and admitted that Surratt had visited him at his shop in Baltimore.[14]

On January 21 Weichmann accompanied Surratt to Baltimore. They stayed at the Maltby House, room 127. The following morning, according to Weichmann, Surratt told him he had $300 and had to see someone on private business and Weichmann could not come with him. It is possible that Surratt met with Powell and gave him the money. Weichmann later suggested that Surratt had already met Powell prior to this meeting. At the 1865 trial, Weichmann stated: "He [Powell] appeared to be treated kindly by Mr. Surratt, as if he was an old acquaintance. On the occasion of his second visit to the house [Mrs. Surratt's boardinghouse in Washington], Mr. Surratt, when meeting him, recognized him as though he had known him." At the trial of John Surratt in 1867, Weichmann again raised the possibility:

> Q. On this occasion [the earlier trial] did you not state that the following day, that is, the day after Payne's [Powell's] arrival, "Surratt had come back; I was sitting writing; Payne came in and asked, was that Surratt; I said yes. Then Payne said he wanted to see Surratt in private?"

A. I said that. But there was a sort of recognition between the two; I believe that Surratt knew Payne before he ever came to the house.

Only three days later, on January 25, Surratt headed to Richmond. While there, he met with the Confederate secretary of state, Judah P. Benjamin. By the first of February, Surratt had returned to Washington. The testimony of another Confederate agent, James H. Fowle, corroborated this. In May 1866, Fowle testified before a congressional committee headed by Congressman George Sewall Boutwell (1818–1905), R-MA:

Q. Where did you meet him [Surratt]?
A. At Surrattsville.... That was in February, 1865. I was introduced to him and we went in and took a drink.
Q. Was that the only time you met him?
A. I had heard of him before. I knew he was the agent of our government [Confederacy].
Q. When did you first hear of John H. Surratt as a Confederate agent?
A. Ever since the 16th of May 1863. I was detached in the Signal Corps. After the first of the war I entered the 17th Virginia Infantry and went on duty at Manassas but injured myself in unloading [railroad] cars and had to be put on light duty. On the 16th of May 1863 I volunteered again and was put into the 17th Infantry and detailed to signal duties and then put in the Secret Service.
Q. Do you know about Surratt's bearing dispatches?
A. I knew he did carry dispatches. He was in Richmond.
Q. When was he in Richmond?
A. He was in Richmond about January or February [1865].
Q. Was Surratt the secret agent of the State Department; if not what Dept. did he belong to?
A. I think the State Dept. but I will not swear to it. Each agent was kept to himself; we did not know about the other. Mr. Benjamin told me that Mr. Surratt was there, and Quinton Washington told me.
Q. When did they tell you that?
A. When I got back on the 2nd or 3rd of March. They told me he had been there since I came over.
Q. Do you know if he had any special branch of the Secret Service?
A. I believe not. He was connected with carrying dispatches to New York and Baltimore.
Q. Do you know of his carrying dispatches through to Canada?
A. I do not think he carried them further than Washington, Balt. [Baltimore] and NY [New York].
Q. Do you know at what time John H. Surratt bore any dispatches from Richmond north?
A. It must have been in February.... He and Gus Howard [Augustus Spencer Howell (1837–1869)] brought dispatches together.
Q. Who introduced you to John H. Surratt in February 1865?
A. Gus Howard [Howell]....
Q. What did Howard say to you about Surratt? Did he tell you Surratt was in the Confederate service?
A. I had known that before.
Q. Did Howard say anything to Surratt about you?
A. It was always understood between us we were all in the Secret Service.

Fowle's testimony establishes that John Surratt went to Richmond in January or February of 1865 and that Surratt conferred with Secretary of State Judah P. Benjamin. Historian James O. Hall speculated that Surratt might have discussed the kidnapping conspiracy at that time. If so, that would mean that Booth's plan to kidnap Lincoln was known, and possibly supported, by the Confederate government at the highest levels. Adding further fuel to the speculative fire, Hall notes that Col. John S. Mosby was also in Richmond at about the same time Surratt was there.

John Surratt was clearly still involved with the Confederate Secret Service at the same time he was a trusted and useful member of John Wilkes Booth's kidnapping conspiracy. Was this a coincidence? Since it appears that Powell had been sent to Parr, who had contacted Surratt about introducing Powell to Booth, the connection of Booth's group with the rebel underground is all but certain. What may have been coincidence was Colonel Mosby's presence at the same time as John Surratt's. Coincidence, perhaps, but if Booth was making plans to abduct President Lincoln in the first two months of 1865, coordinating the abductors would not only make sense, it would be mandatory considering that the kidnappers would have to pass through northern Virginia, "Mosby country."[15]

About this time, John Surratt's path crossed that of a young woman who was also a courier for the Southern cause. She was known by the name "Mrs. Slater." Her real name was Sarah Antoinette Gilbert. She had been born on January 12, 1843, in Middletown, Connecticut. She moved with her family to Kinston, North Carolina, in 1858. Moving to New Bern, North Carolina, by 1859, Sarah met a dance instructor named Rowan Slater (1835–?). Sarah, known to her friends as "Nettie," boarded at the house of J.L. Pennington, who was a friend and patron of Rowan Slater. When the Civil War broke out, Slater had to close his business. "Nettie" Gilbert married Rowan Slater on June 12, 1861, they having already moved to Goldsboro, North Carolina. Slater accepted work as a purchasing agent for the Southern government, while Sarah's three brothers joined the rebel army. The Slaters moved to Salisbury, North Carolina, around the spring of 1863. Enlisting in Company A of the 20th North Carolina Infantry, Rowan Slater went off to war on July 23, 1864. Sarah moved to Richmond in mid–January 1865 and applied for a pass to go to New York City, where her mother was living. This request may have been a cover story to conceal her real purpose, for Sarah Slater left Richmond on January 31, 1865, carrying documents for Confederate agents in Canada. She arrived at Mattox Creek, Westmoreland County, Virginia, by the first or second of February 1865. There she met a rebel spy by the name of Augustus Howell, who had been released from arrest only four days before. He had taken the oath of loyalty to the Union as a condition of release, but he promptly violated that oath by returning to Confederate service. Howell had had no qualms about breaking his oath; this was not the first time he had done so. He accompanied Mrs. Slater to New York City, arriving around mid–February. She went on to Montreal to deliver documents to the rebel agents there, while Howell went to Washington and stayed at Mrs. Surratt's boardinghouse.[16]

Augustus Spencer Howell (1837–1869), also known as Gustavus Howell, enlisted in the Confederate army on June 27, 1861, at Fredericksburg, Vieginia. He was enrolled in the 1st Maryland Artillery Regiment, First Battalion. He was from Charles City, Maryland, stood 5 feet 11 inches tall, had a dark complexion, blue eyes and dark hair, and gave his profession as clerk. Howell became ill in mid–July 1862, his illness being described as "phthisis, erysipelas, and general disability." He was discharged July 16, 1862. A document dated October 24, 1862, entitled "Captures of the Potomac Flotilla," by H.H. Savage, acting master of a schooner, reported the capture of "six prisoners in the act of rowing to Va to join the so-called rebel army." Their names were listed as follows:

> J.T. Swann   Frank Thornton
> R.B. Dasey   Augustus Howell
> Thomas Hammon   J.H. Parsons

The report also noted that the prisoners had tried to destroy personal letters by throwing them in the river. Howell may have already joined the Confederate Secret Service by this time and may have been taking the others across the river, either as enlistees—as the report says—or as participants in secret operations.

Howell testified as a witness for Mrs. Surratt at the 1865 military trial and had some interesting things to say about Louis J. Weichmann:

> I first became acquainted with Mrs. Surratt and John H. Surratt about a year and a half ago [1863], at Surrattsville.... I called one evening at her house [in Washington], about the 20th of February [1865].... I

met Louis J. Weichmann once at Mrs. Surratt's; I remained there two days or more. I had no particular business, and I went to Mrs. Surratt's because I knew them, and because it was cheaper than at a hotel.

When I saw Mr. Weichmann I showed him a cipher [a device for encoding messages], and how to use it. Weichmann then made one himself [the cipher found among Booth's effects was exhibited to the witness].

The cipher I showed to Mr. Weichmann was the same as this. I had some conversation with Mr. Weichmann with respect to his going south; he said he would like to go south, or intended to go south.

Mr. Weichmann said he would like to go south with me, but he was not ready, he said, to go at that time; but as soon as he got his business arranged he was going. He asked me if I thought he could get a position in Richmond; I told him I did not know.... He told me that his sympathies were with the South, and that he thought it would ultimately succeed. I believe he said he had done all he could for that government—referring to the South.... [H]e stated to me the number of Confederate Prisoners the United States Government had on hand, and the number they had over that of the Confederate Government. I doubted it at the time, but he said it would not admit of doubt; that he had the books in his own office to look at [Weichmann worked at the War Department's Office of the Commissary General of Prisoners] ... [and] he expressed himself as a friend of the South, as a Southern man or a secesh sympathizer would.

I met a lady by that name [Mrs. Slater] in Washington, about the 20th or 22nd of February [1865], and had some conversation with her in front of Mrs. Surratt's house. We went to Virginia together. John H. Surratt was with her [Mrs. Slater] in the buggy.... I staid about two days and a half at Mrs. Surratt's in February. I told them that I had been to Richmond. I do not know that they knew my business. I had some conversation with Mrs. Surratt, and judged she knew I was from Richmond. I think Atzerodt was at Mrs. Surratt's house during the time I was there, but I never saw Payne [Lewis T. Powell]....

I never took the oath of allegiance to the United States [untrue].

Weichmann, as we might expect, had a somewhat different description of Howell's visit:

Mrs. Slater at this time had come from Montreal or New York and was on her way to the South. The same evening she came to Mrs. Surratt's house, she met on the pavement in front of the house one Augustus Howell. She was afterwards taken by him to Virginia, and he again met her in Richmond in the latter part of February. Howell himself had been at Mrs. Surratt's before the arrival of Mrs. Slater there. His visit occupied two days and a half. He came about the 20th of February....

I know nothing of him or his antecedents. He was introduced to me by [John] Surratt as Mr. Spencer. I did not know what his business was, but I soon found out that he was in the habit of running the blockade from Maryland into Virginia. I had a good deal of conversation with him, and endeavored to glean from him all the information I could.... He taught me a cipher which he said he learned from a magician's book, and had been familiar with for six or seven years.... I never made any use of it except to translate a few poems into it.[17]

As questions will arise regarding the stories of both Howell and Weichmann, we cannot say which is the more reliable or whether either should ever be taken at face value.

In early February 1865 John Surratt went to New York City. He told Weichmann that he had visited John Wilkes Booth there and also met Booth's mother, Mary Ann Holmes Booth (1802–1885), along with his brother, Edwin Thomas Booth (1833–1893). According to Weichmann, "Surratt ... was continually on the go and away from home much of the time. He was not now busying himself about getting an appointment or securing work. He always appeared to have plenty of money and had the air and actions of a man thoroughly preoccupied with important business affairs." Samuel Arnold also mentioned Booth and Surratt seeing each other and being busy: "He [Booth] was always pressed with business with a man unknown and then only by name John Surratt. Most of Booth's time was spent with him, we [Arnold and O'Laughlen] were left entirely in the dark." John V. Piles, a witness at the trial of John Surratt in 1867, described his having been visited by Surratt about three months before the assassination:

Q. You were justice of the peace in 1865?
A. Yes, sir; in 1864-'65.
Q. Do you know John H. Surratt?
A. Yes, sir; I know him well enough.

4. Conspiracy

Q. How long have you known him?
A. I have known him ever since he was a boy. His residence is not more than two or three miles from mine [referring to the tavern at Surrattsville].
Q. State whether you had an interview with him in the early part of 1865....
A. About that time I had left home; I was working at my father's, or lower place, some mile or so from there. Mr. Surratt came down there for the purpose of getting me to sign some papers ... as a justice of the peace, in order to make them legal.... The draft was on hand at that time, and I asked him about it. He said either that he wanted to get some money, or fix some papers to leave for his mother, or something of that kind. He told me he wanted to go away.... He said he wanted to go away to avoid the draft.
Q. Where did he say he was going?
A. I think he told me that he intended to go to Canada. It was rumored at that time that there were a great many going there in order to avoid the draft.... He said something about wanting to make his mother safe, or leaving her some money.... It was probably a mortgage or deed to get money on to pay the expenses of his voyage—something like that. I think he said, if he did not return he wanted to make his mother safe, or something like that. I am disposed to think that he was going to make some arrangement to get money, and, perhaps, she was going to be responsible, or something like that.

If this actually happened as Piles testified, it probably was John's signing over his interest in the family property to his mother.

Returning from New York around February 22, John Surratt was accompanying Mrs. Slater. She had brought dispatches to the Confederates in Montreal, Canada, and joined Surratt in New York City. According to George Atzerodt, Surratt signaled her on the sidewalk in front of a hotel on Broadway, using an elaborate stick with a ribbon stuck to it he carried in his hand. The Confederate agents did use recognition signals to identify themselves to each other, but this device was most likely made up by Surratt to impress Atzerodt. Mrs. Slater already knew John Surratt, so a recognition signal would not have been necessary. Weichmann described their arrival at Mrs. Surratt's house:

George Atzerodt was another of the Booth conspirators. His courage failed him and he was unable to go through with plans to assassinate Vice President Johnson (Library of Congress).

About the 22nd of the same month [February 1865] a buggy was driven one evening to the house by John H. Surratt with a lady in it. Mrs. Surratt called to me to assist her in getting out, and to bring into the house her trunk, a very small affair, which I did. The woman was rather diminutive in height, but very active and sprightly in all her movements. She wore what was called in those days a "mask," a kind of short veil, covering the face only as far as the chin. I did not succeed in seeing her face at all, and I believe that it was intended that I should not. She was not introduced to me, but afterwards I ascertained her name to be Mrs. Slater, at least that was the name under which she was traveling. She remained in the house only one night, and I gave up my room to her use. I learned subsequently that she was a dispatch bearer.[18]

Around the same time, late February, Lewis T. Powell appeared upon the scene. Louis Weichmann was, as usual, in the middle of the action:

> It was in the evening.... Mrs. Surratt, Anna, her daughter, Miss Fitzpatrick, and myself were there ... [when] sometime during the evening the doorbell was rung. Answering the summons, I found standing before me a tall and robust individual with very black hair and ruddy countenance. He was a young man and wore a dark felt hat, rather slouchy, and was clad in a seedy black overcoat. His two hands were buried deep in his overcoat pockets. Looking me full in the face, he asked if Mr. Surratt lived there and if he was at home. I replied that it was Mr. Surratt's home but that he was not in. Then he inquired if Mrs. Surratt was at home, and I told him she was. He thereupon expressed a desire to see her and gave his name as Mr. Wood.

Mrs. Surratt asked Weichmann to bring "Mr. Wood" a supper to his [Weichmann's] room. The always inquisitive Weichmann remained with "Wood" and asked him questions: "I asked him whence he came. 'I am from Baltimore,' was his answer, 'and a clerk in the china store of Mr. Parr.'" After eating, "Wood" expressed his desire to sleep. He was put up in the attic. Upon arising the next morning, Weichmann learned that "Mr. Wood" had already left. Years later, Weichmann reflected upon his first meeting with Powell: "How often I have pondered over this event. All unconscious to myself I was entertaining a man in the service and pay of John Wilkes Booth; one who would ever figure as one of the greatest criminals of the world." Powell returned to Baltimore. What purpose his visit to Mrs. Surratt's house was is unknown.[19]

The Booth conspirators were gathering in Washington during the early weeks of 1865, but they seemed to need to move around a lot. George Atzerodt visited in early February, as Weichmann testified: "[A]t that time there was a man there by the name of Howell. Mr. John Surratt had been in the country, and he returned from the country that evening; and John Surratt slept that night with Howell.... [Howell] left the next day. His leaving was owing to the arrival of Mr. Surratt at that time, as near as I could judge. He said he wanted to see John; and as soon as he saw John, he left." Samuel Arnold and Michael O'Laughlen were in town, and also changed their residences often.

> [W]e went to Rullman's Hotel (kept by Lichau) on Pennsylvania Avenue. We remained there a few days and then went to Mitchell's Hotel near Grover's Theatre [the National Theatre, on Pennsylvania Avenue] and remained a few days. We went from there and rented a room from Mrs. Van Tyne, No. 20 D Street and obtained our meals at Franklin Hotel at the corner of D & 8th Streets, and there remained off and on until the 20th of March 1865, during which time I [Arnold] frequently went to Baltimore (nearly every Saturday). O'Laughlen as a general thing always went and returned me on these visits.

Booth himself was spending a lot of time in Washington. On December 20, 1864, he had ridden his horse from Baltimore, only to leave the horse at a stable, returning to Baltimore by train the same day. The following day, he brought one of his many girlfriends, a prostitute named Ella Starr (1846–?), to the capital city, where she boarded at a house of prostitution kept by her sister on Ohio Avenue [what is now known as the "Federal Triangle"]. Booth took a room at the National Hotel, where he usually stayed. Booth went to Grover's Theatre on Saturday, December 24. Matthew W. Canning (1830–1890), Booth's manager, was there, too, and described Booth's reaction to seeing Lincoln at the theatre: "[W]hen the President and lady were passing out, he [Booth] moved after them, eyeing them very intently, while they waited on the steps some moments for a carriage." Canning said he noticed Booth watching the president with the greatest intensity, and when the president had left Booth turned around and said, "Come on."

Between December 25 and 31, 1864, Booth was traveling again, to New York City, Philadelphia, and Baltimore, returning to Washington on the last day of the year. His travels cannot be explained by a busy acting schedule, for after ending the 1863–4 season in Boston on May 27 his only subsequent professional appearances were at Corby's Hall, Montreal, Canada; for dramatic readings on October 24, at the Winter Garden Theatre in New York City on November 25; as Mark Antony in Shakespeare's *Julius Caesar*; at Grover's [National] Theatre in Washington on January 29, 1865; as Romeo in Shakespeare's *Romeo and Juliet*; and at Ford's Theatre on March 18 as Pescara in *The Apostate*, by Richard Taylor Shiel.[20]

On January 10, Booth made a brief trip to Baltimore to see Arnold and O'Laughlen. He brought them a trunk. Arnold described the trunk's contents:

> In his trunk he had two guns (maker unknown) cap, cartridges which were placed in the gun stock (Spencer rifles, I think called) Revolver knife bells cartridge caps canteen. All fully fixed out, which were to be used in case of pursuit, and two pieces handcuffs to handcuff the President. His trunk being so heavy he gave the Pistols knives and handcuffs [to] Michael O. Laughlin [sic] and myself to have shipped or bring to Washington, to which place he had gone, bought Horse buggy wagon and harness leaving the team to drive on to Washington.[21]

Booth obviously did not acquire the weapons and equipment in Washington, where he had been residing for days and weeks with only intermittent short excursions elsewhere. He must have taken delivery of the heavy load in Baltimore, perhaps having arranged it earlier, possibly in late December, when he was in Philadelphia and Baltimore. There was no need to hire anyone to deliver the goods, as they might remember the gentleman purchasing a heavy load of weapons and restraining devices and arranging to have them delivered in Washington just before the president was kidnapped. He needed his team of coconspirators to assemble in Washington anyway. Having Arnold and O'Laughlen bring the weapons down with them would be not only convenient, it would also divert suspicion from Booth himself.

On March 3, 1865, Weichmann suggested to John Surratt that they take a walk around town "to enjoy the sights." It was the evening before the inauguration of President Lincoln, and there were many visitors in town and much festivity: "We went down Sixth Street and along Pennsylvania Avenue to Eighth Street. Here Surratt left me. In a short time I returned to the house of Mrs. Surratt, a little after seven o'clock. I was surprised to find John Wilkes Booth and John H. Surratt together in the parlor and engaged in an animated conversation. I proposed to them that we should go to the Capitol." The three friends went to see the final session of the outgoing Congress. While visiting the Capitol, Booth noticed a bust displayed there and asked Weichmann who

Michael O'Laughlen was a childhood friend of Booth. He became part of the conspiracy only to die in prison at Fort Jefferson (Library of Congress).

the bust depicted. "'Why,' said I, 'that is Lincoln.' 'What is he doing here before his time,' said Booth, as he passed on. What Booth meant by the remark, I cannot surmise nor am I able to conjecture, but it certainly revealed a bitter animus toward the distinguished President.... He had never before spoken to me in an unfriendly manner of Mr. Lincoln."

Plans were being made for the abduction of the president. John M. Lloyd (1824–1892), the tavern keeper at Surrattsville, described some of these preparations:

Q. Will you state whether or not, some five or six weeks before the assassination of the President [between March 3 and March 10], any or all of these men [Atzerodt, Herold, Surratt] ... came to your house?
A. They were there.
Q. All three together?
A. Yes: John H. Surratt, Herold, and Atzerodt were there together.
Q. What did they bring to your house [the tavern at Surrattsville]? and what did they do there?
A. I saw nothing until they all three came into the barroom.... John Surratt called me into the front parlor, and on the sofa were two carbines with ammunition. I think he told me they were carbines.
Q. Any thing besides the carbines and ammunition?
A. There was a rope, and also a monkey-wrench.
Q. How long a rope?
A. I cannot tell. It was in a coil—a right smart bundle—Probably sixteen or twenty feet.
Q. Were those articles left at your house?
A. Yes, sir. Surratt asked me to take care of them, to conceal the carbines. I told him there was no place there to conceal them, and I did not wish to keep such things in the house.... He then carried me into a room that I had never been in, which was just immediately above the storeroom, as it were in the back building of the house.... He showed me where I could put them underneath the joists of the house—the joists of the second floor of the main building.
Q. Were they put in that place?
A. They were put in there according to his directions.
Q. Were they concealed in that condition?
A. Yes, sir.... I put them in there myself.
Q. For what purpose, and for how long, did he ask you to keep these articles? ...
A. He said he just wanted them to stay for a few days, and he would call for them.
Q. What kind of carbines were they?
A. I did not examine them; they had covers over them.[22]

Pryor to the trial, Lloyd had been questioned extensively:

Think I have been acquainted with Mrs. Surratt since November or December [of 1864]. I went down to see about renting her place [the tavern at Surrattsville]; rented her place and moved there. Since that time my business has been keeping tavern at Surrattsville. John H. Surratt has been at my house often during that time.... He never said what he came for. He seemed to come for nothing but pleasure. He knocked around about the country rightly smart there to parties and balls.... The last time I saw Surratt was on the 25th of last month [March 1865], when he came there with his mother. I do not know what he came for.... They had another lady with them, and they seemed to be in company [probably Sarah Slater].

Lloyd described John Surratt visiting the tavern in company with David Herold and George A. Atzerodt, "and left things there," referring to the carbines and other objects:

The evening before, Herold was at my house playing cards. Walter Griffen was one of those playing cards, and two or three others.... I was myself engaged in it too. He [Surratt] drove up and seemed to be very uneasy about his horse and gave my little nephew a quarter to watch his horse to keep it from running away. Griffin wanted him to go down and spend the night with him, but I ... urged him to stay with me. After playing several games he started out and said he was going to T.B. [a nearby town].

The following day Surratt left the carbines with Lloyd.

Lewis Powell and John Surratt visited Ford's Theatre, taking two girls who boarded at Mrs. Mary Surratt's house in Washington, Honora Fitzpatrick (1846–1896) and Mary Apollonia Dean (1855–1894). Booth had arranged the outing for the purpose of enabling Powell and John Surratt to familiarize themselves with the theatre, the future scene of the planned abduction of the president. The two girls were not involved in the conspiracy. They were there to lend the two men the appearance of respectability. They occupied boxes 7 and 8, the same double box the Lincolns and their guests would use one month later. Booth visited the box and conversed with his fellow conspirators out of the hearing of the young girls.[23]

After escorting the girls back to Mrs. Surratt's, the conspirators began to gather at Gautier's Restaurant. It was the night of March 15, 1865. Attending the meeting, in addition to Booth, were Samuel B. Arnold (1834–1906), George A. Atzerodt (1835–1865), David E. Herold (1842–1865), Michael O'Laughlen (1840–1867), Lewis Thornton Powell (1844–1865), and John Surratt. Two of these men, Arnold and Surratt, left written accounts of the meeting, though Arnold's account is far more detailed than Surratt's and probably more accurate.

Booth laid out the plan he had devised and assigned various roles to each of the others. Booth and Powell—alias "Mosby," who had previously served with Col. Mosby's Raiders—would enter the theatre box and seize the president. O'Laughlen and Herold would put out the theatre's gas lights then receive the captive, whom Powell would lower from the box to the stage. Booth would jump down and aid the others on the stage. Atzerodt and Surratt would take up positions on the southern end of the Navy Yard Bridge and help to clear the road south and take the party across the Potomac. Arnold spoke against the plan: "After listening to Booth and the others' comments I firmly protested and objected to the whole scheme, and told them of its utter impracticability. I stated that prisoners were now being exchanged and the object to be obtained by the abduction had been accomplished, that patriotism was the motive that prompted me in joining in the scheme, not ambition. That I wanted a shadow of a chance for my life and I intended having it." This prompted an argument, which rapidly heated up to the point that Booth threatened to shoot Arnold, who coolly responded "two could play at that game."

Samuel B. Arnold was another boyhood friend of Booth. Arnold was recruited by the actor for the kidnapping conspiracy (Library of Congress).

Surratt stated that the attempt should be dropped because "the government had received information that there was a plot of some kind in hand" and that gates were being built at the Navy Yard Bridge: "I was confident the government had wind of our movement, and that the best thing we could do would be to throw up the whole project. Everyone seemed to coincide in my opinion, except Booth, who sat silent and abstracted." Surratt hints that Booth may have implied that he might assassinate Lincoln if he could not take him prisoner. He quotes one of the conspirators (perhaps Arnold) saying to Booth, "'If I understood you to intimate anything more than the capture of Mr. Lincoln I for one will bid you goodbye.' Everyone expressed the same opinion. We all arose and commenced putting our hats on. Booth—perceiving probably that he had gone too far—asked pardon saying that he had drank too much champagne. After some difficulty, everything was amicably arranged and we separated at 5 o'clock in the morning." It must be kept in mind that both Arnold and Surratt were eager, in their post-assassination writings, to portray themselves in as positive and sympathetic a light as possible and to lay the blame for the assassination entirely on Booth.

One of the restaurant's waiters, John Howard, left the following account:

> I did not see him [Booth] come in; I saw him after they was in the room; I know him when I see him; I waited on him; there were six others with him; I did not know any of the others; I never saw them before; they came between 12 and 12½ o'clock, and we [the waiters] went away about one or half past one, and left them there then; while I was there they were eating oysters and drinking champagne; Booth did not say anything to me; I simply waited on the party; they were talking about the oil company pretty much [Booth had investments in oil and may have used that as a cover for his conspiracy plans]. They were talking apparently so that I could hear; I do not know that they tried to make me understand that that was their business; they were simply talking the same as if I was not there, I suppose; I never saw Booth before; he was never at Gautier's afterwards to my knowledge; I knew it was Booth because the headwaiter knew him and told me it was him; they did not get drinking while I was there; I was not there more than a quarter of an hour, I suppose.

Another waiter, John Thomas Miles, had more to add:

> I remember seeing Mr. Booth there, I think about three or four weeks before the assassination in company with six other gentlemen. They had a supper, which was of oysters, wine, and whiskey. Mr. Booth came there I guess about 11 o'clock or a little after and said that he had a room engaged there and he called for one of the waiters to go to the front door and watch for a hack that would come there with four gentlemen in it. He stayed there himself for a while and said he would wait and see if the hack came before he got ready to go away; but he found the hack did not come and he left me at the door to wait there and direct the gentlemen to the room while he went down to the Metropolitan Hotel and informed another friend that he had made a mistake in directing this hack to call at the Metropolitan for him so that he would come up and meet the party while the other gentlemen would come in the hack.... The gentlemen did not come. Business called me in the house. The next I heard of it was that Mr. Booth had come himself and carried the gentlemen up in the side room. They did not go at all into the public restaurant. He hurried me up to get the supper. I got him the supper. He told me to give him his check immediately. I gave him the check, received the money and went down and paid the check.... I came upstairs with the change, and he gave me a dollar for waiting on him and told me I might go to bed. They were talking about playing cards, and had cards actually in their hands.
>
> Booth told me that some friends would be there that had made a large amount of money in the oil business, and he expected to win about one half of it. He said he expected a man from Northwestern Virginia. After a while they were eating oysters and playing for shares, etc., but I did not see any money put up. They stayed there. The watchman let them out, I believe.

Miles was asked if he could recognize any of the other men and was shown photographs but was unable to identify anyone but Booth. He was asked if any of them were there any other time: "I saw Mr. Booth there with two other gentlemen. I could not recognize who the gentlemen were. He got his breakfast there then. It was a day or two before he played Romeo in the theatre to Miss Jones' Juliet [Booth played Romeo at Grover's Theatre (the National) in Washington, on Friday, January 20, 1865, opposite Avonia S. Jones].... It was the only time I ever saw him there before I saw him upstairs. Then he had breakfast in the big saloon." The watchman at Gautier's that night was Thomas Manning. He was able to add little detail to the waiters' reports: "I heard them talk about his [Booth's] being there at supper. That was about two or three weeks before Mr. Lincoln was shot.... I did not [know any of the others]. I only just let them in about 12 o'clock [midnight] and out about five.... I would not know them if I met them. I only let them in and out.... That is the only time I know they were there at a supper or anything like that. They might have come into the bar and got a drink."

From all of this we can surmise that Booth wanted to impress his band of conspirators, to bring them all together, and to reveal to them his plan for the abduction and the parts each would play in the scheme. We can also surmise that, although this was an abduction plot, the idea of assassination, in his mind, was at least a possibility. They used Booth's oil speculations as a cover story and pretended to be playing cards for the same purpose.

It also appears that the supper meeting was deliberately set up to draw attention, perhaps as part of Booth's efforts to implicate the others in the eyes of the authorities as members of the conspiracy. This would bind the conspirators more tightly to Booth and also prevent their testifying against him or each other in the event of a trial.

We should also consider who did not attend and why. Known conspirators not present were John Minchin Lloyd (1824–1892) and Thomas Henry Harbin (1833–1885), both of whom played active parts in the abduction plot or the assassination. Nor did three of the conspiracy suspects later on trial attend the meeting: Edman Spangler (1825–1875), Dr. Samuel Alexander Mudd (1833–1883), and Mary Elizabeth Surratt (1823–1865), John Surratt's mother. There was another possible suspect whose role, if any, in the conspiracy is uncertain—Louis J. Weichmann (1842–1902) did not attend. Of course, had Spangler, Mudd, Mrs. Surratt, or Weichmann been present, the question of their guilt would have been settled, but since they did not attend, we remain in doubt. Mrs. Surratt would not have wanted to attend a meeting late at night with several men. Such a thing would not be considered "proper" by Victorian society. Lloyd, Harbin, and Mudd did not live in the area and would have had to make a special trip to attend, but that circumstance alone is unconvincing as a reason for their absence. If Mrs. Surratt was the crucial connecting link between the conspirators, as her past and present prosecutors would have us believe, why would she be left out? Perhaps this meeting was not that crucial to the development of the plot, so only those actively involved in the abduction were invited. That may be so, but this was the first time Booth met with more than two or three of his coconspirators, and only one other meeting, on March 17, is known to have occurred. That meeting as well was not attended by the above-named suspects and apparently did not involve any substantial planning. The meeting at Gautier's Restaurant was obviously considered important by Booth, given the trouble he went to in arranging it, so it seems reasonable to think that the nonattendance of three people whose guilt remains in question, while not proving their innocence, at least contributes to our doubts over their possible guilt.[24]

March 17 was to be the big day. Gathering his fellow kidnap conspirators, and, after apologizing to Arnold for the rough way he had threatened him at the meeting two days before, Booth informed them that they were going to make an attempt that day. He told them Lincoln was to attend the performance of a play at Campbell Hospital outside the city on Seventh Street. Arnold and O'Laughlen, after having their midday meal at the Franklin Hotel, joined Booth, who took them to a stable near the patent office to get horses. After returning to their hotel room to discuss the operation with Booth, they rode toward the hospital.

The plan was for the conspirators to wait in the woods alongside the road, and when the presidential carriage came along they would surround it and force a halt. John Surratt was to jump aboard and take the reins from the driver then turn the carriage southward, through southern Maryland. When there was no sign of the carriage, Booth, Arnold and O'Laughlen mounted their horses and rode together about a mile, then Arnold and

David Herold was a pro–Confederate fellow conspirator with John Wilkes Booth (Library of Congress).

O'Laughlen headed back to the restaurant while Booth headed on to Campbell Hospital. Arnold and O'Laughlen encountered Atzerodt and Powell soon after returning to the Restaurant. Booth and Surratt soon followed, Booth telling his companions that the president had not shown up at the hospital, so the kidnap attempt was off. The group split up, heading off in different directions. Surratt with Booth, Arnold and O'Laughlen headed back to Washington, where they later encountered Booth and Surratt.[25]

On the following evening, March 18, at Ford's Theatre Booth appeared in a play, *The Apostate,* as Pescara, the villain. The performance was a benefit for actor John McCullough (1837–1885). The audience demonstrated excitement for Booth, cheering and stamping their feet at his appearance. Booth gave John Surratt two passes to attend the play, and Surratt invited Weichmann to go with him. In the street they met Atzerodt, who joined them. Arriving at the theatre, they met David Herold and John Holohan. After the performance, Surratt noticed that Herold and Atzerodt had not joined them. Surratt asked Weichmann to return to the theater and invite the two to join them at Kloman's Saloon on Seventh Street, where they would have an oyster supper. Weichmann found Herold and Atzerodt in the saloon adjoining Ford's Theatre, talking with Booth. The actor invited Weichmann to have a drink with them, but he took Atzerodt and Herold aside to talk with them further before Weichmann took the two to Kloman's, where they rejoined Surratt and Holohan.

On Sunday, March 19, John Surratt received a letter from New York:

Mr. John H. Surratt,
Washington, D.C.
Dear Sir,
   I would like to see you on important business. If you can spare the time to come on to New York. Please telegraph me immediately on the reception of this, whether you can come on or not & much oblige.

                        Yours, etc.
                        R.D. Watson

This "Watson Letter," as it is known, has intrigued researchers ever since the Lincoln assassination. Booth made trips to New York City during the period from late October until April. Only one of these involved an acting appearance. It is difficult to know how many times John Surratt went there. His not being a celebrity in addition to being involved in rebel secret work has left little evidence. An 1861 letter to the governor of Virginia asking about the raising of a company of men from Maryland to serve with Virginians contained an endorsement signed by an "RD. Watson." Comparing that letter with the later one to John Surratt establishes that it is the same R.D. Watson. Roderick Dhu Watson, Sr. (1835–1901), originally from Charles County, Maryland, was a Confederate agent. Arrested on March 18, 1864, in Baltimore, he avoided prison by taking the oath of allegiance to the Union. Moving to New York City, with an address at 178½ Water Street, he was arrested again on May 8, 1864, and held at Fort Lafayette until October 10, 1864. Author William A. Tidwell described Watson as a "cutout," a term in the espionage business for a courier who does not know the agent or case officer but transfers messages; in other words, an undercover go-between. What business Watson had with Surratt is unknown, but it is a safe assumption that it involved the passing of messages to or from the Confederacy.[26]

Weichmann wrote a letter to John B. Menu of St. Charles College, which both Weichmann and Surratt had attended. We do not have Weichmann's letter to Father Menu, but the priest's reply was found in Booth's hotel room after the assassination:

St. Charles College

March 19, 1865

Why do you not speak more fully? Again in the letter I have just had the honor of receiving from you, you speak in an obscure way of Mr. Surratt, as if he were a rebel; could you not have said openly what is the perilous trip point which he is soon to depart? What is that last? What is the meaning of that restrictive? Between us there should be no secret ... [and] if you wish me to comprehend your reticence's, you must provide me, if you can, with quite sharper visions....

My best regards to Mr. Surratt, if he is not gone already on his trip.

Another letter to Weichmann, also found in Booth's hotel room, also mentions Surratt:

New York Feb. 15, '65

I hope you could not possibly have been offended by any part of my reply on Jany 9th, which I suppose our mutual friend Mr. S——tt found in some envelope with his little note. How sorry I should be to have anything disturb the disinterested friendship existing between us, Mr. Weichmann.... Will you please write to me directly & explain why Mr. S has not been to N.Y., or if he is still at home. I have often thought of you lately, and sincerely hope yr prospects are fair for gaining the heart you seemed to covet. You see I understand your affectionate remark about Mr. S——tt & the conslusion, "I love him, indeed I do, & his —— too."

May your future be all you wish. I know & feel Miss S——tt is worthy of you & they are all favorably disposed towards you, I believe....

Most sincerely yr friend,
Clara

We do not know who "Clara" was, but clearly this letter speaks of both John and Anna Surrat, and hints at a possible romantic interest by Weichmann in John's sister.

It is characteristic of Weichmann to hold back, to try to communicate through implication and not speak out clearly. This habit of his can lead one to wonder if he did not write or speak his thoughts clearly because he was afraid to reveal the whole truth about his involvement in Booth's plot. Booth left behind clues implicating his fellow conspirators. Was this letter one of these clues, suggesting that Weichmann knew more than he was telling and might have had a deeper involvement than he ever admitted? We cannot assume incriminating ideas about Weichmann without stronger evidence than this, but put together with other hints regarding his role, if any, in the kidnap/assassination plot it is impossible for us to abandon all doubt.

On the afternoon of March 20, Weichmann encountered John Surratt at the intersection of Seventh and F Streets. Surratt was on his way to the post office, where he went to the delivery window and asked for a letter for "James Sturdy," another of his aliases. Weichmann stated, "This letter he permitted me to read. It was badly written and signed 'Wood.' The writer stated that he was endeavoring to get something to do in New York, that he was stopping at some hotel (I think but am not certain, that it was the 'Revere House'). He stated further that he would soon leave for a private boarding house in W. Grand St., mentioning some number, I think, between 120 & 130." Surratt admitted to Weichmann that the letter from "Wood" was from Lewis Powell. He used Powell's alias of "Payne" in revealing this to Weichmann.

On March 23, Eliza Holohan came to the Office of the Commissary General of Prisoners, bringing a telegram for Weichmann, which read as follows:

> To —— Wickmann, Esq., 541 H St.,
>
> New York, March 23, 1865.
> Tell John to telegraph number and street at once.
>
> J. Booth.

Weichmann was mystified: "I knew of no one in New York to send me a telegram. I had no acquaintances there. I opened the envelope and saw that the telegram was from Booth. Why should he address me in that way I could not comprehend.... When I returned to my boardinghouse in the afternoon I gave it to Surratt, saying that I thought it was intended for him, and took occasion to ask him what number and street were meant. His reply was, 'Don't be so damned inquisitive.'" This enigmatic message further added to Weichmann's suspicions. He had already spoken to another clerk at his office:

> Captain Gleason; and I said to him, "there is a blockade runner at Mrs. Surratt's house: shall I have him delivered up?" ... My suspicions were aroused by John Surratt and this man Payne and Booth coming to the house. My suspicions were aroused by their frequent private conversations, [and] by seeing Payne and Surratt playing on the bed with bowie-knives, [and] by finding a false mustache in my room....
>
> I made a confidant of Captain Gleason, in the War Department. I told him that Booth was a secesh sympathizer: I mentioned snatches of conversation that I would hear from these parties; and I asked him, "Captain, what do you think of all this?"...
>
> I asked him whether they could be bearers of dispatches or blockade runners. At one time I saw in the paper the capture of President Lincoln fully discussed; and I remarked to Captain Gleason, "Captain, do you think any party could attempt the capture of President Lincoln?" He laughed and hooted at the idea.[27]

Daniel Henry Lawrence Gleason (1841–1917) was born in Langdon, New Hampshire, and grew up in Massachusetts. From 1857 to 1861, he worked on mackerel fishing boats. He met Charles Appleton Longfellow (1844–1893), son of poet Henry Wadsworth Longfellow (1807–1882), while in the fishing trade and they became close friends. The two friends served together in the First Massachusetts Cavalry. Young Gleason showed ability in administration and was commissioned a second lieutenant on July 27, 1862. Promoted to first lieutenant on February 1, 1863, Gleason was wounded on May 1 and again on June 3, 1863. On May 11, 1864, he suffered wounds to his head, hip, and leg and was discharged on September 14. He began working at the Office of the Commissary General of Prisoners in Washington at the corner of F and 20th streets on January 28, 1865. Gleason described Weichmann:

> [O]f Pennsylvania German stock, about twenty-eight years old [Weichmann was twenty-three in 1865], tall and broad shouldered, well educated, speaking several languages, and had been intended for the Catholic priesthood, though he never actually entered it, but had taught school in Washington. Physically and intellectually he was a giant, but in bravery I should call him a dwarf....
>
> His face wore a look of misery and fear, and perspiration ran down his cheeks. I thought he had gone crazy when he told [me] he had been carrying a terrible secret, which so weighed on him that he must

confide it to me, but only under a solemn pledge of secrecy.... "I have often told you that Mrs. Surratt's is a rendezvous for Southerners and rebel sympathizers, who come and go at all times, day and night ... [and] they suspect me, and only the old time friendship between John [Surratt] and I makes it possible for me to stay. For some time I have been aware that something unusual is going on. There have been long secret meetings in John's room. Mrs. Surratt, John Wilkes Booth and some others are always there, and I am sure some of them are connected with the rebel government and are here under false names. I found arms—pistols and daggers—and a false mustache, in the room, and John quarreled with me the other day for commenting on Booth's frequent visits, and made me swear not to reveal anything I knew or might hereafter learn....

John told me ... they had planned to kidnap Mr. Lincoln and his Cabinet, take them over the Potomac into rebel territory, and thus force the North to compromise with the South.... The time set was Inauguration Day, March 4....

They had arranged with rebels across the Potomac to have men and horses ready there, to get the captives to Richmond as quickly as possible.

Gleason decided that he should tell Secretary Stanton what Weichmann had told him. He told his roommate, Lieutenant Joshua W. Sharp, who was an assistant provost marshal (military policeman) on the staff of General Christopher C. Augur (1821–1898): "I [Gleason] called on him [Sharp] and told him Weichmann's story. He listened carefully, and we discussed the whole plan. He said it was nonsense—no one would be foolish enough to attempt the abduction ... that Weichmann was being fooled." Gleason appealed to Sharp, who finally agreed to present the details of the plot to Stanton. As a result, Gleason said, the president was given a cavalry guard.[28] It is not known if Lt. Sharp actually passed on Weichmann's information, but on the night of March 24 Federal troops raided Mrs. Surratt's tavern at Surrattsville. They very nearly crossed paths with Mrs. Slater.

Sarah Slater was returning from Montreal and spent the night of March 24–25 at Mrs. Surratt's house in Washington. John Surratt accompanied his mother and Mrs. Slater to the tavern at Surrattsville, where Sarah expected to be joined by Augustus Howell, who would take her on to Richmond; but Howell had been arrested the night before. Sergeant Daniel Seaton notified General Augur that he arrested Howell on the night of March 24 at Surrattsville. The following day, Gen. Augur ordered Colonel Timothy I. Ingraham (1810–1876), provost marshal in Washington, to "confine this man [Howell] in O.C. [Old Capitol] Prison subject my order, the charge being in the rebel service and a blockade runner." Howell remained in the Old Capitol Prison until July 8, 1865, when he was released upon oath of amnesty.

One of the Surratts' neighbors in Surrattsville, David Barry, agreed to go along as far as Port Tobacco and return the team of horses to Howard's livery in Washington. Surratt gave Barry a note for the stableman:

March 26, 1865.

Mr. Brooks [Brooke Stabler, the stableman.]

As business will detain me for a few days in the country, I thought I would send your team back. Mr. Barry will deliver it safely and pay the hire on it. If Mr. Booth, my friend, should want my horses let him have them, but no one else. If you should want any money on them he will let you have it. I should like to have kept the team for several days, but it is too expensive, especially as I have "woman on the brain" and may be away for a week or so.

Yours respectfully,
J. Harrison Surratt

This note suggests that the "woman on the brain" may have been Mrs. Slater. Mary Surratt took the stagecoach back to Washington while John took Mrs. Slater on to Richmond. J.B. Tinsley, Jr., the desk clerk at the Spottswood Hotel in Richmond on March 29, testified that a man giving the name of Henry Sherman registered early that evening: "He came on the 29th of March to supper, and left the first of April after breakfast." David Homer Bates (1843–1926), the closest thing to a handwriting expert the government had, was asked to examine the signatures found in the hotel register:

> A. I believe the signature to have been written by Surratt.
> Q. By John H. Surratt, the prisoner, you mean?
> A. Yes, sir. John H. Surratt.

Another witness at the trial of John Surratt, Henry Hall Brogdon, also identified him:

> Q. Did you see the prisoner [Surratt] there [in Richmond]?
> A. I did.
> Q. Under what name did he pass?
> A. He passed under the name of Sherman.
> Q. You knew who he was?
> A. I knew who he was.

Brogdon was a sergeant in the Confederate Army Signal Corps. Surratt knew him through his undercover courier work. Brogdon was detailed to the Confederate secretary of state Judah Philip Benjamin (1811–1884), and Surratt accompanied him to Benjamin's office. It appears that Mrs. Slater also went with Surratt and Brogdon. They first met with Lucius Quintius Washington of the State Department. John Surratt went back on March 31 and met with Secretary Benjamin. The secretary wanted his courier to deliver instructions to Jacob Thompson (1810–1885), head of the Confederate undercover mission in Canada, or, if Thompson was no longer there, to see his replacement, General Edwin Gray Lee (1836–1870). To cover his expenses getting to Canada, Benjamin gave Surratt $200 in twenty-dollar gold pieces. Surratt later stated that he thought the message he was to deliver had to do with financial matters.[29] Two hundred dollars in gold was a substantial sum of money in 1865. Perhaps Benjamin already knew he would never see Surratt again. We do not know if there were verbal instructions as well as the written message. Surratt himself may have known, or guessed, that he would have need of this money, and more, in the days ahead.

5

Assassination

John Surratt was still very much an active member of the Confederate Secret Services. He had escorted courier Sarah Slater to Richmond and had received a new assignment from Secretary of State Benjamin. Surratt departed from Richmond on April 1, 1865, again escorting Mrs. Slater. In his lecture later he said, "As soon as I reached the Maryland shore, I understood that the detectives knew of my trip south and were on the lookout for me.... At that time I was carrying the dispatches Mr. Benjamin gave me: in a book entitled *The Life of John Brown*" After crossing the Potomac River, they boarded the Leonardtown Stage, arriving in Washington on April 3 at about 4 o'clock in the afternoon. According to Surratt:

> I succeeded in reaching Washington safely, and in passing up Seventh Street met one of our party [one of the Booth conspirators, although he does not say which one; but Booth, Arnold, and O'Laughlen had left Washington by March 31, so it had to have been either Herold, Atzerodt, or Powell. In one of his several confessions, Atzerodt said it was he whom Surratt met that day on the street] who inquired what had become of Booth.... I told him where I had been; that I was then on my way to Canada, and that I had not seen or heard anything of Booth since our separation. In view of the fact that Richmond had fallen [that very day, April 3], and that all hopes of the abduction of the president had been given up, I advised him to go home and go to work.... I went to a hotel and stopped over that night, as a detective had been to my house inquiring of the servant my whereabouts. In the early train next morning, Tuesday, April 4, 1865, I left for New York.

As usual, John Surratt did not tell all of the details. He makes no mention of Mrs. Slater on his return journey. Weichmann says Surratt arrived at the boardinghouse "at about half past six" on April 3. As Surratt mentions being told about the detective looking for him, it is likely that he went home first then took a hotel room after being told the authorities were after him. Weichmann said Surratt did not know Richmond had been evacuated until they spoke together at the house that evening. It seems all but certain that it was Weichmann who told Surratt about the detective. While at the house, Surratt also exchanged for Federal greenbacks two of the $20 gold pieces Secretary Benjamin had given him. Boarder John T. Holohan changed the money for him. Weichmann expressed surprise "that he should have so much money.... I had seen him before with money. He seemed to be always well supplied although he had no means of livelihood during all the time I boarded in his mother's house.[1]

John Surratt did, indeed, have money, before, during, and after his association with John Wilkes Booth. Two hundred dollars in gold was a small fortune in 1865. Surratt and Weichmann went out walking that evening. They had a supper of oysters "in a saloon near Four-and-a-half Street and Pennsylvania Avenue. Then we walked back together as far as the Metropolitan Hotel, where he bade me goodbye. He said he was going to Montreal the next morning and would correspond with me. That was the final farewell. Little did I realize that we would never speak to one another again in this life."

Researcher James O. Hall hinted at the possibility that Surratt was romantically interested in Sarah Slater and suggested that she was staying that night at the Metropolitan Hotel, and that John Surratt "was needed there to—well—protect and comfort Mrs. Slater." They left Washington the following morning, April 4, bound for New York City, where they parted company. In his lecture Surratt stated, "Upon arriving in New York, I called at Booth's house [Edwin Booth's, where John Wilkes Booth was staying], and was told by the Servant that he had left that morning suddenly, on the ground of going to Boston to fulfill an engagement at the theatre. In the evening of the same day [April 5] I took the cars [train] for Montreal, arriving there the next day. Booth had been in New York, and did proceed to Boston, but he had no theatrical engagement in Boston at that time.

Coming to Montreal on the same train with Surratt were two mysterious persons giving the names S.P. Leaton and J.A. White. A memorandum summarizing the later investigation of Surratt's part in the conspiracy stated:

> White's signature resembles J.W. Booth's somewhat in the manner of connecting the capitals. The two last [Leaton and White] register as from Boston. They left Montreal for New York by 3 o'clock P.M. train. John Harrison [the name Surratt used in Montreal] started to go to New York [City] New York on the 10th but came back from the R.R. station; Remained until the 12th when he left for New York by 3 P.M. train. His name again appears on the register at St. Lawrence Hall [Montreal], on April 18th as arriving by 12.30 P.M. train from New York; Residence blank, and remains there until the next day when he paid his bill and told the clerk he was going by train to ... Quebec, but he was not seen to go on the train, but other evidence shows that John Harrison and two others muffled with clothing got in a carriage driven tandem; and drove out St. Lawrence Main St. in the direction of Black River. On the evening of the 20th, the carriage and driver returned, but the driver absconded; supposed to be gone to Troy [New York]. Two detectives started for Three Rivers by boat but failed to get any trace of him. [The detectives] lost track at the first toll gate outside the city....
>
> While Harrison was in the city; during his visit he had frequent interviews with J.B. Corse, of Leicester Place, Cor. University and Burnside, John Porterfield, of Firm of Porterfield and Lyon, 3 Merchants Ex.[change] Sacrament St., and other noted rebels and secessionists. He took the carriage near Porterfield's house.
>
> Clerk at St. Lawrence Hall describes him [Surratt] as being a tall man, 24 or 25 yrs. old [he was actually not quite 21], no beard or whiskers, light brown hair, not very gentlemanly in appearance.
>
> J. Wilkes Booth's name is registered at St. Lawrence Hall; Oct. 1864.

This report was written by unnamed detectives, part of the Union government's effort to keep track of Confederate activity in Canada. John Surratt continued on from New York City to Montreal, Canada, arriving at 10:30 a.m. on April 6, 1865.

The register of the St. Lawrence Hall, Montreal's most elegant hotel at the time and a gathering place for Confederate agents and sympathizers, contains the name "Harrison," who arrived at 11:30 p.m. on January 23, 1865, coming from Toronto and took room 186. Was this John Surratt, whose middle name was Harrison? Another entry, at 11:00 a.m. on January 24, was "E.G. Lee and Lady." Sarah Slater had checked in on February 15, the day after Jacob Thompson. E.G. Lee and Lady returned on March 11 and again on April 4. Signing in on April 6 at 10:30 a.m. was "John Harrison" of Washington, D.C., who was given room 50-13.[2]

John Surratt was being watched in Montreal, and the American consul reported his movements to Washington:

> John Harrison Surratt alias John Harrison arrived at Montreal by 10.30 train April 6, registered at St. Lawrence Hall as from Washington, D.C. Harrison started to go to New York on the 10th, but came back from the station. Remained here until the 12th, when he left for New York by the 3 A.M. train. This name again appears on the register at the St. Lawrence Hall on April 18th, as arriving by the 12.30 P.M. train

from New York. No residence given by the register. He remained here until the next day, when he paid his bill at the hotel and informed the clerk that he was going into the city and would leave by the evening train for Quebec, but he did not go on the train. There is reason to believe that Harrison and two others left the house of Porterfield, a Southern rebel residing in this city, in a carriage driven tandem, which went out of the city by St. Lawrence Main Street in the direction of Black River, about 11½ o'clock on the evening of the 19th. The carriage and driver returned on the morning of the 20th and on Saturday the 22nd the driver left for Troy, N.Y., though a resident of this city.

Two detectives started for Three Rivers by boat, but failed to get any trace of him. Other officers followed them from Porterfield's in the direction which they had taken, but all trace of them was lost about 15 miles from the city, but pursuit is still being made which we hope will soon lead to their arrest....

While Surratt was in the city during his first visit, he had interviews with J.D. Corsep, now of this city, formally of Alexandria, Va. John Porterfield of the firm of Porterfield and Lyon, Brokers, now at this city, Geo. N. Sanders and other noted rebels and villains.

It can be seen that the consul's report must have been taken from the earlier one made by the unnamed detectives, although it contains some additional information.

Edwin Gray Lee (1836–1870) was a brigadier general in the Confederate army. A member of an old and very distinguished Virginia family, Edwin's grandfather, Edmund Jennings Lee, was the younger brother of Henry "Light Horse Harry" Lee (1756–1818), Revolutionary War soldier, later governor of Virginia from 1792 to 1795, and a congressman from 1799 to 1801. "Light Horse Harry" was the father of Robert Edward Lee (1807–1870), commander of the Confederate army in the Civil War. That made Edwin G. Lee a second cousin of General Robert E. Lee. Young Edwin managed to distinguish himself as an aide to General Thomas J. "Stonewall" Jackson (1824–1863) and participated in the battles of First Bull Run, Kernstown, Chickahominy, Slaughter Mountain, Antietam, and Fredericksburg. His battlefield service was curtailed by his gradually worsening tuberculosis. After serving with General Thomas Lafayette Rosser (1836–1910) in the Shenandoah Valley, Edwin G. Lee's last assignment was to run the blockade and go to Canada, where General and Mrs. Lee arrived in mid–March and checked into the St. Lawrence Hall in Montreal only two days before John Surratt arrived.

Lee presented Jacob Thompson with a letter from Secretary of State Judah Benjamin:

> This letter will be delivered to you by Brig. Gen. E.G. Lee who is especially recommended to you by the President as meriting your entire and unreserved confidence. I have stated to Genl. Lee many things which could not well be committed to paper, and he will give you full information of my views which, in this instance, are but the reflex of those of the President.... You are requested by the President to furnish Genl. Lee such funds as he may want and his receipt will be considered as sufficient voucher by this Department. The political objects contemplated at the time of your departure from Richmond being at an end, the President supposes that you may desire to return home. If you should wish to do so, without awaiting news from us, you are at liberty to entrust to Genl. Lee all means remaining in your hands, and he can replace you as our agent for the time being.

If Thompson was hesitating to turn over the direction of Confederate operations in Canada to Lee, a subsequent message from Benjamin advised him "so close an espionage is kept upon you that your services have been deprived of the value which we attached to your further residence in Canada ... [and] as soon as the gentleman arrives who bears you the letter ... it will be better that you transfer to him as quietly and secretly as possible all the information that you have obtained, and the balance of funds in your hands, and return to the Confederacy."

Thompson did leave Canada, but not to go home. Nor does it appear that he turned over all the money to his successor, as we shall discuss in detail later. Thompson appears to have argued with Lee. Perhaps he was unhappy at being replaced by the general. Thompson sent a reply, dated April 9, 1865, which read, "Last evening I estimated that I would return $30,000 until you [Lee] could hear from Mr. Benjamin.... I am unwilling to consent to this arrangement because it will hamper my movements and might prevent me from availing myself of a favorable opportunity of returning home—in other words, when I leave here I intend to be a freeman."

Thompson left Montreal on April 11, in company with William W. Cleary, bound for Halifax, the departure point for Europe.

Lee's diary entry for Thursday, April 6, notes the arrival of "Charley," who delivered to him a letter from Benjamin. Since we know from the hotel register that John Surratt arrived in Montreal on April 6, we can assume the young courier from Richmond called "Charley Armstrong" was John Surratt.[3]

On April 8, John Wilkes Booth returned to Washington. The following day, General Robert E. Lee surrendered his Army of Northern Virginia to General Ulysses S. Grant (1822–1885). Richmond had fallen; the remnants of the Confederate government were breaking up and fleeing. Now the South's principal army had surrendered. The war was all but over, but John Wilkes Booth was not giving up. His plans to kidnap President Lincoln had fallen through and now had been rendered useless. There remained, however, one final act in the great drama that the actor Booth had sought to bring off: assassination. Why did Booth assassinate Lincoln? The authors of *Come Retribution* suggest that a plan to capture Lincoln and exchange him for thousands of prisoners of war in Union camps may have evolved into an assassination plot in order to cause chaos and confusion in the Union leadership. That may not sound very likely, but we must remember that by this time the Southern leaders who had not yet given up were grasping at straws. Whether or not Booth acted out of frustrated rebel patriotism, he appears to have set his mind at least by the evening of April 11 to assassinate Lincoln. In the crowd that listened to Lincoln speak from a White House window, Booth urged Powell to shoot the president then and there. We do not know how close Booth and his companions, Powell and Herold, were to Lincoln that night, but they were not close enough to allow Powell to be confident of hitting his target with a handgun. They also would certainly have been seized, and possibly even killed, by the crowd. Booth was as determined as ever, and he remarked to his companions, "That is the last speech he will ever make." His prediction would prove to be true.[4]

In Montreal, General Edwin Lee summoned John Surratt. He had an assignment for the young courier—a spying assignment. Although the Southern cause was obviously collapsing, Lee was one of those who felt there might still be hope. At Elmira, in western New York State, a large prisoner-of-war camp housed thousands of Confederate soldiers. If a breakout could be successfully accomplished, those men might be able to make their way south to rejoin the rebel armies which were still fighting. If not, they could still force the Union to send thousands of troops north to deal with the escapees, providing some relief for the Confederate armies still fighting in the South. Lee probably had only an incomplete picture of the South's prospects overall and no doubt felt that anything he could do would be helpful. He told Surratt to go to Elmira, take a good look at the prison, make note of its layout, find out about the guarding and general condition of the prison, and bring back the details to Lee in Montreal.

Strategically located to take advantage of rail and canal transportation, Elmira was a military depot from the beginning of the war, a staging point for militia, draftees, and regulars. The Chemung County fairgrounds had twice served for the New York State Fair. By the spring of 1862 the army had a different purpose in mind. Colonel William Hoffman (1807–1884), the Union's commissary general of prisoners, took an interest in the fairgrounds, with their flat fields, racetrack, and large pond.

After his graduation in 1829 from the U.S. Military Academy, located in West Point, New York, Hoffman served in the Mexican War of 1846–1848. The outbreak of the Civil War found Hoffman in Texas, where he was taken prisoner. Released on August 27, 1862, he reported to Washington and was chosen to superintend the Union's prison camps, which were then beginning to fill with many thousands of captured rebels. Elmira's military camp was partially converted to a prison camp in May of 1864. The first prisoners arrived on July 6, 1864. Four hundred prisoners had been transported from the camp at Point Lookout, Maryland, one of whom died on the way to Elmira. Colonel Hoffman's office decided that the facilities at Elmira could accommodate between eight and ten thousand prisoners. Right from the start, the number was far too large. Overcrowding, inadequate shelters, unsanitary conditions, food that was inadequate in both quantity and quality, diseases such as smallpox and scurvy, and a deliberate order to reduce food for prisoners as retaliation for the starvation of Union prisoners in Southern camps resulted in such misery that the prisoners called the camp "Helmira." One prisoner's account, G.T. Taylor's of Co. C, 1st Alabama Battalion of Heavy Artillery, sums up the situation from the point of view of the prisoners: "Elmira was nearer Hades than I thought any place could be. If there ever was a hell on earth, Elmira was [it]."

The total number of prisoners held at the camp in Elmira was 12,122. In its year of existence 2,950 prisoners died there, 24.3 percent of the prisoners. This compares unfavorably with the 11.7 percent average for all Union P.O.W. camps, and even exceeds the Southern camp at Andersonville, Georgia. Of course, the sufferings and deaths at Elmira were known to the Confederates and this was a reason to bring about a prison break, but the effect the release of thousands of soldiers would have on the Union war effort was probably the higher priority.

John Surratt arrived in Elmira, New York, on April 12, 1865, registering at the Brainard House, generally considered the town's best hotel, on that date. On the following day, he was able to enter the prison camp by bribing a guard and made drawings of the camp's layout for General Lee.[5]

Meanwhile, John Wilkes Booth, having returned to Washington on April 8, was making his plans. He visited the Surratt boardinghouse on April 10, where he showed a noticeable interest in a letter received that day from John Surratt, who was then in Montreal. Annie Ward (1834–1916), a friend of the Surratt family, was visiting and showed the letter to the family. Louis Weichmann described the scene: "Presently Booth arose and, advancing towards Miss Ward, said, 'Please let me see the address of that lady again.' Miss Ward handed him a letter, which he read and then returned to her. When Booth and Miss Ward had departed, Miss Anna Surratt said, 'Mr. Weichmann, here is a letter from brother John,' and I read the letter which Booth had returned to Miss Ward. No lady's name was mentioned in it." This incident could suggest that Booth might have been expecting to hear from John Surratt. He probably knew that Surratt was in Montreal. If not, he found out as he examined the letter.

Weichmann asked Booth why he was not acting: "He answered he was done playing; that the only play he cared to present was *Venice Preserved*. I did not know what he meant by this; I had never read the play. Years after, however, when I did read it, I found that the whole gist of the play was to assassinate the officers of the Venetian Cabinet in order to save Venice." If Weichmann is right about this, both the play and the date of this conversation suggest that Booth was planning well before April 14 to assassinate Lincoln. There are numerous clues to indicate that his kidnap scheme had evolved into an assassination plot. In the hours following the assassination, as Secretary Stanton notified Major General

John Adams Dix (1798–1879) in New York City, he stated his suspicions that the shooting had been planned in advance: "It appears from a letter found in Booth's trunk that the murder was planned before the fourth of March, but fell through then because the accomplice backed out until 'Richmond could be heard from.' It would seem that they had for several days been seeking their chance, but for some unknown reason it was not carried into effect until last night." Stanton refers to what is known as the "Sam" letter, written by Samuel Arnold to John Wilkes Booth and dated "Hookstown, Balto. [Baltimore] Co. [County], March 27, 1865." This letter was found in a trunk in Booth's hotel room after the assassination. In it Arnold tells Booth:

> You know full well that the G——t [government] suspicions something is going on there: Therefore the undertaking is becoming more complicated. Why not, for the present, desist, for various reasons, which, if you look into you can readily see, without my making any mention thereof? ... None, no, not one, were more in for the enterprise than myself.... I was one with you. Time more propitious will arrive yet. Do not act rashly or in haste. I would prefer your first query, "Go and see how it will be taken at R——d" [Richmond]; and ere long I shall be better prepared to again be with you.

Louis J. Weichmann as he appeared about the time of the assassination (Library of Congress).

This letter confirms that a conspiracy existed, and that Booth, Arnold, and Michael "Mike" O'Laughlen, also mentioned earlier in the letter, were members of the conspiracy. There are different ways to interpret the reference to "Richmond," but it can easily be seen how one could believe this remark suggests that Booth was, or was planning to be, in contact with Confederate authorities.

We have already noted that Booth had assassination in mind as he listened to Lincoln's speech at the White House on the evening of April 11. There is also the statement of one of Booth's actor friends, Samuel Knapp Chester (c.1836–1921), who testified at the trial of the conspiracy suspects in 1865: "On Friday, one week previous to the assassination [April 7] I saw him [Booth] again in New York ... [and] he exclaimed, striking the table, "What an excellent chance I had to kill the President, if I had wished, on inauguration day [March 4]!" He said he was as near the President on that day as he was to me."[6] Weichmann concluded in his memoir that Booth had abandoned the kidnap plan by April 10. On that day, Mrs. Surratt asked Weichmann to take her to Surrattsville, borrowing buggy and horses from Booth. The actor told Weichmann that he had sold his horse and buggy but gave him ten dollars to rent one: "I quizzed him about the horses, saying, 'I thought they were John Surratt's horses.' 'No,' answered he, 'they are mine.' I then left the hotel and went to Howard's stables, where I hired a horse and buggy."

As Weichmann and Mrs. Surratt were proceeding southeast from Washington, they noticed John M. Lloyd heading in the opposite direction. This took place in Uniontown, the southeast portion of the District of Columbia, now called Anacostia. Weichmann continues: "Mrs. Surratt had her buggy stopped and requested Mr. Lloyd to come to her. She leaned out of the buggy and spoke to him in such a way that I did not hear what they were talking about." This is one of those curious times when Weichmann says he could not hear what was being said only a few feet away. He tells us that Mrs. Surratt "leaned out of the buggy," not getting out, only leaning out. Even if they spoke in whispers, at least some of their conversation should have been audible to Weichmann, sitting beside her in the buggy, probably close enough to touch her.

In his testimony at the trial of the conspiracy suspects in 1865, Lloyd described what he said he and Mrs. Surratt talked about:

> Q. Did she [Mrs. Surratt] say anything to you in regard to those carbines? [The carbines left at the Surratt tavern in March, 1865, by John Surratt, Atzerodt and Herold.]
> A. When she first broached the subject to me, I did not know what she had reference to: then she came out plainer; and I am quite positive she asked me about the "shooting irons."

Lloyd then says something very curious and enigmatic: "I am quite positive about that, but not altogether positive." This contradictory sentence is only part of what Lloyd said and is part of the evidence that his testimony is unreliable. He went on:

> I think she named "shooting irons," or something to call my attention to those things; for I had almost forgotten about their being there. I told her they were hid away far back; that I was afraid the house would be searched, and they were shoved far back. She told me to get them ready: they would be wanted soon.
> Q. Was it so indistinct, that you did not understand what was meant?
> A. It was put in a manner as if she wanted to draw my attention to something so that anybody else could not understand. Finally she came out bolder with it.

Weichmann said he "did not hear what they were talking about," not that they spoke in some sort of code, or indirectly, as Lloyd hints at here:

> Q. And then she said they would be wanted soon?
> A. Yes, sir. I told her at the same time that I had an idea of having them buried; that I very uneasy about having them there.

The purpose of the trip to Surrattsville on April 11 was to see John Henry Nothey, who described the visit in his conspiracy trial testimony: "I reside about fifteen miles from Washington, in Prince George's County [Maryland]. Some years ago I purchased seventy-five acres of land from Mr. John Surratt, sen [Senior]. Mrs. Surratt sent me word that she wanted me to come to Surrattsville to settle for this piece of land. I owed her a part of the money on it. I met her there on Tuesday [April 11] in regard to it."[7]

John Surratt was still in Elmira, New York, on his mission to scout the prisoner of war camp. In Washington, on the morning of April 14, John Wilkes Booth, after having breakfast and visiting the barbershop, met briefly with Lucy Lambert Hale (1841–1915), known as "Bessie." Booth told some of his friends that he was engaged to Bessie but appeared to want the news kept secret for the time being. Bessie was the daughter of John Parker Hale (1806–1873), who had just ended his term as a U.S. senator from New Hampshire. Stopping at Ford's Theatre to pick up any mail being held for him there, Booth learned that President Lincoln would be attending the performance that night. Booth supposedly encountered newspaper editor John Francis Coyle (c.1822-c.1909) and quizzed him about the order of succession to the presidency.

According to Coyle, he told Booth that Vice President Andrew Johnson (1808–1875) would be president if Lincoln died, and next in line would be Secretary of State William Henry Seward (1801–1872). Booth must have been putting together his multiple assassination plot, perhaps for the purpose of throwing the Union government into confusion by simultaneously assassinating its principal leaders. If that was Booth's plan, it would explain the attack that night upon Seward. However, Coyle was mistaken. The order of succession in 1865 was the president, the vice president, the president pro tem of the Senate, and the speaker of the House of Representatives. The secretary of state did not figure in the succession until 1886. Booth may have felt enough hatred for Seward to have added him to the list of victims, anyway, for Seward had been a staunch opponent of slavery and the Southern cause. At any rate, the next people in line to become president after Vice President Johnson were Senator Lafayette Sabine Foster (1806–1880), R-CT, and Representative Schuyler Colfax (1823–1885), R-IN. As far as anyone knows, there were no plans by Booth or anyone else to assassinate Foster or Colfax.[8]

U.S. Secretary of State William H. Seward was a target of Booth's assassination plot and bore large scars on his face from the attempt for the rest of his life (Library of Congress).

Mrs. Surratt received a letter from Charles Calvert, one of her former neighbors in Surrattsville, telling her that John Nothey was prepared to pay his debt to her. She was surprised because Nothey had told her on Tuesday that he couldn't pay her. In spite of her confusion, Mrs. Surratt badly needed the money, so she had Weichmann again hire a buggy and escort her to Surrattsville. Leaving Washington about half past two, the trip took two hours. Weichmann testified as follows: "She [Mrs. Surratt] took two packages. One was a package of papers about her property at Surrattsville; and then another was a package which was done up in paper, about six inches, I should think, in diameter. It looked to me like a saucer or two, or two or three saucers, wrapped in paper. That was deposited in the bottom of the buggy, and taken out by Mrs. Surratt when we arrived at Surrattsville." While there they again encountered John Lloyd, who was returning from Upper Marlboro, where he had been waiting to testify in a court case. The case was postponed, and Lloyd estimated he returned to Surrattsville around five o'clock: "She met me out by the wood-pile as I drove in, having fish and oysters in the buggy; and she told me to have those shooting irons ready that night,—there would be some parties call for them." The "shooting irons" Lloyd referred to in his testimony were two carbines left at the tavern a few weeks before by John Surratt, in company with Herold and Atzerodt, that had been hidden in the tavern. Lloyd went on: "She gave me something wrapped up in a piece of paper. I did not know what it was till I took it up stairs; and then I found it to be a field glass [binoculars].... She said to get two bottles of whiskey also." Mrs. Surratt, questioned after her arrest, described this trip very differently:

Q. What conversation did you have with Mr. Lloyd?
A. I do not remember any particular conversation. Mr. Lloyd was not home until I was going to start.
Q. That is the day of the murder [April 14]?
A. Yes, sir.... I think we started from there about five o'clock to the best of my knowledge. When I got there I learned that Mr. Nothey, the man I had business with, had gone to Marlboro. I remained there as long as I could to see whether he would return. In this I had a letter written to Mr. Nothey stating what he could do. It was directed to the care of Captain Gwynn [Bennett Gwynn (1823–1897), a neighbor in Surrattsville]. Just as I was about to start the Captain drove up. I told him my business and left the letter also.
Q. How long a conversation did you have with Mr. Lloyd?
A. Only a few minutes conversation. I did not sit down. I only met him as I was going home.
Q. Where was Mr. Weichmann?
A. He was there.
Q. He heard the conversation?
A. I presume he did. I do not remember [in his statement dated April 23, 1865, Lloyd also suggested that Weichmann heard his conversation with Mrs. Surratt].
Q. What did the conversation relate to?
A. He spoke of having fish and oysters. He asked me whether I had been to dinner, and said that he could give me fish and oysters. Mr. Weichmann said that he would return home as he was in need of his bread and butter.
Q. What did you say about any shooting irons or carbines?
A. I said nothing about them.
Q. Any conversation of that kind? Did you not tell him to have those shooting irons ready, that there would be some people there that night?
A. To my knowledge, no conversation of that kind passed.
Q. Did you know any shooting irons were there?
A. No, sir, I did not.

Obviously, either Lloyd or Mrs. Surratt was not telling the truth. We have no way of knowing which one was lying, at least not from the above statements; but if we peer more deeply into Lloyd's story, especially the circumstances surrounding his testimony, we can certainly establish reasonable doubt. At the trial of John Surratt in 1867, John M. Lloyd testified again:

Q. I believe you were a witness before the conspiracy trial, were you not?
A. Yes, sir; unfortunately.

Twice, when asked if he knew John Surratt and his mother, Lloyd said, "My acquaintance with them was very short the whole time." When asked to relate again the meetings with Mrs. Surratt, including the "shooting irons" remark, Lloyd said, "I do not wish to state one solitary word more than I am compelled to." Finally, after some prodding by the attorneys and the judge, Lloyd stated, "As well as I recollect, in speaking of the shooting irons, she told me to have them ready; that they would be called for, or wanted soon, I forget now which." When Lloyd said he told Mrs. Surratt he was uneasy about having the weapons at the tavern and was tempted to take them out and bury them, he said she changed the subject and "laughed very heartily" at the idea of John Surratt going to Richmond. If Mrs. Surratt was an active member of John Wilkes Booth's conspiracy, as the government tried to prove at her trial, and as some researchers and authors still believe to this day, why would she respond in such a way? If it was her mission to notify Lloyd to get the weapons out and have them ready for Booth that very night, why would she change the subject and laugh the whole thing off?

At the trial of John Surratt, Lloyd's drinking was brought out:

Q. What did you say to her [Mrs. Surratt]?
A. I do not know that I made any reply to her at all. I was in liquor at the time, and being so, I did not want to have any conversation with her.

> Q. How long did she stay there after this?
> A. I do not remember. I went into my back room and threw myself on the lounge, when I immediately turned sick from the effect of the liquor.
> Q. Had you not been drinking during the day?
> A. I do not think I drank anything until the court adjourned [Lloyd had been to Marlboro to testify in a court case earlier that day, April 14]. I know what effect liquor had on me.
> Q. What effect has it?
> A. A very singular effect, upon my mind chiefly. It makes me forget a great many things.
> Q. How much did you drink after the court adjourned?
> A. I drank enough to make me drunk.
> Q. Were you very drunk?
> A. I was so drunk that when I lay down I felt sick. I could not lie down.
> Q. How long after Mrs. Surratt went away did you lie down?
> A. I lay down before she left.

Lloyd's drunkenness on the evening of April 14, 1865, when he said Mrs. Surratt told him to have the shooting irons ready, was also mentioned at Mrs. Surratt's trial in 1865. Joseph T. Knott, who tended bar at the tavern in Surrattsville Lloyd managed, corroborated Lloyd's drunkenness:

> Q. Did you see Mr. Lloyd on the 14th of last April?
> A. Yes, sir.
> Q. At what time in the day?
> A. I saw him in the morning, and I saw him again just before sundown.
> Q. What was Mr. Lloyd's condition at that time?
> A. He was pretty tight....
> Q. Has he been drunk for almost every day for some time past?
> A. Yes, sir....
> Q. Did he or not really have the appearance of an insane man from drink?
> A. He had at times.

On top of his being drunk and thus forgetful, Lloyd admitted at the John Surratt trial that he had been threatened and coerced into giving his damning testimony against Mrs. Surratt. How much Mary Surratt was involved in John Wilkes Booth's conspiracy to kidnap and then to assassinate President Abraham Lincoln cannot now be known. The evidence against her was entirely circumstantial. There are good reasons to feel reasonable doubt about the testimony given against her by both of the principal witnesses at the 1865 trial. Her actions on April 14, 1865, cast doubt upon her innocence and her explanations given after her arrest often seemed confused and contradictory. Her connections with other members of Booth's gang were difficult for her to explain:

> Q. You mentioned the other day to Colonel Foster you had a man by the name of Wood, a Baptist minister, at your house.
> A. Yes, sir. He remained there for a few days. He came there to board and on Friday evening he left saying that he was going to preach there on Sunday.
> Q. Where did he come from?
> A. I don't know....
> Q. Do you recollect the man who came to your house at the time of your arrest?
> A. I do not.
> Q. You did not look to see whether it was this man Wood?
> A. I only saw a stranger. I never saw him before. I never thought it was the Wood who was at our house.

Curiously enough, in this interrogation, Mrs. Surratt was asked to describe the man using the name Wood:

> A. Stout, black hair and eyes. He was a short stout man of few words. He did not seem inclined to talk. He seemed to be a young man, 20 years and odd.

We now know that the man using the name Wood, posing as a Baptist minister, was the former Confederate cavalryman Lewis Thornton Powell (1844–1865). But the above description of Powell by Mrs. Surratt does not agree with Weichmann's: "Sometime during the evening the door bell was rung. Answering the summons, I found standing before me a tall and robust individual with very black hair and ruddy countenance.... He ... gave his name as Mr. Wood."

This description fits Powell much more closely than the one given by Mrs. Surratt. Both agree that the visitor was young and had dark hair. But Mrs. Surratt said he was a "short stout man." Several photographs of Powell were taken after his arrest, so we can have no doubt that he was not a "short stout man." The famous photos taken at the execution show Powell on the scaffold along with Mrs. Surratt, Herold, and Atzerodt. In those photos Powell towers over the others. Although muscular, he could not be accurately described as "stout."

The "short stout" description could indicate that the man Mrs. Surratt knew as Wood was not Lewis Powell the conspirator. But Weichmann saw Powell many times and could not have been mistaken about his identity. Powell himself confessed to being a member of Booth's conspiracy. Descriptions of Powell were published in the press at the time of the trial: "He was very tall, with an athletic, gladiatorial frame; the tight knit shirt which was his only upper garment disclosing the massive robustness of animal manhood in its most stalwart type. Neither intellect nor intelligence was discernable in his unflinching, gray eyes, low forehead, massive jaws, compressed full lips, small nose with large nostrils, and stolid, remorseless expression."[9] Note that this description states Powell had "gray eyes," while both Mrs. Surratt and Louis Weichmann said his eyes were "dark."

On the night of April 14, 1865, President Abraham Lincoln was shot while attending a play at Ford's Theatre in Washington, D.C. Insensible from a bullet in the head, the president was carried across the street and into a small boardinghouse room. The doctors treating him were unanimous in their judgment that Lincoln could not survive such a wound. Even so, he amazed the medical men by lingering for nine hours, being pronounced dead at 7:22 a.m. on April 15.

Even before the death of the president, detectives and soldiers began the hunt for the assassin and his coconspirators. That the assassination was a conspiracy was not doubted from the beginning. Nearly simultaneously with the shooting of Lincoln, another would-be assassin attempted to take the life of Secretary of State William Henry Seward. Seward was confined to bed at his home in Lafayette Square, near the White House, having suffered serious injuries a few days before in a carriage accident. A large, tall, and strong man forced his way into Seward's bedroom, fighting off the attempts of Seward's sons and an army nurse to stop him. Jumping on the sick bed, the attacker plunged a large knife into Secretary Seward's face and neck, inflicting ghastly wounds from which it was feared Seward could not survive. There were rumors that attempts would be made on the lives of Secretary of War Edwin M. Stanton (1814–1869) and General Ulysses S. Grant (1822–1885). Lincoln's assassin had been identified on the scene. Many witnesses, both on the stage and in the audience, recognized John Wilkes Booth as the man who jumped down from the president's upper box onto the stage and ran out behind the scenes. Detectives searching Booth's room at the National Hotel found clues pointing to others who appeared to be involved in a conspiracy with Booth. Very early in the investigation, John Surratt's name began to be mentioned in connection with the attempted assassination of Secretary Seward: "John Surratt of Prince George's County, Maryland, is said to have been the man who cut Seward, but as yet no clue to the direction he took, unless he went with Booth, has been obtained. From

Ford's Theatre, Washington, D.C., the scene of the Lincoln assassination. Author's collection.

evidence obtained, it is rendered highly probable that the man who stabbed Mr. Seward and his sons is John Surratt.... Surratt is a young man, with light hair and goatee. His father is said to have been Postmaster of Prince George Co."

Secretary Stanton took immediate charge of the investigation and issued orders to round up suspects. In the hours and days that followed, hundreds were arrested and legal

Petersen House, Washington, D.C., the house where Lincoln died on April 15, 1865. Author's collection.

cases were built against anyone implicated. Suspicion fell upon the Surratt family early. Weichmann had noted a visit by Booth to Mrs. Surratt's boardinghouse the day of the assassination, around 2:30 p.m. Weichmann met the actor at the door when leaving to hire a horse and buggy to take Mrs. Surratt to Surrattsville. Returning, he noticed that Booth was still there, talking to Mrs. Surratt. Booth apparently gave Mrs. Surratt something to take

Although President Lincoln's box at Ford's Theatre is a modern reconstruction, it contains some of the original furniture: the chair next to the Lincoln rocker replica, and the sofa on the right (Library of Congress).

with her: "She went into the house and presently returned with two packages in her hand, both done up in coarse brown paper and wrapped with twine. One of these was from six to eight inches in diameter. This she deposited in the bottom of the buggy, remarking that it was glass.... She also carried another package, some of her business and legal papers."

Weichmann went on to relate various things he thought were very suspicious, which contributed to the guilt of Mrs. Surratt, including the meeting with Lloyd, who Weichmann said told Mrs. Surratt to have the "shooting irons" ready. He always maintained that he did not hear that conversation. One can wonder when Weichmann became aware of the alleged conversation, with its very incriminating remarks. Who told him about it, and when? He did not say, only venturing a guess: "Who told her [Mrs. Surratt] that these 'shooting irons' were secreted in Lloyd's house? Who informed her that they would be called for that night? Who but Booth? ... Up to the moment of Lloyd's testimony, I verily believed that she was an innocent woman, but when I read the story of the shooting irons as related by him, the scales fell from my eyes and I could believe so no longer."

Weichmann here made a leap of faith. He said, in regard to the testimony both at the time of the conspiracy trial in 1865 and at the trial of John Surratt in 1867 that he found no trouble believing Lloyd's testimony about the "shooting irons," words he steadfastly maintained for the rest of his days he had not heard: "It has been alleged in Mrs. Surratt's behalf that Lloyd had been drinking 'right smart' that day. That may have been so and

Lloyd himself admits it, but the evidence and the facts show that he was sufficiently sober to take the weapons out of their hiding place and deliver them to Booth and Herold—the parties who called for them."

The idea that Lloyd could have been so drunk he felt sick but had recovered sufficient sobriety to be able to help the fleeing assassins is doubted by Weichmann because he realized that Lloyd's drunkenness cast doubt upon his memory of what, if anything, was said about "shooting irons." It was no later than about six o'clock that the alleged conversation took place, and it was after midnight when Booth and Herold arrived at the tavern asking for "those things"; Lloyd acknowledged knowing what those things were without any mention of "shooting irons." This was a period of six hours, perhaps a little more—certainly enough time for Lloyd, drunk as he had been earlier, to recover enough to be able to help the assassins and thereby become an accessory to their crime.

The two witnesses whose testimony against Mrs. Surratt at the conspiracy trial, Lloyd and Weichmann, must be examined carefully before we accept their credibility and their motives as being without blemish. We have already seen that Lloyd admitted, both at the 1865 trial and at the later trial of John Surratt, that he was thoroughly drunk when he spoke to Mrs. Surratt in the late afternoon of April 14, 1865, and that alcohol made him become forgetful. This does not, all by itself, make it impossible that Mrs. Surratt talked to him about "shooting irons," but it does introduce the element of reasonable doubt. What about Weichmann? There is also a considerable amount of reasonable doubt arising from his testimony. William Patrick Wood (1820–1903), superintendent of the Old Capitol Prison in Washington, had this to say about Weichmann: "Up to his arrest Sunday April 30, 1865, [Weichmann] was in the employ of the government in the Office of the Commissary General of Prisoners. From that office I am satisfied that he frequently purloined important papers which have been forwarded to Richmond by or through John Surratt."

Another witness, a colleague of Weichmann's at the Commissary General of Prisoners' Office, Daniel H.L. Gleason (1841–1917), said Weichmann told him about the goings-on at Mrs. Surratt's boardinghouse:

> He never gave me to understand what the nature of the plot was.... At one time he thought it was the assassination of all the officials.... He spoke to me about this plot before the inauguration [March 4, 1865].... He ... dropped the name of Booth as one of this party.... Although they had not asked him to join them he thought he could.... I said, "You better go to the provost marshal's office here, lay open this plot and then get the sanction of that officer and then join them to expose the whole." He said he thought it would be too much risk. He is a man that I put very little confidence in in regard to what he said.[10]

John Surratt later connected Louis Weichmann with the Booth conspiracy:

> During our whole connection we rarely wrote or telegraphed under our proper names, but always in such a manner that no one could understand but ourselves. One way of Booth's was to send letters to me [John Surratt] under cover of my quondam friend, Louis J. Weichmann.... They were sent to him because he knew of the plot to abduct President Lincoln.... He had been told all about it, and was constantly importuning one to let him become an active member. I refused for the simple reason that I told him he could neither ride a horse nor shoot a pistol, which was a fact.... My refusal nettled him some; so he went off ... and told some government clerk [Gleason] that he had a vague idea that there was a plan of some kind on hand to abduct President Lincoln.... Booth sometimes was rather suspicious of him [Weichmann], and asked me if I thought he could be trusted. Said I, "Certainly he can. Weichmann is a Southern man...." He had furnished information for the Confederate government, besides allowing me access to the government records after office hours.

Of course, we must be cautious about what Surratt said about himself, but our caution should also include Weichmann. Louis Weichmann spent the rest of his life trying to convince the world that he was an innocent bystander, drawn into horrendous events by his friendship with John Surratt. Did Surratt make up the details related above in order to take his revenge against his one-time friend for the harm Weichmann had done to the Surratt family?

We have seen what Colonel Wood and Captain Gleason said about Weichmann, and they were not the only ones to question Weichmann's loyalty and innocence. John P. Brophy (1842–1914) was a friend of the Surratt family and tried his best to prevent the execution of Mrs. Surratt. Years later, he told a newspaper reporter his thoughts about Weichmann:

> When the trial was near its end, Mr. Brophy said, Louis J. Weichmann ... came to Mr. Brophy and wanted to know what the effect of his testimony had been. Mr. Brophy accused him of attempting to have an innocent woman killed, and Weichmann acknowledged to Mr. Brophy that he believed Mrs. Surratt to be innocent.... Mr. Brophy quotes the man as saying...."Stanton gave me the choice between turning state's evidence and hanging. Terrified, I told what I had heard, and, although I believed Mrs. Surratt to be innocent, Mr. Stanton appeared to believe her guilty. I did not want to be hanged."

General Robert Sanford Foster (1834–1903), one of the nine members of the military commission that tried Mrs. Surratt and seven others for conspiracy to murder the president, stated, "It seems extremely improbable that Weichmann was ignorant of the entire plot, if he was not an accomplice." In a letter to Colonel Henry L. Burnett (1838–1916), one of the prosecutors, Weichmann made the following plea: "You confused and terrified me so much yesterday that I was almost unable to say anything.... For God's sake do not confound the innocent with the guilty."

John T. Ford (1829–1894), the theater owner, was among the many arrested after the assassination. He was held at Carroll Prison, near the Old Capitol Prison in Washington, D.C., where Lloyd and Weichmann were among the suspects and witnesses being held before and during the trial. Ford was able to visit both Lloyd and Weichmann. He later described his impressions:

> I was, by what I heard from them, convinced of [Mrs. Surratt's] innocence of any knowledge of or complicity in the assassination of President Lincoln. Weichmann sought advice from [me], saying that Secretary Stanton had, in a threatening manner, expressed the opinion "that [Weichmann's] hands had as much of the President's blood on them as Booth's...." Of Lloyd, several there said that ... he had been threatened with torture, and intimidated that he had to say what he did to secure relief.... Lloyd was quite drunk the evening of the 14th of April ... before he started for home, where he met Mrs. Surratt.[11]

It may never be known whether Mrs. Surratt was a fully involved member of Booth's conspiracy, either to kidnap or to assassinate President Lincoln. The testimonies, especially those of Louis J. Weichmann and John M. Lloyd, hint at the possibility of her guilt, but in the Anglo-American system, a defendant is presumed innocent until proven guilty, and the proof must be beyond a reasonable doubt. As with judges and lawyers, so it should also be with historians. One of Mrs. Surratt's lawyers at the trial of the conspiracy suspects was John Wesley Clampitt (1839–1906). In a later article, Clampitt suggested numerous alternate explanations for her so-called incriminating behavior, sewing many seeds of reasonable doubt: "It was alleged ... that [Mrs. Surratt's boardinghouse] was a secret rendezvous of those who plotted treason against the government. If that be granted, still it can be asserted that, in all the pages of the record of that trial, there can be found no testimony to show that Mrs. Surratt was cognizant of the same, or even participated in a single meeting. The testimony of Weichmann ... nowhere reveals the fact that she ever participated in any plot." Clampitt accused both Weichmann and Lloyd of perjury in their testimony accusing Mrs. Surratt of willing involvement in Booth's plot. His explanation of the "shooting irons" remark, which Lloyd vividly described and the military commissioners found so incriminating, is certainly a possible alternative to their belief that it incriminated her. Even conceding that such a conversation could have taken place, it does not necessarily suggest that she was plotting along with Booth: "[Booth] requested Mrs. Surratt to hand the bundle to John M. Lloyd, the tavern-keeper at Surrattsville.... Booth was a frequenter of that neighborhood, and an intimate of the man Lloyd, to whom was delivered the bundle." Clampitt also suggests that Booth may have visited the Surratt tavern in Surrattsville, and have given the impression that he might want to go hunting there, making use of the stored weapons. Is this an unlikely explanation? Perhaps, but is it impossible to believe? We cannot reasonably rule it out, however weak this explanation may seem. Remember, Mrs. Surratt had to be proven guilty beyond a reasonable doubt. That Lewis Powell should show up at Mrs. Surratt's house after the assassination was considered very incriminating. Powell happened to arrive at just the wrong moment for himself and for Mrs. Surratt: three days after the assassination, detectives were searching the house and questioning its occupants:

> It was just after midnight that he [Powell] reached Mrs. Surratt's house and knocked at the door. It was answered by the officers who had taken possession of the house and arrested its inmates. The question was asked Payne [Powell's alias] what he wanted at that hour. He replied, seeing the state of affairs, that he had been employed by Mrs. Surratt the day before to dig a drain, and had come to see at what hour in the morning he should begin. He was asked where he lived, and replied that he was a poor workingman and had no home. That answer seemed sufficient to cause his arrest, which was accomplished, and he was taken to the office of the Provost Marshal, where he proved to be the assailant of the Secretary of State. This was a part of the chain of circumstances that wound itself about the unhappy woman.

It was Clampitt's conclusion "that the commission was organized to convict. The state of the public mind was such that the desire for revenge had taken the place of justice, and, for a time, a reign of terror prevailed." He believed Weichmann, "having been an inmate of her [Mrs. Surratt's] home during the formation of the conspiracy he [Weichmann] was himself suspicioned and was threatened by the authorities of the War Department, in which for some time he had been a clerk, with arrest and trial with the other prisoners, unless he made a statement implicating Mrs. Surratt; that upon such demand he prepared a statement, which was rejected by the Judge Advocate General [Joseph Holt (1807–1894)] with the remark that 'it was not strong enough'; that his life being threatened, he made out another statement which was in accordance with their wishes and demands, and this 'statement' he swore to on the witness stand, falsely implicating Mrs. Surratt in the conspiracy."[12] The testimonies of Lloyd and Weichmann were crucial to the government's case against Mrs. Surratt. Without these two men, the case against her would have been very thin, almost certainly not strong enough to convict her in any kind of court claiming to have an interest in truth and justice.

The government knew Lloyd had not told everything he knew about the Booth conspiracy. When soldiers first questioned him, shortly after Booth and Herold stopped at the tavern in Surrattsville late on the night of the assassination, Lloyd told them that no one had been there that night. It was a few days before he admitted he knew anything about the assassination. Once he began talking, there was no longer any doubt that he was involved in the conspiracy. A telegram sent by Samuel Beckwith (1839–1916), General Grant's telegrapher, to Thomas T. Eckert (1825–1910), head of the War Department Telegraph Office, read: "Port Tobacco, Md., April 24, 1865 "John M. Lloyd has been arrested, and virtually acknowledged complicity." Detective George Cottingham, who had interviewed Lloyd, wrote as follows:

> John M. Lloyd is accessory to the murder of President Lincoln before and after the deed. He concealed firearms in his house brought by [John] Surratt. He has also given aid and comfort to Booth and Herold and furnished them with additional firearms after Booth had told him that he had murdered the President.

> He ... denied everything until they had [e]ffected their escape and knew where they had gone. He had remained two days in the guardhouse before he made his confession.... Lloyd afterwards admitted to me that he concealed the carbine in the place where it was found [at the Surratt tavern] through fear of being implicated in the affair.

Another detective, J.W. Ridenour, asked Cottingham about Lloyd's confession: "Lloyd [was] charged with aiding and abetting with others in the assassination of the President. I was informed by the said Cottingham that the said Lloyd had made a confession of his guilt. I inquired of the said Cottingham how it was obtained. His answer was, 'I dragged it out of Lloyd.'" Taken together, these statements indicate that Lloyd was as guilty as anyone in aiding the assassins. A case could have been made against him that would have been stronger than that against either Mrs. Surratt or Dr. Mudd. Ridenour's statement also suggests that Lloyd's confession may have been obtained under duress.

Why did the government not prosecute either Weichmann or Lloyd? At the time, a prisoner charged with a crime could not also be a witness. If Weichmann and Lloyd had been charged and placed in the prisoner's dock along with the others at the trial of the conspiracy suspects, they could not have told their stories about Mrs. Surratt. Without Weichmann's testimony regarding Mrs. Surratt's meetings with the conspirators, including Booth himself; without his statements about her vague remarks that seemed to be hints that she knew all about the conspiracy; without Lloyd's "shooting irons," there would have been very little else to support charges against Mrs. Surratt, certainly not enough to hang her. The government needed Weichmann and Lloyd to seal the fate of Mary Surratt, and it was not above threatening them with the noose if they did not cooperate.[13]

Mary Surratt was tried, along with seven men, for conspiring to kill President Lincoln. The trial was by a military commission under military law. It seemed to many observers that the defendants were presumed guilty and had to be proven innocent, the reverse of how it normally was under civilian law. Although their circumstances were different and the evidence against them varied from one to another, they were all tried together by the same court. The judges were also the jury, nine army officers, only one of whom had any legal background.

The military commission convened at ten o'clock on the morning of Wednesday, May 10, 1865. Mrs. Surratt and the other defendants were held at the Arsenal Prison at Greenleaf Point, which is now Fort Lesley J. McNair, in Washington, D.C. One room of the Arsenal was converted into a courtroom, which was overcrowded and very uncomfortable for all concerned, as the weather became hot and humid.

Mrs. Surratt attracted much attention, being a middle-aged woman not previously known as anything but a law-abiding citizen. She was accused, along with the men, of "maliciously, unlawfully, and traitorously, and in aid of the existing armed Rebellion ... combining, confederating, and conspiring, together with one John H. Surratt, John Wilkes Booth, Jefferson Davis [naming other known agents of the Confederacy in Canada] ... and others unknown, to kill and murder ... Abraham Lincoln, late ... President of the United States of America." Only three of the eight defendants claimed to be entirely innocent: Mrs. Surratt, Dr. Samuel A. Mudd, and Edman Spangler. The other five had admitted their participation in a conspiracy headed by Booth. They qualified their guilt, however, by making a distinction between the plot to kidnap Lincoln, to exchange him for Confederate prisoners of war, and the one to kill the president. This was a distinction the court refused to acknowledge.

Throughout the trial, Mrs. Surratt wore a heavy veil that obscured her appearance, except when she was required to raise it in order to be identified. She was described by the reporters as "a belle in her youth, has borne her five and forty years or more bravely [she was actually forty-two]; [and] brown hair.... She was evidently the devoted mother of an attached family, of pious sentiments.... [W]hether she was guilty or innocent, it was easy to perceive that she desired to make a favorable impression upon the Court, and to inspire feelings of pity."

Under military law, conditions were more restrictive than they would have been in a civilian court. Lawyers for the defense were limited in the amount of time for consultation with their clients. Statements made by the defendants, whether in the court or not, were not allowed to be considered, even that of Lewis Powell, who declared that Mrs. Surratt was innocent, or David Herold's written confession, in which it was said that he believed Dr. Samuel Mudd should be pardoned. That confession disappeared.[14]

The trial was a sensational one and remains controversial to this day. For years afterward, partisans of either the prosecution or the defense refought the battles over who was guilty, who was innocent, and whether or not the harsh punishments meted out by the military commission were just. As we have shown, it is entirely reasonable to say that in many instances there is room for reasonable doubt. The outcome of the trial of John Surratt two years later cast further doubt upon the judgment of the military commission of 1865.

Clampitt and Frederick Augustus Aiken (1832–1878), Mrs. Surratt's lawyers, felt confident that they had put up a solid defense for her. Late in the afternoon of July 6, they said, "We were suddenly startled by the cry of the newsboys on the street, 'The execution of Mrs. Surratt!' ... [and] the judgment of the Military Commission had been that of death, and the President had signed her death warrant." They immediately went to the White House to interview President Johnson. As the trial had been a military one, there was no appeal to higher courts. Only the president of the United States could overturn or modify the verdict. The president, whose office was closed and guarded by armed soldiers, refused to see the attorneys or anyone else.

They took Anna Surratt with them to see Judge Advocate General Joseph Holt in hopes that he would intercede with the president to relieve the anguish of Mrs. Surratt's daughter: "Upon her bended knees, bathed in tears, the forlorn girl besought him to go to the President and beg a respite for three days.... [T]he Judge Advocate General agreed to meet us at the Executive Mansion at a given hour. We reached there at the appointed time. He had gone before us, and was just emerging as we came. He said, 'I

Edman Spangler was a stagehand at Ford's Theatre and was convicted as a conspirator and sent to prison. The evidence against him was very thin (Library of Congress).

can do nothing. The President is immovable ... [and] you might as well attempt to overthrow this building as to alter his decision.'" On the advice of their senior colleague, Reverdy Johnson (1796–1876), the lawyers for Mrs. Surratt sought an audience with Judge Andrew B. Wylie (1814–1905), a member of the Supreme Court of the District of Columbia, to obtain a writ of habeas corpus requiring the government to bring Mrs. Surratt before Judge Wylie the next morning. By the time they had drafted their petition and arrived at Judge Wylie's home, it was two o'clock in the morning. As Mrs. Surratt was scheduled to be executed the following day, the young lawyers had no time to spare. They read their petition to the judge, who wore only his dressing gown, having been aroused from sleep. Judge Wylie listened impassively, took the petition, and retired into another room. The lawyers' hopes seemed to be sinking, with all legal courses of action exhausted. In a few moments, however, Wylie returned with the papers in his hand and remarked, "Gentlemen, my mind is made up. I have always endeavored to perform my duty fearlessly, as I understand it. I am constrained to decide the points in your petition well taken. I am about to perform an act which before tomorrow's sun goes down may consign me to the Old Capitol Prison. I believe it to be my duty, as a judge, to order this writ to issue; and [taking up his pen] I shall so order it."

Clampitt and Aiken hurried to the U.S. Marshal's office and requested it be served upon General Winfield Scott Hancock (1824–1886), senior military officer with authority over prisoners. The following morning, the general, accompanied by Attorney General James Speed (1812–1887), presented the following document to Judge Wylie:

Executive Office, July 7, 1865, 10 A.M.

To Major General W.S. Hancock, commanding, etc.

I, Andrew Johnson, President of the United States, do hereby declare that the writ of habeas corpus has been heretofore suspended in such cases as this, and I do hereby especially suspend this writ, and direct that you proceed to execute the order heretofore given upon the judgement of the Military Commission, and you will give this order in return to this writ.

(signed) Andrew Johnson, President.

The writ of habeas corpus, requiring that a person accused of a crime be brought before a court to present a defense, had been suspended by President Lincoln in 1861. The Constitution of the United States reads as follows: "The privilege of the writ of habeas corpus shall not be suspended, unless when in cases of rebellion or invasion the public safety may require it." Lincoln's suspension of the writ of habeas corpus was very controversial because it was stated that the president did not have the power to do so, since the clause quoted above appears among the powers assigned to Congress. With no elaboration of who has the authority or how far that power may extend, it can be argued that this clause allows the overthrow of virtually all the rights guaranteed in the Bill of Rights, allowing the president to use the military to make arrests and detain citizens for an indefinite time without their being able to defend themselves. This is a situation more or less identical to a dictatorship. Lincoln agreed to invoke this clause of the Constitution as a way of strengthening the government's ability to suppress the Southern rebellion. Feeling uneasy about it, he intended that the suspension should be lifted when the rebellion was over. The power claimed by Lincoln was inherited by his successor, Andrew Johnson, who had not yet declared the rebellion over. Eventually, the United States Supreme Court unanimously ruled that civilians could not be tried by military courts or commissions when they were not members of the military, in states that were not in rebellion, and when the civil courts were open and functioning.

Although all nine members of the military commission voted to convict Mrs. Surratt and the other seven defendants, only four believed she should be executed. It is said that the other five were tricked into voting for the death sentence by Holt and Stanton, who told them that if they voted for execution a petition would be sent to the president, signed by the five dissenters, calling for commutation of her sentence to life imprisonment. The petition read as follows:

> To the President: The undersigned, members of the military commission appointed to try the persons charged with the murder of Abraham Lincoln, etc., respectfully represent that the commission have been constrained to find Mary E. Surratt guilty, upon the testimony, of the assassination of Abraham Lincoln, late President of the United States, and to pronounce upon her, as required by law, the sentence of death; but, in consideration of her age and sex, the undersigned pray your Excellency, if it is consistent with your sense of duty, to commute her sentence to imprisonment for life in the penitentiary.[15]

The petition, Holt always insisted, was attached to the records of the trial he showed to the president, who nevertheless ordered the execution of four of the defendants, including Mrs. Surratt. Johnson afterwards maintained that he had not seen the petition. Holt tried for years to enlist the aid of members of Johnson's cabinet to corroborate that they had known of and discussed the petition. Holt never succeeded in this effort. The balance of proof and logic leans in the direction of Holt. Johnson always had the power to commute Mrs. Surratt's sentence, with or without the petition. If he hadn't known that, he could have asked Holt, Stanton, or Attorney General Speed. Johnson's attitude toward the defendants, including Mrs. Surratt, was very severe, and having profited from Lincoln's assassination in gaining the presidency he may have felt he could not show mercy to those accused of Lincoln's murder out of concern that he might have been suspected of being a part of the conspiracy.

On the evening of July 6, 1865, Major General John Frederick Hartranft (1830–1889), the officer in command of the Washington Arsenal Prison, read the findings and sentences of the military commission to the four prisoners who had been convicted of conspiracy to kill President Lincoln. They were Lewis Thornton Powell, George Andrew Atzerodt, David Edgar Herold, and Mary Elizabeth Surratt. All four of these prisoners had been sentenced to be executed the following day, July 7. Each of them requested they be allowed to see clergymen and relatives and friends, except for Powell, whose relatives were too far away. Mrs. Surratt requested the presence of her daughter Anna and close friend John P. Brophy, and that two

Jacob A. Walter, a Catholic priest and friend of the Surratt family, stood beside Mary Surratt at her execution (Library of Congress).

Catholic priests see her. They were Jacob Ambrose Walter (1827–1894) and Bernardine Francis Wiget (1821–1883). These two priests stayed with Mrs. Surratt through the afternoon of July 6 and were beside her at the scaffold the following day.

At 1:00 p.m. on July 7, 1865, the condemned were brought from their prison cells into the prison yard beside the building where they had been held and had stood trial. Mrs. Surratt was the first to emerge into the light and heat of the day. Accompanying her were military guards and Fathers Walter and Wiget. The prisoners were seated in chairs on the scaffold platform while the attending clergymen said prayers over them. Then, as the prisoners stood they were bound and hooded. Nooses were fitted around their necks. At 1:30 p.m., the props were knocked out from beneath the scaffold and the hinged floor dropped. Twenty minutes later the bodies were taken down, examined by the prison doctor, and pronounced dead.

Attorney Clampitt later stated that Mrs. Surratt had asked Father Walter if she could not make a statement of her innocence in her last moments before hanging. According to this account, Walter advised her not to, as it would do no good and "might disturb the serenity of your last moments." General Hartranft, explaining his last-minute action on behalf of Mrs. Surratt, wrote to General Hancock:

> U.S. Arsenal Mil. Prison
> Washington, D.C.
> July 15, 1865
>
> Maj. Genl. W.S. Hancock
> Com'dg M.M. Div.
> Wash. D.C.
>
> About 10 o'clock in the afternoon of the day of the execution July 7th 65, Mr. Brophy came to my quarters saying that Judge Holt desired Father Walter to put in writing the statement which Payne [Powell] had made to him relative to the innocence of Mrs. Surratt. I immediately called Father Walter who was then in the cell of—Mrs. S——, into my room, and he proceeded to write the statement. Believing that Judge Holt desired the best possible evidence as to Payne's sayings, I remarked to Father Walter that perhaps it would be better for me to add what Payne had said to me; to which he assented. I then made the endorsement which I presume is in the possession of Judge Holt as nearly in the words of Payne as I could remember and added that I believed Payne had told the truth in this matter. In this, I did not by any means intend to express my own opinion of the guilt or innocence of Mrs. Surratt, but simply that I believe Payne had told the truth according to the best of his knowledge and belief.
>
> I am Genl.
> Your Most ob't. Sv't.
> Bvt. Maj. Genl.
> Com'dg Prison[16]

John Surratt's mother died leaving many questions unanswered. Although new information continues to be found and ideas and opinions are voiced one way or another, we probably will never know the whole truth about her part, if any, in the conspiracy to kidnap or assassinate Abraham Lincoln.

6

Hiding

John H. Surratt had been examining the prison camp in Elmira, New York, making sketches of it to bring back to Canada for General Edwin G. Lee, new chief of the Confederate spy mission in Canada. He had arrived in Elmira on Wednesday, April 12, and had spent the next day carrying out his mission. He did not say, but he may have continued scouting the prisoner of war camp on Friday. Getting up on Saturday morning, April 15, he went down to breakfast. He later described what happened next:

> When I took my seat at the table about nine o'clock A.M., a gentleman to my left remarked: "Have you heard the news?" "No, I've not," I replied. "What is it?" "Why, President Lincoln and Secretary Seward have been assassinated." I really put so little faith in what the man said that I made a remark that it was too early in the morning to get off such jokes as that. "It's so," he said, at the same time drawing out a paper and showing it to me. Sure enough, there I saw an account of what he told me, but as no names were mentioned, it never occurred to me for an instant that it could have been Booth or any of the party, for the simple reason that I had never heard anything regarding assassination spoken of during my intercourse with them. I had good reason to believe that there was another conspiracy afloat in Washington, in fact.

In hope of finding out more, Surratt sent a telegraph to New York:

> J.W.B., in New York:
> If you are in New York telegraph me.
>
> John Harrison, Elmira, N.Y.

Overhearing a woman saying, "That actor Booth killed Lincoln," Surratt hurried back to Brainard's telegraph office and sought to retrieve his telegram to Booth. Not being able to withdraw the incriminating telegram, Surratt changed his original plan, which had been to head south to Richmond, staying over at the Booth residence in New York City on the way. He later stated, "The town [Elmira] was in the greatest uproar, flags at half mast, bells tolling, etc., etc. Still I did not think that I was in danger, and determined to go immediately to Baltimore to find out the particulars of the tragedy." John Cass, a witness at John Surratt's trial, testified to his being in Elmira the day after the assassination and what he was doing there:

> Q. Where were you residing in April, 1865?
> A. In Elmira. I kept a clothing store at the corner of Water and Baldwin Streets.
> Q. Do you remember any particular incident which occurred on the morning of the 15th of April, after the news of the assassination of the President was received in Elmira?
> A. That morning I got the paper about half past seven o'clock with the news of the assassination.... I got down to the store about quarter to eight or perhaps eight o'clock. My store was directly opposite the telegraph office, and when I got down there I went over to the telegraph office and inquired the news of an operator who was a personal friend of mine. He told me they had received nothing since the news of the assassination, but as soon as they did he would let me know.... Shortly after nine o'clock news

came of the death of Abraham Lincoln. I immediately walked over to my store and told the clerks to close up.... I ... noticed a gentleman coming across the street whom I thought, from his dress, was a friend of mine from Canada ... but I soon saw it was not, and I then turned and started to go back into the store. I had not, probably, got more than ten feet into the store, when this party whom I had observed, came in. He inquired for some white shirts. He asked me for a particular make, which make I did not keep, and told him so, but proceeded to show him some other descriptions of white shirts. He examined them, but said he would rather have those of the make which he had been accustomed to wearing. At that time I made a remark that we had received some very bad news. He asked, "What?" I said to him, "Of the death of Abraham Lincoln." The party made an answer to my remark which at the first commencement I took to be a little disrespectful, and I felt rather incensed, but before he concluded I was satisfied no disrespect was intended. My idea was that he was a Canadian and had no sympathies with our people.

Q. Can you describe his dress?
A. He had on dark pants; a kind of mixed blue coat—I should call it—pleated, with a belt around the waist.
Q. Have you ever seen that man since?
A. I have.
Q. Where have you seen him?
A. In the jail down here [in Washington, D.C.].
(The prisoner was requested to stand up)
Q. Look at that man (pointing to the prisoner) and state if he is or not the man.
A. That is the man I saw there.

Cass was closely cross-examined by the prosecutor, and a few more details came out. Surratt wore chin whiskers, called a goatee, which Cass said appeared to be a darker color than he had later at his trial. If so, that could mean that Surratt had dyed his hair for the purpose of a disguise. Surratt's defense lawyers had more questions for Cass:

Q. Tell us, if you please, what is the basis of your opinion that this is the man you saw in the store?
A. Well, the first thing is, that the minute I saw him I recognized him as the man I saw in my store. I did so before I got near him. I saw at once that he was the man I had seen there.
Q. When you came to talk with him, did you recognize a similarity of voice and of action?
A. Yes, sir...
Q. What made you think he was a Canadian when you saw him?
A. I had a friend of mine from Canada the fall before, wearing the same kind of a coat.

Another witness, Frank H. Atkinson, "bookkeeper for the house of Stewart & Ufford, in Elmira [the trial transcript refers to "Stewart & Ufford," but Brightman's Elmira City Directory spells it "Stuart & Ufford"], also testified to having seen John Surratt in Elmira, particularly remembering Surratt's coat:

It was, as I remember it, a coat buttoned up with a full row of buttons in front and on the sides; with a belt fastening about the waist, and the skirt gathered into it below the waist.
Q. Do you remember the color?
A. It was some dark color, either quite a dark gray or a dark blue; I think more likely the former.

Atkinson remembered Surratt's visit to Stewart & Ufford's as coming between April 12 and 15, 1865:

Q. Is that the same man? (pointing to the prisoner, who had been requested to stand up.)
A. I have no doubt but that is the same man.

Asked what time of day Surratt visited the store, Atkinson suggested, "It might have been 2 o'clock." Another employee of Stewart & Ufford, Joseph Carroll, also testified at the Surratt trial and likewise remembered Surratt by his unusual "Canadian" style coat:

Q. State if you can find the date with any degree of certainty.
A. The first time was the 13th. He came in on the 14th also.

Q. Is that the man? (pointing to the prisoner).
A. That is the man.

The defense was attempting to prove that John Surratt was in Elmira, New York, at the time of the assassination and thus could not have been in Washington on the night of the crime and could not have participated directly in the attacks upon President Lincoln and Secretary of State Seward.

There can be no doubt that John Surratt was in Elmira, New York, between April 12 and April 15, 1865, and that he did some shopping there for clothes. He had been given $200 in gold by Judah Benjamin in Richmond and had changed part of that money in Washington in early April. Hotel registers bear his name in Montreal and Elmira, corresponding with the dates given at his trial. There is also the Canadian diary of General Edwin G. Lee, who wrote that "Charley," Surratt's alias, brought him a letter from Benjamin on April 6.[1]

John H. Surratt, Jr., wearing what was referred to as his "Canadian jacket" (Library of Congress).

Surratt said in his lecture that he heard of the assassination at breakfast at the hotel, but the testimony of John Cass seems to indicate that he first heard the news later in the day. He seemed surprised at what Cass told him, and we can surmise that if he knew he was a wanted man he wouldn't waste time visiting clothing stores. It is possible, as he said in his lecture, that the report he got at breakfast did not name the suspects and that he heard the name of Booth later.

Surratt realized that he had to return at once to Canada, where he could avoid being arrested. The most direct route was to take a train from Elmira to Canandaigua, New York, about seventy miles to the northwest. From there he could get a train to Rochester, New York, and take a boat across Lake Ontario, arriving in Cobourg, Ontario, Canada, a distance of sixty miles across the lake. Cobourg is about fifty miles northeast of Toronto. One hitch in his escape plan prevented his taking this shortest route to comparative safety. April 16 was a Sunday, and not all trains ran

General Edwin G. Lee, cousin of Robert E. Lee and head of the Confederate spy mission in Canada in 1865. Lee sent Surratt to examine the prisoner of war camp in Elmira, New York (Library of Congress).

on that day of the week. Surratt checked into the Webster House hotel in Canandaigua, signing the register "John Harrison." Monday morning's paper said Surratt was believed to be the assailant of Secretary Seward, and rewards were being offered for information leading to his arrest.

The authorities were looking for Surratt. Although they were mistaken about his being the man who attacked Seward, they did have information that Surratt was involved in John Wilkes Booth's conspiracy. Years later, Almarin Cooley Richards (1827–1907), superintendent of the Washington, D.C., Metropolitan Police, wrote to Louis Weichmann regarding how he got on Surratt's track:

> If I remember rightly, the man from whom we got the first information connecting Payne [Powell], Herold and Atzerodt with Booth was a saloon keeper under or near the theater [Ford's Theatre] named Ferguson [James P. Ferguson (1828–1897), restaurant keeper at 452 Tenth Street, N.W., next door to Ford's Theatre], I think. We soon thereafter obtained information that John H. Surratt was often in company with these men and then that Booth had often visited or called at Mrs. Surratt's house. Those facts led me to pay that house a visit that night [April 14–15] at about one o'clock.

Weichmann told the detectives that a letter from Canada had been received that very day, April 14, from John Surratt in Montreal. Weichmann volunteered to help in the search for Surratt. He later wrote, "Afterwards I asked McDevitt [James A. McDevitt (1836–1912), a police detective] how it was that they came to Mrs. Surratt's house so soon after the assassination and he informed me that they had come across a man on the street who said to them, "If you want to find out all about this business go to Mrs. Surratt's house on H Street." I have often queried why the officers did not arrest that man." Reading in the next day's paper a description of Seward's assailant, Weichmann realized that the description of the man did not fit his friend John Surratt and "a heavy weight was rolled from my heart." Weichmann and another of Mrs. Surratt's boarders, John T. Holohan (1829–1877), went to police headquarters to give whatever information they could about the conspirators. Soon, rewards were announced, such as these:

War Department,
Washington, April 20, 1865

$100,000 Reward.

The murderer of our late beloved President Abraham Lincoln is still at large.

Fifty thousand dollars reward will be paid by this department for his apprehension, in addition to any reward offered by municipal authorities or state executives.

> Twenty-five thousand dollars reward will be paid for the apprehension of John H. Surratt, one of Booth's accomplices.
>
> Twenty-five thousand dollars will be paid for the apprehension of David E. Herold, another of Booth's accomplices.
>
> Liberal rewards will be paid for any information that shall conduce to the arrest of either of the above named criminals or their accomplices.
>
> All persons harboring or secreting the said persons, or either of them, or aiding or assisting their concealment or escape, will be treated as accomplices in the murder of the President and the attempted assassination of the Secretary of State, and shall be subject to trial before a military commission and the punishment of death.
>
> Let the stain of innocent blood be removed from the land by the arrest and punishment of the murderers.
>
> All good citizens are exhorted to aid public justice on this occasion. Every man should consider his own conscience charged with this solemn duty, and rest neither night nor day until it be accomplished.
>
> > Edwin M. Stanton,
> > Secretary of War

There followed descriptions of the suspects named, including this one: "John H. Surratt is about five feet nine inches. Hair rather thin and dark; eyes rather light; no beard. Would weigh 145 or 150 pounds. Complexion rather pale and clear, with color in his cheeks. Wore light clothes of fine quality. Shoulders square; cheek bones rather prominent; chin narrow; ears projecting at the top; forehead rather low and square, but broad. Parts his hair on the right side. Neck rather long. His lips are firmly set. A slim man."[2]

On Monday morning, April 17, John Surratt checked the New York newspapers, where he read the following: "The assassin of Secretary Seward is said to be John H. Surratt, a notorious secessionist of Southern Maryland. His name, with that of J. Wilkes Booth, will forever lead the infamous roll of assassins." Abandoning his original intention to go to Baltimore, he boarded a train for Albany at noon and arrived in Albany early the following morning, April 18. Canandaigua is roughly 180 miles from Albany, Albany another 130 miles from St. Albans, Vermont, and St. Albans another fifty miles or so from Montreal, Canada, where Surratt said he arrived at 2:00 a.m.:

> When I stepped on the platform at the depot at St. Albans I noticed that one of the detectives scanned everyone, head and foot, myself as well as the rest. Before leaving Montreal for Elmira, I provided myself with an Oxford cut jacket and a round-top hat, peculiar to Canada at that time.... I believe that costume guarded me safely through St. Albans. I went in with others, and moved around, with the detectives standing there most of the time looking at us. Of course I was obliged to talk as loud as anybody about the late tragedy. After having a hearty meal I lighted a cigar and walked up town. One of the detectives approached me, stared me directly in the face, and I looked him quietly back. In a few moments I was speeding on my way to Montreal.

After registering at the St. Lawrence Hall, "soon after I called on a friend," Surratt tells us, and discussed the details of his association with Booth and of the danger he now perceived from the U.S. government. Although he does not name his "friend," it must have been General Edwin G. Lee, who was in a position to help him escape from the American authorities and their agents in Canada. The Civil War was in its final stages, and the Confederate agents in Canada were scattering. Lee, only recently having arrived in Canada and having taken over Confederate interests from the departing Jacob Thompson, was the obvious person to see for help in hiding while in Canada and to arrange Surratt's passage to Europe.

Lee's diary is blank for April 7 and 8; notes "Lee surrendered" on April 9; the 10th, 11th and 12th are missing; the notation, "Good Friday—went to St. George's church" appears on April 14; Saturday, April 15, Lee wrote, "News of Lincoln's death, came this morning, exciting universal horror and amazement." On April 16, he noted, "Easter Sunday—Attended

St. George's." April 17 and 18 are blank. For Wednesday, April 19, Lee wrote, "This day or the 20th—Gave messenger $200 Greenbacks & $100 services. (Charley) see May 4." As Surratt in his lecture stated, "soon after" his arrival in Montreal on April 18 he "called on a friend," and we have Lee's diary entry on the 19th that he saw "Charley." We would seem to have all the proof we need to affirm that "Charley Armstrong" was John Harrison Surratt, Jr. This also supports the assertion that the "friend" mentioned by Surratt was Edwin G. Lee. Further, it disproves Surratt's later claim that the two hundred dollars in gold he received from Judah Benjamin in Richmond amounted to the only monetary help he ever received from the Confederacy.[3]

Fearing that Union agents would too early find Surratt at the St. Lawrence Hotel, Lee arranged for the fugitive to move to the residence of a former Nashville, TN, banker, John Porterfield (1820–?). There is the mention of a "Mr. Potterfield" in the conspiracy trial testimony of Sanford Conover when naming Confederate agents he knew in Canada. On a later page, Conover names "Mr. Porterfield." The earlier reference was probably a misspelling. On another page of the trial transcript, Conover is asked about Surratt:

> Q. Have you seen John H. Surratt in Canada since the assassination of the President?
> A. Yes, sir.
> Q. On what day did you see him, do you remember?
> A. I think it was three or four days after the assassination.
> Q. Where at?
> A. I saw him in the street with Mr. Porterfield.
> Q. Who is Mr. Porterfield?
> A. Mr. Porterfield is a Southern gentleman, now a British subject. He was made a British subject, I believe, by special act of the Canadian Parliament.
> Q. He is from the South?
> A. Yes, sir: he has been for some time a broker or banker there. He is the gentleman who took charge of the St. Albans plunder [from the Confederate raid on St. Albans, Vermont, on October 19, 1864] for the Ontario Bank, when prematurely given up by Judge Coursol.
> Q. He is one of the intimate associates of the Southern traitors of whom you have spoken?
> A. Very intimate; on the most intimate terms with [Jacob] Thompson and [George N.] Sanders.
> Q. Did you learn from any source there when he [Surratt] had arrived in Canada?
> A. I did not; but I learned immediately after that he was suspected, and that officers were on his track, and that he had decamped.

Of course, we cannot depend on what Conover said, as he was a notorious liar. Even his name was a lie. "Sanford Conover" was only one of his many aliases. His real name was Charles A. Dunham (c. 1832–1900). Arrested by Canadian authorities as a suspect in the Confederate raid on St. Albans, Vermont, Dunham met George Nicholas Sanders (1812–1873) in a Canadian jail. Testifying at the trial of the St. Albans raiders, Dunham used the name James Watson Wallace. Before the trial of the Lincoln assassination conspiracy suspects had ended, the prosecutors received information from Canadian authorities that Dunham had lied about nearly everything he had said in his testimony, including his own name. They determined that Conover, Wallace and Dunham were all the same man, and that his loyalty to the Union was totally unreliable. Dunham tried to lie his way out of trouble, but he tried too often. Eventually, he was convicted of perjury in 1867 and received a ten-year sentence, only to be pardoned by President Johnson in 1869. Even though a perjurer, Dunham may have occasionally told the truth about some things. He knew the names of many of the Confederate agents in Canada, including Porterfield, and he knew that John Surratt was in Canada and was in association with Porterfield.[4]

Two of the boarders at Mrs. Surratt's house in Washington were sent to Canada to find John Surratt. Louis J. Weichmann and John T. Holohan went to police headquarters in Washington and were interviewed by Superintendent Almarin Cooley Richards (1827–1907). Weichmann related that Mrs. Surratt gave them a photograph of John Surratt, "with but little persuasion." Weichmann and Holohan were accompanied by James A. McDevitt, a police detective. McDevitt described their first solid lead in pursuing the conspiracy suspects: "With some other detectives I visited Mrs. Surratt's house and searched it; we then turned it over to the military to watch.... I found there a young man named Wickham [Weichmann], who proved so useful that I kept him under arrest for some time, not letting him out of my sight—even taking him home with me for his meals. It was on the strength of what I learned from him that I made an expedition to Canada in search of the trail of John H. Surratt." After searching in southern Maryland and north to Baltimore, McDevitt, Weichmann, and Holohan received orders:

> Headquarters, Department of Washington,
> Washington, D.C., April 16, 1865.
>
> Special Orders No. 68—Extract.
>
> Special officers James A. McDevitt, George [John] Holohan and Louis J. Weichmann are hereby ordered to New York on important Government business and after executing their private orders to return to this city [Washington] and report at these headquarters. The Quartermaster's Department will furnish the necessary transportation.
>
> By Command of Major General Augur
> T. Ingraham, Colonel and Provost Marshal
> General, Defenses North of the Potomac

Confusion was created by the simplest of things. Returning to the Surratt boardinghouse before the departure for Canada, Holohan "changed [his] shirt and got a couple of handkerchiefs off the bed." He continued:

> The washerwoman came in on Sunday [April 16] morning just about the time my wife was leaving. She did not come on Saturday. The clothes were spread out on the bed, the various articles, shirts, handkerchiefs, etc., being in piles to themselves.
>
> Q. You say you got a couple of handkerchiefs. State if either of those handkerchiefs was marked; and if so, how it was marked.
> A. John H. Surratt ... before leaving, by the afternoon train, Clarvoe one of the detectives of the Metropolitan Police force, went with me to the house to get my overcoat. I thought I might want it on the road, as it was a little cool. While there he saw me take the handkerchief off the bed. We then went to the depot and took the train for Philadelphia. We got to Philadelphia about half past 11 or 12 o'clock, stopped all day Tuesday [April 18] in Philadelphia...
> Q. What time did you go to New York?
> A. Wednesday morning.
> Q. Where from there?
> A. Kept on to Canada.
> Q. Where did you stay that night?
> A. In Burlington, Vermont.... We stopped at the hotel, at Burlington, and got supper, and then went out and bought some things.... We then went to the depot. We were either ahead of time, or the train was late; so I laid down on the settee there until the train started.
> Q. Did you afterwards discover that you had lost that handkerchief, and if so, when and where?
> A. I discovered at Essex Junction that I had lost it.... The way I came to miss it was, I had my tobacco in my overcoat pocket, and in searching for my tobacco, I found my tobacco and handkerchief were both gone.

The testimony of another detective, Daniel R.P. Bigley, accompanying McDevitt, Weichmann, and Holohan, further explained the handkerchief incident:

> We were called very early to take the early train from Burlington to St. Albans.
> Q. Who was present when he spoke of the loss of the handkerchief?

A. The loss of the handkerchief was mentioned, either by the American Consul, [John Fox] Potter [1817–1899], or his secretary, I do not recollect which; they were both in the room; I am not certain. [John Alexander W.] Clarvoe [1831–1879], [John F.] Kelly, Weichmann, myself [i.e. Bigley], and Holohan were in that office; it was right opposite the Ottawa Hotel.

Bigley testified that the handkerchief was found at St. Albans, not at Burlington. The night watchman at the Burlington station, Charles H. Blinn, said he found the handkerchief on the morning of April 18, and that the man who left it was traveling with another man. We know that John Surratt signed his name at the St. Lawrence Hall on April 18, coming by way of St. Albans. It does not seem to matter who lost a Surratt handkerchief—Surratt or Holohan—and on what day. It is intriguing that Surratt may have been traveling with someone, but if so, the other man may have been merely an innocent man, unaware that Surratt was a wanted fugitive.

In a later account, Charles H. Blinn elaborated on his story. He had served in Co. A, 1st Regiment, Vermont Cavalry. As the war was ending, Blinn got a job at the Vermont Central Railroad office in Burlington. He worked the night shift at the freight depot at the wharf on Lake Champlain. The first steamer of the season arrived about 2:00 a.m. on April 16, 1865. Only one passenger disembarked, a man later identified as John Surratt. Blinn gave him permission to wait in the depot because Surratt told him he was recovering from an illness: "In repose, he looked emaciated and sick, and his wretched appearance really bore out his story that he had just come from a hospital. I aroused him, with some pity, when the train pulled in. He awoke in much agitation. The startled and scared expression which crossed his face for a second I can still see."

Surratt told Blinn he was a Canadian returning home. "His manner was cordial and friendly, his conversation very entertaining, his whole demeanor that of a gentleman." Blinn claimed it was he who found the handkerchief, under a bench. The name "John H. Surratt" was written in its corner: "Quicker than wind I flew to the telegraph office, and sent the following message: [to] Carrol T. Hobart, Conductor, Montreal Express, St. Albans, Vt.—John H. Surratt on your train. $100,000 reward. Answer. Chas. H. Blinn." The answer came a half hour later: "Train crossed the border fifteen minutes ago."

Blinn positively identified Surratt at his trial. If Blinn's story is at all true, it tells us about the route Surratt took between Albany, New York, and Burlington, Vermont. If he took the ferry across Lake Champlain, arriving at Burlington, the lake ferry would have crossed from Keeseville, New York, about ten miles southeast of Plattsburgh. He must have traveled north from Albany, rather than northeast through Vermont.

Arriving in Montreal on April 20, detective McDevitt and his two charges checked into the St. James Hotel. They began their search for John Surratt at the most obvious place, the St. Lawrence Hall. Examining the hotel register, Weichmann spotted Surratt's handwriting, using the name John Harrison. He had signed in on April 6, signed out April 12, bound for the U.S., and returned on April 18 but left the hotel that same day, not leaving a destination. Subsequent investigation revealed that he had been taken in and hidden by John Porterfield.

"One day I walked out and I saw Weichmann on the lookout for me," John Surratt related later. "He had little idea I was so near." The danger of his being spotted made it mandatory that he be moved. Porterfield's house was being watched; Surratt's old friend was in the neighborhood. A means had to be devised to get him out without being recognized. Porterfield told Surratt that he had been offered $20,000 to tell them where he was. It appears that Weichmann mistakenly told McDevitt that Surratt had already left Porterfield's house, heading north. Surratt saw his opportunity and fled. Another man was dressed in an Oxford jacket, and that man left the house at the same time as Surratt. They each boarded a different carriage and departed in different directions, further shielded by the approaching darkness. At first, Surratt was hidden at the house of John J. Reeves, a local tailor. After two days he was moved again, this time entirely out of Montreal.

At a point about ten miles outside of Montreal, Surratt boarded a canoe and was taken across the St. Lawrence River, in a southerly direction. He was met by Joseph F. du Tilly, a farmer who had about fifty acres in Shefford. Du Tilly took Surratt east about nine miles to the village of St. Liboire, to the home of a priest, Charles Boucher (1832–1914), on the evening of April 22, 1865. Boucher described Surratt: "He was in very poor health; he had fever and ague, [feverish, feeling cold, and shivering]. The first time he remained at my house he had a disease once or twice a week, and the rest of the time he remained in Canada he had it every other day. We used to call it the 'chills.' His health was very poor. He remained in bed whole days at a time. At such times he could hardly move. He was very pale and weak. Sometimes I was apprehensive that he might not live."

Charles Boucher was born May 10, 1832. His parents were Joseph, a carpenter, and Angelique Boucher. Charles attended the seminary of St. Hyacinthe from 1846 to 1854. He was ordained a priest by Mgr. Demers on September 6, 1857. He served as an assistant at St. Cesaire from 1857 to 1858, and at St. Hughes from 1858 to 1859. He was named pastor at West Shefford and St. Joachim, serving from 1859 to 1864, then moving to St. Liboire, where he served from 1864 to 1866.

Du Tilly and Surratt arrived around nine or ten o'clock at night, rousing Father Boucher from bed. Surratt was not wearing a disguise, nor was his hair darkened. According to Boucher. Surratt said he had come from Montreal and introduced himself as Charles Armstrong. "I was told that he was coming to the country on account of his health, and because of being compromised in the American war." Boucher stated, "They had written to me before sending him to my place." He said he did not know that Surratt was being sought as one of the Lincoln assassination conspirators until ten or twelve days after his arrival.

> Q. Had you any suspicion that the man who came there that night was John H. Surratt?
> A. Not before he told me.
> Q. How long after he came there before he went out of the house?
> A. Three months.
> Q. Did he go out of the house at all?
> A. Yes, sir.
> Q. Did anybody come to see him at the house?
> A. Yes, sir.
> Q. His friends?
> A. Yes, sir.
> Q. Did people that you didn't know come to see him?
> A. Yes, sir.
> Q. How many came to see him?
> A. Only once four or five came.
> Q. When?
> A. I know it was in the course of the summer [1865]; I cannot state the date.

Who were the "friends" of John Surratt who visited him at Father Boucher's? Father La Pierre and Lachey came once only, stayed "about three days" and "boarded at a private house." This group of "friends" visited Boucher's house "several times" during a three-day period, all coming together. John Surratt went hunting with the "friends" once. Who were these mysterious friends? Pierre-Larcille La Pierre (1835–1888) was a Canadian priest from Montreal at the Bishopric between 1862 and 1866. It seems that Joseph F. Du Tilly, who had brought Surratt to Boucher's house, was also one of the friends. The name Lachey leads nowhere. It is possible that General Edwin Lee may have visited Boucher's house, but his diary makes no mention of such a visit at that time. The diary often has no entry for one or more successive days. Whether or not Lee went there in person, we can assume that the friends knew the identity of "Charley Armstrong" and so must have had some connection with the Confederates in Canada.[5] Boucher went on to explain Surratt's behavior while hiding at the Priest's house:

Q. How often did he go hunting while he staid [sic] with you?
A. He went frequently during a week.
Q. How long was he gone?
A. When he went in the morning, it was a part of the forenoon. He then came for his dinner and again went in the afternoon.
Q. What was he hunting?
A. Birds.
Q. Did he walk or ride?
A. Walked.
Q. Did sometimes other people hunt with him?
A. Yes, sir.
Q. Did any other party beside this party of which you have spoken come there?
A. No, sir.
Q. Did any other individual come there to see him while he was at your house?
A. Nobody.
Q. Did he go out to see anybody?
A. He went out to go to Montreal when he left my house.
Q. How often did he go out to hunt?
A. During a week he went twice in one day. The next day he could not go because he was sick in bed. He had this fever and ague which prostrated him, and he could not move. Neither could he go the day after. It was only on the third day that he was enabled to go....
Q. What sort of chills was it you said he had?
A. Fever and ague, as I hear it is called here. We do not call it so in French.
Q. What do you call it in French?
A. Fievres tremblantes. [Fever and trembling]
Q. What physician attended him during all this time that he lived with you?
A. No physician at all.

John F. Potter, the American Consul General in Montreal, having been directed to question a doctor H.M. Ross of Toronto, sent his report to the State Department on May 22.

> I found Dr. Ross immediately, and ascertained from the following facts.
> About the first of April Ross was called upon to attend a young man about 22 or 23 years of age who was suffering with inflamation of the lungs. He gave his name with some hesitation of manner as James L. Harrison. In the course of a day or two Harrison asked the Doctor to read him two letters that had been brought in, addressed to Harrison and signed "Booth." The letters all purported to be in relation to the oil business, advising Harrison that the business "was successful"—"was prospering"—"that they were doing well," and urging him to come at once to Baltimore, where the letters were dated and mailed.
> While Harrison remained under Ross' care other letters came from the city of New York signed "Brown"—two from Montreal signed "B.A.," one from Pittsburgh written by a female urging him to give up the business he was on—to this letter only the first name was signed.
> The man Harrison left Toronto, as Ross alleges, on the 9th or 10th of April leaving his bill unpaid. On the 13th Harrison wrote from Baltimore to Ross enclosing $20 of the amount of the bill. The envelope and letter Ross destroyed.
> He describes Harrison as follows: height 5'10", dark complexion, long black hair, no beard, eyes black, bright and piercing, face thin, slight thin moustache, chin small and pointed, hair falls over the left eye, cut across the nose near the point, nose straight, lips thick, mouth large, upper lip long and full, age apparently 22 or 24.
> Ross does not know where he is, and can give no clue to him.

All of this is problematical; it gives a great deal of information that seems to apply very well to Surratt, but there are inconsistencies. We know that John Surratt had health problems while he was in hiding, but he could not have been in Toronto before April 9, 1865, and it is not likely that he was in Baltimore on April 13. The physical description is partially accurate but also inconsistent. Surratt might have dyed his hair "black," but his "dark" complexion might only be a reference to suntan. It is an intriguing story but also an uncertain one. On the same day, May 22, 1865, Consul Potter followed up on his previous message: "Surratt is, I think, secreted in this city [Montreal] in some of the Roman Catholic institutions."

Boucher stated that Surratt returned to Montreal in "the latter part of July" 1865. A stove had been installed in the wall between Boucher's sitting room and a bedroom so that heat could be fed into the bedroom where Surratt was hiding. The stove stood about six to eight inches off the floor, leaving an open space in the wall. Boucher's housekeeper got down on the floor one day and peered into the bedroom, spotting Surratt. She must have made enough noise to arouse Surratt's attention, for he jumped out of bed and approached the hole in the wall, frightening the housekeeper, who ran from the house, screaming. Fearful that he might be enveloped in scandal, Boucher had to terminate Surratt's residence at the priest's house.

Keeping up his contact with Surratt, Boucher took the train to Montreal "about twice a week." Surratt was staying at the house of the father of Pierre LaPierre in Montreal. Andre J. LaPierre had a business selling boots and shoes at 234, 236 and 238 St. Paul Street. His house was at 116 Old Cemetery Street, in back of the Bishop's Palace. John Surratt must have gone on and found another refuge near Quebec City. He made more than one return trip to Montreal during the months of August and September. In his diary Edwin Lee wrote, "Mr. Armstrong arrived from Quebec. Took Miss Young to see Kean as Richard 2nd, and as Felix in 'the Wonder.'—Farewell benefit." Charles Kean and his wife were performing at Montreal's Theatre Royal, in plays by Shakespeare and others. "Miss Young" was an attractive young New Yorker Surratt evidently met when visiting the home of John Lovell, a pro-Confederate Canadian friend of Lee. Lovell was well to do and socially well-connected. His house was on Linden Place at St. Catherine Street. Lee described Miss Young as "remarkably pretty, sings, is said to be rich, tries to be a belle," Another entry in the Lee diary reads, "Mr. Armstrong very devoted. Made an opportunity for him in the Library and after his departure at 8 P.M.... Had very confidential conversation with 'The Young' after returning from theatre at 11 P.M." From these diary entries we can see that John Surratt was very attracted to Miss Young, and seeing this Lee must have discouraged her interest in the young man during their "very confidential conversation."[6]

Father Boucher testified that he visited John Surratt in Montreal, in a rear room on the second floor at the house of LaPierre's father, and sometimes ate with Surratt in the dining room: "I saw strangers and visitors there from Quebec." Boucher went there, staying overnight, "every week, until he [Surratt] took the steamer for Europe." Father LaPierre would sometimes go there with Boucher. General Edwin Lee was another visitor. On Friday, August 11, he wrote in his diary, "Dined with Armstrong," and the following morning, "took walk with Armstg." A week later, Friday, August 18, Lee noted, "Mr. Armstrong arrived from Quebec." On Friday evening, August 25, Lee attended a party and saw Surratt and Miss Young again: "Armstrong arrived at 7 P.M. The Young left at 12 M[idnight]." On Friday, September 1, Lee "made inquiries about a boat." Although he doesn't say so, these inquiries could be for passage for Surratt to go to Europe. On Tuesday, September 5, Lee wrote, "Sent Charley $100 per Buch." "Charley" is Charley Armstrong, i.e., John Surratt. "Buch" is one of Lee's associates in Canada, William Jefferson Buchanan, Jr. He was a Confederate courier for the Confederate commissioner in Brussels, Ambrose Dudley Mann (1801–1889), and was staying at Miss Wickham's boardinghouse at 580 St. Catherine Street. Lee met with Buchanan and the following day gave him the one hundred dollars to pass on to John Surratt. Ten days later, Father Boucher arrived at the LaPierre house to escort Surratt to Quebec along with Father LaPierre. They left on September 16, according to General Lee's diary.

On Thursday, September 14, Lee "made some purchases and called at Porterfield's ... for a moment at Tucker's and on M. LaPierre, Pretse [Priest]. Saw Charlie Armstrong." Lee was making last-minute arrangements, having LaPierre take Surratt to Quebec, where he would board the ship for Europe. Nathaniel Beverley Tucker (1820–1890) joined them but did not leave for Europe at this time. It thus appears that Tucker was involved in some way in helping Surratt to escape. The final entry in Lee's diary referring to Surratt is the one for Saturday, September 16: "Charley leaves Quebec today." The steamer for Europe, the *Peruvian*, was docked at Quebec. Boucher said he did not board the *Peruvian* but said his goodbyes to Surratt while on the boat from Montreal. Surratt had dyed his hair a dark brown and was wearing eyeglasses. Although LaPierre was wearing ordinary clothes, Boucher wore his usual "clerical suit."

Tucker also visited the *Peruvian* that day. He had been sent to Canada in 1864 to try to arrange a deal to exchange cotton for Union meat. Having tried his hand as a newspaper publisher—founder and editor of the *Washington Sentinel* from 1853 to 1856 and printer for the U.S. Senate from 1853 to 1857. Tucker had also been involved in munitions manufacturing during the Mexican War of 1846–1848. He had served as United States consul in Liverpool, England, from 1857 to 1861. Though not supporting Southern secession, Tucker, like other Southerners, resigned and returned to his home state of Virginia. Upon arriving in Richmond, he was sent back to England, this time on a mission to arrange to ship munitions through the blockade of Southern ports. Returning to Richmond again in early 1864, he was recruited by President Davis to go to Canada. As Tucker had been acquainted with many Northern businessmen, Davis hoped he could work out the cotton-for-meat deal, which would benefit the speculators as well as the Confederacy, as food was becoming more and more scarce. Soon Tucker came into connection with the Southern "commissioners" in Canada: Jacob Thompson and Clement C. Clay. An entry in John Beauchamp Jones' (1810–1866) A Rebel War Clerk's Diary, dated October 31, 1864, reads: "Beverly Tucker is in Canada, and has made a contract for the Confederate States Government with —— & Co., of New York, to deliver bacon for cotton, pound for pound. It was made by authority of the Secretary of War, certified to by Hon. C.C. Clay and J. Thompson, both in Canada. The Secretary of the Treasury don't like it."

Tucker always insisted that, although he was friendly with Thompson and Clay, he took no part in their undercover activities. He considered himself to be strictly a commercial agent. Tucker's connections with Surratt—if there were any—came as Surratt was riding down the St. Lawrence River from Montreal to Quebec. Tucker did not board the S.S. *Peruvian* as Surratt did, but left Canada for Europe a few weeks later.[7]

Another passenger on the steamer *Montreal*, from Montreal to Quebec, was Roswell Sabine Ripley (1823–1887). It does not appear that General Ripley had any part in aiding John Surratt's escape to Europe. He does not appear later in Surratt's life, as far as is known. As they rode the boat taking them out to the S.S. *Peruvian*, Ripley apparently did speak with the disguised young fugitive.[8] A letter published in the *New York Times* two years later defended Tucker and Ripley: "[T]he fact of Mr. Tucker and Gen. Ripley having been on the same tug on which Surratt was disguised, has been tortured into irrefragible proof that those gentlemen, and especially the former, were implicated in the assassination.... I went to Montreal specially to see Mr. Tucker, in September, 1865, and saw him a short time after his return from Quebec.... I remember he told me that he had heard that Surratt had been concealed in Montreal, and that he had never, to his knowledge, seen or spoken to him. Alexander Dixon, M.A., Rector of Louth and Canon of St. James Cathedral, Toronto, Pt. Dalhousie, July 12."

Upon arriving at the *Montreal*, Father LaPierre took Surratt to a cabin and locked him in. He returned with the *Peruvian*'s surgeon, Dr. Lewis Joseph Archibald McMillan, whom LaPierre showed inside the cabin and introduced to Surratt, using the alias "Mr. McCarty" for Surratt.

Dr. McMillan would prove to be one of the strongest witnesses against Surratt at his trial in 1867. LaPierre had sought out Dr. McMillan in Montreal several days prior to the commencement of the voyage to Britain. According to McMillan, LaPierre arranged for the doctor to look after the young man during the voyage across the Atlantic. Locking the cabin door on the *Montreal* was apparently intended to protect Surratt from his fellow passengers. Although disguised, he might still be recognized. LaPierre remained with Surratt throughout the voyage from Montreal to Quebec, even riding the tug out to the S.S. *Peruvian* with him and leaving him in the hands of Dr. McMillan. On September 16, 1865, the S.S. *Peruvian* departed the harbor of Quebec City, bound for Liverpool, England, with a brief stop in Londonderry, Ireland.

7

Flight

John Surratt was on his way to Europe. The facts of his voyage across the Atlantic and through the European continent are sketchy. He gave virtually no information about this part of his life. In his lecture, all he said was this: "After visiting Quebec and other places, with the reward of $25,000 hanging over my head, I did not think it safe to remain there, and so I concluded to seek an asylum in foreign lands. I had nothing now to bind me to this country [the United States], save an only sister [Anna], and I knew she would never want for kind friends or a good home. For myself, it mattered little where I went, so that I could roam once more a free man. I then went on a venture."

In his lecture he stated that he had not heard anything of his mother's fate until shortly before leaving Canada. His "friends" in Canada had, he said, kept the news from him. Another question, and one of considerable importance, is that of his finances. The Confederate secretary of state, Judah Benjamin, had given him $200 in gold just before Surratt left Richmond, certainly more than he needed to travel from Richmond to Montreal. General Edwin G. Lee gave Surratt $140 on April 19, 1865, $100 on May 4, and $100 on September 5. We know nothing about who paid Surratt's expenses while biding in Canada or how those costs were paid. If Surratt had to pay his way himself, that would account for some of the money but not all $540, unless he traveled in the most luxurious, opulent way possible. Even then, it is difficult to account for his needing so much from Lee. Of course, Lee may have given Surratt the final $200 to pay for his expenses in Europe. That would seem to be reasonable, but, as we shall see, Surratt appears to have had very little or no money on him after his arrival in Italy. Where did the money come from, and where did it go? It appears that Surratt's passage, first on the *Montreal* downriver to Quebec, then on the *Peruvian* from Quebec to Liverpool, was arranged by his Confederate "friends," most likely General Lee. While Lee does mention giving Surratt—under the alias Charley Armstrong—money, he offers no details about purchasing steamship tickets. As for his legal documents, Union colonel George Henry Sharpe (1828–1900), who later traced Surratt's path from Canada to Italy, determined that Surratt traveled on a British passport: "Surratt's passport showed that it was obtained by some influence from the provincial government of Canada, and had received the visa of the United States Consul general there."

The S.S. *Peruvian*, a coal-fired steamship built in Britain, had made her maiden voyage in 1864, only a year and a half before. Her length was 312 feet, her beam (or width) 39 feet. Although John Surratt might have avoided recognition if he mingled with the passengers, we can assume that he traveled in style, sharing the cabin of Dr. McMillan.[1] The doctor's testimony at Surratt's trial is the only account we have of the voyage across the Atlantic and of Surratt's strange behavior. Dr. McMillan said that he had no idea who the young man really was, having been introduced to him as "Mr. McCarty," by Father LaPierre: "I believe we had breakfast on board the steamer [S.S. *Montreal*] in the morning, probably at seven or eight o'clock. Between nine and ten the company sent a tug to take the passengers and their luggage on board the steamer *Peruvian*. We all went on board.... After we arrived on board, LaPierre ... said he wished me to let [Surratt] remain in my room until the steamer had left. I did so; I got the key of my room, let him in, and went with him."

The *Peruvian* departed Quebec soon after this, with LaPierre returning to Quebec.

> After lunch or after dinner (lunch was at twelve and dinner at four) [Surratt] came to me, and pointing to one of the passengers, asked me if I knew who the gentleman was. I told him I did not; that I supposed he was a passenger as he was himself; that that was all I knew about the man. He then said he thought the man was an American detective, and that he thought he was after himself. I ... did not see why he should be afraid of an American detective ... [but] he said that he had done more things than I was aware of, and that very likely, if I knew, it would make me stare.... I said that he need not be afraid of an American detective; that he was on board a British ship, in British waters, and that if an American detective had been after him, he would have tried to arrest him before he left port. He said that he did not care whether he was or not; that if he tried to arrest him this would settle him—and in saying that, he put his hand into his waistcoat pocket, and drew a small four-barreled revolver.

This behavior is difficult to explain, if it happened as Dr. McMillan testified. We know that Surratt did not know Dr. McMillan before embarking on the trans-Atlantic voyage, for Father LaPierre had introduced them only that first morning. It appears that LaPierre did not know Dr. McMillan prior to their meeting in Montreal, no more than a few days before the departure for Europe. We are asked to believe that Surratt volunteered to McMillan that he was a wanted fugitive. It is possible that Surratt had been told by LaPierre or by General Ripley that he could trust the doctor, but we know that LaPierre had very little knowledge of McMillan before the voyage and we know nothing at all about whether General Ripley knew Dr. McMillan. Surratt was very young at this time and perhaps impetuous; he might have been bursting with the desire to reveal his great secret. Surratt was young but not stupid. Why would he take such a risk? He knew that he was wanted and had a high price on his head. He had at least partially disguised himself shortly before the voyage. And yet, McMillan tells us, Surratt could not wait to reveal his secret. We can be suspicious of Dr. McMillan, but he must have known something about Surratt, for, as we shall see, he alerted the American authorities in England as soon as the *Peruvian* arrived in England. According to Dr. McMillan, he—the doctor—did not know General Ripley by sight: "[Surratt] told me afterwards that General Ripley was a general in the rebel army.... [Surratt] told me he was General Ripley, of South Carolina.... I believe he knew nobody else on board.... There was among the passengers William Cornell Jewett."

William Cornell Jewett (1823–1893), also known as "Colorado Jewett," was born in New York City. He went west as a young man and prospered, having amassed enough money to be able to devote himself to the cause of pacifism. He represented the area of Pike's Peak, Colorado Territory, at a peace convention in 1861. He made several voyages to Europe during the American Civil War, trying to get the European powers to arrange a peaceful resolution to the war. One of these voyages coincided with John Surratt's escape. There is no evidence that Jewett knew Surratt or sympathized with the Booth plot. His being a passenger on the S.S. *Peruvian* on the same voyage as Surratt is apparently a coincidence. Another passenger mentioned by Dr. McMillan was "a colored man who had been in the service of Jefferson Davis":

> Q. Did you hear [Surratt] speak of him?
> A. No, sir; [Surratt] did not know anyone else. This man [the "colored man"] told me so himself.
> Q. Will you tell us where you saw Beverley Tucker on that day [September 16, the day the *Peruvian* left Quebec]?

A. I met him on the tug going from the steamer *Montreal* to the steamer *Peruvian*.
Q. Will you state whether he went on board the *Peruvian*?
A. He did go on the *Peruvian*, but not to cross.

McMillan does not report observing or knowing about Surratt's speaking with Tucker, who did not make the voyage to England on the same vessel with Surratt. McMillan was asked about John Surratt's disguise and stated the following:

> After I got on board the steamer [*Peruvian*] I perceived that his hair had been dyed ... and also his moustache; it was very thin.... He wore a pair of spectacles.... I remember his saying that he did not wear spectacles because he was short-sighted, but because they aided in disguising him a little.
>
> I had conversations with him every day from the 16th until we arrived at Londonderry; that was about nine days.... I remember his saying to me that he had been in the habit for some time during the rebellion of going to Richmond with dispatches, and bringing dispatches back to this city [Washington], and also to Montreal [this may indicate that Surratt made several trips to Montreal, perhaps well before 1865, but it is unclear].

Moving on to the subject of money, McMillan was asked to relate what he remembered about Surratt's receiving money: "He told me he had received money in Richmond from the Secretary of State, Benjamin, several times.... I remember two amounts, $30,000 and $70,000. I do not remember at what times he received them; he stated particular times. I remember these amounts." Of course, we know that while he admitted being given money by Benjamin Surratt said the amount was $200, far less than the huge amounts mentioned by McMillan. We have already observed that Surratt had no reason to make such an open confession to Dr. McMillan. Indeed, common sense would dictate that he say as little as possible about his experiences since he knew that there was a huge reward on his head. Yet, we cannot dismiss McMillan's testimony, for it is far too detailed. How would he know so much about Surratt? Indeed, how could he have known all of this unless he had heard it from Surratt himself? The errors in his testimony can easily be explained by lapses of memory. McMillan could have been telling the truth about the money, for Surratt might have grossly inflated the amounts in order to impress the doctor. It is also possible that the prosecution at Surratt's trial coached Dr. McMillan, feeding him details obtained from others.

As the *Peruvian* came in sight of the Irish coast, McMillan testified that Surratt, after repeating much of his story to the doctor, made a vow to complete the work of the conspiracy: "[H]e said, pointing to the coast of Ireland, in sight of which we were then sailing, 'Here is a foreign land at last.' Then, said he, 'I hope I shall be able to return to my country in two years. I hope to God,' at the same time holding a revolver in his hand, 'I shall live to see the time when I can serve Andrew Johnson as Abraham Lincoln has been served.'" This sounds a little too melodramatic, even for John Surratt. McMillan even told the story of the handkerchief lost in the station at St. Albans, Vermont, testifying that Surratt had told him all about it in detail while crossing the ocean many weeks later. McMillan related further details of Surratt's hiding in Canada, even naming Porterfield as one who had taken him in and Father Boucher, too: "His general conduct was gentle. He would, however, show signs of nervousness whenever anyone came suddenly behind him. He would turn round and look about as if he expected some one to come upon him at any moment." Why should Surratt have felt uneasy about being caught when he had been constantly telling all the little details of himself to the doctor, a man who had been a total stranger to him prior to this voyage?

McMillan claimed that Surratt asked his advice on whether to leave the *Peruvian* at their first stop at Londonderry, in the north of Ireland, or to remain aboard and continue on to Liverpool. McMillan said he could offer no advice on this, and that Surratt told him he was going on to Liverpool: "I was a little surprised, therefore, when I came into the after-square and saw him all ready to leave.... He says, 'I have thought over the matter, and I believe it is better for me to get out here. It is now dark, and there is less chance of being seen.' Says I, 'You have been telling me a great many things about what you have done and seen, and I believe the name under which you travel [McCarty] is not your name. Will you please give me your own name?' He looked about to see if there was any one near, and then whispered in my ear, 'My name is Surratt.'"

After this, McMillan said, Surratt and the doctor went to the ship's bar and drank a large quantity of brandy, so much that McMillan was concerned for Surratt's safety and asked a ship's officer to escort him off the ship. That was around midnight on September 24 or just after midnight the morning of Monday, September 25, 1865. Londonderry, Ireland, is about 180 miles from Liverpool, England. Since the top speed of the *Peruvian* was eleven knots (or twelve miles per hour), it would require a minimum of fifteen hours to reach Liverpool, longer if the ship did not go at full speed. Surratt would have had to lose at least half a day in stopping off at Londonderry. He was on the run with a price on his head, and he had just told everything about himself to a stranger. Under those conditions, why would he stop and lose a day unless he had an important reason to do so? Was there someone in Londonderry he needed to see? Dr. McMillan continued: "I next saw the prisoner on Wednesday following [September 27] ... in Birkenhead, at my own boardinghouse. Birkenhead is right opposite the city of Liverpool.... When he came to my house that evening to find a house to which he had been directed and recommended ... I told him I would go, and we came across to go to Liverpool, and I went part of the way to this house with him. Then I called a cab and told the cab where to drive him. He went away; that was the last I saw of him that night."

McMillan went to the United States consulate in Liverpool the day after his arrival and met with the vice consul, Henry J. Wilding (? –1872), to whom he told his story about John Surratt. Under cross-examination, Dr. McMillan was questioned closely:

- Q. How many affidavits have you made upon this subject?
- A. I made an affidavit before Justice Meely in Liverpool. I was called before the [U.S. House of Representatives] Judiciary Committee last February [1867], I believe.
- Q. How long have you been in the city [Washington] attending to this matter?
- A. I arrived in Washington on the 21st of January last.
- Q. Have you been here ever since?
- A. I have.
- Q. What have you been doing here?
- A. Nothing.
- Q. How have you sustained yourself?
- A. I have had money to pay my board.
- Q. Who has furnished it to you?
- A. I had it from the State Department.
- Q. Have you had anything further than money to pay your board since January from the department?
- A. Here, within a few days, I wanted some more money, and I called on the deputy marshal and got some from him.
- Q. How much has the State Department paid you?
- A. I have received $350 since I have been here, and $100 from the marshal; $450 in all.

The questioning turned to more central issues:

- Q. Did you ever ask him [Surratt] his name before he got to the end of the voyage?
- A. I never did.
- Q. Did you feel no curiosity to know it?

A. I did.
Q. Why did you not ask him?
A. Because I had my suspicions as to who the man was from his conversation.
Q. If you were suspecting why did you not develop your suspicions, and satisfy yourself by asking him?
A. I did not want to.
Q. Why did you do it finally?
A. Because I wanted to make sure. The passenger had interested me.... I do not remember asking him during the whole passage a half dozen questions ... [as] he seemed to be so free in expressing everything that he had done, that I thought he would tell me enough without my questioning him. He was quite free; seemed to be overflowing with the subject....

Since October, 1865, when Mr. Wilding told me that this government was not going to prosecute the prisoner; that they had not anything against him. I thought the matter never would be brought up before the public again, and so I made no secret of it. I told it to whoever wanted to know it. The first time I saw Mr. Wilding I made the affidavit that you have there. Then he told me not to sail back to Canada again without calling and seeing him....

On the Wednesday previous to my sailing to Canada I went and saw Mr. Wilding, and he then told me that he had received news from Mr. Adams, American Minister at London, that he was not going to do anything in the matter.

Q. What induced you to make this affidavit as soon as you landed?
A. Because I thought the prisoner was guilty of a crime not only against society, but against civilization. I thought it was my duty as a man to go and give him up to the proper authorities.... I had no intention of giving this information until after we arrived in Liverpool, and he gave me his name. I made up my mind after I found out positively who the man was, that he was guilty of a great crime, and I should give him up.
Q. Did you expect any reward in giving him up?
A. No, sir. I did not then know that a reward had been offered for him.
Q. Have you ever stated that you expected a reward?
A. I have stated that since, many times.... At the time I went to Mr. Wilding I was in the service of the [steamship] company.... I did not want my name to go before the public in any way whatever. He then gave me his promise it would be so. I then made my affidavit.... When I saw him next he says, "I know who you are," and added "If you are afraid of losing your position I will state that there is a heavy reward offered for his capture, and you will be entitled to it if he is taken." That was a week after I had made my affidavit.... I said ... that if any one was entitled to a reward for his arrest, I thought myself as much entitled to it as anybody else.

McMillan was asked a series of questions about what he said, or was reported to have said, about Surratt having been in Canada or in New York State or that Surratt could have been guilty of assassination but was merely a political offender. To all of these questions he replied that he had not made any such statement:

Q. I ask you whether you have ever made any statement contrary to what you have made on the stand [at the trial of John Surratt]?
A. I never said anything contrary to it. I have said something "different," but not "contrary."

Under probing cross-examination, McMillan admitted that he saw Surratt in Liverpool three times, but he insisted it was Surratt who came to him in the days immediately following their arrival:

Q. Did Surratt say anything to you about his being in want of money?
A. He did. He said that he was hard up for money; that the parties where he lived seemed to be tired of him.

Here again arises the mystery of Surratt's money. We know that he had received a few hundred dollars between his departure from Richmond and his arrival in England. As he was in hiding most of that time, and we can assume that General Edwin Lee paid Surratt's expenses while in Canada, what happened to his money? It seems reasonable that he would have had at least some money with him upon his arrival in Liverpool. And, we must remember,

McMillan had said that Surratt had tens of thousands of dollars. Either Surratt was lying about it to the doctor or McMillan was lying in his testimony. McMillan's testimony has to be taken with a healthy dose of reasonable doubt. He admitted that the reward money offered for Surratt was a motivating factor, but even if we discount that we are still left with the question of why Surratt would take such a chance as telling a perfect stranger his true identity and even making threats of future criminal acts. Because we do not know the whole story of who McMillan was, and what, if any, connection he might have had with the Confederacy in Canada, we cannot accurately evaluate the doctor's role in Surratt's story. His testimony is included here because he is the only person who can tell us anything about Surratt as he crossed the ocean and arrived in England. How much of that story we can believe to be true is for the reader to decide.[2]

Upon learning of Surratt's presence in Liverpool, U.S. vice-consul Henry J. Wilding sent a dispatch to Washington:

> Hon. William H. Seward
> Secretary of State
> Washington, D.C.
>
> Sir: Yesterday, information was given me that Surratt, one of the persons implicated in the conspiracy to murder Mr. Lincoln, was in Liverpool, or expected there within a day or two. I took the affidavit of the person who gave me the information, and transmitted it to Mr. Adams, and I herewith transmit a copy.
>
> [McMillan] described himself as a passenger, but I have ascertained that he is [the ship's surgeon].
>
> He expects a letter or a visit from Surratt in a day or two, and has promised to acquaint me with his, Surratt's location.
>
> Should there be really anything in it, and a warrant be obtained for Surratt's apprehension, we should scarcely get him delivered up without other evidence than we can obtain here, we should have to ask his remand until you could send us the necessary evidence.
>
> Very respectfully, I am, Sir, your obedient servant,
>
> H. Wilding, Vice-Consul
> United States Consulate, Liverpool
> September 27, 1865
> No. 538

Notice Wilding's expression of doubt regarding the trustworthiness of Dr. McMillan's statement. The word "remand" in the above dispatch means to have a suspect arrested awaiting trial. Wilding obviously thought McMillan's affidavit would not be considered sufficient to satisfy British authorities, perhaps for the same doubts expressed here.

Henry J. Wilding served for many

John H. Surratt, Jr., in Zouave uniform, c.1867 (Library of Congress).

years at the United States consulate in Liverpool, England. Although he worked for the United States, he was a British subject. Nathaniel Hawthorne (1804–1864), the great American author of *The Scarlet Letter* and *The House of the Seven Gables*, was appointed U.S. consul in Liverpool in 1853 by his old school friend Franklin Pierce (1804–1869), who became the fourteenth president of the United States and served from 1853 to 1857. Hawthorne was happy to find Wilding among his staff in Liverpool. Holding the position at that time of second clerk, Wilding was described by Hawthorne as "honest and capable" and as "a man of English integrity." He stated, "It would have been a sore mischance to me, had any better fortune on his part deprived me of Mr. Wilding's services." The great majority of official documents, dispatches, depositions, and financial records were in Wilding's hand. By the end of Hawthorne's tenure in Liverpool, 1857, Wilding was also involved in legal work for the consulates as well as arranging Hawthorne's personal affairs. Wilding was married and had a child. He ignored Hawthorne's instructions to dismiss the English clerks in favor of Americans, saying that he was "little inclined to open the Consular doors to a spy of the State Department or an intriguer for my own office." Just before leaving for home, Hawthorne wrote a letter of recommendation for Wilding in case the clerk, by this time serving as vice-consul, should lose his job: "He is a man, in my judgment, worthy of all trust. While I held the Consulate, there was no limit to the confidence which I reposed in his integrity, and I can now look back and see that it was always justified.... He was a treasure to me, (indeed, I could not possibly have done without him,) and he will prove the same to any man who may be lucky enough to secure his services. If I knew how to say more in his favor, I would say it, and feel it not more than true."

Hawthorne described the American consulate in Liverpool:

> [It was] a shabby and smoke-stained edifice of four stories high ... at the lower corner of Brunswick Street, contiguous to the Goree Arcade, and in the neighborhood of some of the oldest docks.... A narrow and ill-lighted staircase gave access to an equally narrow and ill-lighted passage-way on the first floor ... [that] were often thronged, of a morning, with a set of beggarly and piratical-looking scoundrels ... purporting to belong to our mercantile marine, and chiefly composed of Liverpool blackballers and the scum of every maritime nation on earth; such being the seamen by whose assistance we then disputed the navigation of the world with England....
>
> Any respectable visitor, if he could make up his mind to elbow a passage among the sea-monsters, was admitted into an outer office, where he found more of the same species, explaining their respective wants or grievances to the Vice-Consul and clerks, while their shipmates awaited their turn outside the door. Passing through this exterior court, the stranger was ushered into an inner privacy, where sat the Consul himself....
>
> It was an apartment of very moderate size, painted in imitation of oak, and duskily lighted by two windows looking across a by-street at the rough brick-side of an immense cotton ware-house, a plainer and uglier structure than ever was built in America.

A decade had passed since Hawthorne had served as consul, but it is doubtful that much had changed in the building and the neighborhood. Coincidently, Hawthorne's successor as consul in Liverpool had been Nathaniel Beverly Tucker, whom we have already encountered as a Confederate business agent in Canada and who shared the S.S. *Montreal* steamer from Montreal to Quebec with John Surratt. Tucker had been appointed consul in August 1857 but was delayed in arriving to relieve Hawthorne until October. Tucker held the post until 1861, when he returned home to join the Confederate effort.[3]

On September 30, 1865, Wilding sent another dispatch to Secretary of State Seward:

> Sir: Since my dispatch No. 538, the supposed Surratt has arrived in Liverpool and is now staying at the Oratory of the Roman Catholic Church of the Holy Cross. His appearance indicates him to be about twenty-one years of age, rather tall, and tolerably good looking....

7. Flight

 I know that clergymen of that persuasion on their way to and from America have frequently lodged, while in Liverpool, at that same oratory, so that the fact of this young man going there somewhat favors the belief that he is really Surratt.

 I can, of course, do nothing further in the matter without Mr. Adams' instructions and a warrant. If it be Surratt, such a wretch ought not to escape.

The "Mr. Adams" referred to was the American minister to the United Kingdom, Charles Francis Adams (1807–1886), son of the sixth president of the United States, John Quincy Adams (1767–1848), and grandson of the second president, John Adams (1735–1826), continuing the family's distinguished tradition of diplomatic service. In a follow-up dispatch, Wilding told Seward, "Mr. Adams instructed me that he did not consider it advisable, with our present evidence of identity and complicity, to apply for a warrant for the arrest of the supposed Surratt." Wilding received a prompt reply to this dispatch:

Lewis T. Powell (right) with guard was a Booth conspirator who attacked Secretary of State Seward and four others in the Seward household. He was executed standing beside Mary Surratt, John's mother (Library of Congress).

> Sir: Your dispatches from 533 to 541 inclusive, have been received. In reply to your No. 538, I have to inform you that, upon a Consultation with the Secretary of War [Edwin M. Stanton] and the Judge Advocate General [Joseph Holt], it is thought advisable that no action be taken in regard to the arrest of the supposed John Surratt at present.
>
> W. Hunter
Acting Secretary

William Hunter (1805–1886) became acting secretary of state on the night of April 14, 1865, when Lewis T. Powell attacked Secretary of State William Seward and his son, Assistant Secretary of State Frederick W. Seward (1830–1915), seriously wounding both of the Sewards. Considering their zeal in arresting and prosecuting the suspects in the Lincoln assassination, including John Surratt's mother Mary, it is curious that Secretary Stanton and Judge Advocate General Holt would back off from ordering the arrest of John Surratt. Perhaps they were influenced by the doubts expressed in Wilding's dispatch.

The United States consul general in Montreal, Canada, John Fox Potter (1817–1899), sent a dispatch to Secretary Seward on October 25:

> Sir: I sent a telegram in cipher yesterday informing the department that John H. Surratt left Three Rivers some time in September for Liverpool, where he is now awaiting the arrival of the steamer *Nova Scotian*, which sails [from Canada] on Saturday next, by which he expects to receive money from parties in this city, by the hand of [name deleted, likely it was Dr. McMillan, who had been transferred from the *Peruvian* to the *Nova Scotian*] of whom Surratt made a confident [*sic*] in Liverpool.
>
> I have the information from [Dr. McMillan] it is Surratt's intention to go to Rome....
>
> I requested instructions in my telegram, but hearing nothing yet, I scarcely know what course to take. If an officer could proceed to England in this ship [the *Nova Scotian*], I have no doubt but that Surratt's arrest might be effected.... If I hear nothing from Washington, I shall go to Quebec tomorrow to see [Dr. McMillan] further on the subject.[4]

Whether or not Dr. McMillan told the truth to Wilding and Potter, or, for that matter, if John Surratt told the truth to McMillan, it was known that John Surratt was in Liverpool, England, for a time after late September. And again, according to McMillan, Surratt was once again short of money. Wilding had reported that Surratt was staying at the Oratory of the Holy Cross in Liverpool. It is likely that Surratt was referred to this institution by his "friends" in Canada, Fathers LaPierre and Boucher, perhaps by way of General Edwin Lee. If Surratt was again in need of money and had sent word by way of McMillan, Lee would be the likely source of the money. But if Lee was in touch with McMillan, that would make the doctor a Southern sympathizer, unless McMillan was either a traitor to the Confederates or some sort of a double agent pretending to be the helpful messenger and guardian of Surratt while all the time reporting to the Union authorities.

The Oratory of the Holy Cross was established in 1849 and the building where Surratt stayed was built in 1860. The six priests there in 1865 were either Irish or French, and none of them had ever been to Canada or the United States. Father Charles Constant Jolivet (1826–1903) seems to have been the priest who dealt with Surratt. It appears that Surratt was hidden, or partially hidden, for in a letter to Father Jolivet, written eight years later, Surratt stated, "I have never forgotten your kindness to me at a time when I was without friends and penniless.... It seems impossible that only a wall separated us, and I should not have known anything about it. I marvel that some priest did not whisper to me, 'without stands your best friend.' There would have been no risk to you or to myself, though at that time my friends did not know it as well as I."

No sooner was a national government established for the Southern Confederacy than efforts began to court the European powers to support the Confederacy. Southern attention was focused on England and France, nations which imported vast amounts of American cotton. The British textile industry obtained three-fourths of their cotton from the United States by 1860 and possessed the military and naval power to break the American blockade of Southern ports. The Confederates adopted a policy of an embargo on their cotton. Public opinion in the South recognized the importance of cotton to the Europeans and, without urging from the Confederate government, began to withhold their cotton from the markets. Land that had been devoted to cotton was converted to food crops. By 1862, the British were importing about 3 percent as much American cotton as they had before the war. Although there was a good deal of British support for the South, there was little desire for war with the United States, especially within British political leadership.

Britain faced a legal and political issue in challenging the Union blockade or declaring it ineffective or illegal. Blockading had been—and would be again—Britain's principal strategy against her enemies. With their island nation and their large navy, it was a natural way to deal with continental enemies such as Napoleon I. The British could not match the large armies of their opponents, but by blockading their ports they could make them very uncomfortable. Thus, the British could not denounce the American blockade without undermining their chief weapon and means of defense. The large importation of cotton in the years before the American Civil War broke out provided Britain with a surplus, making the Confederate embargo ineffective. Even the seizing of British ships by the American navy did not provoke the British into war, for they had done the same thing with American ships and sailors before the War of 1812.[5]

In spite of these obstacles to Confederate recognition by the European powers, the Southerners did not give up hope of foreign intervention in their favor. If the British and French would not intervene militarily on their behalf, the South could at least obtain weapons and supplies from Europe. A very capable agent for this purpose was Caleb Huse (1831–1905). Huse had graduated from the U.S. Military Academy in 1851 and was an instructor there before the Civil War. Although born in Newburyport, Massachusetts, Huse became a loyal and effective purchasing agent for the Confederate army.

Another of the more important figures in the economic story of the Civil War was George Alfred Trenholm (1807–1876) of Charleston, South Carolina. Going to work for John Fraser & Co., a major cotton broker, Trenholm became head and principal owner of the company by 1853. In addition to cotton, he had holdings in steamships, railroads, banks, hotels, and other areas, and was thought to be the richest man in the South. During the Civil War, Fraser, Trenholm & Co. became the Confederacy's overseas banker and financial agent, with their overseas headquarters in Liverpool, England. Trenholm was an important advisor to the Confederate secretary of the treasury and was appointed to that post on July 18, 1864.

Confederate diplomatic representatives to Britain at the beginning of the war were William Lowndes Yancy (1814–1863), Pierre Adolphe Rost (1797–1868), and Ambrose Dudley Mann (1801–1889). Initially well received, these three proved to be relatively ineffective. Although they were popular with those inclined to support the Southern cause, they were unable to coax the British or French governments to intervene in the American war. They were succeeded by James Murray Mason (1798–1871) and John Slidell (1793–1871). Mason and Slidell are best remembered today as the two principal figures in the "Trent Affair."[6]

John Surratt arrived in England in late September 1865. As we have seen, he told Dr. McMillan that he was short of money. That being the case, to whom could he apply for help—financial and otherwise? As a former courier for the Confederate Secret Service, he may have received instructions from General Edwin Lee in Canada, and as he was Catholic the priests LaPierre and Boucher may have steered him toward the Oratory of the Holy

Cross in Liverpool. But now that he was there, to whom could he apply for further assistance?

Many former officials of the Confederacy fled, unwilling to accept total defeat and several fearing for their lives should they be captured by Union forces. Some went southwest, toward Texas and Mexico, some went north to British Canada, and several crossed the ocean to Europe. Secretary of State Judah P. Benjamin ordered Jacob Thompson, head of Confederate secret operations in Canada, to close out operations on March 2, 1865. The funds in Thompson's care were to be used to assist Confederate agents to return to the South. Benjamin, in a letter to Thompson, who was then at the Hotel Castighone, Paris, stated, "I am endeavoring to gather all the remnants of the funds for the purpose of paying the most sacred claims against the [Confederate] government, among which the first and most pressing is that of the President [Jefferson Davis] and family, as I know Mr. Davis was utterly destitute of resources when I left."

Benjamin also provided Thompson with at least some partial protection against claims that Thompson had made off with a great deal of Confederate wealth when he left Canada: "I recognize in advance your right (and the propriety and justice of your exercising it) to retain such amount as shall be necessary to your own maintenance while proscribed by the Federal Government for your action as a servant of the Confederacy."[7]

When Benjamin arrived in England he sought to cash a draft for £25,000 drawn on Fraser, Trenholm & Co., the chief business agents for the Confederacy in Europe. Benjamin was seeking to pay John K. Gilliat & Co. In this letter to Thompson in Paris, Benjamin stated that Fraser, Trenholm & Co. "admit receiving remittances from you [Thompson] of more than £103,000 sent from Canada in compliance with my instructions to you in March last."

One of the Confederate agents in Canada, Thomas Henry Hines (c. 1840–1898), sent Benjamin an accounting of receipts and expenses that he knew about regarding the Confederate Canadian operations. He estimated the amount brought to Canada by Thompson at $200,000. Adding to that money stolen from the banks at St. Albans, Vermont, and various other robberies, Hines' grand total came to $2,530,000. From that, he subtracted the amounts required for various operations and miscellaneous expenses, totaling $215,000. What remained, or should have remained, came to $2,315,000. Even allowing for Thompson's generosity in funding many fraudulent schemes, it is hard to believe that Thompson squandered such a huge sum prior to leaving for Europe, but Benjamin's letter to Thompson on September 13, 1865, acknowledges £103,000 deposited by Thompson with Fraser, Trenholm & Co. The British pound was equal to $4.85 in 1865. Thus, if the £103,000 is multiplied in Union currency, we have $499,550. An unofficial rate in Confederate money was $13.33 to the pound; if that was the rate used by Fraser, Trenholm & Co., we have $1,372,990 in Confederate money. If we subtract that amount from Hines' estimate, we have a remaining total of $942,010. Allowing for Hines' estimates, and perhaps expenditures he may not have known about, this seems relatively realistic, though we have no way of knowing if Hines' total was in Union or Confederate money. It is logical that he meant Union dollars, since most of that money was stolen from Union sources. Regardless of how the numbers add up, or fail to add up, it is known that Thompson had a great deal of money with him while he was in Europe.

Whatever accounting we use, Benjamin clearly believed that Thompson had not stolen the Confederacy's money for his personal use; Benjamin wrote a receipt, also dated September 13, 1865, in which he said:

> Received from honorable Jacob Thompson twelve thousand pounds sterling ... to be applied to the partial payment of a bill of exchange for twenty-five thousand pounds, now in the hands of John K. Gilliat &

Co., and for which the said Jacob Thompson was directed to make remittances to Fraser, Trenholm & Co., the drawees, by letter addressed to him from Richmond in March last, by the undersigned Secretary of State of the Confederate States. The payment now made is in full of all claims of the Confederate Government on account of the undersigned as Secretary of State of said government against the said Jacob Thompson for money deposited in his hands as agent of said government.

[signed] J.P. Benjamin[8]

How much money did Thompson have? There seems no way now to determine that with any assurance of accuracy. A remnant of a "Secret Service account book" survived the war—not intact but still containing important information. In the surviving pages, we learn that Thompson received a payment on April 27, 1864, in the sum of $100,000, and two days later another payment of $900,000—both payments in gold. This was his budget for operations in Canada, although it is unclear whether the dollar amounts mentioned in the surviving records refer to U.S. dollars or Confederate dollars. If the latter was meant, it would be closer to $3,000,000 in Confederate gold. This figure is much more similar to Hines' reckoning of two and a half million.

The Confederates had the money and the desire to aid them in their fight for independence. Act 73, dated March 15, 1861, designated $840,000 for "Necessities and Exigencies" of the Confederate Secret Service. An additional $5,000,000 was appropriated for "Secret Service" without specifying for exactly what activities it would be used. All expenditures of gold had to be authorized by President Jefferson Davis. These authorizations did not always specify what currency was involved, but it is assumed that gold was the medium. A warrant for $1,000,000 exists, dated April 25, 1864, "payable out of the appropriations for 'Secret Service,' act of 15 Feb. 1864." Davis specified that it be "payable in foreign countries £206,185. 11S, 4p [two hundred six thousand one hundred eighty-five pounds, eleven shillings, four pence], exchange on England requested." This leaves no doubt that this was the one million dollars for Thompson to use in Canada, which was then under British rule.

The "Secret Service Account Book" lists the following individuals as recipients of funds: Jacob Thompson, Captain George Dewson, John Slidell, James M. Mason, James P. Holcombe, James L. Capston, the Rev. Father John Bannon, Major N.S. Walker, Colin J. McRae. There is also a reference in another appropriations act of 1863 "to provide for the compensation of certain persons therein named ... to pay officers, non-commissioned officers and privates not legally mustered into the service of the Confederate States, for services actually performed," naming a "Captain Booth." However, we cannot say that this "Captain Booth" is John Wilkes Booth because 1863 was prior to his organizing the Lincoln kidnap plot, but we are strongly tempted to do so.[9]

John Surratt, newly arrived in Europe and evidently short of funds, planned to go to Rome. Where was he to get the money to finance this journey? Father Charles Jolivet of the Oratory of the Holy Cross in Liverpool was the source of some funds, though it is not known how much he gave Surratt. It is doubtful it was enough to finance all of his expenses for the journey. Even if General Edwin Lee hadn't told him of contacts in Europe, Surratt must have known of, or assumed, Confederate diplomats and agents there would be an obvious source. On our list of names from the "Secret Service Account Book" we have several potential sources of funds in Europe in the fall of 1865. Heading the list is Jacob Thompson. Before leaving Canada, Thompson got word to his wife, Catherine (1822–?), to come to him and to bring the receipt for his investments in British stocks, amounting to $200,000. After a difficult and dangerous journey, she joined her husband. Thompson closed the account with the Ontario Bank in Montreal on April 10, 1865, withdrawing $649,873.20, and left Montreal on April 14, the day of the assassination of Lincoln. Thompson headed to England by way of Halifax. The Thompsons lived in style in Europe, staying at the Grand Hotel in Paris and touring Europe, Egypt, and Palestine. Thompson always claimed that his finances came from his own personal wealth.

John Surratt knew Jacob Thompson, having carried messages to and from him in Canada. We know that Thompson was in Europe by the time Surratt made his journey from Liverpool to Rome, and we know that Thompson had money—a lot of money—whether his own or purloined from the Confederate treasury or both. Surratt would not have had to meet Thompson face to face but could have contacted him through others. There is no evidence that Surratt contacted Thompson while they were in Europe, but Surratt's money while in Europe had to have come from somewhere, and it is reasonable to suspect that the well-heeled Thompson may have been the contributor—or one of the contributors—of it. Thompson was in London by early April of 1865 and was in Paris by July.[10]

Another Confederate refugee who was in Europe at the same time as John Surratt was John Cabell Breckinridge (1821–1875). Breckinridge had served in the United States Congress before the Civil War. He was in the House of Representatives from 1851 to 1855, vice president of the U.S. from 1857 to 1861, and the United States senator from Kentucky from March 4 to December 4, 1861. Serving as a general in the Confederate army, he was appointed the Confederate secretary of war in February 1865. Escorting the fleeing President Jefferson Davis part of the way, Breckinridge fled through southern Georgia and across Florida to Cuba, from which he departed for Europe, arriving in England on August 25, 1865. Breckinridge was in Europe only until September of 1865. Although Breckinridge had helped to escort and disburse much of the money Davis and other officials with him brought with them in their flight from Richmond, it appears that Breckinridge kept very little of it for himself. He returned to Toronto by September 13, and therefore could not have directly met Surratt in Europe.

The two Confederate representatives made famous by their capture in the "Trent Affair," John Slidell and James Murray Mason, arrived in Europe in 1862. Slidell remained there after the war until his death in 1871. Mason returned to Canada in April 1865 then went home to Virginia in 1868. Thus, of the two, Slidell, Confederate commissioner to France, would have been the much more likely to help Surratt in the fall of 1865. Again, it would not have been necessary for Surratt to deal directly with Slidell. There is no proof that any such contact occurred, but the cash-short Surratt would certainly have known about Thompson and Slidell and could have gotten word to them. They would, of course, have known who Surratt was and could have given him money, if only a modest amount.[11]

Another name from the "Secret Service Account Book" is Colin John McRae (1813–1877). After service in the Confederate Provisional Congress, representing the State of Alabama from 1861 to 1862, McRae became involved with the Alabama Ordnance Bureau, receiving an appointment with the Confederate States of America Ordnance Bureau in the summer of 1862. To secure a major loan for the Confederacy from the French banker Emile Erlanger & Company, McRae was sent to France, arriving on May 13, 1863. John Slidell was happy to welcome McRae, whose administrative skills were by this time well known. James Mason was so eager to secure McRae's help that he traveled to Paris to meet McRae at the earliest possible date. When another Confederate purchasing agent in Europe, Caleb Ruse (1831–1905), was told that McRae would examine his records, Ruse stated, "It will be sufficient for me to say that in Mr. McRae I find a clear-headed man, desirous of doing everything in his power to promote the best interests of the Government." By mid–September 1863 Colin J. McRae was appointed the "sole depository and co-ordinator of Confederate finances abroad." Hearing of the legal difficulties of President Davis, imprisoned at the end of the war, McRae deposited £10,500 with a London bank to be used to pay Davis's lawyers. So if John Surratt needed money upon his arrival in Europe, Judah P. Benjamin, Jacob Thompson, John Slidell, and Colin McRae were four obvious persons on hand and with money available to them.[12] They perhaps would not have wanted to give Surratt any large sum of money but could easily have supplied his immediate needs.

In the Liverpool offices of Fraser, Trenholm & Company, another possible source of funds for fugitive John Surratt could have been found. James Dunwoody Bulloch (1823–1901) was a Confederate naval officer who proved to be so successful an agent for the acquiring of ships for the South that he spent most of the war on land, especially in England. Bulloch was the senior Confederate naval officer in Europe, with seventy-two men under his supervision and millions of dollars passing through his hands. He traveled all over Britain and France, procuring weapons and supplies. Living in Britain from the spring of 1862 until his death in 1901, Bulloch would have been well known and could have furnished money to John Surratt. Bulloch wrote afterward:

> At the time when hostilities actually ceased and the authority of the United States over the whole country was resumed, the Confederate finances in Europe were in a condition of actual depletion. The only department which had a balance in the hands of the bankers was that of the navy; but that balance was not sufficient to make good the deficits in other accounts. Messrs. Fraser, Trenholm and Co., acting with their accustomed liberality and public spirit, informed me that they would pay any liabilities of the Navy Department for which I had given a personal pledge, but they thought that I should make the best practicable arrangements with contractors, so as to leave as much as possible for transfer to the general account.... [T]he final statement of account exhibited a considerable amount still to the credit of the Navy Department, which helped to reduce the general balance against the defunct Government.

Here we have a first-hand admission that Bulloch had money at his disposal at the end of the war. Although Bulloch says the money in his hands was used to settle accounts, it is possible that he could have given a small amount of it to Surratt. Again, we have no proof that Surratt contacted Bulloch or any other Confederate agent in Europe; it is only logical speculation that he did.

Ambrose Dudley Mann, one of the first Confederate commissioners sent to Europe, moved to Paris after the collapse of the Confederacy. He entertained former Confederates at his apartment in Paris, including former President Jefferson Davis and his wife. An unrepentant ex-rebel, Mann kept in touch by writing others of like mind and thus was well known and quite prepared to receive visiting Southerners, perhaps even John Surratt. We know that Surratt traveled across Europe, stopping in Paris, on his way to Italy. The report of Colonel George Henry Sharpe (1828–1900) to the State Department established that in 1867: "I was informed, through our legation in Paris, that the [Papal] Nuncio [official representative of the Pope] stated his [Surratt's] visa had been obtained, not through any letter or special recommendation, but upon the personal presentation of the passport by Surratt, whom that official remembers to have seen, and upon the formal statement that he was going to Rome for the purpose of enlistment." Sharpe notes that he consulted the American diplomatic representatives in Paris and Brussels in his efforts to trace Surratt's path through Europe without learning anything more. He said, "Every inquiry which I had seen directed to make was completed, so far as there were means to do it." The fact that Surratt passed through Paris lends further support to the idea that he may have been helped, financially and perhaps in other ways, by Jacob Thompson or others there in a position to help him. Surratt did not need money to obtain a visa to go to Italy. Sharpe reported to Seward, "The visa was ... given gratis, which is unusual." The visa issued in Paris was dated September 24, 1865. His arrival at Civita Vecchia was dated December 5, 1865.[13]

We cannot say for sure how he traveled from Liverpool to Civita Vecchia and whom he may have seen along the way, but we do know that he wrote from Civita Vecchia to Doctor Frederick Neve, rector of the Venerable English College in Rome. Surratt was again asking for money. Dr. Neve apparently did advance him money; researcher Alfred Isacsson (1932–2011) said it was fifty Francs. This was enough to pay his expenses in getting to Rome, where he found the English College willing to give him shelter.

The venerable English College in Rome is a seminary for training priests who are to serve in England and Wales. It is the oldest English institution not in Britain, having been founded in 1579. Its predecessor institution, the English Hospice of the Most Holy Trinity and St. Thomas, dates back to 1362 and welcomed many English people to Rome. When Rome was sacked by the army of the Holy Roman Emperor, the hospice suffered the loss of gold and silver, as well as its archives. The Protestant Revolution in England, under the auspices of King Henry VIII (1491–1547), reduced the flow of English pilgrims to a trickle. Trouble did not cease upon the establishment of the college, as 44 of its students were martyred between 1581 and 1679, and 139 others were imprisoned or exiled during those dark years. When Napoleon's army entered Italy in 1798, the college was again sacked. Pope Pius IX (1792–1878) laid the first stone for the college church in 1866, while Surratt was in Italy. Surratt apparently had letters of introduction to individuals in Rome by his hosts at the Oratory of the Holy Cross in Liverpool. Their favorable reception must have encouraged the fugitive. Little did he know that his troubles were very far from being over.[14]

8

Capture and Escape

When John Surratt arrived in Italy, the peninsula was in turmoil. After many centuries of being a fragmented collection of small states, subject to the whims and desires of the larger nations, a movement to achieve the unification of the Italian people into one nation was gaining strength. Called Risorgimento, or resurgence, the movement for Italian unification was sweeping the land. By only 1860, the northern provinces of Piedmont, Lombardy, Parma, Modena, Romagna, Tuscany, and the island of Sardinia had united to form the Kingdom of Italy, led by King Vittorio Emanuele II (1820–1878). In the south between the twelfth and the nineteenth centuries the Kingdom of Naples gradually joined the southern lands with Sicily. In between were the Papal States, ruled by the Roman Catholic Church, with the pope serving as both religious and secular leader. Although over the centuries the pope's leadership had been challenged many times, even to the point of driving him from Rome for a while, the papacy had always managed to restore itself. Pope Pius IX (1792–1878) was in the middle of his thirty-one-year reign, having ascended the throne in 1846. The little kingdom he ruled stretched across the middle of the Italian peninsula but was scarcely one hundred miles wide from north to south. As the revolutionary factions fought each other toward the goal of Italian unification, the church and its leader held on to what was left of their earthly holdings with a grip that was determined yet tentative.

The papal army had been reorganized beginning in 1851 and comprised mercenaries. As the sons of prominent Italian families seldom were interested in a military career, there was no officer corps that could be depended upon. Corruption was rampant, with smuggling and payoffs to papal officials siphoning away resources. Although many revolutionaries throughout the gradually unifying parts of Italy espoused the liberal idealism to which revolutionaries in America, France, and elsewhere aspired, the new propertied class gradually ascended, replacing the high-minded ideals of brotherhood and equality for all with the freedom of the prosperous to grow ever wealthier.

When King Vittorio Emanuele II was able to persuade the French to remove their troops from Rome, the pope began expanding his army.[1] Part of the Pope's army consisted of Zouaves. Zouaves were considered elite troops whose training, as well as especially their uniforms, set them apart from the rest of a nation's army. The Zuavi Pontifici were established in 1860 by Christopher Leon Louis Juchault de Lamoriciere (1806–1865). They had an international nature, making it easy for a young foreigner wanted by the law of another country to lose himself in the anonymity of a foreign army. That John Surratt was a Catholic also made it easier. Among the Pope's Zouaves were Belgians, French, Dutchmen, Bavarians, Americans and Canadians. They wore gray uniforms trimmed in red and topped with either a French-style kepi or an Arab-style fez. Being a Zouave was considered a distinction and was sought by many, including Americans. Both Union and Confederate armies in the American Civil War contained Zouave units.

Arriving in Rome, John Surratt probably had letters introducing him to those in a position to help him. The likelihood is that priests where Surratt had stayed in Liverpool had given him such references. He was residing at the English College in Rome by mid-November 1865.[2] His whereabouts were known to American authorities, who were receiving information from Dr. McMillan and other pursuers. Secretary Seward sent a message dated November 13, 1865, to Attorney General James Speed (1812–1887: "I have the honor to transmit herewith for your perusal dispatch No. 237 from John F. Potter, esq. ... relative to an interview with [McMillan] in relation to John H. Surratt, the conspirator. In this connection I beg leave to request that you will procure an indictment against the said John H. Surratt as soon as convenient, with the view to demand his surrender." Before anything could be done officially, the following order was issued by the War Department:

> Adjutant General's Office
> Washington, November 24, 1865.
>
> Ordered that—
> 1. All persons claiming reward for the apprehension of John Wilkes Booth, Lewis Payne [Powell], G.A. Atzerodt, and David Herold, and Jefferson Davis, or either of them, are notified to file their claims and their proofs with the Adjutant General, for final adjudication by the special commission appointed to award and determine upon the validity of such claims before the first day of January next, after which time no claims will be received.
> 2. The awards offered for the arrest of Jacob Thompson, Beverley Tucker, George N. Sanders, William G. [sic] Cleary, and John H. Surratt are revoked.
>
> By order of the President of the United States:
>
> Edward Townsend

John H. Surratt Jr., age about 17. This photograph was used on "wanted" posters after the assassination of Lincoln. Some believe it is a photograph of John's older brother, Isaac (Surratt House Museum/MNCPPC, Clinton, Maryland).

Beginning on the day of Lincoln's death (April 15, 1865), rewards were offered for the conspiracy suspects. The first rewards offered did not name John Surratt, but on April 20 a poster was issued that not only included Surratt's name but also featured a photograph of him. It stated, "$25,000 reward will be paid for the apprehension of John H. Surratt, one of Booth's accomplices" (this poster is often reproduced).

The question arises as to why this reward was revoked seven months after it had been offered. Surratt was still at large, and the government was well aware of where he had gone. It will be remembered that while Surratt was in England the U.S. government had shown a strange reluctance to have him apprehended and extradited. The usual explanation for this mystery is to note that time had passed and the passions

Wanted poster for Booth, Herold, and Surratt. The huge reward offered would be the equivalent of tens of millions of dollars in today's money (Library of Congress).

of the war and the thirst for vengeance had abated, together with the dilemma of another trial, whether military or civil, reigniting the controversy over the 1865 military trial. There was also the concern that Surratt might point his finger at hitherto unknown conspirators. If the authorities didn't know what to do with Surratt and needed time to decide, it was better not to press the pursuit of the fugitive until they could make their decisions.[3] This was discussed in later congressional testimony:

> A. [by Stanton] I have a recollection one time of Mr. [William] Hunter [acting secretary of state] bringing or sending to me some correspondence in relation to Surratt. My impression is that at that time Mr. Seward was absent. A few days afterwards Mr. Hunter called and said the steamer was about to go out and wanted to know if I had any instructions to give in regard to Surratt. I told him I had not, that I did not think at present the information was sufficient to warrant any instructions for the arrest of the person supposed to be Surratt. I thought he ought to be fully identified before any arrest was made.... I thought the matter might as well lie over for the present....
>
> Q. Were there any persons employed by the War Department for the purpose of discovering and arresting Surratt in Europe in the year 1865 or 1866?
>
> A. No, sir, not for his arrest in Europe. Persons were employed while he was supposed to be in Canada to get information on the subject, but without authority to make arrest there. I did not consider that the War Department was authorized to make any arrest in a foreign country.... I am not aware of any disposition upon the part of any officer of the government to delay or hinder or throw any obstacle in the way of Surratt's arrest, and I do not know of anything more that could have been done, than was done to accomplish that object.

There is no reliable information of Surratt's whereabouts until the spring of 1866. He may have spent several months hiding out in Rome at the English College. On April 21, 1866, an old acquaintance of John Surratt's, Henri Benjamin Ste. Marie (1833–1874), visited the Legation of the United States in Rome and had a talk with the U.S. minister to the Italian states, Rufus King (1814–1876). King's message to Secretary Seward describes the substance of their talk:

> John H. Surratt, who was charged with complicity in the murder of President Lincoln, but made his escape at the time from the United States, had recently enlisted in the Papal Zouaves, under the name of John Watson, and was now stationed with his company, the 3rd, at Sezze [Italy]. My informant said that he had known Surratt in America, that he recognized him as soon as he saw him in Sezze; that he called him by his proper name, and that Surratt, taking him aside, admitted that he was right in the guess. He added that Surratt acknowledged his participation in the plot against Mr. Lincoln's life; and declared that Jefferson Davis had incited, or was privy to it. [Ste. Marie] further said that Surratt seemed to be well provided with money and appealed to him [Ste. Marie] not to betray his secret; and he expressed an earnest desire that if any steps were taken towards reclaiming Surratt as a criminal, he [Ste. Marie] should not be known in the matter.
>
> He spoke so positively in answer to my questions as to his acquaintance with Surratt, and the certainty that this was the man; and there seemed such entire absence of motive for any false statement on the subject, that I could not very well doubt the truth of what he told me. I deemed it my duty, therefore, to report the circumstance to the department and ask for instructions.

The reader may remember John Surratt's meeting Henri B. Ste. Marie, described in Chapter 2. Ste. Marie had been having significant adventures since then. While living in Montreal between 1860 and 1862 he was said to be studying law while working in "the education office." This would have been in the Ministry of Public Information in Quebec. Leaving Montreal for the United States, "taking away with him a certain sum of money, but ... the money had been refunded; that he had sent back a portion, and that the balance was paid by his father." Louis Weichmann found Ste. Marie a job in the school where Weichmann worked in Washington after his arrival in the U.S. Weichmann and Surratt met Ste. Marie in 1863. According to Weichmann, Ste. Marie "conceived a great desire to join the Confederate army and fight for its cause. He came to New York and sailed from that point on a vessel that intended to run the blockade. The ship, however, was captured by a United States war steamer and Sainte Marie with his fellow voyagers was thrown into Fort McHenry as a prisoner of war. Thence he was released as a British subject through the intervention of the English Consul resident in Baltimore."

After being forced to accept employment as a farm hand, Ste. Marie was able to become a teacher at the Catholic parochial school in the village of Little Texas, Maryland. Weichmann said he and Surratt met Ste. Marie there on April 3, 1863. Ste. Marie followed Weichmann to Washington, and Weichmann, who was then teaching at the St. Matthew's institute, secured Ste. Marie a position there as an assistant teacher. Weichmann said he was surprised to find Ste. Marie gone after only three weeks. Ste. Marie had enlisted in the Third Delaware Regiment, but he deserted when the regiment was sent to the front. After being captured by the rebels and accused of spying, Ste. Marie spent time in the notorious Castle Thunder Prison. According to New York newspaper correspondent Albert D. Richardson, Ste. Marie secured his release by informing on other prisoners to General John H. Winder (1800–1865), Confederate provost marshal in charge of prisoners. Released after a time, Ste. Marie was able to return to Canada.[4]

John Surratt escaped to Italy and enrolled in the Papal Zouaves. While serving there, he was spotted there by a former acquaintance (Ste. Marie) who then informed on him to American diplomatic authorities. Ste. Marie was aware of the large reward offered for Surratt, though mistaken in the amount: $25,000, not $50,000. Ste. Marie proceeded to track down Surratt in order to claim the reward. If Surratt was traveling more or less openly, as he seems to have been doing, it would not have been too difficult for Ste. Marie to follow his trail. Ste. Marie appears to have been unaware that the reward offered for Surratt was cancelled on November 24, 1865.

Ste. Marie was anxious to have the government arrest Surratt, claiming that he feared retaliation from Surratt's friends in the Zouaves. His real motivation may have been to ensure that his claim to reward money was acknowledged. On April 23, 1866, Rufus King sent another message to Secretary Seward, enclosing another message from Ste. Marie:

> Honorable Sir: With reference to the information I had the honor to give you Saturday last [April 21] I most respectfully state and suggest that it would be advisable to proceed at once and ascertain if such information is correct, as I understand that [the Zouaves] may be soon under orders to go further in the mountains, and it would be more difficult for me to communicate with you. As to the identity of the party [Surratt] I can assure you on my most sacred honor it is lost time to acquire further proofs. I am truly convinced that it is the same individual. I have known him in Baltimore. I have seen him here; have spoken to him; recognized him at once; when he made himself known to me and acknowledged he was the same party I thought he resembled to. He related several particulars of our first meeting at Ellengowan, fifteen miles from Baltimore, where I was then engaged as a teacher, which no one but himself could have remembered. This is about a year before the assassination of President Lincoln; all this occurred about a fortnight [two weeks] ago....
>
> I am fully aware of the danger of my position ... and the utmost caution must be used both in securing him, and for my personal safety. I have told you it is my desire to leave [the Papal Zouaves] as soon as possible, and that I can do by paying a sum of five or six hundred francs. I think I have done my duty in conscience, and trust in you not to be forgotten. I shall expect an answer at your earliest convenience; in writing to me use ordinary paper and envelope, and take a form and turn of expression as none but myself will be able to understand.

Ste. Marie continued to communicate with King, letting him know that Surratt was still with the Zouaves. On May 19, Secretary of War Stanton received a message from Joseph Holt, the judge advocate general of the army: "Bureau of Military Justice, May 19, 1866. It is recommended that the American Minister at Rome be urged to procure without delay, if possible, a full statement of John H. Surratt's confession to [Ste. Marie], verified by oath.... [I]t is believed that it can be shown here that he [Ste. Marie] is a man of character and entitled to credit in his statements."

Word got around Washington that Surratt had been located. Congressman James Falconer Wilson (1828–1895) R-IA, chairman of the House Judiciary Committee and at that time serving the third of his four terms in the House of Representatives, sent a message to Secretary Seward inquiring after suspects in the Lincoln assassination. Seward replied to Wilson on May 25: "Sir: In transmitting an official reply to your letter of the 23rd instant, it is proper that I should add in this form that we have information from United States agents in foreign countries in regard to John H. Surratt. It would not now be advisable to communicate this, as the communication might tend to defeat our wish to arrest Surratt for the purpose of bringing him to this country to be tried." It has been suggested that the U.S. Government, or certain individuals in it, displayed a curious reluctance to bring Surratt to justice. Author Otto Eisenschiml (1880–1963) is not the only one to raise these questions, but he is a good representative of this point of view. He stated that "fear of embarrassing political entanglements" motivated those in the U.S. government; Vatican officials did not want to turn over "a foreigner to a country where capital punishment was still in vogue"; and England's ambivalent attitude can be explained by the complications which would have been presented under the extradition treaty. Eisenschiml quotes a "representative of the British government at Malta": "Without some evidence ... that the man ... is indeed Surratt, and connecting him with the murder of Mr. Lincoln as an accomplice, that man, if apprehended, would within a very short time be discharged, and might then bring an action of damages for unlawful arrest."

Stanton's withdrawing of the reward for Surratt prompted Eisenschiml to question whether Surratt's capture was actually wanted. He wrote that the diplomatic personnel abroad might have interpreted the canceling of the reward as a sign to those diplomats not to bother with the fugitive. Eisenschiml quotes a newspaper editorial of the period:

> [There is] a laxity on the part of the Executive which would be culpable enough if the humblest citizen had been murdered, but which was criminal under the ... circumstances.... No demand was made upon England for [Surratt's] return to this country, nor is there any evidence of the procurement or attempted procurement of an indictment against him.... No agent or detective was sent to England to dog the footsteps of the supposed assassin, to identify him if necessary, and secure his capture; for all of which it appears there was ample opportunity. Although our government officials were sufficiently well informed of his purpose to know that Surratt was going to Rome, no notice of the fact was given to our minister there, Mr. King.... No steps were taken to identify or secure the arrest of the supposed conspirator and assassin up to October 16, 1866, when the rumors of his known presence in Rome had been rife long enough for everybody to have heard them.... The facts are bad, and the world is censorious enough to believe that bad facts have a motive behind them.

Of course, Otto Eisenschiml's books on the subject attempt to make a case for a wider conspiracy in the assassination of Lincoln, so he was motivated to interpret his information as suggesting that idea as much as possible. More recent research and accounts have tended to dismiss Eisenschiml's theory that a Union government conspiracy was behind the assassination, which would explain the apparent reluctance to apprehend Surratt and put him on trial. William Hanchett (1922–), one of the first professional historians in modern times to take a hard critical look at Eisenschiml's theories, has been particularly forceful in his conclusions:

> He rigged his case against Stanton, and he says at the beginning and at the end, that he can't prove it. And he pointed out a number of times that he called his book, *Why Was Lincoln Murdered?*, not *Why Lincoln*

Was Murdered.... After having twisted and distorted evidence all through the book, then he can hide behind this shield that [he is] just asking questions that have never been asked before.... I don't think Eisenschiml was an honest man.... He invented a theory to explain Lincoln's assassination.... I don't think that he can be accepted at face value.... And remember, it was a time [the 1930s] when history of the Civil War was extremely antiradical, so charging Stanton with this crime would be carrying antiradicalism to its logical extreme.... I hold professional historians responsible for not having analyzed his theory [prior to the 1980s]. They rejected it but without an analysis, and that's what made it possible for his theory to get such a hold over the public.[5]

The seeming hesitation by the U.S. government in the pursuit of John Surratt probably represents uncertainty over whether the evidence against him was strong enough to secure a conviction in a civilian court of law. In light of subsequent events, as we shall see, this proved to be true. The military trial and execution of Surratt's mother had been very controversial—and remains so to this day—so the U.S. government must have realized that only a civil trial, with a jury, would be accepted by the public. The old questions about the 1865 trial would have been raised again, resulting in political consequences. But can we say that the U.S. government's reluctance to pursue Surratt is evidence of either conspiracy or gross incompetence? The communications quoted above, from Joseph Holt on May 19, 1866, and from William Seward on May 25, both urged action to prevent Surratt's escape. The time required for trans-Atlantic communications, together with a busy government's priorities and the necessity to verify and evaluate the statements of Ste. Marie, must be weighed in the balance with conspiracy theories.

The first trans-Atlantic telegraph cable had been completed in 1858, but it proved to be very slow in transmitting signals. When the voltage was increased to improve the speed of the signal, the cable ceased to function altogether. It had been in operation a mere three weeks. A new cable was laid in 1865 and it became operational on July 28, 1866. We can see from that date that it should have been possible to make use of the cable for the pursuit of John Surratt. That it was not was likely due to difficulties with the cable. The first cable required seventeen hours to transmit the first message. The new cable was greatly improved, though there was considerable distortion of the message. Because of this, it is understandable that sensitive diplomatic messages could not yet be trusted to the cables, as they were in 1866.

Having been instructed to obtain from Ste. Marie a full statement of his knowledge of and actions in the pursuit of Surratt, Minister King sent the statement to Seward on June 21. Ste. Marie summarized his early acquaintance with Surratt and Weichmann as well as his experiences in the army. Ste. Marie had some interesting things to say about Louis Weichmann, probably the most important witness at the military trial in 1865 and whose testimony had been crucial in bringing about Mrs. Mary Surratt's conviction:

> About six months before the end of the war I had removed to Washington, and ... Weichmann, who was a friend of Surratt, was there with me. I had occasion to see him [Surratt] several times. He and Weichmann ... were intimates....
>
> After ... the unfortunate assassination of President Lincoln took place I immediately went to the United States Consul at Montreal, and informed him what I knew about Surratt and Weichmann, and told him that in my opinion I thought one was as guilty as the other, and acted only through fear in selling his accomplice. I have met Surratt here in Italy. He has acknowledged to me that he was the instigator of the murder, and had acted in the instructions and orders of persons he did not name, but some of whom are in New York, and others in London. He told me a party in London offered him £10,000 to publish a statement of the affair, but he refused.
>
> I beg to say I am prepared to go to the United States, and give all the evidence I know in the unfortunate matter.

The reader will note that in this statement Ste. Marie casts much doubt upon the character and actions of Louis Weichmann. Here is, perhaps, a further explanation for the U.S.

government's indecision and slowness of action in the pursuit of Surratt. Weichmann had been a crucial witness at the trial; it can be said that Mary Surratt was hanged largely upon his testimony. With this statement, Ste. Marie casts doubt upon Weichmann's testimony. Having him make such statements at a public trial would add powerfully to the doubts about her guilt and the fairness of the trial. That would not be something that Holt, Stanton, and Seward would have wanted to happen. Also, Ste. Marie's statement about Surratt saying he refused a huge sum of money to publish his story in London sounds more like fantasy than a credible statement of fact, whether invented by Surratt or by Ste. Marie. Remember, Ste. Marie always had a motive in his pursuit of Surratt—the reward money. Even after the reward was cancelled, he continued to seek money from the government, as we shall see later.

Minister King obtained another sworn statement from Ste. Marie, longer and more elaborate than his previous ones:

> At that first interview [between Ste. Marie, Surratt, and Weichmann] a great deal was said about the war and slavery; the sentiments expressed by these two individuals being more than strongly secessionists. In the course of conversation, I remember Surratt to have said that President Lincoln would certainly pay for all the men that were slain during the war. About a month after I removed to Washington at the instigation of Weichmann.... Surratt visited us [Ste. Marie and Weichmann] weekly and once he offered to send me south; but I declined.
>
> I have met Surratt here in Italy, at a small town called Velletri. He is now known under the name of John Watson. I recognized him before he made himself known to me, and told him privately, "You are John Surratt, the person I have known in Maryland." He acknowledged he was, and begged of me to keep the thing secret. After some conversation, we spoke of the unfortunate affair of the assassination of President Lincoln, and these were his words: "Damn the Yankees, they have killed my mother; but I have done them as much harm as I could. We have killed Lincoln, the nigger's friend." He then said, speaking of his mother, "Had it not been for me and that coward Weichmann, my mother would be living yet. It was fear made him speak. Had he kept his tongue there was no danger for him; but if I ever return to America, or meet him elsewhere, I shall kill him."
>
> He then said he was in the Secret Service of the South. And Weichmann, who was in some department there [U.S. War Department, Office of the Commissary General of Prisoners], used to steal copies of the dispatches and forward them to him, and thence to Richmond. Speaking of the murder [of Lincoln], he said he had acted under the orders of men who are not yet known, some of whom are still in New York, and others in London. I am aware that money is sent to him yet from London. When I left Canada, he said [he] had but little money, but [he] had a letter for a party in London. [He] was in disguise with dyed hair and false beard; that party sent [him] to a hotel where he told [him] to remain till [he] would hear from him. After a few weeks he came and proposed to me to go to Spain, but I declined, and asked to go to Paris; he gave me £70 with a letter of introduction to a party there, who sent him here to Rome, where he joined the Zouaves. He says he can get money in Rome at any time. I believe he is protected by the clergy, and that the murder is the result of a deep laid plot, not only against the life of President Lincoln, but against the existence of the republic, as we are aware that priesthood and royalty are and always have been opposed to liberty. That such men as Surratt, Booth, Weichmann, and others, should, of their own accord, plan and execute the infernal plot which resulted in the death of President Lincoln, is impossible. There are others behind the curtain who have pulled the strings to make these scoundrels act. I have also asked him if he knew Jefferson Davis, he said no, but that he had acted under the instructions of persons under his immediate orders. Being asked if Jefferson Davis had anything to do with the assassination he said "I am not going to tell you."
>
> My impression is that he brought the order from Richmond, as he was in the habit of going there weekly. He must have bribed the others to do it, for when the event took place he told me he was in New York, prepared to fly as soon as the deed was done. He says he does not regret what has taken place, and that he will visit New York in a year or two, as there is a heavy shipping firm there who had much to do with the South, and he is surprised that they have not been suspected.

Although it appears that Rufus King believed that Henri Ste. Marie was telling the truth, one might think that this longer statement might have aroused at least some doubts. The new version of the story contains contradictions, especially the revelation that Surratt was,

8. Capture and Escape

according to Ste. Marie, the instigator of the assassination plot. Just as in the testimony of Dr. McMillan, who said that Surratt confessed to him his guilt, we must ask the critical question. Why would John Surratt confess? Why would he endanger himself so? At least with Ste. Made, unlike his earlier confession to Dr. McMillan, he was talking to someone he knew, not to a stranger. But Surratt could not have considered Ste. Marie to be an intimate friend, as they had only a casual acquaintance, meeting only occasionally over a period of more than two years. On the other hand, as with the statement of Dr. McMillan, this enlarged account of Ste. Marie's contains many details that can cause us to wonder how he would have known about them unless Surratt told him of them himself. Certain details, such the Roman Catholic Church's possible involvement in planning the assassination, may have been added by Ste. Marie, he wishing to provide the government with that which he knew they wanted to hear.

These two accounts, by McMillan and by Ste. Marie, are our only source of information about Surratt between the time he left Canada and the time he arrived in Italy, a period of about seven months. Surratt never denied that he met with and talked to these two men, though we have to depend entirely upon them as to what he said to them. Both men confessed to monetary motivations, which ought to arouse our suspicions, and both men were anxious to add additional details to their statements when pressed by authorities. No motive is apparent for Surratt's self-incrimination in either case, and even if the statements are accurate we cannot dismiss the possibility that Surratt lied or exaggerated about what he told the two men.

Rufus King served as the American minister to the Papal States and was involved in the search for the fleeing John Surratt (Library of Congress).

Seward passed on a copy of Ste. Marie's newest statement on August 7, 1866, pointing out "John H. Surratt's acknowledged complicity in the assassination of the late President Lincoln." The following day, Rufus King sent Seward another message: "I availed myself of the opportunity to repeat to the Cardinal [Giacomo Antonelli (1806–1876), the Vatican secretary of state] the information communicated to me by [Ste. Marie] in regard to John H. Surratt. His eminence was greatly interested by it, and intimated that if the American government desired the surrender of the criminal there would probably be no difficulty in the way." It is curious that Rufus King would seem to have been so credulous in accepting everything Ste. Marie told him, even setting aside any doubts he may have had about Ste. Marie's contradictory statements. Perhaps he felt so strongly that Surratt must be punished that he was blinded to the doubts that should have been obvious in the statements.

Rufus King was born in New York

City on January 26, 1814. Entering the United States Military Academy at West Point at the age of fifteen, he graduated at age nineteen. He served as an assistant to Captain Robert E. Lee (1807–1870), working on the construction of Fort Monroe, Virginia. Resigning from the army in 1836, King assisted in the survey for the New York and Erie Railway. In 1838, he became an associate editor of the *Albany Evening Journal*, which was managed by New York political power Thurlow Weed (1797–1882). Weed must have been impressed by King, for when William H. Seward (1801–1872), a close friend of Weed, became governor of New York in 1839, he appointed King the state's adjutant general. Moving to Milwaukee, Wisconsin, in 1845, King became editor and part owner of the *Milwaukee Sentinel and Gazette* and helped create the new state's constitution as a member of the Wisconsin constitutional convention. He also served as Milwaukee's first superintendent of schools. Impoverished by the Panic of 1857, King had to sell all of his property and holdings in the newspaper.

Rufus King was appointed United States Minister Resident to the Papal States by President Lincoln in 1861, having been recommended to the president by King's friend Seward, the U.S. secretary of state. The outbreak of the Civil War moved King to ask for a military command instead of the diplomatic appointment, and he subsequently commanded a brigade with the duty of occupying the Lee Mansion in Arlington, Virginia, where he attempted to preserve the Lee family's personal property. Given command of a division in March 1862, by the fall of 1863 he was again offered the diplomatic post at the Vatican, which he accepted.[6]

As we have seen, at the time of Ste. Marie's contact with King the Atlantic cables had not yet been perfected and communication between Washington and Rome had to be carried out by physically conveying the documents on ships. Secretary Seward sent a message to King on October 16, 1866, with instructions on how to proceed in the Surratt matter:

> I think it expedient that you do the following things:
> 1. Employ a confidential person, not [Ste. Marie] to visit Veletri, and ascertain, by comparison with the photograph herewith sent, whether the person indicated by [Ste. Marie] is really John Surratt.
> 2. Pay [Ste. Marie] in consideration of the information he has already communicated on the subject.
> 3. Seek an interview with Cardinal Antonelli, and referring to an intimation made by him to Mr. King in conversation ... "that if the American government desired the surrender of the criminal [Surratt] there would probably be no difficulty in the way," ask the Cardinal whether his Holiness [Pope Pius IX] would now be willing, in the absence of an extradition treaty, to deliver John H. Surratt upon authentic indictment and at the request of this department, for complicity in the assassination of the late President Lincoln, or whether, in the event of this request being declined, his Holiness would enter into an extradition treaty with us, which would enable us to reach the surrender of Surratt.
> 4. Ask as a favor to this government that neither [Ste. Marie] nor Surratt be discharged ... until we shall have had time to communicate concerning them after receiving a prompt reply to this communication from you.

In his next dispatch, King reported on his progress:

> I lost no time in seeking an interview with the Cardinal Secretary of State ... and ... proceeded this morning to the Vatican, accompanied by Mr. Hooker, acting Secretary, as well that he should hear the conversation between the Cardinal and myself, as that he should repeat to his Eminence in Italian what I proposed saying to him in French, relative to the wishes and expectations of our government in reference to Surratt. We were fortunate in finding the Cardinal alone and disengaged, and I proceeded at once to state the business upon which we had called. His Eminence was greatly interested in the matter, the more so as I showed him the portraits of the "conspirators," contained in the volume published by "Ben Pitman," and entitled "Assassination of President Lincoln" ... and in reply to my question whether, upon authentic indictment or the usual preliminary proof, and at the request of the State Department, he would be willing to deliver up John H. Surratt, frankly replied in the affirmative. He added that there was, indeed, no extradition treaty between the two countries [United States and the Vatican], and that to surrender a criminal,

where capital punishment was likely to ensue, was not exactly in accordance with the spirit of the Papal government, but that in so grave and exceptional case, and with the understanding that the United States government, under parallel circumstances, would do as they desired to be done by, he thought the request of the State Department for the surrender of Surratt would be granted.

After promising his swift compliance with Seward's previous message, King added, "I may also hold out to him [Ste. Marie] the hope of some further remuneration, should Surratt be identified and surrendered, as also of his speedy discharge, in order to be a witness against Surratt, if required in the United States."

King followed this message with a suggestion that an American warship be sent to Italy to take Ste. Marie and Surratt back to the United States, the former as a witness, the latter as a prisoner.[7]

Alfred Isacsson (1932–2011), a Catholic priest, visited Rome in the 1980s and made an attempt to locate records relating to John Surratt's service in the Papal Zouaves. He found pay records for the 3rd Regiment, Company C, stationed at Sezze in 1865 and 1866 that listed "Giovanni Watson," Surratt's alias. Listed as a Zouave 2nd class, Surratt spent his leave time in Rome on two occasions. There are no indications of his having had any trouble. In May 1866 he was transferred from Sezze to Veroli. Surratt served in the Papal Zouaves from late 1865 until November of 1866, when he was arrested.

On November 6 an order was sent to Lieutenant Colonel Allet, commander of the Zouave battalion at Velletri, to arrest the Zouave using the name John Watson and send him to Rome's military prison. After a search for "Watson" at Trisulti, his duty station, he was located at Veroli, where he was on leave. On November 8 the following message was received in Rome: "I received the following telegram ... from Captain Lambilly: At the moment of leaving the prison, surrounded by six men as guards Watson plunged into the ravine, more than a hundred feet deep, which defends the prison. Fifty Zouaves are in pursuit.... Lieutenant Colonel Allet." There are two versions of the story of Surratt's escape. The first version, widely known and generally accepted at the time and still most commonly heard, had Surratt, as he was being led from the prison at Veroli, asking permission of his guards to use the latrine. They allowed him to do so, and as he approached the latrine, which sat along the wall overlooking the valley below, he leaped over the wall and fell twenty-three feet onto a projection of rock. Waste from the latrine above cushioned his fall. Although sore and dirty, he was able to flee his pursuers, who were unable to chase him after he reached the border separating the Papal States from the Kingdom of Italy.

Some years later, a different story of Surratt's escape appeared in a New York newspaper. Henry Lipman (c. 1846–?) answered the call for recruits for the papal army early in 1867. He joined Company 6, 1st Battalion, of Pontifical Zouaves, and was stationed at Velletri. On his return from leave in Rome [his] "attention was called to a handsome young soldier with a black mustache and goatee, who wore a uniform like mine.... After a while, thinking that he might be one of my comrades, I approached him and spoke to him in French." The soldier did not respond to the several languages Lipman tried until Lipman spoke English:

> We then had a pretty long conversation together, in the course of which I learned that his name was Watson; that he was an American by birth, and that he was serving in the 3rd Company, 1st Battalion, Pontifical Zouaves stationed at Veroli. More he would not say....
>
> Two months later ... my company was transferred to Veroli. I then met Watson for the second time, and became very intimate with him. In fact we shared the same room in the barracks ... [but] try as I might I never succeeded in making him speak of his past. Sometimes in the middle of the night I would hear him sobbing and praying. Then again he would be murmuring something about his "poor mother," and "her terrible end."

About this time an American named St. Mary [Ste. Marie], who had shortly before enlisted in our battalion, attracted some attention by the persistency with which he inquired whether any of his countrymen were serving with the Zouaves.... I noticed a change in Watson's demeanor. He was paler, more nervous, and more reserved than usual.... We ... all learned that our melancholy comrade was none other than John H. Surratt....

When De Monsty [Captain De Lambilly] heard of Watson's departure he concluded that the fugitive had not gone to Veroli, but was on his way to the frontier. The detachment started immediately in pursuit, and after a sharp ride caught up with Surratt at a village not far from Tuscany. He was brought in irons to Veroli and thrown into the barrack dungeon.... De Monsty detailed twelve of us ... to guard the dungeon and its inmate. Ten of us were posted on the narrow staircase, and two ... were outside. Soon night fell upon us, and all around became as quiet as death. Next to the dungeon was a small compartment containing the entrance to the barrack sewer. As had been arranged between Surratt and ourselves, as soon as the clock struck twelve he was allowed to enter this compartment, as prisoners were in the habit of doing. Apparently we forgot him, but at ten minutes to two we all made a rush to the dungeon, and as several among us expected, Surratt had disappeared. He had lowered himself into the sewer and had made his way out at an opening into the neighboring rivulet. The discovery led to a furious fusilade on our part, its object being naturally to divert suspicion and to make believe that we were trying to stop the fugitive. As soon as the Lieutenant heard of the escape, he ordered the entire party on watch to be put under arrest, but I remember that a smile of satisfaction seemed to play around his lips, and there is no doubt in my mind that he secretly rejoiced at what had occurred....

The most curious part of the story is, that when I attended a lecture He [Surratt] gave in this city [New York] in 1870, he singled me out among the audience and embraced me with gratitude.

Which of these two versions sounds more credible? We may point to several problems in Lipman's account, but there is a great deal of detail in it, including descriptions of the interior of the prison, the names of some of the guards, etc., to suggest a kernel of truth. Surratt was a celebrity, a wanted fugitive known around the world. There was a great deal of public interest in him and sensational accounts of his involvement with Booth and of his escape—dressed in the gaudy uniform of a Zouave—were appearing in the press.[8]

John Surratt had escaped and crossed the border into the Kingdom of Italy, which took him out of Rufus King's territory. King accordingly referred the matter to the American minister in Florence (then the capital of the kingdom), George Perkins Marsh (1801–1882). On November 18, 1866, Marsh wrote to Secretary Seward: "I lost no time in seeing the Secretary General of the Ministry of Foreign Affairs ... [and] stated to him such facts as I was possessed of, and inquired whether he thought his government would surrender Surratt to the United States for trial if he should be found in the Italian territory. He replied that he thought the accused would be surrendered on proper demand and proof, but probably only under a stipulation on our part that the punishment of death should not be inflicted on him. Having no instructions on the subject, knowing nothing of those which Mr. King might have received, and having, moreover at that time no reason to suppose that Surratt had escaped into the territory of the King of Italy, I did not pursue the discussion further."

Marsh received further information from King after a few more days, and he again met with the secretary general of the Ministry of Foreign Affairs: "The Secretary ... appeared to me less favorably disposed to the application than I had expected from my former conversation with him.... I doubt whether, in case of the surrender of Surratt, a formal stipulation to exempt him from the punishment of death will be insisted.... I suppose the government of Italy would strongly recommend Surratt to mercy, if he is surrendered to us. The public sentiment of all classes in Italy is decidedly adverse to the infliction of capital punishment.... The universality of this feeling will have its weight with the government." Information on Surratt seemed to dribble in to Marsh from King, the dates on the communications indicating a delay of several days from the day they were written. It appears that they were going through the mail, which would account for the delays. King sent Marsh

8. Capture and Escape

a photograph of Surratt in his message of November 12, and the following day supplied more details:

> I had another interview and long conversation with Cardinal Antonelli this morning [November 13] in reference to the arrest and escape of John H. Surratt. The Cardinal gave me the reports of the various officers charged with the investigation of the facts in the case. They certainly show, on the surface, perfect good faith on the part of the Papal authorities, and an earnest desire to arrest the criminal of whose guilt the Cardinal expressed himself fully satisfied. He added that Surratt had, beyond doubt, made good his escape into the Italian territory, and was now, doubtless, at Naples.... I still think and hope we may catch the fugitive.

A few days later, King had more news for Marsh: "I have just heard that Surratt has been admitted, wounded, into the hospital at Sora." Marsh immediately sent a message to the Italian Minister of Foreign Affairs: "I am credibly informed, and confidently believe, that John H. Surratt, a leading actor in the assassination of Abraham Lincoln, late President of the United States, who escaped from justice after that event, and has been serving as a Zouave in the Papal army at Rome, is now in a hospital at Sora (supposedly Sora Tena di Lavoro), where he is said to have been admitted in consequence of a wound received in some manner of which I am not informed."

It has been assumed that Surratt's injuries were the result of his having jumped over the cliff when escaping from his guards at Veroli. But we have seen that he probably escaped with the assistance of the guards by crawling through a sewer pipe. It is possible that he may have injured himself in the pipe, but there can also be doubts about whether he sought medical attention at all. Marsh went on:

> [T]his legation, as well as the government and people of the United States, have received such abundant proof of the intense horror with which this great crime was regarded by the Italian government and nation, that I cannot doubt the entire readiness of the public authorities of this Kingdom to use all proper measures to bring to justice any of the participators in the offence who may be found within their jurisdiction....
>
> I pray, therefore, Mr. Minister, that the local authorities at Sora may be instructed to hold the accused in safe custody until further proceedings can be had to insure his surrender to such officers of the United States as shall be authorized to receive him.

Marsh followed this message the next day with another, enclosing a photograph of John Surratt to be compared with the man in Sora: "[A]s it is not apparently of the most recent date, it is not improbable that time and the circumstances of Surratt's life for the last eighteen months may have produced some change in his features and expression, which will render the likeness between the original and the portrait less striking. The point of identity ... can, it is believed, be satisfactorily established by the testimony of persons at Rome, who have known Surratt familiarly on both sides of the Atlantic." This last comment is an obvious reference to Henri B. Ste. Marie.[9]

At this point, Rufus King sent a lengthy dispatch to Secretary of State William Seward, describing all of the efforts in the pursuit of Surratt and adding a few details not previously reported. The tip that Surratt had stopped at the hospital at Sora for unspecified wounds had been given by the Papal minister of war, General Kanster, to King:

> Regarding, however, the identification and apprehension of Surratt as of the first importance, I dispatched Mr. [J. Clinton] Hooker, acting Secretary of legation, by the earliest train to Sora, furnished with all the necessary documents and a photograph of Surratt, and also with instructions, if he found Surratt there, to ask, in the name of the American Government, that he should be held in close custody until a proper demand could be made upon the Italian authorities for his surrender as a fugitive from justice. Mr. Hooker executed his mission with intelligence and dispatch. Arriving at Isoletta, the frontier station, and communicating by telegraph with the commanding officer at Sora, he ascertained that one of the Pontifical

Zouaves, calling himself Watson, of Richmond, United States, twenty-two years old, tall, fair complexion, blue eyes, high forehead, reddish (sandy) hair, moustaches and goatee, had passed Sora for Naples, on the 8th instant, the same day that he escaped from Veroli, only a few miles distant. Mr. Hooker at once telegraphed this intelligence to our Consul at Naples. The officer at Isoletta did the same to the Neapolitan chief of police. Both asked that Surratt should, if possible, be arrested. I received a prompt reply from Mr. [Frank] Swan [appointed U.S. consul May 14, 1866, and serving until 1867] at Naples, acknowledging receipt of Mr. Hooker's telegram, and stating that they were on the lookout for Surratt. Our hopes were strong, therefore, that we should succeed in catching him somewhere in the vicinity of Naples. But yesterday a second dispatch from Mr. Swan apprised us that Surratt had left the preceding day, November 17, for Alexandria [Egypt], by a steamer which stopped at Malta to coal, and that he had telegraphed the facts to our Consul at that point. I also immediately telegraphed to Mr. [William] Winthrop [appointed October 7, 1834, under the name William W. Adams, name changed to William Winthrop on September 2, 1845, died at his post on July 3, 1869] at Malta, urging the arrest of Surratt.... The probabilities, I fear, now are, that Surratt will make good his escape.

The message of Consul Swan to King is dated November 18: "I received your dispatch this morning about 8 o'clock. I immediately had the police at Naples and the small towns about here hunting for Surratt, and learned, about 2 o'clock, that he left last evening at 9 o'clock, on the steamer *Tripoli*, for Alexandria, under the name of Walters. The steamer stops tomorrow at Malta to take on 300 tons of coal, and as the quarantine is in force there, he cannot get on shore." Swan notified the consul at Malta, William Winthrop, to have Surratt arrested when the steamer's quarantine was lifted. He also had an interesting bit of additional information on Surratt's escape: "Surratt has been about Naples in his Zouave uniform some days. Passed himself at the British Consulate as a Canadian, and was taken on this steamer through the influence of the Consul."[10] In his dispatch on November 21, 1866, Swan provided more details: "Surratt came here [Naples] about the 8th, dressed in the uniform of the Papal Zouaves, having no passport, but stating that he was an Englishman who had just escaped from a Roman regiment. He stated that he had no money, and the police being somewhat suspicious of him, gave him (at his own request) lodgings in the prison, not exactly as a prisoner, but holding him for three days in surveillance, and questioning him as opportunity offered."

Surratt told the police a story that approximated his actual experiences without revealing his true identity or the real reason he was being sought as a fugitive. He told the police the story of his escape by jumping over the wall, claiming he had injured his arm and back in the process:

> On the third day he asked to be taken to the British Consulate, to which place one of the police went with him ... stating that he was a Canadian, and the Consul claimed his release as an English subject. In the mean time the police had found that he had twelve scudi with him, and on asking him why he went to prison, he replied that he wished to save his money. He remained here till Saturday [November 16], giving them some trouble at the English Consulate and exciting sympathy by his position as a young man of good appearance, without means, they not knowing of the money which the police had found. He expressed at the Consulate the greatest desire to return to Canada, and through the influence of the Consul he obtained passage on the steamer to Alexandria [Egypt], some English gentlemen paying for his board during the voyage, and giving him a few francs. He still wore his uniform when he sailed.

Here again, as we have seen before whenever we have been looking into Surratt's sources of income, we confront a mystery. Swan mentions "some English gentlemen" paying for his passage to Egypt. Bear in mind that Surratt was known to be a wanted fugitive who had recently been jailed in Naples. He had no money, he said, and had only his Zouave uniform to wear. We must ask why "some English gentlemen" who did not know him would believe his story and assist him to escape and why they would not wonder, if he wanted to go to Canada, why he would board a ship bound for Egypt. We do not know who these "English gentlemen" were; it is entirely reasonable to wonder if there actually were such "gentlemen." Someone was helping John Surratt in his escape. There can be no doubt about that. It is possible—though unlikely—that wealthy Englishmen were impressed enough with Surratt's intelligence, manner, and good looks to give him money. Is it not more plausible that Surratt was able to get in touch with someone who had already aided him before, such as Jacob Thompson in Paris or Dr. Neve of the English College in Rome? It should also be noted that after telling his story freely to Dr. McMillan, a man he had not known before, onboard the S.S. *Peruvian* crossing the Atlantic, and to Henri B. Ste. Marie, whom Surratt knew only casually from a few years before and who found him serving in the Zouaves, Surratt now felt the need to conceal his identity. Of course, he knew by this time that the authorities knew who he was and would arrest him if they had the chance, but this does not explain his earlier risk-taking in bragging about what he had done.

Swan telegraphed the U.S. Consul in Malta, William Winthrop, who soon reported on Surratt's progress to Secretary Seward:

> [T]he English steamship *Tripoli* ... coming from Naples had fifteen days quarantine, and the regulations are so severe as to absolutely prevent my having any communication with her while she remained....
>
> It was only yesterday [November 21] afternoon that I heard this individual ... hailed from Canada, and not "Candia" [the Greek island of Crete], as stated in the honorable Mr. Legh's [a consular employee] note No. 4,600, having been thus informed by this gentleman, who stated it was a clerical error ... the name John Agostini, given by the person who was dressed as a Zouave, is an Italian, and not an American or Canadian name.

Winthrop explained that he had not been told who "Agostini" was and had not been requested to interrogate him and hold him under guard. He pointed out that the consul in Alexandria had greater powers to act, "having judicial powers ... and not be hampered by legal quibbles, as I think I have been here." Winthrop sent a message to the American consul at Alexandria to intercept Surratt upon his arrival there. In his follow-up messages, he continued to defend himself: "[T]he man who was dressed as a Roman Zouave, by whatever name he went, was the person I wanted, and would have been arrested, had I the power to do it."

Some of the legal issues involved in this international incident were explained in a reply to Winthrop from an official in Malta:

> I am directed by the officer administering the government to acquaint you that a conspiracy to commit murder is not one of the offences included in the 6th and 7th Vic., c.76, unless the murder intended, or an assault with intent to commit it, was actually perpetrated, so as to make the conspirator responsible for the murder or an assault with intent to commit murder. In your letter you do not say that the conspiracy in which Surratt had taken part was the same which obtained its object by the murder of the late President, Mr. Lincoln. Nor does your letter point to any evidence that the man going by the name of Walter or Watson is the conspirator Surratt.
>
> Without some evidence ... connecting him with the murder of Mr. Lincoln as an accomplice, that man, if apprehended, would within a very short time be discharged, and might then bring an action of damages for unlawful arrest, for which you would be responsible.

With insufficient evidence upon which to make an arrest and having no reliable description of the wanted man, the British authorities felt they could not arrest Surratt. Although they admitted that there was only one passenger aboard the *Tripoli* wearing a Zouave uniform, they stated that he gave them the name of John Agostini, not John Surratt, so they did not feel justified in arresting him. The *Tripoli*, with a fresh load of coal, proceeded on its way to Egypt with John Surratt still onboard.[11]

Winthrop, not wanting it to be said that he had not done enough to apprehend the fugitive, sent a message to the Alexandria, Egypt, American consul, Charles Hale (1831–1882): "If Surratt came in the vessel *Tripoli*, he is on board now. I do not see his name Walters, or Watson, among the list of passengers; but as there are seventy-nine laborers, it is difficult to tell if he is among them [how could it be difficult, since Surratt was the only one onboard dressed in a Zouave uniform?] I have no doubt you will do the needful, that such a murderer may not escape." Further frustrating Winthrop was the news that the undersea cable to Alexandria was broken, so that no communication was possible. He did find out that the line to Constantinople—modern-day Istanbul, Turkey—was operating, and a cable could be sent to Egypt from there. He also managed to get a letter to Hale to be delivered by the consignees of the *Tripoli* when it arrived in Alexandria. To be doubly sure, Winthrop gave a message to the Peninsular and Oriental Company's steamer S.S. *Pera*, also to be given to Hale, stating, "On the afternoon of the 19th of November I sent you a telegram via Constantinople, requesting you to arrest Surratt, which I hope will reach you before the Tripoli arrives in your port…. I think it very possible, if this Surratt lands safely in Egypt, that he may hurry off to India, but perhaps through the assistance of the Peninsular and Oriental Company he might be discovered on the voyage, and arrested on his landing."

While John Surratt was sailing to Egypt, Rufus King was still busy, sending all the information he could find about the fugitive to Secretary Seward in Washington:

> In my last dispatch I mentioned that I had telegraphed to our Consul at Alexandria in regard to John H. Surratt…. [T]he chief of the telegraphic bureau in Rome appris[ed] me that in consequence of the interruption in the wires, my dispatch to Alexandria was forwarded thither from Malta by steamer. The probabilities are that it was sent by the same steamer in which John H. Surratt is supposed to have sailed.
>
> I obtained … from a clerk in a Roman bookstore, who knew Surratt quite intimately as John Watson, an original letter of his…. This clerk told me that Watson, alias Surratt, claimed to be a Canadian by birth, and represented that he had been a spy in the Confederate service.

The letter written by Surratt referred to in King's dispatch read as follows:

> Ceroli, August 30, 1866
>
> Dear Sir: Will you be so kind as to send me a French and English grammar—the best method you have. I think Ollendorf's is most in use. When I come to Rome I will settle with you. I shall be in in the course of two or three weeks. If you should have the time to reply to me, please give me all the news you can. By so doing you will greatly oblige your friend,
>
> John Watson, 3rd Compagnie, Veroli.
>
> Edward T. O'Connor, Esq.[12]

Once again it appears that John Surratt was not afraid to confess potentially damaging facts about himself, even while being pursued by American and Italian authorities. We can only ascribe this to his youthful sense of adventure and lust for excitement. Later in life, as we shall see, he had entirely the opposite impulse, refusing to discuss his youthful notorious adventures, even with his own family. The details revealed would seem to make it obvious that he was telling these witnesses at least something related to the truth.

Shortly before Surratt arrived in Egypt, Secretary Seward wrote to General Rufus King, summing up the case thus far:

> Your dispatch of the 26th of November [1866], which relates to the case of John H. Surratt, has been received. I commend and thank you for the useful and very interesting details concerning the ways of that offender which you have given me. Among the papers which accompany the dispatch is a memorandum which is inscribed "A copy" and the text of which is as follows:
>
> "About twelve months ago Surratt came to Rome, under the name of Watson. In Canada he procured letters from some priest to friends in England. Having left England for Rome, he got letters for some

people here, among others for Rev. Dr. Neane [sic], rector of the English College. Being detained for some days, at Civita Vecchia, and having no money to pay expenses there, he wrote to Dr. Neane [sic], from whom he received fifty (50) francs. On his arrival here he went to the English College, where he lived for some time. After that he entered the Papal service."

Rome, November 25.

The paper bears no signature. The only information you give me from which to determine its authenticity is, that you have received it from good authority. I do not know that the statement thus recited would in any case have any value. Certainly, unauthenticated, it can be of no use other than to awaken curiosity. I think you ought to have given the authority to which you allude. I am aware that the person who imparted the information to you may probably have given it to you as confidential, and that he might even have declined to give it to you at all if you had not agreed to receive it under an injunction of secrecy. Such an injunction neither you nor I have in any case a right to accept. We are agents of the President, in whom executive power of the United States is vested. Clearly the information contained in the paper was designed for him, and not for yourself or for me personally. No one can rightfully claim to impose upon us an injunction to conceal from the President facts which concern the public safety and welfare. I have acted upon the principle which I thus inculcate throughout all the excitement of a civil war. Better to reject all information whatever than to receive it with limitation inconsistent with official duty. What I have written is not to be taken, however, as conveying censure for the past, but rather as an instruction for the future.[13]

9

In Custody

William Seward, secretary of state of the United States, received the following message from the American consul at Alexandria, Egypt, Charles Hale (1831–1882), dated November 27, 1866:

> Sir: I have the honor to report that, in consequence of a telegram received, via Constantinople [Istanbul, Turkey], from Mr. King, United States Minister at Rome, and of several letters received from Mr. Winthrop, United States Consul at Malta ... I have this day arrested a man calling himself Walters, dressed in the uniform of a Zouave, who arrived at Alexandria on the 23rd instant in the steamship *Tripoli*, from Naples, and who is believed to be John Harrison Surratt, one of the conspirators for the assassination of President Lincoln....
>
> I was fortunate in finding the man still in quarantine among the third-class passengers, of whom there is no list whatever. It was easy to distinguish him among seventy eight of these by his Zouave uniform and scarcely less easy by his almost unmistakable American type of countenance. I said at once to him, "You are the man I want; you are an American." He said, "Yes, sir; I am." I said, "You doubtless know why I want you. What is your name?" He replied promptly, "Walters." I said, "I believe your true name is Surratt," and in arresting him mentioned my official position as United States Consul general. The director of quarantine speedily arranged a sufficient escort of soldiers, by whom the prisoner was conducted to a safe place within the quarantine walls. Although the walk occupied several minutes, the prisoner, close at my side, made no remark whatever, displaying neither surprise nor irritation. Arrived at the place prepared, I gave him the usual magisterial caution that he was not obliged to say anything, and that anything he said would be at once taken down in writing. He said, "I have nothing to say. I want nothing but what is right." He declared he had neither passport, nor baggage, nor money except six francs....
>
> The appearance of the prisoner answers very well the description given of Surratt by the witness Weichmann.... Mr. King and Mr. Winthrop speak in confident terms of the identity of the Zouave Walters with Surratt, and, after seeing the man, I have not a shadow of a doubt of it.... The prisoner's quarantine will expire on the 29th; he will then be received into the prison of the local government, which cordially gives me every assistance.
>
> It will readily occur to you that the only convenient way of transferring the prisoner to the United States will be by an American man-of-war....

This lengthy message contains much interesting information. It is noted that Surratt continued to wear his Zouave uniform throughout his escape, both in Italy and on the ship to Egypt. Consul Hale prominently mentions how easy it was for him to pick out Surratt among the passengers because he was in uniform. How difficult would it have been for Surratt to purchase clothing in Italy? Once again, as noted earlier, he took unnecessary risks as he fled to Europe and the Middle East. Although we have no reliable information on where, when, and how he received money or how much he was given, it could not have been very expensive to acquire clothing. We have seen how he was concerned about his dress and appearance prior to leaving the United States, and his use of disguises, wearing a "Canadian" style jacket and eyeglasses, and darkening his hair, and yet, in Italy he seemed entirely uninterested in such obvious and rudimentary precautions. Consul Hale also tells us that he pointedly explained to his prisoner his rights, very similar to those from the Miranda Decision (not saying anything, any statements he made would be taken down and could be used against him), which are familiar to us all. Charles Hale was born June 7, 1831, into a prominent Massachusetts family. His brother was Edward Everett Hale (1822–1909), author of *The Man Without a Country*. Charles attended Boston Latin School, then Harvard University, from which he graduated in 1850. After working as an editor for the *Boston Daily Advertiser*, he was elected to the Massachusetts General Court in 1855. While visiting Egypt in an effort to improve his health, he was named U.S. consul there in 1864.

The arrest of Surratt was a big story at the time, both in America and in Europe:

> He stands as the only known representative of a conspiracy which, though it was formed and culminated within the last two years ... is to-day wrapped in as dense and unfathomable mystery as covers any similar plot in the dimness of the middle ages.... All the facts in the case are known to John Surratt, and to no other man who can be named; and with his person in our possession the nation could well afford to offer him his life, his liberty, or any other price which might be sufficient to secure it, to obtain from his lips the information which will shed the light of day upon the most difficult as well as the most interesting criminal mystery of our time [*New York Times*, November 26, 1866].
>
> He has no chance of escape, as orders have been telegraphed to Admiral Goldsborough, who is cruising in those waters, to bring the criminal directly here. Those familiar with the character of John H. Surratt have believed that he would never be taken alive, but the event has shown that either the burden of his great crime has completely cowed him, or that he was never possessed of the desperate nerve which has been attributed to him. We have heretofore expressed the opinion that the earth did not possess a hiding-place so secret as to secure any one of these great criminals from detection, and the events have so proved [*Washington Evening Star*, December 4, 1866].
>
> In the present state of our information on the subject, it is impossible to pass any opinion on the conduct of our authorities at Malta.... If, however, it should be anywhere assumed that we, either through negligence or indifference, lost an opportunity of doing what the Egyptians have done, the conclusion would assuredly be wrong. The law of extradition is full of difficulties at the best, but it is perfectly clear that the evidence and authority required for the arrest of a fugitive would be the same in all cases, whatever might be the nature of the crime imputed. As good reason must be shown for apprehending a murderer as for apprehending a fraudulent bankrupt, we could not strain the law in Surratt's case, whatever might be our detestation of the crime laid to his charge.... Not in the whole of this kingdom would there have been any party found to sympathize with an assassin....
>
> [I]t would be universally admitted that murder is a crime unworthy of asylum, and yet universally required that political refugees should be sheltered. What, then, was to be done with a political murderer? What was to be the treatment of a man whose offence was murder, but whose offending, nevertheless, was in its origin and circumstances entirely and purely political? ... We answer without hesitation that it would have deserved no such shelter.... There are things which are not to be done in any cause, and murder is one of them ... [and] a murder committed with political views deserved hanging as much as any other murder....
>
> The Americans may assure themselves that no party of Englishmen would wish either to palliate the deed or shield the assassin [*London Times*, December 6, 1866][1]

Consul Charles Hale assured Secretary Seward that "Surratt remains in safe custody and subject to no jurisdiction other than of the United States." Although John Surratt and Louis J. Weichmann had been close friends, Weichmann, having already struck his blows upon the Surratts, now seemed unable to stand aside. He seemed eager to do whatever he could to further damage them. If he was trying to save himself, perhaps in response to threats if he didn't cooperate, or if he was seeking to gain advantage by pleasing those who had become his masters, we perhaps can feel some sympathy for him, but little admiration or honor. He wrote the following to Judge Joseph Holt: "I hereby tender my services to you in case it should be necessary to send someone to Egypt to positively identify John H. Surratt, who, so says the cable, has been arrested at Alexandria in that country. I make this offer on account of my former friendship for this man, but inasmuch as his actions have destroyed my prospects in life, and rendered me an object of mean hatred and suspicion to the copperheads [Democrats] and rebels, and especially to the people of my own church [Roman Catholic], I cannot but consider it my duty to do all I can to advance the interests of justice, and to do all I can to effectually and forever wipe out that suspicion." Strange logic he offers us now. Those who believed him honest and patriotic above all bounds of his shattered friendship did not need convincing, and those who doubted, and still doubt, cannot be convinced otherwise.

After a few more days, Rufus King was able to inform Seward:

[T]he United States corvette *Swatara*, Captain Jeffers, arrived at Civita Vecchia on Wednesday last, 12th instant [December 12, 1866], and was followed next day by the *Frolic*, Captain Upshur. The latter brought dispatches from the admiral, directing the *Swatara* to proceed forthwith to Malta. She sailed accordingly at noon next day. At Malta, no doubt Captain Jeffers will receive further instructions from Admiral Goldsborough, who must be in that neighborhood. The *Frolic* remains at Civita Vecchia awaiting orders.

Ste. Marie, who first informed me of Surratt being in the corps of Zouaves, has been discharged from the Papal service at my request. I have paid him the sum specified [amount unknown—Ste. Marie had asked for $50,000, but Seward authorized King to pay him $250, "in consideration of the information he has already communicated"] in the dispatch from the State Department of October 16. Threats have been made against him by some of his old comrades [presumably in the Zouaves], and thinking that his life was not altogether safe, and that he might be wanted in Alexandria as a witness to identify Surratt, I put him in charge of Captain Jeffers, and he sailed in the *Swatara* on Friday last [December 21, 1866]. His great desire seems to be to return to America and aid in bringing Surratt to justice. I have seen, as yet, no reason to doubt his good faith or question the truth of his statements.

On December 24 Consul Hale sent a brief message to Secretary Seward: "I delivered Surratt board corvette *Swatara* twenty-first (21st) December. No trouble." The U.S.S. *Swatara* was a screw-driven gunboat of the Resaca class built at the Philadelphia Navy Yard and the ship's machinery being built at the Washington Navy Yard. The keel was laid in 1864 and the ship was launched on May 23, 1865, and commissioned on November 15, 1865. Displacing 1,129 tons, it was 230 feet long, 30 feet in width, and had a draught of 12 feet 10 inches. Her speed was twelve knots. *Swatara* carried a crew of 213 officers and men and was armed with one 60-, six 32-, and three 20-pound guns. The *Swatara* had served with the West Indies Squadron in 1866 before being transferred to the European Squadron, where it served from 1866 to 1869.

Swatara's commanding officer was Commander William Nicholson Jeffers (1824–1883). A graduate of the U.S. Naval Academy at Annapolis in 1846, he was a veteran of service in the Mexican War. After the war, he served at Annapolis as an instructor and as a member of surveys and explorations in Latin America. In the Civil War, he participated in the blockade of the Southern states and also commanded the *Monitor* following its battle with the Confederate ship *Virginia* in 1862. As a lieutenant commander he served in Philadelphia and Washington in the Bureau of Ordnance.

Commander Jeffers took charge of the prisoner John Surratt at 1:00 p.m. on December 21, 1866. The ship's log stated, "At 1 P.M. received on board a person delivered by the U.S. Consul General, Mr. Charles Hale, supposed to be John H. Surratt, one of the conspirators implicated in the assassination of the late President Lincoln." The *Swatara* departed Alexandria on December 26, 1866. Jeffers' treatment of his prisoner was governed by the following orders:

Orders Relative to the State Prisoner
For Executive and Watch Officers

He is not to be allowed to converse with any person whatever.... No person is to be permitted to converse within his hearing upon any other subject than ship's duties.

The orderly and a sentry specially charged with his guard will be responsible that he does not escape.

He will be kept in the room arranged, for his reception, in single irons only, so long as he keeps quiet and makes no attempt to escape.

The room door to be kept locked.

He will, when necessary, use the Captain's water-closet [restroom].

His meals will be supplied by the ward-room mess. The food to be cut up, and a spoon only to be allowed with which to eat it.

He is to be carefully guarded against attempts at suicide, whether by jumping overboard or otherwise. If he attempts to escape he is to be fired upon by the sentry, the orderly, and the officer of the watch. The upper tier of carbines in each chest is to be kept loaded, and daily examined to see that they are in good order.

It is to be carefully borne in mind that the prisoner is put on board for safe keeping and transportation to the United States, and that his death is preferable to his escape.

If the prisoner becomes violent he is to be placed in double irons, hands behind him.

He will be provided with a mattress and two blankets.

The sentry will be relieved every two hours, and he, with the corporal of the watch, will assure himself of the presence of the prisoner before relieving. The [officer of the] poop [deck] will be present when he is taken to the water-closet, will see the door locked on his return, and hand the key to the officer of the watch.

When in port the officer of the watch will be present whenever the door is opened.

Meals may be passed in through the window. At the discression [sic] of the commander the window may be left open in the daytime in sunny weather.

Years later, an account by one of the *Swatara*'s officers, George DeForest Bruton, was published:

I ... accompanied Commander Jeffers to Rome to arrest John H. Surratt. They learned Surratt had escaped and gone to Egypt. Once there, an officer and a file of marines were sent to the corral. Surratt, a tall, straight, self-contained young man, was marched, a prisoner, on board, handcuffed between two marines. The ship was not a large one and there was a quandary just where to put him. He was a state prisoner and had to be treated with consideration.

Commander Jeffers finally concluded to relinquish his bathroom, which was outside of his cabin with a door opening on the spar deck, and it was fitted up as a stateroom and the prisoner made as comfortable as he could be; his meals were served to him from the wardroom table.

The ships were not kept together in those days, but were scattered about in European waters. Then came a hunt to find Admiral [Louis Malesherbes] Goldsborough [1805–1877]. The *Swatara* chased him around the Mediterranean looking for the flagship and finally located the [U.S.S.] *Colorado* in Villefranche. A few days afterwards the *Swatara* started homeward under orders to proceed to Washington and report to the Secretary of the Navy.

The *Swantata* and its crew encountered heavy seas in the Mediterranean Sea, slowing them down. The need to conserve fuel for the Atlantic crossing called for the use of sail power, requiring "forty five days from Villefranche to the Cape of Virginia": "Surratt's personal condition when brought aboard the ship was frightful, but plenty of hot water and good soap with fresh new [sailor] clothes from the ship's stores soon made him quite comfortable in that respect. He was a wretched sailor, however, and suffered greatly from seasickness on the long voyage. During the time he was on board the *Swatara* an armed sentry was at his door and no one but the commander, the executive officer, the surgeon and the officer of the deck ever spoke to him. Their conversation was limited to inquiries for his health and comfort."

On the voyage home, the *Swatara* stopped at Villa Franca—modern day Villefranche, near Nice, France—where Henri Ste. Marie left the ship. He had boarded at Rome, but Jeffers reported that Ste. Marie complained that he was not being allowed to go ashore at any of the ship's stops. Admiral Goldsborough told Jeffers to let their reluctant passenger go. Ste. Marie would sail back to the United States on a commercial steamer.[2] Newspaper articles reported on the crossing of the *Swatara*:

Surratt on the *Swatara*

A Letter has been received in this city [Washington] from an officer of the steamer *Swatara*, who writes from Lisbon that Surratt is very reticent, speaking only in answer to questions, and then in monosyllables. He is still clad in the Zouave uniform. He seems to be in good health, and is entirely self-possessed.

Surratt

The steamer *Swatara*, with Surratt, the conspirator, on board, is expected to arrive here [Washington] about the latter part of the month [January, 1867]; but should the ice continue in the river, she will probably stop before reaching the Potomac and communicate with the Navy Department. Commander Jeffries [sic], of the *Swatara*, was directed by Admiral Goldsborough to procede [sic] immediately to the Washington Navy Yard and await orders from the Department.

Surratt

The steamer *Swatara*, with Surratt, the conspirator ... sailed from Lisbon on the 8th instant, and the usual time for the trip from that place to New York being twenty days, it is very probable that *Swatara* will be heard from in less than forty-eight hours.

Surratt

No information has yet been received at the Navy Department from the steamer *Swatara* with Surratt, the conspirator, on board.... She will come immediately to the Washington Navy Yard, should the river permit, and the prisoner will be handed over to Marshal Gooding for safe keeping until the trial. It is not improbable that the *Swatara* may be used for the prison-ship should the jail not be deemed sufficiently secure.

Arrival of Surratt

The United States gunboat *Swatara* ... was near Fortress Monroe yesterday morning, where, after taking a pilot on board, she proceded on towards this city [Washington], and was this morning expected at the Navy Yard, where considerable numbers of persons were waiting her arrival.

She had not up to 2½ o'clock this afternoon hove in sight, and the impression among the officers at the Yard was that she received orders yesterday to remain below the city until she received further orders; and at that hour the tug *Primrose* was at the wharf with steam up, waiting to take down dispatches from the Department.

The officers at the Yard are certain that she is in the Potomac, and think that the prisoner Surratt will be landed sometime to-night and be immediately delivered to the Marshal.

The officers of the jail have recently cleaned out one of the iron-cased cells for his reception, and it is probable that by to-morrow morning he will be safely lodged there.[3]

While the *Swatara* was picking its way through the icy waters of Chesapeake Bay and the Potomac River, Henri B. Ste. Marie was also returning to America, still hoping to collect a lot of money for having exposed John Surratt in Italy. Arriving in New York on February 15, 1867, Ste. Marie took a train to Washington. He had time to give a short interview to a *New York Times* reporter, saying that Surratt confessed his identity "when excited with wine" and "engaged in braggadocio concerning the Canadian raids, [and] the assassination plot" in front of other Zouaves, who enjoyed the revelations. Ste. Marie said Surratt "was well supplied with funds, and gave the impression of perfect serenity—a serenity and security that could only be procured by protection." It was also stated that Surratt "recognized Ste. Marie, who stood among the spectators," when Surratt was brought onboard the *Swatara*.

The *Swatara* finally arrived at the Washington Navy Yard on February 18, 1867. Seward wrote to the U.S. Marshal, David S. Gooding: "It is the request of the President that you take the prisoner at once into your custody and detain him for trial according to law. You will call at the Navy Department for an order on the Commander of the *Swatara*." An indictment of Surratt had already been issued, on February 5, 1867, and contains some rather curious language:

John H. Surratt, Jr., arrives at the Navy Yard in Washington, D.C., February 18, 1867 (*Harper's Weekly*, March 9, 1867).

District of Columbia, County of Washington, to wit:

The jurors of the United States of America for the county of Washington aforesaid, upon their oaths present that John H. Surratt, late of the county aforesaid, yeoman, not having the fear of God before his eyes, but being moved and seduced by the instigation of the devil, on the fourteenth day of April, in the year of our Lord one thousand eight hundred and sixty-five, with force of arms, at the county of Washington aforesaid, in and upon one Abraham Lincoln, in the peace of God, and of the said United States of America, then and there being, feloniously, willfully, and of his malice aforethought, did make an assault; and that the said John H. Surratt, a certain pistol of the value of ten dollars, then and there charged with gun powder and one leaden bullet, which said pistol he, the said John H. Surratt, in his right hand then and there had and held, then and there feloniously, willfully and of his malice aforethought, did discharge and shoot off against and upon the said Abraham Lincoln; and that, the said John H. Surratt, with the leaden bullet aforesaid, then and there by force of the gunpowder aforesaid, shot and sent forth as aforesaid the aforesaid Abraham Lincoln, in and upon the left and posterior side of the head of him, the said Abraham Lincoln, then and there feloniously, willfully, and of his malice aforethought, did strike, penetrate, and wound, giving to the said Abraham Lincoln then and there, with the leaden bullet aforesaid as aforesaid, so as aforesaid, shot, discharged, and sent forth out of the pistol aforesaid, by the said John H. Surratt, in and upon the left and posterior side of the head of him, the said Abraham Lincoln, one mortal wound of the depth of six inches and of the breadth of half an inch, of which said mortal wound the said Abraham Lincoln, from the fourteenth day of April , in the year of our Lord one thousand eight hundred and sixty-five, until the fifteenth day of the same month of April, in the year last aforesaid, and at the county aforesaid, did languish, and languishing did die, on which said fifteenth day of April, in the year last aforesaid, the said Abraham Lincoln, at the county aforesaid, of the mortal wound aforesaid, died. And so the jurors aforesaid, upon their oath aforesaid, do say that the said John H. Surratt the said Abraham Lincoln then and there ... feloniously, willfully, and of his malice aforethought, did [commit] murder, against the form of the statute is ... made and provided, and against the peace and Government of the United States of America.

In the second count against Surratt, John Wilkes Booth is named as the principal, with Surratt: "[T]hen and there torturously, willfully, and of his malice aforethought, was present, aiding, helping and abetting, comforting, assisting, and maintaining the said John Wilkes Booth the felony and murder aforesaid, in manner and form aforesaid, to do and commit." In the third count, the names of other accomplices appear: "David E. Herold, Geo. A. Atzerott [sic], Lewis Payne, and Mary E. Surratt ... listing them as fellow conspirators."

If the language seems unclear and awkward, it is because the indictment was written to describe the crime, and Surratt's involvement in it, in the manner called for by law, to avoid the charges being challenged. Of course, the first count stated that John Surratt actually held the pistol and fired it into the back of Abraham Lincoln's head. We know that was not so, and it certainly can be questioned how Surratt could have "aid[ed] and abett[ed], comfort[ed] and assist[ed]" Booth in the assassination when he was hundreds of miles away at the time. The fourth count tries to erase the ambiguity and tie up all of these loose ends, stating that Surratt and the others named "did conspire and confederate together to kill and murder Abraham Lincoln."[4]

The religious references in the indictment have more to do with custom and tradition than with literal belief. "Not having the fear of God" might be taken to mean that Surratt displayed no scruples or feelings of right and wrong in committing the crime. "Being moved and seduced by the instigation of the devil" could be understood to mean that he was a person of bad character. It could not have been proven in a court of law that Surratt did not fear God or that he was motivated to commit a crime by the devil. Clearly, such language was not to be taken literally. If it had been, constitutional issues might have been raised by the defense based on the first amendment, which states that "Congress shall make no law respecting an establishment of religion." An examination of Surratt's motives might well have led to a characterization of the kidnap and assassination plots as political acts.

A reporter described Surratt on the eve of his trial:

Richard T. Merrick was a lawyer who advised the defense team at John Surratt's trial in 1867 (Library of Congress).

John Surratt seems in excellent health, sleeps well and eats heartily, but speaks little, and then only in regard to his personal wants. He cannot see or have any intercourse with any of the other prisoners, and is very closely watched by the guards. It is now stated that the Messrs. Bradley and Mr. Merrick have been retained as his counsel, and yesterday [February 21] Mr. Bradley, Jr., had an interview of some length with him. The sister, Miss Anna Surratt, was last fall the governess in the family of Captain B[ennett]. Gwynn [1823–1897], in the lower part of Prince George's County, but for several weeks past she has been in this city [Cincinnati], stopping with some relations.

Secretary of State Seward was involved behind the scenes in the organization of the Surratt trial. He sought to have former Massachusetts governor John Albion Andrew (1818–1867) appointed counsel for the government. Although Andrew was a staunch Union man, he had not approved of the 1865 trial by military commission that had resulted in the hanging of John Surratt's mother. Andrew declined the offer, refusing, as he said, "to help the Government put a rope around the neck of a fellow man."

On the morning of February 23, 1867, John Surratt changed out of his well-worn Zouave uniform and put on a suit. He met at the jail with two of his attorneys, Joseph Bradley and Richard Merrick.

Surratt was being held at the city jail at 4th and G streets. The courtroom where the trial took place was in room 222 at the city hall. As word got out around town that Surratt would be arraigned that morning, a crowd gathered, eager to obtain entry into the courtroom. So many people pressed into the room that some climbed over the railing and sought to obtain seats in the prisoner's dock. Those not able to get inside stood at every window, hoping to see the prisoner. Once the prisoner's dock had been cleared of spectators, John Surratt was brought in, and District Attorney Carrington announced that as the grand jury had indicted Surratt for murder the trial could begin at an early date. Merrick objected to Surratt's being manacled in court, and Judge Fisher ordered their removal. The clerk, after reading the indictment, asked, "What say you, are you guilty as indicted, or not guilty?"

> THE PRISONER: "Not guilty"—distinctly, but with a slight clearing of the throat.
> THE CLERK: "How will you be tried?"
> THE PRISONER: "By my country."
> THE CLERK: "May God send you safe deliverance."

While awaiting his trial, John Surratt was reported to have been interviewed by a newspaper correspondent. The interviewer was not named, lending further skepticism to the alleged interview. The article does, however, include details that, though not enough to lift our skepticism, at least leave some degree of doubt. Dated April 2, the interviewer states:

> It is unnecessary to dwell here upon the means used to obtain this interview, despite the stringent regulations, which forbid any intercourse with Surratt by others than the officials of the jail and his sister when admitted under surveillance. Suffice it to say that in the case of my admission the officers of the jail in nowise exceeded their authority or instructions in the premises....
> I found him occupying temporarily the watchman's lodge in the jail yard, accompanied by a veteran keeper.... The little building ... was a small octagonal structure of wood, with large, open windows on seven sides and a glass door on the eighth....
> The prisoner ... sat in a chair by one of the open windows reading a small volume, the character of which I did not inquire.... In stature I should judge him to be five feet nine or ten inches high, rather slender in form—almost delicate, perhaps—and apparently twenty-eight years of age [he was twenty-three at the time].... He has a very pleasant voice, in conversation used good language.

The interviewer, after making small talk for a few minutes, tells us the following:

> I ventured to ask him a leading question in regard to his escape to and concealment in Canada ... [but] he replied, "I have nothing to say about that...."
> He spoke of meeting St. Marie in France. He claims that he recognized St. Marie first, and that they traveled to Italy together.... Surratt says that he had information of St. Marie's "treachery" before it was fully accomplished, and was kept advised from time to time of the steps taken to secure his arrest. Had the actual arrest been delayed one day longer, as Surratt had reason to expect it would be, he would have been beyond the reach of his pursuers, his arrangements for desertion and flight being nearly perfected at the time of his arrest. He is careful to abstain from saying what those arrangements were, who were his accomplices and informers, or where he was to find a place of refuge....
> The wonderful leap off the precipice in Italy, of which so much has been said and written, is a source of great amusement to him.

Whatever our doubts about the truthfulness of this article, it sounds as if it could be at least partly true. The jail is described in such detail that it is certainly possible the author had visited it, either in the company of Surratt or not.

> An entire corridor, full thirty feet in length, and eight in breadth, with three large cells, are placed entirely at his disposal. In this corridor he is excluded from the gaze of the common prisoners and the curious visitors by a tight door closing within the usual door of iron grating whenever it is not agreeable to him to seek the open air of the prison courtyard. At night only does he have occasion to feel at all the doors of confinement, when he is locked in the central of the three cells, a commodious apartment at least ten feet square. True, the furniture is scant, consisting merely of a stool, and a mattress laid upon the stone floor, though amply provided with coverings.

We are told by our interviewer that Surratt was allowed his choice of food, and he had much reading matter of all types: "Moreover, the comforts of home are provided for him in the frequent and protracted visits of his sister, who calls at least each alternate day, and spends the time with him, cheering him by her presence and ministering to his comforts."[5]

John Surratt was arraigned under federal law and tried in a federal court. This ignored, as had the 1865 trial, the fact that the murder of the president was not a federal offense in 1865 or in 1867. Indeed. it would not be a federal crime for a full century. In spite of this, no one seems to have objected to having the case in a federal court under federal law. The trial was described by a newspaper reporter:

> It is ... Washington as it was—a room forty feet square, dingy with age and neglect, and dirty with much use and many feet. There are three great windows on the south, from which one can dimly see the old arsenal ... within which the other assassins were tried and executed; and three great windows on the north, from which one can easily see the old jail in which Surratt is confined, and the path up which he walks, the Marshal on one side and a deputy on the other.... The Judge's bench is on the east—a high, ungainly, old fashioned concern, within which His Honor sits in solitariness and incongruousness.... On the right of the Judge is a door into the little room where the witnesses are kept. On the left is another door through which enter lawyers, prisoner, reporters, and such other ... persons as can pass the grizzley moustache keeping guard there. In front of the Judge is the Clerk—old and methodical and inoffensive, of course, as the clerks of courts always are. At his immediate right is the stenographer of the court—young and nimble and knowing, of course, as shorthand writers always are. Just at his right ... eighteen inches above the main floor, is the witness box.... In the northeast corner ... are the jury benches, long and uncomfortable. The lawyers are in front of the Clerk.... Within the bar can be seated about seventy-five persons.... Outside the bar is standing room for two to three hundred. The windows are dirty, the ceilings are cobwebby, the whole place is seedy and slovenly.

The arraignment was held on the morning of February 23, 1867. News of the first appearance in court of the famous fugitive attracted large crowds, the eager onlookers crowding into the relatively small courtroom, each one intent on securing a seat with good visibility. Those onlookers who had climbed over the bar had to be removed before the prisoner could be brought in.

The presiding judge for John Surratt's trial was George Purnell Fisher (1817–1899). Fisher had attended St. Mary's College in Baltimore and graduated from Dickinson College, class of 1838. After studying law with family friend John Middleton Clayton (1796–1856) of Dover, Delaware, he was admitted to the bar in Delaware in April of 1841. He became clerk of the Delaware senate in 1843 and was elected to the state house of representatives. In 1846, Fisher was appointed Delaware secretary of state and became a confidential clerk to John M. Clayton when the latter became United States secretary of state in 1849. Fisher was temporarily private secretary to President Millard Fillmore (1800–1874) in 1850. In 1855 Fisher was appointed attorney general for the State of Delaware, serving until 1860. Running for Congress in 1860, as a candidate of the "People's Party," former Whigs not wishing to identify too closely with the new Republican Party, Fisher narrowly defeated his Democratic opponent, Benjamin Thomas Biggs (1821–1893) by 247 votes. In the election of 1862 Fisher lost to Democrat William Temple (1814–1863) in an even closer election, 8,014 to 8,051. After his defeat for reelection to Congress, Fisher served briefly in the Union army as colonel of the First Delaware Cavalry.

In 1863 Congress established a new federal district court called the Supreme Court of the District of Columbia, not to be confused with the United States Supreme Court, and abolished the old district and circuit courts covering D.C. The court made use of the D.C. city hall. President Lincoln named four men to the D.C. Supreme Court: Chief Justice David Kellogg Cartter (1812–1887); Justice Abram B. Olin (1808–1879); Justice Andrew B. Wylie (1814–1905); and Justice George P. Fisher. The trial of John Surratt was to take place before the D.C. Supreme Court, and Justice Fisher was assigned to preside.[6]

John Surratt's sister, Anna, tried to raise money for John's defense by selling photographs of him wearing his Zouave uniform. The photographs were popular but were of small financial help. The defense lawyers had to take Surratt's case pro bono, meaning without charge.

Heading the prosecution was federal district attorney Edward C. Carrington (1825–1892). Carrington was described as "quite an experienced practitioner, a fluent speaker, and had been for six years the prosecuting attorney for the District of Columbia." Carrington, born in Virginia of a distinguished family whose ancestors had fought in the American Revolution and the War of 1812, was a great-nephew of Patrick Henry (1736–1799). Carrington had followed the family's military tradition, commanding a company in the Mexican War. He moved to Washington and remained loyal to the Union, in spite of having a brother who served in the Confederate army. Personal wealth enabled him to raise and equip a company of Carrington's Volunteers for the Union numbering over one hundred men. Early in 1861, as Carrington was raising his company, his name was proposed for United States attorney for the District of Columbia. The choice was between Carrington and Edwin M. Stanton. Attorney General Edward Bates (1793–1869), a friend of the Carrington family, recommended Carrington and continued to advise his retention in office for another term in 1865. Carrington had many enemies who sought to blacken his record, and Carrington even maintained that he had been stabbed twice during his term as district attorney but the support of his influential friends prevailed.[7]

Carrington was assisted at the Surratt trial by his deputy district attorney, Nathaniel Wilson (1836–?), an Ohioan who had been a judge advocate in the army, and by Edwards Pierrepont (1817–1892). Pierrepont, a Yale graduate, who had been admitted to the bar in 1840 and tutored at Yale for a year. Moving to Columbus, Ohio, Pierrepont practiced law for five years before moving to New York in 1846. Moving into a new house in 1852, Pierrepont and his wife, son, and daughter became well established and Pierrepont was doing well enough to build a country house at Garrison, New York. Pierrepont was elected a Superior Court judge, serving from 1857 to 1860. He made the acquaintance of Abraham Lincoln and became one of his advisors, supporting his election as president although he himself was a Democrat.

Another aide to the prosecution was Albert Gallatin Riddle (1816–1902), a congressman from Ohio. Riddle was born in Massachusetts, and his parents moved the family westward when Riddle was still a baby. Admitted to the bar in 1840, he became the prosecutor of Geauga County, Ohio, in 1840, following that with service in the Ohio house of representatives. Moving to Cleveland in 1850, he became a prosecuting attorney there in 1856. Elected to Congress in 1860, Riddle served from March 4, 1861, to March 3, 1863. Leaving

Edwards Pierrepont was one of the prosecutors at John Surratt's trial (Library of Congress).

Congress, he was appointed United States consul at Matanzas, Cuba, returning in 1864 to Washington, where he practiced law. He was hired to assist the prosecution of Surratt by the State Department.[8]

Against this formidable team of prosecutors, John Surratt was defended by Joseph Habersham Bradley (1803–1887). He was born on March 23, 1803, in Washington, D.C., to a prominent family. Bradley's father, Abraham Bradley (1767–1838), served as assistant postmaster general of the United States from 1793 to 1829 and was responsible for creating some of the earliest maps of the United States, laying out the postal routes on them. Joseph Bradley attended public schools in Washington, then enrolled at Yale, from which he graduated in 1821. He was admitted to the bar in Montgomery County, Maryland in 1824, and to the D.C. bar in 1825. He married Lucy Sherman Tuttle (1804–1870) in 1825. They had five children, including Joseph Henry Bradley (1831–1874), who also became a lawyer and assisted his father with the Surratt case. By the time of the Surratt trial, Joseph Habersham Bradley was one of the more prominent lawyers in Washington. He had been requested by David E. Herold (1842–1865) to defend him at the military trial of the conspiracy suspects in 1865, but Bradley had declined. Bradley's son, Joseph Henry, had been arrested at the time of Lincoln's assassination because of his supposed resemblance to John Wilkes Booth.

The Bradleys also had the help of Richard Thomas Merrick (1828–1885, a member of a distinguished family. His father, William Duhurst Merrick (1793–1857), had served as United States senator of Maryland from 1838 to1845, and his brother, William Matthew Merrick (1818–1889), had served as a federal judge and would later be a member of the U.S. House of Representatives from 1871 to 1873. Richard Merrick had raised a regiment for the Mexican War, though he was only eighteen years old. Taking up the practice of law after the war, he had been elected to the Maryland legislature. By 1860 Merrick changed his political orientation, becoming a delegate to the Democratic National Convention in Chicago in 1860. He supported Senator Stephen Arnold Douglas (1813–1861) for President. Lincoln's debates with Douglas in the Senate contest of 1858 that had brought him national prominence. By 1864, Merrick had married Nannie McGuire (1837–1885) and returned to Washington and the practice of law.[9]

Shortly before the trial began, John Surratt was told that a deal was being worked out in behalf of members of Congress opposed to President Andrew Johnson (1808–1875). It was said that if Surratt would implicate Johnson in the plot to assassinate Lincoln, Surratt would be saved and the charges against him dismissed. Surratt's lawyers urged him not to cooperate, as they felt that he would be cleared without such a deal. This was one of the schemes of Sanford Conover, who had aided the prosecution in the 1865 trial of the conspiracy suspects, and was eventually convicted of perjury. Conover—one of his many aliases—was actually Charles A. Dunham (c. 1832–1900). Taking the advice of his lawyers, the closest Surratt ever got to Dunham was on the day Surratt was first brought into court. Dunham's case was also being heard, and the two men found themselves seated side-by-side on the same bench. The newspaper reporters wrote, "All eyes were riveted upon the prisoners whose past histories had been so strangely connected [in rumors, not in fact], and it was thought they might possibly recognize each other, but neither exchanged the slightest look of recognition. It was considered strange indeed that both these men … should meet today upon the prisoner's bench, linked in the same fatal chain of circumstances, one to be arraigned [Surratt] and the other to be sentenced [Dunham].[10]

The trial of John H. Surratt, Jr., opened on June 10, 1867. It was the first civil trial for the murder of a president of the United States. The 1865 trial of the conspiracy suspects, including John Surratt's mother, Mary, had been a military trial under military law. In that trial, the panel of nine military officers, only one of whom had any legal background, acted as both judges and jurors. The 1867 trial would be very different. A jury of twelve white men would decide the guilt or innocence of the accused. The judge was a civil federal judge, and the normal rules of civilian law would be followed.

Days were consumed in selection of a jury. A full week passed and one hundred and four men were questioned before a dozen were accepted. Before any witnesses were called to testify, defense attorney Joseph Henry Bradley read an application to the court: "The petition of John H. Surratt shows that he had now been put on his trial in a capital case in this court; that he has exhausted all his means, and such further means as have been furnished him by the liberality of his friends, in preparing for his defense, and he is now unable to procure the attendance of his witnesses. He therefore prays your honor for an order that process may issue to summon his witnesses, and to compel their attendance, at the cost of the government of the United States, according to the statute in such case made and provided." This document was accepted by the court.

Nathaniel Wilson made the opening statement for the prosecution:

Andrew Johnson was vice president for only forty-one days, and became the seventeenth president upon Lincoln's death (Library of Congress).

[F]or the first time in our existence as a nation a blow was struck with the full purpose of destroying not only human life, but the life of the nation, the life of liberty itself....

We shall prove to your entire satisfaction, by competent and credible witnesses, that ... the prisoner at the bar was then aiding and abetting that murder, and that at twenty minutes past ten o'clock that night he was in front of that theatre in company with Booth.... You shall know that his cool and calculating malice was the director of the bullet that pierced the brain of the President and the knife that fell upon the face of the venerable Secretary of State. You shall know that the prisoner at the bar was the contriver of that villainy, and that from the presence of the prisoner, Booth, drunk with theatric passion and traitorous hate, rushed directly to the execution of their mutual will ... [and] the butchery that ensued was the ripe result of a long premeditated plot, in which the prisoner was the chief conspirator. It will be proved to you that he is a traitor to the government ... a spy in the employ of the enemies of his country in the years 1864 and 1865 passed repeatedly from Richmond to Washington, from Washington to Canada, weaving the web of his nefarious scheme, plotting the overthrow of this government, the defeat of its armies, and the slaughter of his countrymen....

When the last blow had been struck, when he had done his utmost to bring anarchy and desolation upon his native land, he turned his back upon the abomination he had wrought, he turned his back upon his home and kindred, and commenced his shuddering flight....

[I]n law flight is the criminal's inarticulate confession ... [and] in some moment of fear or of elation or of fancied security, he, too, to others, confessed his guilty deeds.

When the prosecution's lengthy statement was concluded, the defense, rather than challenge point by point, merely said they "would reserve their opening remarks to the jury."[11]

The prosecution's case opened with Dr. Joseph K. Barnes (1817–1883). Barnes was surgeon general of the army and was one of the doctors who had tended the stricken president. He described the fatal wound. Subsequent witnesses' purposes were to establish that a crime had been committed and describe the events surrounding it. Various articles connected to the assassination were displayed and described. Colonel Henry Reed Rathbone (1837–1911) testified to what he saw and heard in the theatre box that night. His testimony closely followed the testimony he had given at the 1865 trial. "A particularly important witness was Sergeant Joseph M. Dye (1843–?)":

Q. Were you in the Army in April, 1865?
A. I was.
Q. Where was your regiment stationed on the 14th of April, 1865?
A. I belonged to Battery C, independent Pennsylvania artillery, stationed at Camp Barry.
Q. Tell me where Camp Barry was.
A. It was at the junction of H Street and the Baltimore Turnpike.
Q. At what time in that evening did you come to Ford's Theatre?
A. I arrived there about half past nine o'clock.
Q. Who was with you?
A. Sergeant Cooper.
Q. Were you at the theatre?
A. I was in front of the theatre.
Q. What was the condition of the street in front of the theatre that night as to its being light?
A. It was light directly in front of the door.
Q. In what way?
A. There was a large lamp there.
Q. While you were sitting there, state whether there was any change in the inside of the theatre as to persons coming out at the end of any act?....
A. Parties came down—I presume it was about ten or fifteen minutes after we got there....
Q. State whether you know John Wilkes Booth.
A. I do, sir.
Q. State whether John Wilkes Booth was one of the persons who entered into that conversation.
A. He was.

The defense at this point sought to interrupt the testimony because it related to Booth, and no connection had yet been established between Booth and Surratt. The court ruled that it would decide whether there was a connection:

> A. The first who appeared on the scene was John Wilkes Booth himself.... [He] was conversing with a low, villainous looking person at the end of the passage ... [and] it was but a moment before another person joined them. The person was ... neatly dressed—and entered in conversation....
>
> Booth said to this other person that he would come out now, as I supposed, referring to the President. They were then standing facing the place where the President would have to pass in order to reach his carriage, and watching eagerly for his appearance. He did not come.... He [Booth] appeared in a moment again. This third party, neatly dressed, immediately stepped up in front of the theatre and called the time.
>
> Q. Where was the clock?
> A. The clock was in the vestibule of the theatre.... As soon as he called the time to the other two, he went up the street towards H Street. He did not remain there long, but came down again, stopped in front of the theatre, looked at the clock, and called the time again, looking directly at these two, and seemed excited....
> Q. Did you see that man distinctly?
> A. I did....
> Q. Do you see him now?
> A. I do.... He sits there.... (pointing to the prisoner)
> Q. Please state what occurred as you and Sergeant Cooper hastened up H Street.
> A. As we were passing along H Street out to Camp Barry, a lady hoisted a window and asked us what was wrong down town.... I told her that President Lincoln was shot....
> Q. Please describe this woman who opened the window....
> A. She resembled the lady on the trial of the conspirators—Mrs. Surratt.
> Q. Have you seen the house since?
> A. I have.
> Q. Do you know the number?
> A. I do—541.

541 H Street was, of course, the boardinghouse of John's mother, Mrs. Mary E. Surratt, who was convicted of conspiracy at the 1865 military trial and was hanged. This testimony connected John Surratt directly with Booth and his conspiracy, if, that is, the testimony was true. The defense lawyers, Merrick and Bradley, questioned Sergeant Dye at considerable length. Clearly, this testimony presented a considerable danger to Surratt unless it could be shaken. Initially, they tried to make Dye look unreliable by questioning whether he had official permission to be out of camp that night. Later, they encouraged him to speculate about the men he had seen, about their drawing attention to themselves by calling out the time in a loud voice. Dye's speculations made his testimony seem more uncertain, guessing as to their motives.

Dye had stated that he had seen Surratt in his dreams after the assassination. The defense now tried to suggest that his testimony might be unreliable, confusing dreams with reality. Next Dye was questioned about his descriptions of the men he saw in front of the theatre:

> Q. Can you describe his dress as to color and appearance?
> A. No, sir, I cannot describe it.
> Q. How was the well-dressed man as to size?
> A. He was not a large man—about five feet six inches high.
> Q. He was not a large man then, but is a large man now. The man you saw has not changed so much as that, has he?
> A. I call a man a large man if he be only five feet high, if he is heavily built.
> Q. When you said this man was the smallest man of the three, did you mean that he was the slimmest man of the three?

A. I meant he was the lightest man....
Q. Then you told the [military] commission that the smallest man of the three called the time; that he was five feet six; the other five feet eight, and the other, again, five feet ten, and never explained that you did not mean the height?
A. No, sir; with regard to the man standing against the wall I could not tell what his height was, but I judged him to be the height mentioned there, when straightened up. I did not consider my judgment then as to height worth anything at all; now, however, I do.

It can be seen how Dye's judgment in trying to describe the men he said he saw seemed imprecise and questionable.[12] The defense produced a sworn statement, seeking to question the statements of Sergeant Dye:

> John H. Surratt being duly sworn says: that since the cross-examination of Sergeant Joseph M. Dye is now under bonds to answer in the city of Philadelphia to the charge of passing counterfeit money. That the testimony of said Joseph M. Dye as he is informed may be of much importance in this cause and that it is essential to the ends of justice that he should be interrogated as to said charge.
>
> (signed) John H. Surratt
>
> Sworn and subscribed this 21st day of June
>
> Test: R.J. Meigs, Clerk.

The prosecution called other witnesses to try to establish that Surratt was in Washington the night of April 14, 1865. James Sangster, a clerk at the St. Lawrence Hall hotel in Montreal, Canada, described how the man who used the name "John Harrison" left the hotel on April 12, taking a train for New York, and returned on April 18. The younger Mr. Bradley asked:

Q. You say he left the hotel instantly on the 18th. What is the entry on the 18th?
A. There is no entry excepting the name on the register.
Q. He may have been there or somewhere else?
A. He may have been; he paid no bill....
Q. Do you identify this gentleman at the hotel as the prisoner at the bar?
A. No, sir; I cannot say that I identify him.

Thus it was shown that if Surratt was not at the St. Lawrence Hall between April 14 and 18 it does not prove that he was not in Montreal. Sangster remembered a man wearing a certain style of jacket, but he could not identify Surratt as being that man.

In a further effort to prove that Surratt was in Washington on the night of the assassination, further witnesses were called. Robert H. Cooper was another soldier who said he was in front of the theatre with Sergeant Dye. Cooper corroborated everything Dye said. Detective John Lee (1815–?) also said he saw Surratt that night, but his testimony proved shaky:

Q. Now tell us what notice you had ever taken of him.
A. They would go along and say, "There goes a rebel"; I would look at him so that I would know him again when I saw him.
Q. You would know him so well that, in the course of a year or two, having never exchanged a word with him, and seeing him pass by on the street, you would say that was him?
A. I might be mistaken in that, too.

An important witness for the prosecution was William E. Cleaver, a veterinary surgeon and stable-keeper:

Q. Did you know J. Wilkes Booth?
A. Yes, sir.
Q. Did you know John H. Surratt?
A. Yes, sir.
Q. How long have you known John H. Surratt?

A. About twelve years, I think—ten or twelve years.
Q. Have you had a speaking acquaintance with him?
A. Yes, sir.... He came down to hire a horse of me at the time Booth kept his horse with me....
Q. State whether you saw him [Booth] and Surratt together.
A. Yes, sir....The first time I saw Surratt there with Booth, Booth came, I think, and paid one or two weeks' livery. Then, three or four days after, he came down and I hired him a horse to go into the country. [Surratt] came and hired a horse two or three times....
Q. When he [Surratt] had met Booth there [the stable], had he any conversation with him?
A. He always came with him.... [On another occasion] he told me he was going down in the country to T.B. [a town in southern Maryland], to meet a party and help them across the river; that he and Booth had some bloody work to do; that they were going to kill Abe Lincoln, the d——d old scoundrel; that he had ruined Maryland and the country. He [Surratt] said that if nobody did it, he would do it himself, and pulled out a pistol and laid it on the desk....
Q. Were you in Washington on the day of the assassination?
A. Yes sir.... I got to the stable, I reckon, at four o'clock, or a little after four.
Q. Before you got to the stable, when you came down H Street, did you meet anybody that attracted your attention?
A. I met John H. Surratt.

Asked at some length in the defense's cross examination about Cleaver's testimony at the 1865 military trial, Cleaver's answers were somewhat confusing:

Q. Did you tell them [the military commission] you saw John H. Surratt in this city [Washington] on the afternoon of the 14th, the day of the murder?
A. No, sir, I did not.
Q. Did you not know it was of importance to find out whether John H. Surratt was concerned in the murder or not?
A. Yes, sir.
Q. Then why did you not tell them what you knew?
A. I was well acquainted with Surratt and inclined to shield him.
Q. Yet you told them that he was with Booth at your stable.... Did you tell them about Surratt being tight [drunk] that night...?
A. No, sir.... I told them all they asked me.... I think they asked if anybody used Booth's horses besides himself, and that I told them he let Surratt use his horses....
Q. Then you think it is possible that they might have asked you about Surratt?
A. I think so; I do not know.

Having made confusion of Cleaver's testimony, Bradley moved in for the kill:

Q. I ask you whether you are the same Dr. Cleaver who was indicted, tried, and convicted for rape upon a poor little girl in this city....
A. I cannot answer that question.

The Judge ruled that Cleaver did not have to "answer that question" or any question related to where he had been or what he had been doing the past two weeks. Bradley tried another tack:

Q. Have you recently seen a man by the name of Sanford Conover, otherwise known as Dunham?
A. Yes, sir....
Q. Have you talked with him about this case?
A. Yes, sir; I told him all I knew about it two or three months ago....
Q. During the conspiracy trial [of 1865] you knew it was an important fact to ascertain whether he [Surratt] was in the city on that day or not?
A. Yes, sir; and I should not have told it now if it had not been for Conover. He soon told somebody, and the first thing I knew, somebody came to the jail to see me. I got very mad at Conover. I told him I did not want to answer the question....
Q. Who came to see you?
A. I think it was Mr. [James Mitchell] Ashley [1824–1896], a stoutish gentleman. I asked him, and he told me how he came to know of it.

Q. Who was the Mr. Ashley who called on you at the jail?
A. I don't know him only by that name. I believe he is a member of Congress [a congressman, R-OH, from 1859 to 1869, friend of Stanton, involved with Benjamin Franklin Butler (1818–1893) and Conover-Dunham to discredit President Johnson]. I never saw him before in my life.
Q. Did you understand he was a member of Congress?
A. Yes, sir; he told me who he was.
Q. Have you received any offer of favor or reward for the testimony you have given in this case?
A. I have not, from anybody.

Another stableman, Brooke Stabler, testified that Surratt knew Booth and Atzerodt:

Q. Did you see them at your stable?
A. Frequently.
Q. Did you see them all together there?
A. I have seen them together, and separately.
Q. In reference to their [Surratt's horses] use, what did he direct?
A. That they were not to be used except by his order.... His directions were that Booth and no one else was to have his horses, but that Booth could get them at any time....
Q. Did you have any written order from Surratt?
A. I had one.... It is Surratt's handwriting.
[Mr. Pierrepont read the note.]

March 26, 1865.

Mr. Brooks: As business will detain me for a few days in the country I thought I would send your team back. Mr. Bearer will deliver in safety and pay the hire on it. If Mr. Booth, my friend, should want my horses, let him have them, but no one else. If you should want any money on them, he [Booth] will let you have it. I should have liked to have kept the team for several days, but it is too expensive, especially as I have women on the brain and may be away for a week or so.

Yours respectfully,
J. Harrison Surratt[13]

Numerous witnesses were called to testify that John Surratt knew and associated with Booth and the other conspirators. Among these witnesses was Miss Honora Fitzpatrick (1846–1896), a boarder at Mrs. Surratt's house in Washington at the time of the assassination:

Q. Do you remember when you first formed his [Booth's] acquaintance, and where he was?
A. I met him at Mrs. Surratt's.
Q. Where was Mrs. Surratt living at that time?
A. On H Street, between Sixth and Seventh.
Q. Do you remember the number of the house?
A. 541.
Q. How often did you see him at the house, to your recollection?
A. I met Mr. Booth there several times. I do not know how often I saw him.
[She was asked about the other members of Booth's gang, Atzerodt, and Powell, and replied that she met both of them at Mrs. Surratt's house.]
Q. You know the prisoner, John H. Surratt?
A. Yes, sir.
Q. Do you recollect when was the last time you saw him at his mother's in April [1865]?
A. The last time I saw Mr. Surratt was two weeks before the assassination.
Q. During these visits by Atzerodt and Payne [Powell] to Booth, did you see John at the house? And if so, did you ever see or hear them conversing?
A. I have seen them, but never heard them conversing together.
Q. Do you recollect in the month of March of going to Ford's Theatre? And if so, state in whose company you were.
A. I went with Mr. Surratt, Mr. Wood [an alias of Powell's] and Miss [Mary Apollonia] Dean [1855–1894, another boarder at Mrs. Surratt's].
Q. State in what part of the theatre you were seated—whether you occupied a box or seat in the orchestra.
A. We occupied a box, sir [the same box, numbers seven and eight, which would be occupied by the president's party one month later].

Q. When you say Mr. Surratt, you mean John H. Surratt, the prisoner?
A. Yes, sir.
Q. While your party was in the box, did you see J. Wilkes Booth? If so, state what he did.
A. Mr. Booth came there and spoke to Mr. Surratt. They both stepped outside the box, and stood there at the door.
Q. You mean spoke to the prisoner?
A. Yes, sir.
Q. State if anyone else joined them while they were standing there.
A. Mr. Wood.
Q. Lewis Payne [Powell], you mean?
A. Yes, sir.
Q. How long were these three talking together?
A. They remained there a few minutes.
Q. Could you hear what they said?
A. No, sir. I was not paying attention; they were conversing together.[14]

An important witness was John Minchen Lloyd (1824–1892). Lloyd's testimony had been very instrumental in convicting Mrs. Surratt in the 1865 trial. Although Lloyd testified reluctantly at both trials, what he had to say was very important:

Q. I will ask you if you ever saw David E. Herold, George A. Atzerodt, and the prisoner at the bar in company together?
A. One morning, probably about five or six weeks before the assassination, Surratt and Atzerodt came to my house [Lloyd was renting the tavern at Surrattsville from Mrs. Surratt]; Herold had been there the night before, and said that he was obliged to go to "T.B." that night; He stopped in there, and was playing cards; he played several games; the next morning Surratt and Atzerodt drove up.... There were several other persons besides them there at the time.... After a while Surratt called me into the front parlor, and said he wanted to speak to me. There I saw lying on the sofa what I supposed to be guns. They had covers on them. Besides there were two or three other articles.... One was a rope.... It was coiled rope. I should think from the size of the bundle that there was not more than 18 or 20 feet of it. I took it to be an inch and a quarter rope.
Q. What other articles do you think of?
A. There was a monkey wrench.... He [Surratt] wished me to receive those things and to conceal the guns. I objected to it, and told him I did not wish to have such things in the house at all ... [but] finally, by assuring me most positively that there would be no danger in taking them, he induced me to receive them.... I told him there was no place about the premises to conceal such things ... [and] he told me then of a place where he knew it could be done. He then carried me up into a back room from the storeroom.
Q. Had you ever been in that room before?
A. Never. I supposed the place was finally closed up. I did not know that there was anything kept there at all.
Q. After you and the prisoner went into this room with these articles, state what you did.
A. I put them in an opening between the joists of the second story of the main building....
Q. State whether or not there was any ammunition brought there.
A. There was a cartridge-box brought there. Whether it was full of ammunition or not, I am not able to say.
Q. State how long Surratt wanted you to keep these articles.
A. He told me that he only wanted me to keep them two or three days, and that he would take them away at the end of that time.
Q. When was the next time you saw the prisoner?
A. I think I met him two or three days after that, going down to Surrattsville, and I supposed at the time that he was going to take those things away and I said nothing to him about them.
Q. Did you have any conversation with him at all?
A. Nothing more than that he asked me if he could get his breakfast down there. I told him I thought so—some ham and eggs. I was on my way to Washington when I met him.

Further questioning centered on Mrs. Surratt, and Lloyd was asked to repeat what he had testified to at the 1865 military trial. He expressed reluctance to do so; the judge had to instruct him to answer. A seemingly harmless detail would later be seen to have considerable significance in judging the truthfulness of both Lloyd and Weichmann:

> She [Mrs. Surratt] was in company with a young man whose name I did not know. Since that time, however, I have discovered his name to be Weichmann.
> Q. Where was she standing or sitting?
> A. She was sitting in the buggy alongside of Mr. Weichmann, in one of these high narrow buggies.
> Q. State if you had any conversation with her; and if so, state what was said by you both at that time.
> Mr. Bradley: Tuesday or Friday?
> The District Attorney: I am referring to Tuesday [April 11, 1865].
> A. She made use of a remark to me—called my attention to something that I couldn't understand.
> [Asked to state what Mrs. Surratt said to him, Lloyd was again reluctant.]
> A. I do not wish to state one solitary word more than I am compelled to
> [After more prompting, Lloyd continued.]
> A. She finally came out and asked me about some shooting irons that were there.... She told me to have them ready; that they would be called for, or wanted soon.... The conversation then ... turned on John Surratt. I told her I had understood that the soldiers were after John to arrest him for going to Richmond. I had understood that he had gone there. She laughed very heartily at the idea of anybody going to Richmond and back again in six days, and remarked that he must be a very smart man indeed to do it.

Later, Lloyd was recalled, and he testified regarding his second meeting with Mrs. Surratt, on the afternoon of Friday, April 14. Again he met Mrs. Surratt and Louis Weichmann in a buggy at Surrattsville, and again Lloyd stated that she told him to have the "shooting irons" ready:

> Q. Had you drank [sic] anything?
> A. I do not think I drank anything until the court adjourned [he was returning from court in Marlboro]. I knew what effect liquor had on me.
> Q. What effect has it?
> A. A very singular effect upon my mind chiefly. It makes me forget a great many things.
> Q. How much did you drink after the court adjourned?
> A. I drank enough to make me drunk.
> Q. Were you very drunk?
> A. I was so drunk that when I lay down I felt sick. I could not lie down.
> Q. How long after Mrs. Surratt went away did you lie down?
> A. I lay down before she left.[15]

In his testimony before the military commission in 1865—which he repeated at the Surratt trial—Louis J. Weichmann corroborated Lloyd's account of the two meetings with Mrs. Surratt during the week of the assassination. Weichmann admitted that he had escorted Mrs. Surratt on both occasions—on Tuesday, April 11, and again on Friday, April 14—but one detail, the most crucial one, Weichmann would not corroborate. Both times he stated he could not hear what they were talking about. Had he admitted to having heard any mention of the "shooting irons," as Lloyd called them, it would have cleared away any reasonable doubt. In a like manner, in Weichmann's testimony about the meeting in Booth's hotel room with Booth, Dr. Mudd, and John Surratt, Weichmann said he had heard their voices but could not make out what they were saying, even though he was in the same room with them, only eight feet away. As far as is known, Weichmann—only twenty-three years old in 1865—did not suffer from any sort of hearing loss and seemed to have normal hearing at other times. Why would he deny having heard the crucial words from the mouths of those accused of conspiracy—words which would have eliminated any doubt of their guilt? The answer to that question is obvious: if he admitted to hearing their conspiratorial talk he would be admitting to his own involvement in the conspiracy. Had he heard and understood Booth, Mudd, Surratt, Lloyd, and Mrs. Surratt talking together of conspiracy he would have had to report it to the authorities. His failure to do so made him guilty of conspiracy as well. Since he admitted to being present on those three occasions, close enough to the conspirators to have easily heard them, his excuse that he couldn't hear them is simply not credible. As we shall see, there were those at the time who doubted Weichmann's innocence but did not question his hearing because his testimony was crucial to the prosecution of Mary Surratt, Dr. Samuel Mudd, and John H. Surratt, Jr.[16]

10

A Jury of His Peers

The flight, capture, escape, second capture, and trial of John Harrison Surratt, Jr., was a story as sensational as any modern crime drama could be. No one could avoid knowledge or discussion of it. Among the papers of poet Walt Whitman (1819–1892) are references to Surratt. The first is a letter to Louisa Van Velsor Whitman (1795–1873) (Whitman's mother): "Washington, Feb. 26, 1867 ... Surratt is here in jail—his sister Anna goes to see him most every day—poor girl." Next is a letter to Louisa Van Velsor Whitman: "Washington, March 26, 1867 ... It is likely Surratt's trial will come on before long—I have become acquainted with [Henri B.] St. Marie, the man who discovered Surratt in Rome.... He goes here by a false name—he is very unhappy, and is in dread of assassination, from Surratt's friends—He came to me for advice, and wanted me to intercede for him with some members of Congress, as he says the government is treating him very coldly, as if they didn't consider he had done them any favor. I declined to mix up at all in the matter, in any way. He talked a good deal, and told me a good deal about Surratt. It is quite an interesting story...." A letter to Alfred Pratt reads as follows: "Washington, July 25, 1867 ... Alfred, I suppose you read in the papers about the trial of John H. Surratt for taking part in the murder of President Lincoln. I went down to the trial, day before yesterday. Surratt is very young—I sat near him and looked at him a long time—he sits most of the time fanning himself with a big palm leaf fan, and watches the witnesses with his sharp eyes—and his brother [Isaac], a young farmer-looking man from Texas, sits close by him. The lawyers on both sides are very smart—sometimes the evidence goes strongly against him, and then again for him. It is very interesting to sit and hear the witnesses and the speeches of the lawyers. It has been a tedious trial, and it is hard to tell how it will end...."

Washington was still a relatively small city in the 1860s. It should not be surprising that Walt Whitman, who worked in the attorney general's office and was friendly with Attorney General James Speed (1812–1887), was also well acquainted with the Surratt trial judge, George P. Fisher.[1] A newspaper article originating from Montreal on July 25, 1867, speculated on Surratt's connections with the Confederate authorities:

Davis and Surratt

The Surratt trial is watched here [Montreal] with keen interest.... There ... [are] opinion[s] in certain circles of this place, plainly showing that there are parties here who know more on the topic of the day than they choose to tell ... some of these parties who, from their past and present positions, can be correctly entitled well-informed persons, and who have been behind the curtains. They say that Surratt was dispatched to Richmond to procure commissions [as Confederate soldiers] for the [St. Albans, Vermont] raiders; that he was paid there for his services; but never received any money from [Clement C.] Clay or [Jacob] Thompson. The latter denies the charge against him of having drawn from the Montreal bank a large sum of money for the express purpose of giving it to Surratt, that much-talked-of draft having been solely for the purpose of stocks.

He states that he never saw Surratt but once, and then for a moment only, as he delivered to him dispatches in reply to a communication he had forwarded by a lady to the Richmond authorities, that he could not recognize him if he were to see him.

The parties mentioned, proceeding in their accounts, assert that it is very "probable" Surratt was engaged in the attempt to abduct Lincoln, as that scheme had first been started in 1863, as a legitimate piece of warfare....

Subsequently, towards the close of the war, Surratt, Booth, & Co. hit upon the abduction scheme, which was freely talked over in knowing circles at Richmond, months before the evacuation occurred; and this plan, they assert, Booth, on the strength of events, suddenly changed into one of assassination upon his own responsibility and without Surratt's participation or knowledge ... [and] they express a confident belief that more about it could be extracted from men now in high office than from anybody else if these gentlemen were disposed to mount the stand.

The witness in a position to do the most harm to Surratt was his one-time friend Louis J. Weichmann. Surratt had told Weichmann a good deal about his involvement with the Confederate Secret Service:

Q. Now on the 3rd, what occurred?
A. On the 3rd of April, after the excitement and noise of the day, I was seated in Mrs. Surratt's parlor in the evening, on the sofa, when, about half past six o'clock, John Surratt walked into the room. He was very neatly dressed. He had on a new pair of pants. I asked him where he had been. His answer was to Richmond. I then said, "Richmond is evacuated. Did you not hear the news?" "No, it is not," he said. "I saw [Judah] Benjamin and [Jefferson] Davis in Richmond, and they told me it would not be evacuated...." He went up before me. I went up a few minutes afterwards; I think he called me up stairs.
Q. When you got to the room with him, what did he say?
A. He did not say very much. He said that he wanted to exchange forty dollars in gold. He did exchange this forty dollars in gold for forty dollars in greenbacks [paper money]. He showed me in the room nine or eleven twenty-dollar gold pieces, and fifty dollars in greenbacks.

It will be remembered that John Surratt had been to Richmond at the beginning of April 1865 and that he was given $200 in gold by Secretary of State Judah P. Benjamin to carry dispatches to Canada.

Q. Did he say anything as to where he had got the money?
A. I did not ask him where he got it. I expressed a sort of surprise. He said that he had an account in the Bank of Washington, but he did not say that he had gotten this money from the Bank of Washington.... He always appeared to have plenty of money in his pockets—five dollars and ten dollars. He seemed to be always well supplied.... He told me that same evening that he was going to Montreal.... He said he would correspond with me when he got to Montreal....
Q. How often was Booth at Mrs. Surratt's house two or three months prior to the murder?
A. He came very frequently. It was a very common thing for me to see him in the parlor with [John] Surratt, when Booth was in town after 4 o'clock. They appeared like brothers.

After establishing Weichmann's ability at identifying the handwriting of Booth and Surratt, he was shown a letter, which was read into the record: "Surrattsville, (November) 12, 1864. Dear Al: ... Next Tuesday, and the jig's up. Good by, Surrattsville. Good by, God forsaken country. Old Abe, the good old soul, may The devil take pity on him. John H. Surratt." Would this letter not suggest that Surratt believed Weichmann had knowledge of John's involvement in some sort of plot against Lincoln? It could even suggest that Weichmann was involved in such a plot. "Al" was a nickname for Weichmann. This letter was followed by one from James Rowan O' Beirne (1838–1917), provost marshal of the District of Columbia, and dated May 10, 1865. Weichmann later compared his testimony at the military trial of 1865 with the trial of John Surratt in 1867: "I was on the stand for three days. I repeated the testimony I gave in 1865 with many additional facts which had come to my mind since that time. I also made some corrections in my evidence, notably in relation to the time when I met Dr. Mudd, and stated my reasons for so doing. Mr. Bradley in his cross-examination was very severe, and pressed me very hard; he tried his best to confuse me and make me contradict myself, but his efforts all came to naught."

Weichmann's testimony in the 1865 trial had been particularly harmful to Mary Surratt. At the trial of John Surratt, however, he modified his story about her:

> Q. Did you tell Mr. [John P.] Brophy (1842–1914) or Mr. [Louis J.] Carland (1845–1900), or either of them, that on one occasion Mrs. Surratt called her son aside, in your presence, and said to him, "John, I am afraid there is something going on, why do these men come here? Now, John, I do not feel easy about this, and you must tell me what you are about."
> A. Yes, sir; I told them shortly after Booth and Atzerodt commenced coming to the house, that Mrs. Surratt was very much exercised about their coming there. I did hear her say, "John, what are these men doing here? What business have they with you?" or something to that effect. And she stated to me that she would know what John had to do with it, and she took John into the parlor and closed the door. Whether John disclosed his business or not I do not know. I afterwards asked her what business John was engaged in, and she said he told her he was engaged in cotton speculations.

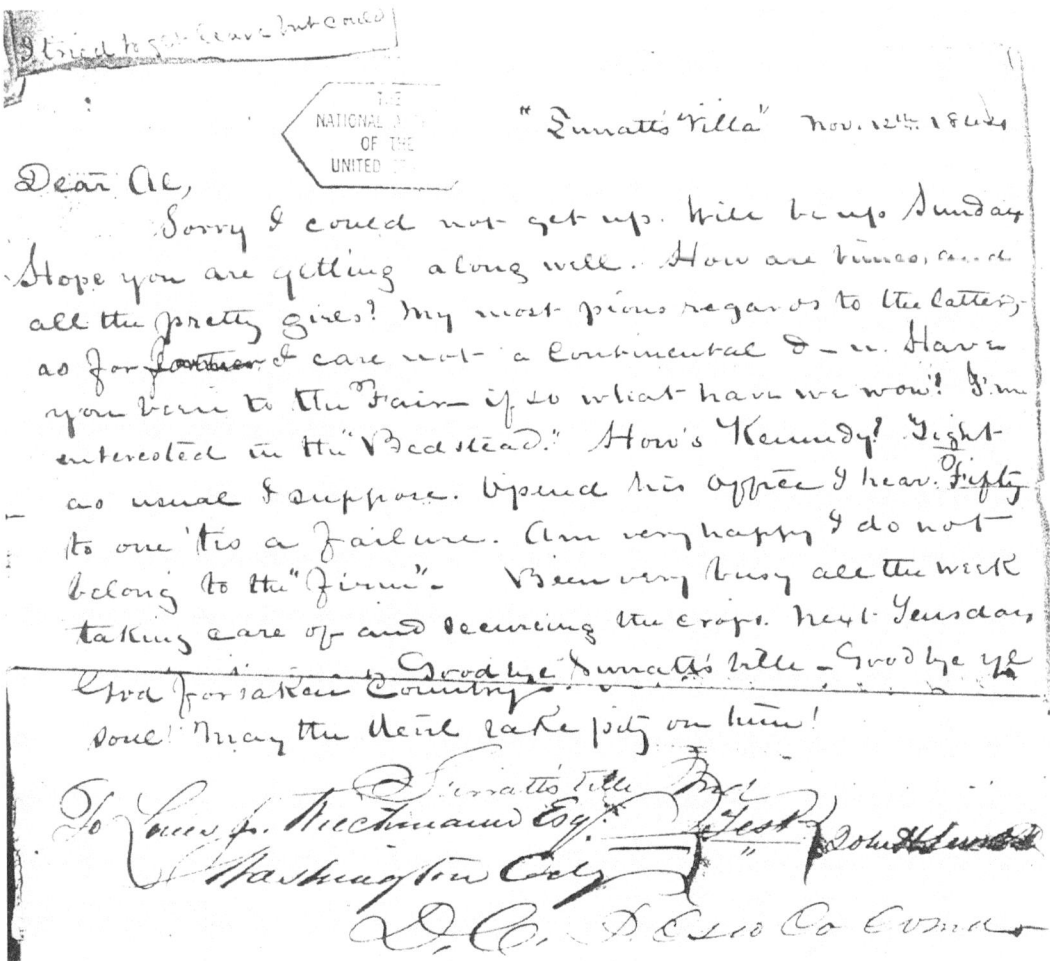

John Surratt's handwriting from a letter he wrote to Louis Weichmann, November 12, 1864 (National Archives).

If this is an accurate account of what happened and what was said, it either indicates that Mrs. Surratt and her son staged the scene to fool Weichmann or suggests that Mrs. Surratt was ignorant of her son's connection with Booth's conspiracy and was therefore innocent of the charges against her. Either way, it creates reasonable doubt. The questioning continued:

> Q. Was anything said between you and [Augustus Spencer] Howell (1837–1869), the blockade runner, about your going to Richmond?
> A. I said I would like to go to Richmond for the purpose of continuing my theological studies. I would have crossed the river for that purpose.
> Q. Is there any college there?
> A. No, sir; it was not necessary to have a college there; I could have studied in a bishop's house.... I sent two letters by a flag of truce boat to Bishop [John] McGill [Bishop of Richmond from 1850 to 1872] during the war, and I received an answer to one of them January 15, 1865.
> Q. And you were at the same time talking with Howell about how you could get across [through the blockade]. Didn't you tell him all your sympathies were with the South?
> A. O, I have talked secesh very often in my life for buncombe, especially with such men as Mr. Howell.

These answers may or may not have been true. Why would Weichmann need to travel along the risky and illegal route to Richmond, risking being arrested or even shot amid the contending armies? There were Catholic colleges or bishops in the North that would have been just as good and without such risks. In his history, written later, Weichmann changed his story again: "I made application in August to the Catholic bishop of Richmond, Virginia, for his permission to begin my theological studies in the seminary at Baltimore, but he took no notice of my letter, and it remained unanswered." It is also curious that Weichmann should be so anxious to study theology, given what he had said about it earlier in his book: "My preferences were for the drug business, but my mother overruled my predilections in this respect.... I yielded to my mother's wishes although I confess I had but little heart for the profession selected."[2] As we shall see, a great deal of doubt was raised about the truthfulness of Weichmann's testimony.

Another witness who was carefully questioned at length was Lewis J.A. McMillan, the ship's doctor of the S.S. *Peruvian*, who said that John Surratt told him much of his story while they crossed the Atlantic from Canada to England:

> Q. Haven't you stated in this city [Washington] since his [Surratt's] arrest, that you would be entitled to the reward, and intended to claim it?
> A. I said ... that if anyone was entitled to a reward for his arrest, I thought myself as much entitled to it as anybody else....
> Q. Did you ever say to any one in conversation, in which the question of your intimate relations with Surratt on shipboard came up, that Surratt could not have been guilty of the charge of assassination, and therefore you regarded him merely as a political offender; the victim of compromising circumstances, and felt no scruples in extending aid to him?
> A. I never did.
> Q. I ask you whether you have ever made any statement contrary to what you have made on the stand?
> A. I have never said anything contrary to it. I have said something "different," but not "contrary."

McMillan steadfastly denied telling anyone anything that might have indicated he had any sympathy for Surratt at any time.

Several more witnesses were called to corroborate testimony that Surratt was in Washington on the night of the assassination, and especially that he was in Booth's company in front of the theatre. The testimony of the theatre's carpenter, James Johnson Gifford (1814–1894), was especially damaging to the prosecution's contention that the conspirators, especially Surratt, were out together:

Q. Were you out there at the commencement of the third act?
A. Yes, sir.
Q. Did you see Booth out there?
A. No, sir.
Q. How long did you remain there...?
A. [A]bout twenty or twenty-five minutes.... I did not see Booth that night at all.
Q. Did you know Mr. J. Wilkes Booth?
A. Yes, sir; I knew him from his boyhood.
Q. Did you ever see the prisoner at the bar before you saw him here?
A. No, sir, I never saw him.
Q. That night when you and Mr. Carland were out in front of the theatre, did you see him [Surratt], or anybody resembling him come down in front of that place?
A. No, sir.
Q. Did you see any one come there and ask what time it was?
A. Yes, sir ... the gentleman's name was Hess.... He came and asked what time it was. Mr. Carland stepped in the door, came out and said it was ten minutes past ten.
Q. Was Booth anywhere about then?
A. Not that I saw; I did not see him.
Q. Did you see anybody sitting on the carriage platform in front of the theatre that night?
A. I did not.... We allowed no persons to sit there at all, nor to loaf about the front of the theatre. It would have been my duty to see that they were put away if they had been there.

Another witness, Courtland Van Rensalaer Hess (1839–1887), was called to back up Gifford's testimony. Hess's name has been mixed up with Dwight Hess, who was the partner of Leonard Grover of the National Theatre:

Q. State whether you had any part in the performance that night, and at what time you were to appear.
A. I was not in the *American Cousin* [the name of the play was *Our American Cousin*], but was in a song that was to be sung after the performance of the *American Cousin*.
Q. A national song?
A. Yes, sir; written expressly for the President.
Q. State whether you were in front of the theatre in the course of that evening.
A. I was in and out of the theatre several times during the evening.
Q. Do you recollect of, at any time, talking with Mr. Gifford or anyone else in front of the theatre?
A. While I was talking with Mr. Gifford and Mr. Carland, there was a gentleman standing on the curbstone, dressed, it seemed to me, like an officer....
Q. When you came out and spoke to them, was anything said about the time?
A. Yes, sir. I asked them what time it was. Mr. Carland walked as far as the first door in front of the theatre, leading into the audience department, looked at the clock, and came back and told me it was ten minutes past ten. Says I, "Ten minutes past ten; I will be wanted in a few minutes," and left them immediately and went back into the theatre again....
Q. At any time in the course of the evening, and shortly before this, had you come from the direction of F Street down to where they were standing?
A. Yes, sir; I walked up as far as F Street, to Mr. Ferguson's I think it was, and got a cigar. I then walked back again to the door.
Q. Was that announcement of the time in an audible tone of voice, or was it said in a private way?
A. I asked it in a kind of very loud tone myself, knowing that I had, at least I supposed I had, about a quarter of an hour in which to dress up
Q. Did you ever see Mr. Surratt before? (The prisoner was requested to stand up.)
A. No, sir; never.
Q. You did not see him out there that night?
A. No, sir.
Q. You did not see him go up and come down and speak to Carland and Gifford?
A. No, sir; he did not while I was there.[3]

Thus was the testimony of Sergeant Dye, if not demolished, at least thrown into doubt. The same shadow of doubt was cast upon the testimony of William E. Cleaver, who had testified to seeing Surratt together with other Booth conspirators. The testimony of Thomas Geary was typical:

> Q. Do you know W.E. Cleaver, a witness in this case?
> A. Yes, sir.
> Q. Do you know his general reputation for truth and veracity among the people with whom he associates and in the community where he lives?
> A. Yes, sir, I do.
> Q. What is his reputation as a truthful man?
> A. It is generally bad.
> Q. From his general reputation among the people with whom he associates, would you believe him on his oath?
> A. No, sir; I would not.

Geary was one of nine witnesses, one after another, who described Cleaver as unreliable as to his speaking the truth.

Honora Fitzpatrick was recalled to testify in regard to whether or not John Surratt was at his mother's house on April 14, 1865:

> A. I know Mr. Surratt was not in the house that night.

She was asked about events at Mrs. Surratt's house on the night of April 3, 1865.

> Q. Did John Surratt come into the parlor?
> A. No, sir.
> Q. If he had come in you would have seen him?
> A. I saw him in the back parlor....
> Q. Did you see him anywhere else after he ate supper?
> A. No, sir.
> Q. Was that the last time you ever saw him until you saw him here?
> A. Yes, sir.

An important witness in establishing that John Surratt was not in Washington on the night of April 14, 1865, was John Cass., who spoke to Surratt in his store in Elmira on the morning of April 15:

> Q. Look at that man (pointing to the prisoner) and state if he is or is not the man.
> A. That is the man I saw there ... [and] the minute I saw him I recognized him as the man I saw in my store. I did so before I got near him. I saw at once that he was the man I had seen there.[4]

Other witnesses from Elmira also identified the prisoner in court as being the same man they had seen in Elmira only a few hours after the assassination. Although an effort would be made to suggest that Surratt might have managed to travel through the night and arrive at Elmira in time, there was more than a reasonable doubt that such a thing could have been done.

The defense presented General Edwin Gray Lee (1836–1870) as a witness for John Surratt. Lee was questioned on whether Surratt had brought dispatches with him for Lee. The prosecution objected to the question. Lee was asked whether Jacob Thompson had money belonging to the Confederate government. Again the prosecution blocked an answer by objecting. When asked whether Surratt had received any money from Thompson, the prosecution again objected: "'Did you employ him [Surratt] while he was in Montreal, on any business calling him into the United States, on or before the 12th of April, 1865?' (Same objection as heretofore had, with a like ruling. Exception reserved.)"

> Q. Did you see him when he left Montreal to come to the United States, on the 12th of April, or whatever day he came away?
> A. I did not.

Q. Do you know upon what business he came to the United States (Same objection, with a like ruling. Exception reserved.)

Several more questions were asked, only to be objected to:

Q. Do you know at or about what time you arrived in Montreal after you had left the scene some time?
A. At the close of the interval of the several days that I mentioned just now he arrived in Montreal. I next saw him either on the 17th or the 18th of April. My own impression has been, ever since I have thought over the matter at all, that it must have been the 17th, though I am not positive. I am positive, however, that it was one of those two days.
Q. Do you recollect at all how he was dressed when you first saw him in Montreal?
(Objected to by Mr. Pierrepont on the ground that they had given no evidence with regard to his dress in Montreal. Objection overruled.)
A. I recollect nothing of his dress except that he wore a large ordinary traveling shawl that covered his shoulders and his body below his waist, and nearly to the skirt of his coat.
Q. Do you remember whether he then had a moustache or a goatee?
A. He had a very light moustache. It looked to me like one that had never been shaved off at all, but just allowed to grow. It was like a boy's moustache. The goatee was very light. When I say light I mean in quantity. I do not remember whether it included an imperial or not. I know that there was not an imperial alone; but whether the goatee grew to the lip or not I do not remember.

Lewis J. Carland (1845–1900) was recalled to cast further doubt upon the truthfulness of Louis J. Weichmann. He was asked about a conversation after the 1865 trial:

Q. Did Mr. Weichmann state to you … that he was very much troubled in his conscience about the testimony he had given at that trial?
A. He did. He wished me to go with him to St. Aloysius church, as he said he wished to make a confession; that his mind was so burdened with what he had done, that he had no peace.
Q. Did you say to him, "That is not the right way, Mr. Weichmann, You had better go to a magistrate and make a statement under oath?"
A. I did.
Q. Do you remember his replying to you, "'I would take that course if I were not afraid of being indicted for perjury?"
A. He did make that remark to me, and I then asked him the particulars. He said if he had been left alone, and had been allowed to give his statement as he had wanted to, it would have been quite a different affair with Mrs. Surratt than what it was.
Q. Did he say who troubled him?
A. Yes, sir; he said the parties who had charge of the military commission.
Q. Did he say to you that he had been obliged to swear to the statement that had been prepared for him, and that he was threatened with prosecution for perjury—threatened with being charged as one of the conspirators unless he did?
A. Yes, sir; he did; that it was written out for him, and that he was threatened with prosecution as one of the conspirators if he did not swear to it.... He said that a detective had been put into Carroll prison [where he was being held as a witness] with him and that this man had written out a statement … and that he had to swear to that statement. I asked him why he swore to it when he knew it was not true? He said part of it was true, but not all the points that he could have given, if he had been let alone, were contained in it.
Q. There is no doubt about this being the man (Pointing to the witness Weichmann).
A. No, sir. I have met him frequently.
[James J. Gifford was recalled to comment further on Weichmann.]
Q. Were you in Carroll prison with him?
A. Yes, sir.
Q. This is the man here? (Pointing to the witness, Louis J. Weichmann)
A. Yes, sir.
Q. Did he say in your presence that an officer of the government had told him that unless he testified to more than he had already stated they would hang him too?
A. I heard the officer tell him so.
(Subsequently ordered to be stricken out by the court)

10. A Jury of His Peers

Q. Who was present at that time?
A. James Maddox.
(Subsequently ordered to be stricken out by the court)
Q. Did Weichmann ever say anything to you about wanting to go south?

Mr. Pierrepont objected, and, at the same time, asked that the answers to the first two questions be stricken out, as they did not relate to this trial and were not contradictory of anything Weichmann had said, as would appear from a reference to his testimony. The testimony of Weichmann on this point was referred to and commented upon by the counsel, when the court said he thought the objection that had been made a proper one and directed the answers already given to be stricken out.

Although Carland's and Gifford's testimonies were obviously harmful to Weichmann, as to both what he had said and his motives in saying it, the prosecution and, it appears, the judge as well, sought to eliminate it or to reduce its impact. It is surprising, in view of that, that the government published the statements of Gifford in the official record of the trial, in spite of their having been ordered stricken out by Judge Fisher. Weichmann, in his memoir, did not mention Gifford at all and did not say anything about this incident at the 1867 trial, including Maddox's testimony.[5]

There was more testimony regarding Surratt's presence in Montreal in April 1865, which was mostly not precise enough to establish that he was in Canada at the time of the assassination. The Canadian witnesses also remembered seeing Henri B. Ste. Marie in Montreal, working in a bank. Sarsfield B. Nagle testified that, in addition to Ste. Marie, he also knew Dr. Lewis J.A. McMillan, the ship's doctor who gave so much detailed and damaging testimony about what he said Surratt told him as they sailed together across the Atlantic.

A. I knew of his [McMillan's] going to the university [in Montreal], and taking his degree of Doctor of Medicine.
Q. State, if you please, whether you thus had opportunities of learning and knowing the general character, among those with whom he associated, of the witness McMillan.... I speak of his general character ... for truth and veracity ... was it good or bad?
A. It was not good.... I should consider it was bad from common report.
Q. From that general reputation as to his truth, would you believe him on his oath?
A. I would have great doubt about it if I were interested myself.... I will explain what I mean: From what I know of him, not personally but from hearsay in that locality, if I had a lawsuit wherein I wanted a witness, I would not certainly take his oath.

Dr. McMillan wrote to Secretary Seward, early in 1867, inquiring about the reward offered for Surratt. Seward replied: "Sir, your note of yesterday claiming the reward offered in a proclamation of the President, for the apprehension of John H. Surratt, has been received.... Your letter has ... been referred to the Secretary of War, whose province it is to decide upon the claims to the reward adverted to." It will be recalled that McMillan, at first maintaining that his interest was that justice be done, decided that if a reward was offered, his information ought to have qualified him to be the recipient.

Another Canadian witness was Louis W. Sicotte, who testified about H.B. Ste. Marie:

A. I did not meet him in 1858; but I have seen him since 1859, and from then up to 1862.... From 1860 to 1862 he was employed in the educational office [in Montreal].
Q. Was his general character for truth and veracity good or bad?
A. Very bad.
Q. From that general character—from what was said of him by people with whom he associated—would you believe him on his oath?
A. No, sir....
Q. After the arrest of Surratt in Rome, did you hear anything about it?

A. Yes, sir; many people spoke of it then.
Q. Did you know the fact that Surratt was arrested in Rome on the information given by St. Marie?
A. Certainly.
Q. Now state what you did say about St. Marie when you heard of the betrayal [of Surratt]?...
A. When I heard that St. Marie had made the deposition against Surratt, I said to the curate and others, that it was mean or unprincipled in him to have made that deposition.

Portions of Sicotte's testimony had to be given in French, which was translated by Col. James Rowan O'Beirne (1838–1917), provost marshal of the District of Columbia. O'Beirne also interpreted the other French-speaking witnesses.

Joseph Du Tilley had more testimony to add, especially about Dr. McMillan:

Q. Do you know Dr. McMillan, who has been examined as a witness in this case?
A. Yes, sir.
Q. Do you know the Canadian people who are acquainted with Dr. McMillan?
A. O, yes, sir....
Q. Have you ever heard them speak of Dr. McMillan's character for truth?
A. Yes, sir.
Q. What kind of character did they generally give him for truth—good or bad?
A. It is bad....
Q. State whether, from what people say generally of him, you would believe him on his oath?
A. No, sir; I would not.

At this point, Mr. Merrick, attorney for the defense, argued against the prosecution's contention that a conspirator need not be present at the scene of the crime. Merrick cited a case from Massachusetts: "That a co-conspirator, in order to be charged as a principal, must be within such distance that he could render material aid in the consummation of the act, or render the party who struck the blow, fresh from the deed, assistance in his escape. The same rule was laid down by Chief Justice [John] Marshall (1755–1835) in the case of [Aaron] Burr (1756–1836)." The court decided to hold these questions over for future consideration.

John Surratt's brother, Isaac Douglas Surratt (1841–1907), was called as a witness for the defense. His only contribution to the case was to state that John was twenty-three years old, having been born on April 13, 1844. Isaac had been noticed among the spectators. Another defense witness was Charles Boucher (1832–1914), who described Surratt's stay with him in Canada, as described in Chapter 6. Boucher also testified about Dr. McMillan:

Q. State, if you please, whether you had opportunities to know his [McMillan's] general character among those with whom he associated as a man of truth and veracity.... Was his character for truth good or bad?
A. As well as I can say, I do not think his character was very good.
Q. Was it good or bad?
A. Bad.

Boucher also described a quarrel he had with Dr. McMillan over the issue of abortion:

I said to him at that time that I would like to advise him not to practice abortion nor to argue the point before the people; that it would be a great scandal. He then made an insulting reply, and I took hold of him by the collar and put him out.

Q. State whether you have any hostile feelings towards Dr. McMillan now in consequence of that quarrel, or from any other cause.
A. No, sir; I never had any spite against him....
Q. Would you, or not, from [his] general reputation believe him on his oath in a matter in which he was interested?
A. No, sir; I would not.

Of course, when Dr. McMillan was recalled to testify about Boucher's charges, he disagreed with everything the priest had said about him.

As the trial dragged on, the newspapers reported on Surratt's life as a prisoner: "Since the trial of Surratt, his quarters in the jail have been moved, and he now has one of the rooms on the second story, fronting south, which he occupied in common with Henry Johnson, who is charged with the killing of Thomas Smoot, for seducing his (Johnson's) wife. Surratt has of late much improved in health. They are well fixed in this room, each having a cot on which they sleep. They have some books and papers, and when not reading, conversation is engaged in. Surratt alludes but seldom to the charge against him, but speaks of general topics. He seems to think much of his Zouave uniform and wears it nearly all the time."[6]

After a long parade of witnesses, many of them testifying only to the truthfulness or untruthfulness of one or another witness, it was at last time for the summations of the prosecutors and defense attorneys. Carrington began, describing Lincoln and his assassination. He pointed out that conspiring to abduct bears full responsibility for the murder of the victim. He went over a few points of law for the jury:

> An accessory before the fact is defined ... as one who, being absent at the time of the commission of the felony, advised and counseled another to commit the crime.
> Absence is necessary to make him an accessory. If he be present he becomes a principal; whether he be constructively or actually present is immaterial....
> The offense your honor will observe, is complete when the conspiracy is formed, and every one who engages in it is a conspirator, and is guilty of a misdemeanor. But if in engaging in a conspiracy to commit felony, the conspirator performs some act towards the commission of the felony, continuing a member of the conspiracy until the felony is committed, he is a felon.
> I maintain that when a conspiracy is formed to commit murder or any other felony, and murder is actually committed by one of the conspirators, every other conspirator who has cooperated—and mark, if your honor pleases, that is a question of fact for the jury—who is cooperating in the conspiracy and acting his part in the general plan at the time the felony is committed, is in legal contemplation constructively present, no matter where he was at the time of the murder or felony was committed.

Carrington also cited part of Chief Justice John Marshall's statement in the treason trial of Aaron Burr: "Judge Marshall expressly declares in the Burr trial, that a party to a treasonable conspiracy, who performs any part in the general plan, however minute or however remote from the scene of action, is constructively present." He also contended that attacking the President was not the same as an attack upon any ordinary citizen: "I boldly affirm as an American lawyer, proud of our country and our institutions, that when war is levied against the federal government, either by foreign enemies or domestic foes, the man who strikes at the commander of the American army is a traitor, and deserves a traitor's doom. If a number of persons conspire together to engage in an unlawful act, and, while thus engaged, one takes life, his act is equally the act of everyone co-operating in the conspiracy at the time the act or crime was committed, though not originally intended."

In summarizing the testimony of several witnesses, Carrington spent the longest time on Louis J. Weichmann. It was, and remains, evident that Weichmann was the most important witness against John Surratt, as he had been against John's mother at the earlier trial. Whatever one chooses to believe about Weichmann and his testimony, then as now it should be remembered that a great deal of what Weichmann said was not corroborated by anyone else. The dark interpretations he put upon the words and deeds of Mrs. Surratt were denied by her when alive and became empty echoes after her death. Likewise, much of what he said about John Surratt, his one-time friend, could not be supported by anyone else.

About another witness, Carrington made an extraordinary statement: "I say frankly that I would not convict any living man upon the uncorroborated testimony of William E. Cleaver.... When I understand a bad man knows a fact, to put him before you, and it is for you to say whether you will believe him or not. Wrapping up his lengthy summation, Carrington brought religion into the argument:

> I read from the thirteenth chapter of Romans, commencing with the first verse:
> "Let every soul be subject unto the higher powers; for there is no power but of God. The powers that be are ordained of God.
> "Whoseever, therefore, resisteth the power resisteth the ordinance of God, and they that resist shall receive to themselves damnation.
> "For rulers are not a terror to good works, but to evil. Wilt thou then not be afraid of the power? Do that which is good, and thou shalt have praise of the same.
> "For he is the minister of God to thee for good. But if thou do that which is evil, be afraid; for He beareth not the sword in vain; for he is the minister of God, a revenger to execute wrath upon him that doeth evil."[7]

Carrington sought to eliminate any reasonable doubt the jurors might still be entertaining by addressing the Almighty. "The true question, therefore, in trials of fact, is not whether it is possible that the testimony be false, but whether there is sufficient probability of its truth; that is, whether the facts are shown by competent and satisfactory evidence. Things established by competent and satisfactory evidence are said to be proved." Carrington finally concluded his summation and Pierrepont began his. He mostly reiterated what Carrington had already stated, adding, "[C]onspiracy to kidnap, abduct, or murder the President of the United States in time of rebellion, or other great national peril, is a crime of such heinousness as to admit of no accessories, but such as to render all the conspirators, their supporters, aiders, and abettors, principals in the crime. That such is the common law of England, and is the law of this country.... [A]ny man, and any judge, who will treat this as a mere ordinary crime, having no other qualities in it than those of a common murder ... do not understand the principles of law which should govern nations, or the laws which bear on governments.... That the personal presence of the prisoner in Washington is not necessary to his guilt in this case. He could perform his part in the conspiracy as well at Elmira as at Washington, and be equally guilty at one place as at the other."

This statement is especially interesting, since the prosecution had gone to considerable trouble to try to prove that Surratt was, or could have been, in Washington the night of the assassination. Now, with this remark, Pierrepont seems to be supporting the defense's contention that Surratt was not, and could not have been, in Washington that night. But to save that part of the case, he said that Surratt was involved in the conspiracy no matter where he was. Surratt had certainly been involved in a conspiracy to kidnap the president but not to murder him. It had not been shown by testimony that Surratt's business in Elmira was related to the conspiracy. The prosecution had prevented the testimony of General Edwin Lee, the only person aside from Surratt himself who knew what that business was, and could have testified to it.[8]

Now it was the turn of the defense to make their case. Mr. Merrick spoke first:

> The prisoner is here arraigned for a particular crime, and the jury are charged with an investigation of his guilt or innocence as to the crime with which he thus stands charged. Prejudice should find no place in your hearts. Feeling should raise no cloud to obscure your judgment, and the United States should stand, represented by its attorney, the impersonation of a stolid logic, with the utter absence of every emotion. Instead of representing the United States in that capacity and in that character, every feeling that could rock the human heart upon its foundations has been invoked to influence you; and every sentiment calculated to excite your prejudice has been urged upon you with a violence which I have never seen equaled in a court of justice.

Our civil war is over. Let there be no triumph, no jibes, no animosities, no invectives. Let me say to the North, "Extend the hand of friendship; renew the relations temporarily interrupted by the clash of arms. Take back the estranged brother to your arms, and feel that, in doing so, you are accomplishing the great purpose of Christian charity implanted in your hearts, as Christian men, and the great purpose of patriotic citizens in reuniting your divided land." My learned brother is mistaken in representing God as a God of vengeance and a God of wrath.

He is a God of love and kindness.

Merrick then turned to the heart of the case, the actual charges against Surratt:

Gentlemen of the jury, what are you trying? Are you not trying John H. Surratt for the murder of Abraham Lincoln? Is there anything else in the case? Is there anything else in the indictment? What is to be your verdict…? He is charged in the indictment with the murder of Abraham Lincoln. The only question for you to decide is, did he commit the murder…?

They want to try him apparently for carrying dispatches; for being in sympathy with the rebel government; for being in some sort of conspiracy; anything and everything but the charge which we have come here to meet—that of murder.

There may have been some legal reason to charge Surratt with murdering Lincoln, but in wording the charges that way the prosecution left open a door by which Surratt might escape. They meant that to conspire with others to commit a crime is the same as having himself committed it (a dubious proposition), but the charges do not say that; they say that Surratt fired the shot at Lincoln, ignoring the common-sense proposition that two men could not have fired the same pistol at the same time, nor could one of them (Surratt) have vanished into thin air. Merrick rejected the idea that to kill the president is more of a crime than the murder of any other person: "The President is a simple American citizen, the representative of the free people of America. The monarchy of this country, grand and sacred beyond the touch or the reach of an assault, is the embodied will of the people in the Constitution of the United States; our only emperor, our only king, is the Constitution of the United States. It is the only sovereign of a republic." Many years later, in our own time, laws were passed to recognize the status of the president of the United States, making it a federal offense to assault or murder the president. But this was done to establish legal jurisdiction of the federal government in such cases, not to maintain that the president has a superior status to that of a private citizen: "[A]lthough the consequences of this crime might have been disastrous beyond the killing of an ordinary individual, yet, in contemplation of law, the killing was but the killing of an individual, and the charge is murder, and nothing but murder."

In discussing the concept of reasonable doubt, Merrick defined it this way: "There must be no lurking apprehension, no latent doubt, no slumbering fear, no possibility in your minds that hereafter your dreams will be disturbed and your waking hours haunted by the ghost your verdict is to make."

The long argument of Merrick, like that of Carrington, must have seemed nearly without end. Bradley the elder, following Merrick, made his remarks relatively short. He noted that he was acquainted with all of the jurors. He pointed out that the indictment was not specific. He argued that the government knew of the conspiracy before the assassination. He maintained that Weichmann knew everything the conspirators knew. He pointed out that Lloyd was also involved.[9] After Bradley's argument for the defense was completed, Pierrepont again rose and began a summation:

Has the counsel explained to you why he [Surratt] was concealed? Not at all. Why was he concealed? It was either because he was innocent or because he was guilty. Which was it? …

God does not allow those who commit such deeds as his to be safe anywhere…. [S]omething still haunted him and told him that there was no hiding place for treason and for murder…. Now, this was the strange flight of an innocent man, as my learned friend [the defense counsel] says, or rather argues it was. Now, what do you think about it? Do you think that an innocent man would do those things? Do you think he fled because he did not engage in murder, or because he did—which? ... It is certainly a mystery as it now stands—that an innocent man should thus flee....

Every lover of freedom, every lover of constitutional liberty, every lover of our free and blessed government is ready to fall upon his knees and pray that no such calamity may befall our country as to have a jury of twelve men, or one out of the twelve, refuse to find a man guilty when the law and the evidence say that he is guilty.

Pierrepont introduced the bizarre idea that if the jury did not convict Surratt, Washington would no longer be the capital of the nation, for "every such man of all things wants to be able, at the top of his voice, to say.... 'You see it is just as I told you. You cannot get justice in the city of Washington; a jury of the city of Washington refuses even to find guilty the assassin of the President, who is overwhelmingly proved to be guilty.'"

Dragging on extensively over the testimony, often quoting it from the record, Pierrepont sought to review what he considered the most important points. However, at least once, he seemed to damage his own case: "the testimony of Mr. John M. Lloyd. Mr. Bradley, if I remember correctly, charged him with being a liar, and in the conspiracy. He also charged him, with being a drunkard. I believe he drinks; I have no doubt about that." Pierrepont maintained that Lloyd lied in order "to shield her" [Mrs. Surratt], since by associating himself with her some of his own guilt might rub off onto her. A very curious tactic, using your own witness to protect the other side: "He would have concealed every important fact in this case if he could have done it. I believe no man rejoiced more at this murder than he [Lloyd]. I believe that no man would have assisted in the murder sooner than he, and I agree with Mr. Bradley that he was a party knowing to this crime, and believing himself implicated, made every effort to conceal it."

After thus destroying the reputation and credibility of Lloyd, one of the more important witnesses at both trials, Pierrepont asked the jury to consider Lloyd's testimony about Mrs. Surratt's telling him to get the "shooting irons" ready to be true, helping to establish her son's connection with the conspiracy and therefore guilt. If the jurors were able to follow this argument they must have thought it strange and unreasonable. Pierrepont went on and on, reviewing what had already been covered by Carrington. One can imagine the thoughts of the jurors as they sat, hour after hour. When Pierrepont had finally finished, the defense lawyers expressed the desire to comment on the prosecutors' lengthy statements. Judge Fisher would not accept any further statements, saying that if misstatements had been made, the defense could address them to the court and he would see that the jury was informed.[10]

On Wednesday, August 7, 1867, all testimony having been heard and the summations of the counsels for the prosecution and defense concluded, the judge presented the case to the jury to decide. Mr. Merrick was able to get a review of certain testimony into the record, and at last all that remained was the judge's charge to the jury. Ordinarily, the judge would explain to the jury certain points of the law they needed to consider and advise them of any special circumstances that might affect their decision. But Judge Fisher went beyond that—well beyond. After referring to the leader of the Confederate army as "the traitor Lee," he characterized the crime in these inflammatory terms:

[T]he executive head of this great nation, the Commander-in-Chief of your army and navy, by the most foul and wicked conspiracy the record of which has ever stained the pages of history, was stricken down at the hands of the assassin John Wilkes Booth, in the metropolis of the republic, and under the very shadow of its Capitol.

Why should the people be less proud or less regardful of the life of a ruler selected by themselves, from

The jury at John Surratt's trial, standing left to right: William W. Berth, B.E. Gittings, C.G. Schneider, William McLean, Columbus Alexander, James Y. Davis. Sitting: Benjamin F. Morell, George A. Bohrer, Thomas Berry, J. Russell Barr, Robert Ball, William B. Todd (Library of Congress).

> among themselves, than they would be of the life of him who claimed to rule over them of his own light? When this question can be sensibly answered, I shall be willing to admit that the life of a President is less worth preserving than that of a king, and that to destroy the life of a President is a crime of less atrocity than to merely desire the death of a prince; but not till then; nor do I believe will you.

He argued for the rightness of the military commission that had tried and punished eight people, depriving them of many of their rights through the substitution of military law for civil, and had executed four of them, including a woman, the mother of the defendant in the later trial:

> The right of self-defense needs not to be inscribed upon parchment, either for individuals or for sovereign states ... [and] these powers are but the incidents of sovereignty, requiring no warrant in written governmental charters; they are derived from the common law of nations, and are coexistent with sovereignty.
>
> It is not alleged in the present indictment that Abraham Lincoln was a reasonable creature [a creature capable of reason], nor has any proof been adduced to show it; and yet we take cognizance of the fact that at the time of his murder he was the President of the United States, because it is something known to every man, woman, and child in the country capable of knowing anything; and, taking such judicial cognizance of it, it need neither be alleged in the indictment nor proved by witnesses.

Judge Fisher, in his very lengthy charge, made many references to religion, including quotations from the Bible. This was much less problematical in the nineteenth century than it might be today, but it is clear the judge was suggesting that Surratt deserved not only the full weight of the law upon him but also the wrath of Heaven as well. After much further discussion of points of law and revision of the testimony, he eliminated any doubt that might have existed that his judgment was entirely on the side of the prosecution:

> In giving these matters your attention you will not fail to remember that flight from the scene of crime, the fabrication of false accounts and contradictory statements, the concealment of instruments of violence, are all circumstances strongly indicative of guilt. You will further bear in mind that a confession of crime, when freely and fairly made, the body of the crime being proved, (which is, in this case, the fact of murder,) is one of the surest proofs of guilt, because it is the testimony of the Omniscient speaking through the conscience of the culprit.
>
> If John H. Surratt, in the honest and intelligent conviction of your judgment and consciences, is not guilty, so pronounce him by your verdict, thus giving a lesson of assurance that a court of justice is the asylum of innocence. On the contrary, if guilty, pronounce him guilty, and thus by your verdict furnish a guarantee of protection to the intended victims of guilt, and a testimonial to the country and the world that the District of Columbia, set apart by the Constitution of the United States as the theatre for the exercise of federal power, gives the judicial guarantees essential to the protection of the persons of the public servants commissioned by the people of the nation to do their work, safe and sacred from the presence of unpunished assassins within its borders.

The bailiffs, William S. Ross and Robert Hughes, escorted the jury to the jury room to begin their deliberations.

On Saturday, August 10, 1867, at one o'clock in the afternoon, the jurors returned to the courtroom. The clerk asked them, "Gentlemen of the jury, have you agreed on a verdict?" The foreman, W.B. Todd (1810–?), replied that they had not. A note from the jury to the court was then read:

> To the Hon. George P. Fisher, Judge of the Criminal Court:
>
> Sir: The jury in the case of the *United States vs. John H. Surratt* most respectfully state that they stand precisely now as when they first balloted upon entering the room, nearly equally divided, and they are firmly convinced that they cannot possibly make a verdict. We deem it our duty to the court, to the country, and in view of the condition of our private affairs and situation of our families, and in view of the fact that the health of several of our number is becoming seriously impaired under the protracted confinement, and to make this statement, and to ask your honor to dismiss us at once.
>
> Most respectfully submitted:
>
> > William B. Todd
> > Robert Ball
> > J. Russell Barr
> > Thomas Berry
> > George A. Bohrer
> > C.G. Schneider
> > James Y. Davis
> > Columbus Alexander
> > William McLean
> > Benjamin F. Morell
> > B.E. Gittings
> > William W. Berth

Judge Fisher inquired whether the attorneys for the prosecution and defense had anything to say about the jury's statement. Bradley replied that the prisoner, John Surratt, must protest that to dismiss the jury would be against his will. Carrington stated that the matter was up to the judge. Noting that the jury had requested dismissal due to their inability to reach a verdict and there seemed no likelihood that they would agree, Judge Fisher declared them dismissed.

The votes of the jurors were as follows: For conviction: Todd, Barr, Schneider, McLean.

For acquittal: Davis, Berry, Ball, Bohrer, Alexander, Morell, Gittings, Berth. This tally of the jurors remained the same throughout their deliberations. The jury had reached an impasse, eight voting to acquit Surratt and four voting to convict him. It has been supposed, as seven of the eight voting to acquit had been born in southern states and all of those voting to convict were northern born, that it was a biased jury. There is no way to know if this was so or to what extent it may have been so, but in the end a decision was made. Surratt had not been acquitted. The judge dismissed the jury, not the charges against Surratt. The marshal led him back to his jail cell.

Passions had been aroused among more than just the jurors. Judge Fisher stated that during the course of the trial the elder Joseph Bradley had made a threat against the judge. As a consequence, Fisher ordered Bradley "be stricken from the rolls of attorneys practicing in this court." Bradley protested, but Fisher rose and left the courtroom. Bradley followed Fisher, handing him a note that seemed to be a challenge to a duel. Fisher ignored the note. Bradley the younger caught up to Judge Fisher and apparently managed to cool down the judge's ruffled feathers. They even shook hands before parting.[11] Bradley appealed Fisher's charge of contempt to the District Supreme Court, which consisted of three judges, David Kellogg Cartter (1812–1887), Abram B. Olin (1808–1879), and Andrew B. Wylie (1814–1905), who ruled against him. Bradley then took his case to the United States Supreme Court, which ruled that the District Supreme Court had "no power to disbar an attorney for contempt."

It was reported in the newspapers that "if the prisoner [Surratt] had been indicted for conspiracy to murder they would have unanimously convicted him." The failure to establish that Surratt was in Washington at the time of the murder prevented the jury's being able to agree that he was "present aiding and abetting the murder" of the president. John Surratt had not been convicted, but neither had he been acquitted. His trial was over, but he was not a free man. He had been arrested on November 7, 1866, in Italy. The following day he escaped and was at large until his arrest in Egypt on November 23. His trial had commenced on June 10, 1867, and ended August 10, 1867. He was still in jail while lawyers on both sides of his case planned their strategy. Edward Carrington decided that he might be able to get a conviction of Surratt for treason. He sought the opinion of Orville Hickman Browning (1806–1881), whom President Johnson had appointed to his cabinet as secretary of the interior in 1866. Although a friend of Lincoln's, Browning found himself more in agreement with Johnson opposing the Radical Republicans, who sought a harsh punishment for the defeated South. Browning neither encouraged nor discouraged Carrington.

The murder charge was declared nolle prosequi, which means to be unwilling to pursue the charge. Carrington obtained two treason indictments against Surratt from two different grand juries. The first indictment, No. 5920, was voted on June 18, 1868. Because the date of the crime was April 15, 1865, Judge Fisher ruled that the two-year statute of limitations for the District of Columbia had expired. He therefore dismissed the case. Carrington appealed to the Supreme Court of the District of Columbia. The decision, delivered by Justice Olin, on November 14, 1868, stated the following:

> The Government has no right in a criminal case to an appeal or writ of error when judgment has been rendered in favor of the prisoner.... The accused was indicted under the second section of the act of July, 1862, for engaging in the rebellion, by conspiring to abduct or murder the President of the United States on or about the 6th day of March, 1865. The indictment was found on the 18th of June, 1868. The accused was arraigned, and in the first instance pleaded "not guilty," but was subsequently allowed to withdraw that plea when he interposed the special plea of a pardon growing out of the President's proclamation of amnesty, as he claimed. To that plea a demurrer [the formal mode of disputing the sufficiency in law of the pleading of the other side] was entered on the part of the United States....

> The defect relied on in the indictment ... arose under the statute of limitations, which required an indictment of this description to be found within two years after the commission of the offence....
>
> We think that, in the absence of any statute, the United States cannot bring up by writ of error or appeal a cause where final judgment has been given.

The second indictment, No. 6594, came before the grand jury the following day, November 5, 1868. The words "true bill" on the indictment were crossed out by the jury foreman, who wrote "ignoramus," meaning to ignore it. With that action, taken in recognition of the other indictment being dismissed, the United States government's legal proceedings against John Harrison Surratt, Jr., were ended.

Richard Merrick questioned the court and was told by the judges that the defendant was discharged. Friends of Surratt crowded around him, congratulating him. Carrington sought to have Surratt held while a new indictment was prepared. The court replied that the district attorney could apply to another grand jury for another indictment, but as the crime had occurred more than two years before he could not be prosecuted. Carrington began to speak but was interrupted by Judge Wylie, who said that the court had announced its ruling and Carrington need not say anything more. Doubt was expressed by newspaper reporters that no further action was likely in the Surratt case since so much money had already been spent. Horace Greeley (1811–1872) expressed his opinions in an editorial: "As was expected, the trial of John Surratt has ended as we expected, in a postponement of the question. From the first it was conducted with little dignity or force, and has been for weeks one of those dragging bores—news without news—which at once interest and weary the public. The Government will, we presume, order a new trial, and in that case the court may profit by the errors of that just closed. The counsel will not be again allowed to bully either the judge or witnesses." Another reporter concentrated on the jury:

> A curious fact about the Surratt jury has just come to light. It is stated by one of them that from the first moment they were locked up together between the adjournments each day they were divided in their sentiments about the prisoner, eight favoring and four condemning. While the arguments of the counsel for the defense were going on, these eight continually sneered at Judge Pierrepont and Attorney Carrington in their rooms, and when they were locked up to find a verdict, they balloted, the result being eight votes for acquittal and four for conviction. Each side tried to convince the other, but without success to either. Then one of the jurors proposed three propositions, and asked that a vote be taken on them separately. These were, first, that Lincoln was assassinated; second, that the assassination was the result of a conspiracy; and third, that Surratt was in that conspiracy. Upon the first two propositions the vote was unanimous, but upon the latter the eight favoring acquittal refused under any circumstances to vote. These same men, however, tried to induce the four to pledge their word that nothing which took place in the jury room should be divulged, especially the votes. The other four, however, would not agree to this.

The passions aroused by the military trial of 1865 were still simmering three years later, as suggested by this article:

> The motive of this trial was not the vindication of justice, but the vindication of the government and its famous Military Commission. The prisoner had not, therefore, the ordinary chances of a person on trial for his life. His acquittal would have been a condemnation of the government. If this prisoner could be convicted by an ordinary court of justice, the impression meant to be given by the country was that the military commission, though perhaps irregular, had not violated substantial justice, since the result was precisely similar to what took place in an ordinary tribunal, in a case almost identical, and resting on much of the same evidence.... [T]he trial has failed to accomplish its object. Instead of proving that a military tribunal is as safe a tribunal for persons accused as a jury, it proves the reverse.... It is clear, therefore, that Mrs. Surratt and the others had not the chances which the law would have given them. That being the case, no matter whether they were innocent or guilty, they were murdered. Any life taken without warrant of law is murder.

District Attorney Carrington did not give up with the dismissal of John Surratt's first trial. As late as June 1868, he was still looking for a way to obtain a conviction for Surratt:

> Judge [Andrew B.] Wylie, I am well satisfied, will rule that in order to convict the prisoner of murder the jury must be satisfied from the evidence that at the time the murder was committed the prisoner was near enough to render physical assistance if called upon....
>
> We have no statute in the District of Columbia abolishing the old common law distinction between principals and accessories....
>
> I have no hope of securing his [Sgt. Dye's] attendance at the next term....
>
> My opinion is that it would be best to indict the prisoner for conspiracy and enter a nolle persequi to the present indictment, which charges him with murder.

The trial was over. Even though it had ended in a manner not approved of by Surratt and his lawyers it was, nevertheless, over. The cost of the trial was reported by the press. Jurors had been paid $2 each per day, beginning when they were empanelled. The cost of boarding in hotels by jurors had been paid by the government. Hiring carriages and omnibuses for the jurors totaled $730. Witnesses had been paid a total of $11,964.51—$1.25 per day and $0.05 per mile travel allowance. Henri B. Ste. Marie had been paid $668.15, Dr. McMillan had been paid $343.80, and Weichmann had been paid $96.30. The press reported that "the whole expense of the trial cannot fall short of $100,000, if it does not largely exceed that amount."

John H. Surratt was admitted to bail in the sum of $20,000 on June 22, 1868, and required to appear in court on June 29, 1868. The session of the District of Columbia Supreme Court resumed pursuant to adjournment. Present *The United States versus John H. Surratt*, Criminal Court No. 5920, were Chief Justice Cartter and Justices Olin and Wylie: "And now comes here as well as the United States by the District Attorney as the defendant by his attorney, Mr. Merrick, whereupon it is considered by the Court that the appeal prosecuted by the United States from the judgment of the Criminal Court be and the same is hereby dismissed."

For engaging in the Rebellion—the indictment of June 18, 1868—Surratt was arraigned and pleaded not guilty on June 22. This indictment was marked "ignoramus"—to be ignored—on January 4, 1869. At long last, John Surratt was a free man.[12]

11

A Long Twilight

Although John Surratt was free, and the charges against him now no longer a danger, he still had to face serious problems and possibilities. Money, as usual, was a continuing problem. Even while the trial had been going on there were legal expenses pressing upon him and his family. Even before the last of the legal moves against him sputtered out, John, aided by his sister, Anna, worked on a translation from the French of *The Life, Labors and Times of Christopher Columbus*, by Alphonse de Lamartine (1790–1869). Lamartine was one of the early romantics, subjectively presenting his ideas about nature, religion, and love. Although he was very well known in his time as a writer of poetry and prose as well as a statesman of distinction, the Columbus book must have been one of his lesser works, as it is quite forgotten today. A newspaper account offers little additional information on the book: "Since last November [1867], he [Surratt] has been busily engaged in helping his sister, Miss Anna Surratt, in the translation of Lamruline's last great literary production, "The Life, Labors and Times of Christopher Columbus," the only work of the kind ever published. The manuscript is nearly ready for the printer, and those who have examined the translation and read the original pronounced the work well done. The style of the author has been admirably followed, and this historical work cannot fail to be acceptable to the American public." In spite of this praise, the book, if it was in fact published, seems to have vanished, even from the Library of Congress.

John and Anna were slightly more successful selling photographs of John wearing his Zouave uniform. Others were seeking to profit from John Surratt's celebrity. Even before his capture and trial, books began to appear about him. In 1866 a volume was published entitled *Private Journal and Diary of John H. Surratt the Conspirator*, edited and arranged by Dion Haco, Esq., author of *Booth the Assassin, The War Novels: The Lives of Grant, Sherman, Sheridan, Lincoln, Butler*, and *Grant and His Generals* (New York: Frederic A. Brady, 22 Ann Street near Nassau, Price: 25 cents). Leading authorities on the Lincoln assassination have denounced the Haco book. James O. Hall (1912–2007) called it "the work of a hack writer, using readily available sources such as trial records and newspaper accounts. In short, it is a fabrication of the 'penny dreadful' variety." John C. Brennan (1908–1996) denounced it as "a complete forgery and fabrication produced by a diabolical, money-mad, two-bit liar of the vilest hue." A somewhat more reputable book appeared at the conclusion of the trial: *Life, Trial, and Adventures of John H. Surratt, the Conspirator*, without an author or editor listed. This one was more carefully written, though it also made extensive use of newspaper accounts and the trial record.[1]

While John was in custody and during the trial, his sister, Anna, was forced to deal with creditors. Mary Surratt had not been able to pay her husband's debts, and both her trial and John's trial involved legal expenses. The property of the Surratt family represented the only things of real value, but when Anna could not pay all the debts, the property was seized and sold at a loss. Anna could not manage all of this, and on September 1, 1865, she turned over the legal affairs to Edward W. Bett. The tavern in Surrattsville was rented to Edward Roby for $550 a year. By November 1865, the house on H Street in Washington was taken over to settle a debt of $162.08, which had gone unpaid since 1852. This sale was ratified two years later.[2]

While these legal and financial proceedings were taking place, Isaac D. Surratt returned home. He had not been seen by his family since the spring of 1861, when he went south to join the Confederate army. Isaac had joined the Texas 33rd Cavalry Regiment at San Antonio and served in Capt. Richmond Taylor's Company, Duff's Texas Partisan Corps. Colonel James Duff commanded what had been the 14th Cavalry Battalion, which increased in size to become a regiment in 1863. The regiment had patrolled west Texas, as well as northern New Mexico and Arizona. Isaac became the acting quartermaster sergeant in August 1864. The 33rd Cavalry Regiment was surrendered on May 26, 1865, as part of the forces of General Edmund Kirby Smith (1824–1893), the last Confederate army to surrender. In a message dated October 19, 1865, Major General Philip H. Sheridan (1831–1888) wrote to Secretary Stanton the following warning:

Anna Surratt, John's sister, in middle age (Surratt House Museum/MNCPPC, Clinton, Maryland).

> Isaac Surratt, another son of Mrs. Surratt, left Monterey, Mexico some three or four weeks ago to assassinate the President [Andrew Johnson]. This resolution was taken after he heard of the execution of his mother, and the rebels at that place made up a purse for him. The young man was very frantic when he left Monterey some four weeks ago, traveling toward the Rio Grande on horseback.
> Isaac Surratt is about thirty-two years of age [born in 1841, making him 24 in 1865], olive complexion, five feet nine or ten inches in height, full beard, dark eyes, black curly hair, and good looking. Was a member of Duff's regiment of cavalry.

If this warning was accurate, Isaac must have cooled down by the time he returned home, for there is no record of an attempt being made on President Johnson's life or of Isaac's being arrested and tried for such a thing. It is possible that he was only boasting to his friends or that the friends in Mexico imagined he was serious about his threat against the president. Isaac arrived in Washington in 1866. He attended at least some sessions of John's trial.[3]

The tavern at Surrattsville and the surrounding property was sold after legal action on March 11, 1869, for $3,500, with the debts owed to George H. Calvert, Jr., along with

Private Journal & Diary of John H. Surratt, the Conspirator (F.A. Brady, 22 Ann Street, New York), one of several unauthorized biographies of Surratt that appeared soon after his trial.

other creditors, never being fully repaid. Even the name of the town of Surrattsville was changed, first to Robystown after the new postmaster, Andrew V. Roby, who was appointed November 17, 1863, the name Robystown becoming official on May 3, 1865. Then it was changed to its present-day name of Clinton on October 10, 1878.

The need for money, affecting the whole Surratt family, remained acute for several years. Virtually all the property was sold, and even that did not produce enough money to satisfy the family's creditors. The Surratt brothers and their sister moved to Baltimore. We know from a letter John wrote to Major William Norris (1820–1896), former head of the Confederate signal corps, that John Surratt had been in the "Produce and General Commission" business at 80 Light Street, Baltimore. The letter is dated June 24, 1869, and states that John had returned from South America around the preceding April, having spent about six months there. He apologized for not writing before, claiming to have been busy starting his new business. He was still short of funds, for he asked Norris for financial help. No explanation was made for how he could finance a trip to South America or why, exactly, he was there. An indirect reference to his improving health is made, so it is possible that bad health was the reason for the trip. There is no information about whether Norris helped John or if anyone else did, though John was looking for assistance among former Confederates and Southern sympathizers, a search that would eventually pay off.[4]

Anna Surratt, who had tried to save her mother's life and whose agonized cries had been heard by all those attending the execution, continued her demonstration of family loyalty to give her mother's remains a decent burial. She wrote to President Johnson:

> His Excellency the President of the United States:
>
> The undersigned most earnestly and respectfully address your Excellency on a matter which has been for more than three years a source of great affliction. She seeks the privilege of removing the remains of her deceased mother, to have them interred in consecrated ground.
>
> She fondly hopes that your Excellency will not allow your authority in the premises to expire without granting this request, prompted only by filial love and devotion to the memory of her dear mother.
>
> Annie E. Surratt
>
> [The letter was endorsed.]
>
> Anne E. Surratt asks authority to remove the remains of her deceased mother.
>
> Received Feb. 4, 1869.
>
> The Honorable Secretary of War will cause to be delivered to Annie E. Surratt the remains of her mother, Mary E. Surratt, for the purpose set forth in the within communication.
>
> Andrew Johnson

Making the arrangements on behalf of Anna was the Reverend Jacob. A. Walter, pastor of St. Patrick's Church in Washington, D.C., and the same man who had ministered to Mrs. Surratt during her imprisonment and execution.

Isaac D. Surratt, John's older brother, in middle age (Surratt House Museum/ MNCPPC, Clinton, Maryland).

On February 9, 1869, the Rev. Walter delivered the president's order to General George D. Ramsay (1802–1882), commandant of the Washington Arsenal, where the trial and execution had been held. The remains of George Atzerodt, David Herold, Lewis Powell, and Mary Surratt had been buried close to the scaffold upon which they had been executed. When the original arsenal was torn down in 1867, the remains were removed to a warehouse known only as No. 1, in new graves beneath the warehouse floor stones, with Mrs. Surratt's coffin placed next to the building's north wall. A crew of workmen supervised by a Mr. Tatspaugh disinterred the coffin and it was placed in the care of Richard Harvey, undertaker, of the firm of Messrs. Harvey and Marr, 335 F St., Washington. Witnesses present besides the workmen were William P. Tonry, Anna's fiancé, Major Hill (USA), and Harvey. Newspaper accounts described the scene:

> The box containing the remains was of rough pine boards. Upon the top was a strip of wood, painted white, with the name "Mrs. Surratt" painted upon it in black letters. The box was opened, and although the body was somewhat decomposed, it was not offensive. The dress, gaiters and black silk bow at the neck were all in a perfect state of preservation. The hair was also perfectly preserved, and did not seem to have been disarranged in the least. A steel arrow pin, which Annie Surratt fastened the bow about her mother's neck just before she was led to execution, was also in place. A lock of the hair was clipped off for Annie Surratt at her own request.
>
> The remains were placed in a new casket and taken to Mount Olivet Catholic Cemetery, where they were buried, in lot 31, section F, at the junction of Olivet and St. Dominick avenues, near the cemetery's northwest corner, with a ceremony conducted by Father Walter, and attended only by Anna, her brother Isaac, and a few close friends: Mrs. Cantatori, a niece of former President John Tyler [1790–1862], Honora Fitzpatrick, who was boarding at Mrs. Surratt's house in Washington at the time of the assassination, Rev. Father J.J. Kean, Assistant Pastor at St. Patrick's Church, Miss McCalla, Mrs. J.F. Ellis, Mrs. Thomas Berry, Mrs. Kelly, Mrs. William L. Wall, Mrs. T.A. Stephens, Mr. Kelleher, Mr. Tonry, Mr. Drane, and others.

Newspaper accounts stated that Anna planned to move to Baltimore, "where she ha[d] many friends," and become a schoolteacher. The absence of John Surratt was explained as his having gone to South America, "whither he went some time ago for the benefit of his health." Mrs. Surratt's original coffin was apparently chopped up into fragments and distributed to memento seekers. Father Walter took charge of the glass bottle containing a note with Mrs. Surratt's name, which had been put in the original coffin.[5]

Around this time, John's sister married. An account of the wedding appeared in newspapers:

Marriage of Miss Annie Surratt

Washington, June 17 [1869]

Miss Annie Surratt was married today at St. Patrick's Church [in Washington] to Mr. William P. Tonry, a chemist employed in the Surgeon General's office. The ceremony, which was very private, was conducted by Rev. Father [Jacob Ambrose] Walter [1827–1894], assisted by Rev. J.J. Kane.

The happy couple started immediately on a bridal tour north. The bride appeared in better health than she has enjoyed for years. It was the desire of the parties that the marriage should be strictly private, and the usual publication of the bans was for this reason dispensed by Archbishop Spalding. There were no bridesmaids or groomsmen. The bride was attended by her brother Isaac, while John H. Surratt occupied a seat in a pew in front of the altar. These and a few intimate acquaintances of the bridal party were the only witnesses to the nuptial ceremony.

Anna's husband was a "chemist" named William P. Tonry (1840–1905). Born in Sligo, Ireland, he came to Boston in 1848. After early schooling in Boston, he came to Maryland around 1856 and attended St. Charles College in Howard County. Attending Georgetown College (now Georgetown University), he was appointed adjunct professor of chemistry in 1865. In 1866, Tonry became assistant chemist for the surgeon general of the U.S. Army. After his marriage to Anna Surratt, Tonry was discharged by special order dated June 21, 1869. A newspaper article fills in the background on Tonry's dismissal: "It appears that Mr. Tonry, late a chemist in the Surgeon General's office ... was notified shortly before his marriage that he would be sent to the Northwest to take solar observations during the coming eclipse in August [1869]. In fact, he had made preparations to go, and was greatly surprised when on return from a brief honeymoon trip he was presented with a letter of dismissal, assigning no cause whatever therefore. Mr. Tonry and his friends are firm in the belief that he was certainly removed because of his marriage with Miss Surratt." The Tonrys traveled around the United States, looking for somewhere to settle. Returning to Baltimore, Tonry established a chemistry laboratory there and soon won a reputation as being highly capable. He was awarded an honorary degree of doctor of philosophy from Georgetown College.

William P. Tonry and Anna Surratt Tonry had five children: William S. Tonry (c. 1870–1944); Albert S. Tonry (c. 1872–?); Reginald I. Tonry (1874–1946); Charles S. Tonry (c. 1876–?); and Catherine Tonry, who was born in 1879 and died after just three months.[6]

A list of schoolteachers in the Montgomery County, Maryland, public school system states that "Surratt, John H.," taught school there from "Nov. 1870 to Feb. 1873." Various sources indicate that John Surratt taught school at Rockville, Maryland, beginning in the later part of 1870. However, Father Alfred Isacsson (1932–2011) stated:

After being set free, John Surratt was given a position between 1870 and 1872 as a teacher in St. Joseph's School at Emmitsburg [Maryland] (Green and Gettysburg Streets) by a sympathetic pastor. The school used Fireman's Hall located opposite the church. He was a poor teacher who rattled his classes and resorted to physical punishment and French profanity to preserve order. Despite this conduct, Surratt was remembered, in Emmitsburg as loving young children and attending local dances.

Surratt was fond of discussing and debating topics of the day with the men who were accustomed to gathering in the local drug store. He was remembered as a good shot in local contests using live pigeons, clay pigeons and glass balls.

Rockville is about forty miles south of Emmitsburg—rather far from Baltimore to commute back and forth in those days. It is possible that he taught in each location at different parts of the same year. The sources of information for both towns are reliable. A newspaper article from 1919 repeats the story of Surratt's teaching school in the Rockville area at a place called the "Upper School" "A few hundred yards west of the site of the school and on the south side of School House Lane is an old frame house set in a shady garden.... Here it was that John Surratt boarded while a teacher at the "Upper School," and [Conrad Franklin] Maught was one of his pupils.... Mr. Maught has a very clear remembrance of John Surratt, and says he was a good teacher, a good man, and [was] affectionately remembered by all the people who took their lessons under his guidance."

On December 6, 1870, John Surratt delivered a lecture at the courthouse in Rockville, Maryland, about twenty miles northwest of Washington, D.C. His financial problems still a long way from being resolved, he spoke on the one subject which he knew the public would pay to hear. A reporter from the *Washington Evening Star* attended and took down the lecture in shorthand. The lecture was published in the paper the following day:

A Remarkable Lecture! John H. Surratt Tells His Story.

A vivid narrative—His story of the Abduction Plot—Surratt's Experience with J. Wilkes Booth—Booth Hints of the Murder of Lincoln—the Other Conspirators Threaten to Withdraw—The Assassination—Surratt's Escape to Canada—He Implicates Weichmann in the Assassination Plot—He Denounces Weichmann, Judge Fisher, and Edwin M. Stanton—"John Harrison"—Surratt and the Confederate Government—Why Surratt Did Not Come to the Aid of his Mother.

[The article described Surratt's actions from the time his trial.]

[H]e has spent a portion of his time in Lower Maryland, been in the commission business in Baltimore, and now has turned up a school teacher in Rockville, where he has availed himself of leisure hours to prepare, in the shape of a lecture, a history of the events which brought him so prominently before the public....

The village looked deserted of everything save horses and empty vehicles of all kinds....

At 7 o'clock Surratt entered and passed up the side platform in unceremonious style to the judge's desk. He was unattended, wore a mixed grey suit, and with the exception of having grown much stouter, looks the same as during the trial here [in Washington]. He has rather a mild and pleasant face, and a decidedly intellectual head; and does not look like the sort of stuff for a performer of desperate deeds.

On his entrance the Rockville Comet Band in attendance struck up a lively air. Surratt then threw off his overcoat, revealing a manuscript book, which he drew from under his arm and laid open on the desk before him. He referred to it but little, however, having his lecture well in his memory. Without any introduction he was on, speaking very rapidly but distinctly for an hour and a quarter. He has a good voice and easy delivery, to which he occasionally added great warmth of feeling, particularly when he referred to his mother, and his alleged desertion of her in her darkest hour.

He opened the lecture with an explanation: "In presenting this lecture before the public I do it in no spirit of self-justification. In a trial of sixty-one days I made my defense to the world, and I have no need or desire to rehearse it; nor do I appear for self glorification. On the contrary, I dislike notoriety, and leave my solitude and obscurity unwillingly." He explained that it was the need of money which had prompted him to embark on a lecturing career. Describing little of his early life, he did state that he met Booth "in the fall of 1864" and not at Christmastime, as Weichmann had stated. As to his motive, he related how Booth proposed to kidnap Lincoln and exchange him for Confederate prisoners in Northern camps: "I was led on by a sincere desire to assist the South in gaining her independence. I had no hesitation in taking part in anything honorable that might tend towards the accomplishment of that object." Upon stating this, it was reported that Surratt received "tremendous applause." We must remember that the majority of Marylanders during the Civil War had been sympathetic to the Southern cause, with a number of them going south and serving with the rebels. This explains Surratt's acceptance in Maryland and his being able to find employment there. He added this firm statement, which, it was reported, caused a "sensation": "Such a thing as the assassination of Mr. Lincoln I never heard spoken of by any of the party [of conspirators]. Never." Surratt made sure to deny any help from the Confederate government "in any shape or form," although he did mention having been in Richmond just before it fell to the Union and having received "$200 in gold with which to pay my way to Canada."

Surratt's lecture is remarkable both in what he chose to reveal and what he chose to conceal. He mentioned, for instance, that following their unsuccessful attempt to abduct Lincoln in mid–March, "a separation finally took place, and I never saw any of the party [of Booth conspirators] except one, and that was when I was on my way from Richmond to Canada.... I succeeded in reaching Washington safely, and in passing up Seventh Street met one of our party." The identity of "one of our party" causes one to speculate. Arnold and O'Laughlen left Washington on March 20, with Powell following soon after. Booth took the afternoon train from Washington to Baltimore on April 1. That left only Herold or Atzerodt. Surratt continued: "I went to a hotel and stopped over that night, as a detective had been to my house inquiring of the servant my whereabouts."

Neither Herold nor Atzerodt were living at Mrs. Surratt's house in Washington. Surratt changed some of his gold for greenbacks through Surratt House resident John T. Holohan. He could have known about the detective and so could Weichmann. But neither of those two men had held meetings with the other conspirators. Or had they? As Weichmann had testified against both Mrs. Surratt at the first trial, and again at the trial of John Surratt against his former close friend, John had no compunction in stating openly in his lecture, "I proclaim it here and before the world that Louis J. Weichmann was a party to the plan to abduct President Lincoln. He had been told all about it, and was constantly importuning me to let him become an active member." His anger at Weichmann could explain his wanting to blacken Weichmann's name, but it is possible that there was some truth in his statement.

Surratt discussed his adventure in Canada, including his tight escapes from detectives. He mentioned "a friend" he told about his connection with Booth and who advised him and helped him. Although he did not name his "friend," there can be little doubt that it was General Edwin G. Lee, the new Confederate commissioner in Canada who had replaced Jacob Thompson only days before Surratt's arrival in Montreal. Later in the lecture Surratt says that his "friend" called him "Charley." General Lee used the name "Charley Armstrong" in his diary, and there can be no doubt that he is referring to John Surratt. His having received help from Lee shows the untruthfulness of Surratt's earlier statement that he received no help from the Confederates except for the $200 from Benjamin.

He ended his lecture with his decision to go to Europe. As we have seen, there is a good deal of information about that we would wish to have. He hinted that he would tell more of his story in later lectures. The newspaper story remarked on this, too: "Really the serious defect in the Surratt lecture was not what he said, but what he failed to say ... [and] it will be noticed that throughout his lecture he is silent in regard to what part she [Mrs. Surratt] took or did not take in the plottings of the conspirators." Upon the conclusion of the lecture, the band played "Dixie," and Surratt socialized among the audience members, "not separating till a late hour, during which time Surratt was quite a lion among the ladies present."[7]

His lecture having been well received in Rockville, Surratt immediately headed for New York City. He spoke at the Cooper Institute on December 9, 1870, to an audience of about 150. Judging from the newspaper reports, it was basically the same lecture he had delivered in Rockville. The citizens of New York apparently gave him a cooler reception than had those of Rockville, stating that he was "with one or two slight occasions of applause, listened to quietly by the small audience."

The next stop on the lecture tour was Baltimore, where he spoke at Concordia Opera House on December 29, 1870: "There was but a slim audience present for so large a hall—about 250 persons—but the intense cold of the night was not favorable to a large attendance.... When he came upon the stage he was received with applause." He seems to have been stung by the publicity he had received so far and began his lecture with a denunciation of the press: "I have often heard of an olden time when every one was bound, as a matter of course, to swallow down with unquestioning belief whatever he saw in print, when every petty scribbler who held the types might be a little despot, swaying public opinion, controlling public action, and making and unmaking reputations at will. Were such the condition of things now it is not at all likely that, after the flood of slander lately poured out against me by a portion of the press, either I could have the hardihood to appear again in public, or you would have the independence to come and hear me."

After a few more hard words, he proceeded to deliver his lecture. Here he told his audience that he was preparing two additional lectures that would relate his entire story.[8] As soon as he had finished his lecture, a United States deputy marshal arrested Surratt "upon the charge of being a retail dealer in leaf tobacco, in this city [Baltimore] without having paid the special tax." They left by the rear door, and many who had attended the lecture knew nothing of the arrest until reading of it in the next day's paper. Surratt was accompanied by William Tonry, his brother-in-law, and by his agent. In a carriage, they went first to his boardinghouse on Saratoga Street and then to the commissioner's office. The warrant had been issued upon information furnished by the deputy collector. Surratt told the commissioner that he had complied with the internal revenue laws during the two years he had been in business in Baltimore [1868–1870]. He told the commissioner he had never been a retail dealer in tobacco and questioned his having been arrested at night, when it was difficult to raise bail. Surratt got word to a lawyer, John B. Tidy, Jr., of the firm of Barnett and Tidy, who advised him to waive an examination and post bail of $1,500, which was posted by Tidy. Surratt's friends expressed the opinion that the arrest was a scheme to prevent him from going on to Washington, where he was scheduled to present his lecture.

Surratt had advertised that he would present his lecture in Washington on the night of December 30, 1870, but he ran into considerable opposition in trying to hire a hall in which to present his speech. His agent at first was able to obtain Lincoln Hall, but the managers of the hall changed their minds about having one of the conspirators speak in a hall named for their victim. He was able to secure the Odd Fellows' Hall, located on 7th and D streets, NW, and had handbills printed and distributed, confidently stating, "J. H. Surratt will most positively deliver his Lecture in Washington.... Thrilling Adventures During the Rebellion, his introduction to J. Wilkes Booth, and the Plan Arranged to kidnap, not Murder President Lincoln ... Arrest! Trial! Acquittal! ... Surratt's Account of Himself! ... Plan to Release Confederate Prisoners ... Life Among the Papal Zouaves in Rome! Arrest and Return to the United States! A Captive in Irons, Trial, Continuing Sixty-two Days and

Honorable Acquittal. Admission 50 cents." It can be seen from this announcement that Surratt was planning to make his lecture longer, including the later portions of his story not included in the lecture at Rockville. He (or whoever actually wrote the handbill) also was falsely claiming to have been acquitted at his trial. His case had been dismissed because the jury had been unable to agree on a verdict, which is not the same as being acquitted. The Washington lecture was scheduled for December 30. On December 29 the managers of the Odd Fellow's Hall withdrew their permission. The Masonic Hall likewise refused him.

Surratt's agent, Corbyn, had paid $75 to hire Lincoln Hall, but the owners revoked the permit. Corbyn then secured the Odd Fellow's Hall, but the governing board cancelled the lecture. Corbyn was advised by Father Walter of St. Patrick's Church "to persuade Surratt from appearing in public here." Corbyn next engaged Carusi's Hall. At five o'clock, December 30, Mayor M.G. Emery presented this letter:

> Mayor's Office, City Hall,
> Washington, D.C. Dec. 30, 1870.
>
> J. H. Surratt—Sir: It is announced in the papers of today, that you are to lecture this evening at Odd Fellow's Hall. Learning from various sources that there is great opposition to your returning in Washington City upon the subject proposed, and if you attempt it, fearing it may cause trouble, I would earnestly advise you officially, to desist from your purpose and withdraw your appointment to lecture.
>
> Respectfully yours,
> M.G. Emery, Mayor

A newspaper ad said the lecture would be given at Carusi's Saloon, but the sixty or so people who gathered in front of that establishment found it closed and dark. After a while, they drifted away. Surratt was located at his hotel, Seaton Hall, room 29, where he told a reporter that he had received a message from the mayor requesting that he not give his lecture due to expected trouble. Surratt spoke of possibly giving the lecture at Fredericksburg, Virginia, but that, too, failed to come about. John Surratt's career as a lecturer was over. His poor showing as a lecturer drew the following comments from one of the most popular lecturers in America, Mark Twain (1835–1910):

> To the Editor of the [New York] Tribune,
>
> Sir, John H. Surratt's manager evidently understands his business, or else Surratt is fortunate above the average of snubbed and struggling would-be lecturers—for every day the newspapers reveal to the people that the gentleman is being persecuted. I am of the lecturing guild, sir, and aware that the cheapest and the surest way to get an undesired or unknown person splendidly before the public and crowd his houses, is to get somebody to persecute him. There are other ways, but this is the surest. One of the most courted lady lecturers of the day is soaring along on a lucrative notoriety nine-tenths of which is the result of industrially supplied two-line personal items, telling how she wore her hair at Long Branch. So you see how easy it is to excite the public interest in an individual, and fill that individual's lecture halls for him. Do you not perceive that Mr. Surratt, who cannot at present induce more than a hundred people to listen to him, is on the high road to a notoriety which in a very little while will cram the largest halls in America with people eager to see the new wonder and hear him? Indeed he is on that very high road. Mr. Surratt's manager, I fancy, is deliberately procuring this persecution, and the deep old fox knows that it is exactly the sort of advertising he needs. It is a hundred thousand times more effective than commonplace commendation in the dramatic column, which makes not the least impression upon the reader. When the telegraph recently spread it over the country that Mr. Surratt had an audience of only a hundred and fifty to hear him at Cooper Institute, it was a most damaging thing. Six more such announcements, unaccompanied by any saving persecution, would have hurried the lecturer Surratt beyond the hope of resurrection; but at a lucky moment there was talk of his arrest (incited by his manager, no doubt) and next there was a story that Attorney General [Judge Advocate General] Holt once offered to save Mrs. Surratt, and set her free, if the son would take her place, and the son refused (more acute managerial intervention, no doubt), and next came the announcement that Surratt's Baltimore lecture was interfered with by his arrest on a charge of

nonpayment of a trifling tobacco tax years ago (this official persecutor being a guileless catspaw of that manager, without the shadow of a doubt); and now at last comes the announcement that the Mayor of Washington has warned Surratt against driving the people of the capital to extremities by attempting to lecture there, and immediately the meek and law-abiding Surratt takes in his sign and closes his hall (the entire thing a crowning triumph of that manager's inventive genius, without question)!

If it is desired to make John H. Surratt a prodigious success as a lecturer, and give him an income of $25,000 a year, it is only requisite that mayors, revenue officers, and hall proprietors continue to stand in front and persecute the lecturer while the ingenious manager stands behind and pulls their strings—and it is further only necessary that the telegraph people get knowledge of the said persecution (a thing which the said manager will attend to). But if it is desired that Mr. Surratt drop entirely out of the public notice in three short weeks, it is only necessary to let him alone and cease to make public mention of him. His little candle would straightway begin to burn weaker and weaker, and the cabbage head would begin to develop more and more prominently on its top, and presently the poor thing would flicker out and pass away in a film of smoke, leaving nothing behind but an evanescent stench! Am I not right![9]

John Surratt's personal life was improving at this time. On May 21, 1872, he married Mary Victorine Hunter (c. 1846–1926), daughter of Thomas Hunter (1812–1854) and Susannah Scott Key Hunter (1820–1885). John's wife was a second cousin of Francis Scott Key (1779–1843), author of the words to what became the national anthem, "The Star Spangled Banner." John and Mary were married

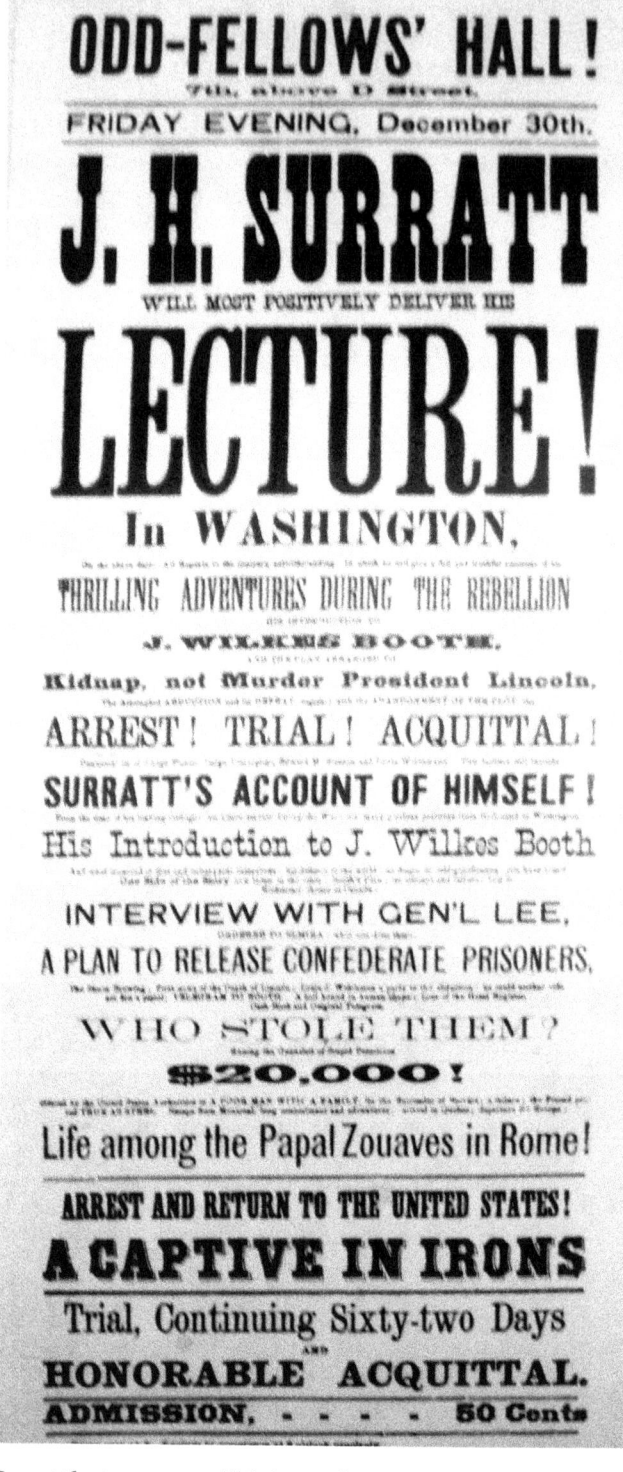

Surratt lecture poster. This is an advertising poster for Surratt's lecture in Washington, D.C., on December 30, 1867. The lecture did not take place (Library of Congress).

at St. Mary's Church in Alexandria, Virginia. Mary Victorine had grown up in Green Spring Valley and lived in upper Montgomery County, Maryland. John may have met her in Montgomery County during his school teaching days. Their seven children were:

John Harrison Surratt III (1873–1920)
William Hunter Surratt (1874–1934)
Mary Eugenia Surratt (1876–?)
Leo Jenkins Surratt (1878–?)
Susanna Scott Surratt (1882–?)
Mary Victorine Surratt (1883–1982)
Ella Key Scott Surratt (1885–1980)

There is some confusion about this period of John Surratt's life. Alexander Crosby Brown's book on the Old Bay Line states that John and Isaac Surratt "came to the [Old Bay] line in 1870," but records in the Montgomery County Historical Society state that "John H. Surratt was living in the Rockville area from about 1870 to 1875." Records of St. Mary's Catholic Church in Rockville show the birth of one of their children, John Harrison Surratt III, born March 7, 1873, and baptized May 16, 1873, and describe the parents as "John H. Surratt, of Prince George County, MD, and M. Victorine Hunter." Another child, William, was "born July 5, 1874, baptised April 8, 1875, at Great Falls, MD," and the record adds the note, "Baptised with ceremonies at the father's home in Great Falls, MD." It cannot be imagined that John Surratt was living in the Rockville area and working in Baltimore, a distance of 34 miles each way. People might travel that far today, over good roads in high-speed vehicles, but not in the mid-1870s. Another discrepancy to be noted is that Great Falls, Maryland, is not in Prince George's County but a good twenty miles upriver in Montgomery County. Also, the marriage register of St. Mary's Catholic Church, which records John's marriage to M. Victorine Hunter, gives the church's location as "Alexandria, Virginia." There certainly is more than one "St. Mary's Catholic Church," but we must try to decide what is the more likely explanation for these mixed-up dates and places.

It appears that the best evidence available indicates that Brown's date is wrong. The Montgomery County Historical Society has a list of teachers in Montgomery County "from Feb.1866 to Nov.1879," and that

Mary Victorine Hunter Surratt, wife of John H. Surratt, Jr. (Surratt House Museum/MNCPPC, Clinton, Maryland).

list includes "Surratt, John H., Nov.1870 to Feb. 1873." This would explain why he gave his first lecture in Rockville, his place of residence. He probably got teaching jobs through ex-Confederates or Southern sympathizers, as with his later employment with the Old Bay Line in Baltimore.[10] John Surratt expressed his discontent with teaching in a letter to Father Charles Constant Jolivet (1826–1903), who had given him shelter in Liverpool, during his escape:

> My greatest desire, Father Jolivet, is to leave this abominable country and go to Europe there to spend the balance of my days in peace and quiet. If I could only feel secure of something to do in France or England that would assure me of a moderate living, I would leave here in less than a week. Ah! Father Jolivet if you could only secure me some kind of employment, you would confer a favor indeed. I have been married about eleven months and am the happy father of a hearty boy.

The following year Jolivet left for South Africa and did not return to England.

John H. Surratt, Jr., with one of his daughters (Surratt House Museum/MNCPPC, Clinton, Maryland).

What John Surratt needed was employment upon which he could build a stable life. But how could he get a decent job when only a few years before he was the most famous fugitive of all time, accused of being a party to the murder of the president of the United States? His name and appearance were very well known, and reporters were keeping track of him wherever he went. Who would consider hiring such a person?

Like the answer to a prayer, enter the fascinating figure of John Moncure Robinson (1835–1893). Born in Philadelphia, Pennsylvania, on October 22, 1835, Robinson was educated at the Virginia Military Institute, the Lawrence Scientific School, and Harvard University. Having had experience with railroads, he became a colonel in the Confederate army's Corps of Engineers, serving as a staff officer to Generals Henry Alexander Wise (1806–1876), John Cabell Breckinridge (1821–1875), William Edmonston "Grumble" Jones (1824–1864), and William Wing Loring (1818–1886). Robinson built bridges and defenses for bridges and supervised the Seaboard and Roanoke Railroad. Sent to England in February 1863, he served as a purchasing agent for Virginia Railroads. After returning from England,

The Old Bay Line offices and terminal as it appeared in 1911 when John H. Surratt, Jr., was employed there. The building was torn down in 1950.

he took charge of the Richmond-Wilmington Railroad in May 1864. He was attached to General Robert Edward Lee's (1807–1870) headquarters on March 18, 1865. His final duties in the Confederate army were removing the wounded and supplies from Goldsboro, in late March 1865. When the war ended, Robinson was chief of confederate railroads with the rank of colonel. After the war ended, he continued his work in railroads, and in 1867 John Moncure Robinson became president of the Baltimore Steam Packet Company—better known as the Old Bay Line—whose headquarters were in Baltimore.[11]

The company had first been incorporated in 1840, taking over two boats from the Maryland and Virginia Steam Boat Company, which ceased operations that year. The Old Bay Line would run passenger steamboats up and down Chesapeake Bay for well over the next hundred years. Robinson was the fourth president of the line, serving from 1867 to 1893. A typical trip from Baltimore to Norfolk took most of a day's or night's travel and cost $8 in 1840, which included meals served aboard.

The Civil War considerably affected the Line's business, with fewer passengers wanting, or being able, to travel. As Norfolk was in rebel territory, it was difficult and largely illegal for civilians to make the trip. Also, some of the Line's boats had been taken over by the naval forces. With the end of the war, the Old Bay Line found itself having to compete with other steamboat lines, but under Robinson's management it grew and prospered, concentrating on making the waterborne trip a comfortable and luxurious one. After 1870 there was a greatly expanded freight business and new boats were acquired to handle it. John M. Robinson directed the line for twenty-six years, overseeing many improvements and expansion of services. Paddle wheels were replaced by screw propellers, iron hulls by higher quality steel, and gas lighting, eventually, by electric lighting. The Old Bay Line grew and prospered and became one of the foremost names in luxurious travel by water in America.[12]

John Surratt and his brother, Isaac, were hired by Robinson. John served as a freight claim agent and later as an auditor for the Old Bay Line. Baltimore had many citizens who favored the Southern cause throughout the Civil War, and Maryland had flirted with secession at the beginning of the war, with large numbers of Union troops stationed in the state or passing through it during the war effectively preventing the success of any pro-Confederate factions. Robinson's willingness to hire the Surratt brothers must have been influenced by his own background and military service with the Confederacy and by the generally more pro-South attitude of Baltimore and Maryland.

By the time the Surratt brothers went to work for the Old Bay Line, steam-powered boats and ships were commonplace on the rivers of the world and steamships were crossing the oceans regularly. Isaac Surratt—after Confederate service in Texas during the war—reportedly spent some time in Europe before returning to America. If he did, he may have been in Europe when John passed through. We can be forgiven for wondering if the two brothers met during that time. No record suggests that such a meeting took place, and it is unlikely that Isaac was in a position to help John at that time. Although Isaac had studied civil engineering before the war, his position with the Old Bay Line was described as "chief receiving clerk." During the years the Surratt brothers worked for the Old Bay Line, the steamboat service in Chesapeake Bay and adjoining rivers and tributaries involved much competition. For instance, there were periods of price wars, in which the competing lines would lower their fares to attract business away from their competitors, even though this might hurt profitability.[13]

In 1878, William P. Tonry, Anna's husband, received a telegram which read, "Tell Ike [Isaac] John and Anna that their grandmother is dead and will be buried at Grimes Cross Roads tomorrow at three o'clock. [Signed] J.Z. Jenkins." The grandmother referred to was Elizabeth Ann Webster Jenkins (1794–1878), the mother of Mary E. Surratt. The sender of this telegram was John Zadoc Jenkins (1822–1896), Mary's brother and uncle of Isaac, John, and Anna. At Grimes Cross Roads, there was a Catholic church with a cemetery. This place is today at the intersection of St. Barnabas Road and Brinkley Road, near the route 495 beltway near Oxon Hill in Prince George's County, Maryland, about two miles south of the District of Columbia line. The telegram has managed to survive, but we do not know if Grandmother Jenkins' grandchildren attended her funeral.[14]

As the years passed, John Surratt was occasionally approached by reporters eager to obtain new details and rehash his story yet again. An unknown reporter who signed himself "Pilgrim" published such an account in the *Philadelphia Times* on October 4, 1885, under the following title:

> John H. Surratt
> Talk with a Once Famous Man Who Narrowly
> Escaped the Scaffold.
> A True Story of His Flight.
> He Would Have Returned Had He Thought His Mother Was in Danger.

An army officer named Colonel Hat Adreon is credited with revealing Surratt's whereabouts to the reporter: "I hear he is a good freight clerk, but he was a most unsuccessful assassin."

Even "Pilgrim" expressed some doubt about Adreon, suggesting the colonel was a drinker. But "Pilgrim" sought out John Surratt at the Old Bay Line offices in Baltimore and claimed to have interviewed him. Surratt was reluctant to discuss the events of his early life that had made him famous. "Pilgrim" described the man before him in some detail:

> His is an interesting face, clear-cut and intelligent, the eyes grayish-blue fringed with dark heavy lashes, but sharp, inquisitorial, and suspicious. In one of them there is dilation of pupil which gives a coquettish, indeed almost uncanny, effect to the half-querulous glance with which he received those who came into the office from time to time as we sat there on the rainy afternoon [September 25, 1885]. Still, his face is a nice one. There are signs of the good blood in him. The nose well developed and shapely. The chin shaded by a tawny mustache which, in color, cuts upon the red line of the straight-lipped mouth. The chin itself full, the high forehead unhaired almost to the crown, but below it all a facial expression which, if interpreted by the knowledge of his history, might suggest weariness of life; but with that knowledge awakens sentimental fancies of flight, pursuit at night without sleep, of fear without alloy, of all that mortal agony can depict upon the human face. These could, at best, be only sentimental fancies, but the impression grew upon me as I listened to the story.... It was coldly related, not as one who sought vindication of a wrong, nor as one might have sought to tell a story of evil-doing and was putting his best foot forward; It was a calm, cold narration of his life between the time of the 10th of April, 1865, and the 21st of February, 1867.

These impressions and observations may be truly related, but they are heavy with skepticism and Victorian moral interpretation.

The story of his flight from Elmira to Canada he related with no meaningful variation from what came from his trial or his lecture, with one startling exception. Surratt mentioned that he had a companion with him as he fled toward the safety of Canada: "'Who was he?' Pilgrim asked eagerly. 'I believe that he has never been identified,' Surratt replied, clearly intending that his secret was not now to be revealed." According to "Pilgrim," Surratt grew agitated when relating his feelings upon learning of the fate of his mother, weeping bitterly over the distant memory. He again confirmed the story that his "friends" in Canada prevented him from returning to Washington and giving himself up in order to save her. Crossing Europe, he said he went through France and Switzerland on his way to Italy. He related that his Catholic "friends" advised him to join the Papal Zouaves: "I was, I daresay, recognized by dozens before one fellow, a French Canadian [Ste. Marie], carried the news to United States Minister Marsh [actually to Rufus King in Rome] that I was in the Zouaves." He repeated the dramatic story of his leap over the wall to escape his pursuers. He described his treatment on the U.S.S. *Swatara* as "brutal." "'Isn't there more I can learn, Mr. Surratt?' Pilgrim asked. 'No, I think not. Certainly nothing that I could permit you to print.'"

Another article appeared in 1898, said to be Surratt's own telling of the abduction plot and his part in it. It is known as "The Hanson Hiss Article," after the name of a reporter for the *Washington Post* who supposedly interviewed Surratt, as "Pilgrim" was said to have done: "For a third of a century prominent writers for newspapers and magazines, in every section of the Union, have realized that could John H. Surratt be induced to tell his story, freely, unreservedly, and fully, it would rival in romantic interest any dramatic detail of anything hitherto published concerning the landmarks of the war between the states." After stating that "countless" attempts to get him to tell his story had all been refused, somehow "Hanson Hiss" had finally been able to induce him to open up. As in the "Pilgrim" article, the reporter gave a detailed description of his subject: "Surratt is very different from the ignorant and blood-thirsty Southerner pictured by an angry press during his trial. On the contrary, he is refined, highly educated, and polished. His manners are stately and dignified. He is a brilliant talker, and every word he utters conveys the exact meaning he intends. He is above the medium height, straight and slender, and has iron gray hair and mustache, and two piercing gray eyes set deep in his head beneath heavy eyebrows. He talks in a low tone of voice, never hesitates for a word, and only twice during my talks with him did he become excited.... [O]nce was when he spoke of Wilkes Booth, and the other time was during his terrible arraignment of Weichmann. He is only fifty-five years old, although he looks seventy [he was actually fifty-four in 1898]." Surratt proceeded, according to the article, to relate his story, with little variation from his own lecture or the earlier "Pilgrim" interview, with a few exceptions: "Wilkes Booth was never introduced to me by Dr. Mudd on the street or anywhere else. Booth came to me with a letter of introduction from a valued and trusted friend.... Weichmann was nowhere near when Booth presented his letter."

In this interview, Surratt said he was sent to Elmira, New York, by "Gen. Wilder." It was actually Brigadier General Edwin G. Lee. "I was in Elmira for several weeks [actually, only a few days] and as my pockets were full of Uncle Sam's gold furnished me by my government, I made hosts of friends." He had $200 in gold, given to him by Judah Benjamin when he left Richmond. This was gold appropriated by the Confederate government from federal accounts at the beginning of the war, and therefore could be described as "Uncle Sam's gold." Surratt implied that he used his money to induce Union officers to tell him what he needed to know about the POW camp, especially an officer he described as "a Union Colonel": "It was on my return from Elmira to Albany that I first learned of Lincoln's assassination." This statement, if true, would mean that Surratt had no involvement in, or prior knowledge of, the plot to assassinate the president, only the earlier kidnapping plot. It also contradicts the account in his lecture, in which he claims he was informed of the assassination by a store clerk in Elmira.

He mentions only one stop on his journey from England to Italy, and that was Paris. He does not mention seeing anyone in Paris. While serving in the Papal Zouaves, he says, "I wrote to one of the most prominent Union statesmen [unnamed] in this country, telling him who and where I was, and asking him if it would be safe for me to return to the United States.... He wrote back saying that, in his opinion, I could not get a jury trial and advising me to remain away from America at least three years. The Judge at my trial refused to admit those letters as evidence of my intention to return to this country voluntarily [no such letters survive and it seems unlikely Surratt would reveal his location by staying long enough to receive a reply by mail]. I determined, however, to return and to take my chances of a court martial, and was on the point of doing so when I was arrested." There is no other mention of his intending to return, and, as we have seen, he fled away from home rather than toward it when he escaped in Italy.

The story of "his sensational escape" by jumping over a cliff is retold, and in the most dramatic fashion. During the telling of his difficult and dangerous travels through Italy, Surratt states, "I was traveling under English passports." Although dressed in the uniform of the Papal Zouaves, he said, according to this article, that he was helped and protected by "Garibaldians," the enemies of the Papal States. In this account he made no mention of being helped by "English gentlemen."

In discussing his trial, he names his attorneys as "Gen. Merrick and John O. Carlisle" with no mention of the Bradleys, who were his principal defenders. There was a prominent lawyer in Washington named J.M. Carlisle, but he is not mentioned in the transcript of Surratt's trial. More believable are Surratt's comments about Louis J. Weichmann: "That man's testimony from beginning to end was outrageously false. He lied ... from the time he took the witness stand until he left it.... That man has done more to bring disgrace and ruin on me and my family than anyone and everyone else, living or dead. Weichmann made up his story out of whole cloth, and when he was in safety he did not have the moral courage to contradict it, as any honest man would." The uncertainties and improbabilities in the "Hanson Hiss" article cause most researchers today to discount it, either as a complete fabrication or as a wildly augmented version of what Surratt may have said.

An article appearing in the *Springfield, MA, Daily Republican* in 1901 contrasted Surratt's adventurous early life with the relative tranquility of his later years:

> Mr. Surratt lives at 1016 West Lanvale Street [Baltimore], and is auditor of the Baltimore Steam Packet Line, better known as the Old Bay Line. He ... is numbered among its most valued employees.
>
> Mr. Surratt is now of middle age and is a man of a quiet and retiring disposition. His friends and his business associates appreciate the mental and physical sufferings that have beset him in the years gone by through his indirect connection with the great crime of 1865, and for that reason the matter is never broached to him.
>
> An acquaintance who met him in Elmira, N.Y., just a few hours before Lincoln was assassinated, and who paid a visit to Baltimore recently for the express purpose of talking to Surratt about his memorable adventures, thus speaks of the interview....
>
> Had he been captured at that time, he would have been hanged with his mother ... so incensed were the people of that time that it does not seem possible that he would have been cleared in 1865 when he came so near conviction in 1867, after time had appeased the wrath of the people and an impartial trial was possible....
>
> He is still a well-preserved man in middle life, with the ease of manner and courtesy that distinguished him as a man of 24 or 25.

The unnamed author relates bits and pieces of the story, revealing nothing previously unknown. He even quotes Surratt on that subject: "[T]here is not much to tell. All the facts came out on the trial, and are, I think, in the main accurate." Surratt mentions that he had a companion part of the way on his escape from Elmira, but will not name him: "[A]ll I know about him is that he was equally poor with myself. It matters not where I met him, but we reached St. Albans, Vt., together, and walked to Franklin, on the other side of the line. This was a walk of a good fifteen miles." This article is no more satisfying than the others. If Surratt actually gave these interviews, their air of unreliability suggests that he was being careful to reveal no more about his story than he already had in his lecture.[15]

In the census taken in Baltimore on June 8, 1880, the following were residents at 161 North Calvert Street:

> John H. Surratt, head [of household], age 36, Clerk at Steamboat Co.
> Neary V. [Mary Victorine], wife, age 33, Keeping house.
> John H. Surratt, Jr., son, age 7
> William H. Surratt, son, age 6
> Marie J. Surratt, daughter, age 4
> Leo J. Surratt, son, age 2
> Isaac D. Surratt, brother, age 38, Clerk at Steamboat Co.
> Cecelia Hunter, sister-in-law, age 28, No occupation
> Clarence Sydney, Boarder, age 24, Clerk in store
> J. Sarriera, Boarder, age 33, Clerk at coal office
> L.D. Saxton, Boarder, age 50, Civil Engineer
> Lloyd Simpson, Boarder, age 50, Lawyer
> Lucky Watkins, Boarder, age 42, Music Teacher
> George Hobson, Boarder, age 19, Clerk at Steamboat Co.
> Joseph E. Smith, servant, age 18, household servant.

With fifteen people living in the same house, either it was a large house, or a very crowded one. Surratt's place of residence changed several times prior to 1903, when he moved to 1004 West Lanvale Street. This house, though not pretentious, must have been relatively spacious, with four floors. Surratt lived at this location for thirteen years. Lanvale Street is located in the western suburbs of Baltimore, well away from the bustle of the busy city.

The offices of the Chesapeake Bay Steam Packet Company, or the Old Bay Line, were located in room 800 of the Equitable Building at the southwest corner of Calvert and Fayette streets. The ticket offices were located at 1129 East Baltimore Street and the shipping offices were at 544 Union Dock, at the foot of Concord Street on the west side of Jones Falls. John Surratt, and possibly also Isaac, initially worked at the Union Dock location. They were described as "freight agents," which were clerical positions. This building burned down in 1898, and the general offices and shipping offices were moved to Piers 9–13 on Light Street. From 1898 until his retirement in 1915, John Surratt's offices were in the Light Street building. By 1910, he was described as the firm's "auditor," or chief bookkeeper, a position that made him one of the senior executives of the Old Bay Line, presumably with a good salary to support himself and his family.

The fire that destroyed the Old Bay Line's Union Dock location began the night of May 17, 1898, and burned large U-shaped buildings containing bales of cotton, hogsheads of tobacco, and other types of freight for shipping. Papers and documents relating to the history of the Old Bay Line were also destroyed. The company was able to obtain the use of buildings at Pier 10 on Light Street on the west side of Baltimore harbor. Soon the Old Bay Line purchased the Light Street property and built their iconic main building, which had a 274-foot frontage on Light Street and was topped with an ornate tower in the middle. Behind this building were the docks numbered 9–13, used by the steamships of the Old Bay Line, which operated between Baltimore, Maryland, and Norfolk, Virginia.

On Sunday morning, February 7, 1904, at 10:48 a.m., a fire alarm was received and Engine Company 15 of the Baltimore Fire Department responded. The fire began at the John Hurst and Company building on Liberty Street and rapidly engulfed the building, causing a huge explosion in the upper floors that shattered windows and showered nearby buildings with debris and burning embers. By midday a call for help went out to other cities, and they responded with firefighting crews and equipment. A hard westerly wind fanned the flames and spread the fire across the city toward the east. Although considerable help arrived over the next few hours, problems with equipment hampered the firemen. Fire hose couplings were not of a standard size at that time, so hoses from Washington and other cities could not be hooked to Baltimore's hydrants.

As the fire spread across the downtown portion of the city it jumped across the narrow streets of the older part of Baltimore. Soon it was decided to use dynamite to clear firebreaks; this was unsuccessful, and the explosions contributed to the fire rather than stopping it. A second fire began in the Center Market area, east of the original fire. As Monday morning went on, this new fire joined forces with the original one. By early Monday morning the fire was burning near Light Street, where it intersected with Pratt Street. A heroic effort by firefighters prevented the fire from spreading down Light Street, where the docks and relatively new main building of the Old Bay Line were located. By midday Monday the fire, still following an easterly course driven by the winds, had burned the piers along Pratt Street.

With fire companies from Washington, D.C.; Philadelphia; Wilmington, Delaware; New York City and other cities joining the Baltimore firemen, the Jones Falls, a waterway that flowed south into the harbor, became the strongest line of resistance to the onrushing flames. Water drawn from the Jones Falls was used as thirty-seven fire engines created a barrier. Although the fire burned all the way up to the Jones Falls, it was unable to cross

Ruined buildings from the Baltimore fire of 1904, one of the worst disasters in American history. Much of the city was destroyed, but firemen were able to save the Old Bay Line offices, where John Surratt and his brother Isaac worked (Library of Congress).

the falls. By the evening of February 8, the Great Fire was defeated, reduced to smoldering ruins. Eighty-six blocks had burned, causing over $70,000,000 in losses. Policemen, firemen, federal agents of the Secret Service, and U.S. Army troops patrolled the city, controlling the crowds of spectators and would-be looters. In spite of the severe devastation, only four fatalities were noted, all of them from exposure to the harsh weather.

John Surratt's office at the Old Bay Line building on Light Street was not burned in the 1904 fire, and neither was his home on West Lanvale Street, well away from the area of the fire. The Old Bay Line building at Union Dock on the west side of Jones Falls, the same building which had burned in 1898, was again burned in the Great 1904 fire.[16]

Around the time of the Great Fire, the Old Bay Line was acquired by the Seaboard Air Line Railway, though it was allowed to continue using its time-honored name. The Union Dock facility, which had twice been burned, was rebuilt and leased again by the Old Bay Line to provide a convenient location for freight business from the eastern side of Baltimore. Accounts stating that the Light Street headquarters had burned in the Great Fire of 1904 are in error, confusing the Light Street building with the Pratt Street Union Dock, which was burned again in 1904. In 1905, Light Street was widened to relieve traffic congestion caused by the busy steamship business.

In 1910 the *Old Bay Line* magazine began publication. Each issue of this monthly magazine featured advertising promoting the line and articles about the sights of Chesapeake

Bay and the places served by the Old Bay Line. The senior officials of the line were listed in each issue including the president of the line, treasurer and general passenger agent, traffic manager, purchasing agent, and the auditor and freight agent. The name of the auditor and freight agent was John H. Surratt. His duties would have consisted of record keeping for the freight business of the line.

Because of the fires of 1898, 1904, and 1911, there are very few documents remaining from the Old Bay Line during these years. Few of these mention Surratt, and those that do give us only a partial picture of what his position entailed. A memorandum from 1906 states that Surratt—the company auditor—made an inspection of the wharf at Norfolk, the southern end of the line. The memo describes freight handled and the cost of labor performed. Surratt wrote a formal report three days later for John R. Sherwood, who was then vice president and general manager, on his Norfolk trip. Chance does not discriminate: another surviving document, a letter from John R. Sherwood, by this time (1908) president and general manager of the line, advises Surratt that the clerks in the Auditor's Department will no longer be paid for their lunch. Of greater moment is a letter from President Sherwood to all department heads and agents, who are named (including J.H. Surratt), regarding a Mr. Key Compton, vice president of the Chesapeake Steamship Company, a major competitor of the Old Bay Line, advising them to refer Mr. Compton to deal directly with President Sherwood. A copy of Sherwood's letter to Compton for the same purpose survives, as well as Compton's reply and Sherwood's further acknowledgment. Another notice to the same department heads and agents closes the matter. A statement of the earnings and

Mr. William B. Hurst presenting medal to Capt. William C. Almy, *Old Bay Line* 3, no. 2 (September 1912), 2. John H. Surratt, Jr., by now an older man, was serving as the auditor of the Old Bay Line. He can be seen in the background on the far right. This photo was published in 1912 and is here reproduced for the first time in more than a century (Mariner's Museum, Newport News, Virginia).

expenditures for the month of March 1910 shows the line was making a profit. The statement does not name Surratt but says it was issued by the auditor. Finally, two communications from J.S. Wilson Jr. & Co., bankers of Baltimore, describing the attractiveness of the Chesapeake Steamship Company 5 percent Gold Bonds as a good investment and listing the assets of that company. Key Compton had by this time, April 1910, become president of the Chesapeake Line.[17]

The Old Bay Line liked to recognize and reward its employees for exceptional service. On the night of November 13, 1911, the Old Bay Line steamship *Florida* was fighting a 45-mile-per-hour wind off Sparrows Point when a red light was seen. A searchlight revealed an open boat containing five men. Captain William C. Almy (1859–1939) carefully maneuvered the *Florida* to approach the boat without swamping it. Ropes were thrown and the men were rescued. On a previous occasion, Almy had rescued four men from a burning boat. The company decided to honor Captain Almy, and a ceremony was conducted on the upper deck of the *Florida* on August 5, 1912, when it was docked in Baltimore. William B. Hurst, director of the company, presented a diamond-studded medal to Almy. Present at the ceremony were directors of the company Douglas H. Thomas, S. Davies Warfield (president of the Old Bay Line), John R. Sherwood, and most of the senior executives of the line, including John H. Surratt, the auditor. A photograph was taken showing Hurst handing the medal to Captain Almy, while several figures can be seen in the background. On the right side of the photo we see an older man, taller than most of the others, standing straight and watching the presentation. Comparison of this photo with other photographs known to be of Surratt in his later years—and who was sixty-eight at the time of this ceremony—show that this man appears to look very similar to Surratt. The light-colored hair, a heavy moustache (also light in color), the shape and size of the ear, all correspond with photos known to be of Surratt. Since we know from a news report that Surratt was there, the odds are very good that this is a photograph of John H. Surratt, not published since 1912.[18]

The recollections of J. Friend Lodge, a collector of Civil War–related literature, appeared in the book *Further Light on Lincoln's Last Day*, by John W. Stan Jr.:

"My recollection of [John] Surratt," said Mr. Lodge, "goes back to a period of about fifteen or sixteen

John H. Surratt, Jr., in old age (Surratt House Museum/ MNCPPC, Clinton, Maryland).

years ago [perhaps 1914–1915].... We invariably used the Baltimore Steam Packet Co., 'The Old Bay Line,' in going down the bay.

"[At the line's headquarters] ... "[t]here was a row of offices up on the second floor of the dock where we were, and I noticed one that was marked 'Freight Auditor' or something to that effect, on the door.

"In response to my knock a voice within said 'come in.' I did so, and there was but one occupant of the room, sitting at a desk on the side farthest from the door. He smiled very pleasantly and asked my business.... He was very courteous.... We conversed pleasantly for perhaps five minutes."

Afterward, speaking to his wife, Lodge said, "Have you ever heard of John H. Surratt?"

"Why yes, certainly. He was mixed up in the Lincoln conspiracy," she replied.

"Well, I just met John H. Surratt in that office."

"Perhaps you are mistaken. Surratt is probably in his grave long years since."

"No, I am not mistaken.... I have seen Surratt's picture many times, and except that his hair and moustache have turned from black to gray, almost white, the features are the same...."

"Upon my return home I wrote Mr. Surratt and thanked him for his courtesy to us, and also asked him for his autograph on a card which I enclosed. He autographed the card for me, and wrote me a very courteous letter, too, saying that it was an old established policy of the 'Old Bay Line' to afford every accommodation and courtesy to its patrons....

"It always seemed rather odd to me that he would favor me with his autograph, for I have been advised by friends in New York in the autograph business, that he would not give his autograph to anyone, and that it could not be had.

"I saw and spoke to him many times after that while on my way to and from the South. He always seemed very courteous and pleasant with me; seemed to want to do what he could for the convenience of the passengers on the line....

"What were my impressions of him? ... I usually had to make the conversation. He would always answer me very nicely and politely, but always there was that 'reserve....'

"He impressed me as a man that always, under any and all circumstances, could be counted on to be in full control of himself. I regarded him as an able, energetic and capable man in anything he might undertake, and I believe he was. He was approximately six feet tall, and sparely built. His forehead was very prominent, and his eyes deeply set. Whenever I met him he was always modestly and neatly dressed. His manner of speech was well regulated, and his tone of voice modulated and pleasing.

"His face, I would say, was a hard one to read; by that I mean that there was nothing that was not agreeable, but just that quiet and dignified look that would afford no indication, as I saw him, of what was in his mind."[19]

Anna Surratt Tonry, John's sister, died on October 24, 1904, in Baltimore, having been an invalid for a number of years. A requiem mass was held at St. Ann's Church in Baltimore, and her remains were taken to Washington, D.C., and buried in Mount Olivet Cemetery, alongside her mother. Her husband, William P. Tonry, and their three sons and daughter, as well as Anna's two brothers, Isaac and John, presumably attended her funeral. The other family members also buried in lot 31 are Anna's husband, William P. Tonry, in 1905; Anna's brother Isaac Douglas Surratt, in 1907; Anna's children, Dr. Reginald I. Tonry, in 1946; Cecelia B. Tonry, wife of Reginald I. Tonry, in 1943; and William S. Tonry, in 1944. The *Baltimore Sun*, of November 4, 1907, reported: "Surratt—On November 3, 1907, Isaac D. Surratt, aged 66 years. High mass at St. Ann's Church on Tuesday [Nov. 5] at 9 A.M. Interment in Mount Olivet Cemetery, Washington, D.C." Another article in the same paper gave the cause of Isaac's death as "indigestion and paralysis of the heart" and that "any reflection over the death of his mother filled him with unspeakable sadness.... For the last thirty five years he had been chief receiving clerk of the Old Bay Line. He never married and for some time had made his home with his nephew, Dr. Reginald I. Tonry [Anna's son], 2206 York Road. He was 66 years old.... Rev. Dr. C.F. Thomas will celebrate a low mass of requiem. The body will be taken to Washington and will be interred by the side of his mother, in Mount Olivet Cemetery. The pall-bearers will be Mr. Surratt's nephews. They are Dr. Reginald L. [I.] Tonry and Mr. William H. Surratt of Baltimore and Messrs. Raymond Thorne, Archibald, Clarence and Milbert Donohoe of Washington, D.C."

The last of the children of Mary E. Surratt, John H. Surratt, Jr., continued to be listed as the auditor of the Old Bay Line in each issue of *Old Bay Line* until the October 22, 1915, issue, which stated, "E.P. Hook, Acting Auditor and Freight Claim Agent." All of the successive issues after that listed Hook in that position, dropping the "acting" from his job title. From this, we can place John Surratt's retirement from the Old Bay Line as sometime in August of 1915. He continued to reside at 1004 West Lanvale Street, Baltimore.

In John Surratt's final years, his son William encouraged him to write down the story of his early life. As articles and purported interviews about him were appearing in the press, John finally agreed and set down an account of his experiences. William sent the manuscript to *McClure's* magazine but received a reply from an unsympathetic editor: "I doubt that anyone would be interested in anything Mr. Surratt has to say." With that rejection, John Surratt decided to destroy the manuscript. The manuscript, along with letters from Father LaPierre, Stephen F. Cameron, Roswell S. Ripley, Harry H. Brogden, Joseph Bradley, Richard Merrick, John W. Clampitt, and others from private individuals were burned in the backyard of the Surratt home. Other items burned reportedly included a document commissioning Surratt into the Confederate Secret Service signed by Jefferson

John H. Surratt, Jr., and his wife (Surratt House Museum/MNCPPC, Clinton, Maryland).

Davis and numerous newspaper clippings, including one that quoted Edward C. Carrington—who had prosecuted Surratt—as acknowledging that John had been in Elmira, New York, on the day of the assassination, and that Carrington had had doubts about John's guilt during his trial. Another letter was to John R. Sherwood threatening to terminate U.S. Mail contracts with the Old Bay Line if they employed Surratt, which Sherwood, a Union veteran, had refused to heed. Also into the fire went the original manuscript of Surratt's lecture, the contents of which had been taken down at the time and thus became one of the very few documents from John H. Surratt, Jr., to have survived until that day.

In February of 1916, Surratt fell ill with pleurisy, an inflammation of the membrane around the lungs. He seemed to be recovering and was able to take walks in his neighborhood, but he was stricken with pneumonia and as his condition deteriorated he passed in and out of consciousness. He was unable to eat during most of this time. On April 13 he achieved his seventy-second birthday, though he was probably too ill to take notice of it. On the night of April 21, 1916, John Harrison Surratt, Jr., died. With him at his passing were his wife, Mary Victorine Hunter Surratt, and two daughters. A brief service was held the next morning at his home at 1004 W. Lanvale Street, Baltimore, with the funeral at St. Pius' Catholic Church, at Edmondsen Avenue and Schroeder Street, officials of the Old Bay Line serving as pall bearers. The Rev. John E. Dunn presided at the funeral service. John Surratt was buried at new Cathedral Cemetery in Baltimore, section J, lot 264. Upon Mary Victorine's death on November 16, 1926, she was buried in the same lot.[20]

It was the end of John Surratt's life, an end to the exhilaration of being involved in "the lost cause" of the Confederacy, an end to the fear of being captured and hanged for his involvement with Booth, an end to the grief at the loss of his mother, an end to the largely peaceful later life with his wife and children and his service with the Old Bay Line. All was ended, except for the fascination and mystery surrounding the fugitive who managed to escape justice but not the suffering that was the consequence of his acts.

Chapter Notes

Chapter 1

1. Marguerite Marie Dubois, *Larousse's French-English, English-French Dictionary* (New York: Washington Square, 1968), 224; Carlos F. McHale, *Vox New College Spanish and English Dictionary* (Lincolnwood, IL: National Textbook, 1984); D.P. Simpson, *Cassell's Latin Dictionary* (New York: Wiley, 1977); Catherine Soanes and Sara Hawker, *Compact Oxford English Dictionary of Current English* (Oxford: Oxford University Press, 2005), 943; *Dictionaire Etymologique des Noms de Famile et Prenoms de France* (Paris: Larousse, 1961); "From Whence Cometh Surratt?," *Surratt Society News* 5, no. 11 (November, 1980), 4.

2. Fernand Braudel, *A History of Civilizations* (New York: Penguin, 1994), 460–464; James O. Hall, with Norman and Laura Sarratt, "Some Surratt Background," *Surratt Courier* 20, no. 10 (October, 1995), 6–8; Bernice Surratt, "A Little Extra on the Surratt Genealogy," *Surratt Courier* 20, No.12 (December, 1995), 3.

3. *Neinton's Map of Prince George County*, Surratt Society (Clinton, MD: J.O. Hall Research Center), copy in papers of J.O. Hall.

4. Hall, with Sarratt, "Some Surratt Background."

5. Prince George's County Stamps and Licenses (1851–1854), M.H.R. Accession No. 6164, folio 17 (Annapolis, MD: Maryland Hall of Records). Historical documents under the jurisdiction of the clerk of the Circuit Court for Prince George's County, Upper Marlboro, MD.

6. John M. Walton Jr., *Historical and Architectural Archaeological Research at the Surratt Dwelling House-Tavern, Clinton, Maryland*, prepared by Contract Archaeology, (J.O. Hall Research Center), 10–11; D.C. Equity Case No. 559 (Suitland, MD: Washington National Records Center); D.C. Land Records, Liber JAS 70 (Suitland, MD: Washington National Records Center), 301–304, 311 et seq.

7. Walton, 11; D.C. Land Records, Liber 70, 311 et seq.

8. Hall, with Sarratt.

9. James O. Hall Papers (Clinton, MD: Surratt Society J.O. Hall Research Center); James O. Hall, *The Surratt Family and John Wilkes Booth* (Clinton, MD: Surratt Society, [1976]), 3.

10. Hall, Hall Papers, Surratt Family, 3–4. James O. Hall to Laurie Verge, October 5, 1978, J.O. Hall Papers, *op. cit.*; Walton, 15; Judge Lee Van Horn, unpublished history of Prince George's County, MD. J.O. Hall Papers, *op. cit.*; *Laws Made and Passed by the General Assembly of the State of Maryland* (Annapolis: E.S. Riley, 1854).

11. Hall Papers; Hall, *Surratt Family*, 4–5; Walton, 15; Phyllis Cox, "The Surratt Physician: A Story of his Own," *Surratt Society News* 8, no. 5 (May 1983), 6; David Rankin Barbee interview with Dr. Riginald I. Tonry, November 13, 1931, in *Surratt Courier* 12, no. 4 (April 1987), 7–10; *Alexandria Gazette* (June 23, 1832).

12. Elizabeth S. Trindal, Mary Surratt, *An American Tragedy* (Gretna, LA: Pelican, 1996), 20; Kenneth J. Zanca, "Was Mrs. Surratt Married in the Church?," *Surratt Courier* 28, no. 1 (January, 2003), 5–7; Hall Papers, *op. cit.*; Hall, *Surratt Family*, 5–6.

13. Hall, *Surratt Family*, 6–7; Laurie Verge, "The Surratt Mill," *Surratt Society News* 4, no. 1 (January, 1979); Walton, 16–17.

14. "With the Rambler," *Washington Evening Star* (October 13, 1912).;Hall Papers, notes on legal papers of Neales and Surratts; Laurie Verge to James O. Hall, January 17, 1978; J.O. Hall Papers, *op. cit.*; Walton, 20; Historical Documents, *op. cit.*; "We Lived Here, Too: Slavery in Prince George's County, Maryland, 1860–1864" (Clinton, MD: Surratt House Museum, n.d.), copy in Frederick Hatch Papers.

15. Hall, *Surratt Family*, 7; "The Surratt House and the Saga of Mary Surratt" (Maryland National Capital Park and Planning Commission, n.d.); Louise Oertly, "The Financial Page," *Surratt Courier* 34, no. 6 (June, 2009), 4; "New Post Office," *Planter's Advocate and Southern Maryland Advertiser* (November 1, 1854), reprinted in *Surratt Society News* 3, no. 4 (April, 1978), 1.

16. *Atlas of Fifteen Miles around Washington Including the County of Prince George, Maryland* (Philadelphia: G.M. Hopkins, 1878), 26; "The Surratt House and the Saga of Mary Surratt," *op. cit.*

17. Jim Walsh, "John Surratt: A Respectable Deadbeat?" *Surratt Courier* 14, no. 4 (April 1989), 1, 6–7; Laurie Verge and Joan Chaconas, *Surratt House Museum* (Greendale, IN: Creative, 1997).

18. Walton, 32; Barbee, Tonry Interview, *op. cit.*

19. Walton, 45–48; *Atlas of Prince George's County, Maryland, 1861, Adapted from Simon J. Martenet's Map of Prince George's County, Maryland* (Baltimore, 1861); Joseph George, Jr., "'A True Childe of Sorrow': Two Letters of Mary E. Surratt," *Maryland Historical Magazine* 80, no. 4, winter (1985), 402–405; Trindal, 45–46.

20. "Sulpician Educational Institutions in Baltimore Area Circa 1850," documents in J.O. Hall Papers, dated 3-26-1990; Rev. John J. Tierney, S.S., "St. Charles College: Foundation and Early Years," *Maryland Historical Magazine* 43, no. 4 (December 1948), 294–311.

21. Louis J. Weichmann, *A True History of the Assassination of Abraham Lincoln and of the Conspiracy of*

1865, ed. Floyd E. Risvold (New York: Alfred A. Knopf, 1975), 14–15; David Herbert Donald, *Lincoln* (London: Jonathan Cape, 1995), 225–229; Samuel Eliot Morison, Henry Steele Commager, and William E. Leuchtenberg, *The Growth of the American Republic*, 7th ed. (New York: Oxford University Press, 1980), 1, 601–607.

22. Weichmann, 15–16; Joseph George, Jr., to John C. Brennan, James O. Hall, and Robert L. Keesler, "Was John H. Surratt a Seminarian?," February 22, 1991, J.O. Hall Papers; Benn Pitman, *The Assassination of President Lincoln and the Trial of the Conspirators* (Cincinnati & New York: Moore, Wilstach and Baldwin, 1865), 115, 131; William C. Edwards and Edward Steers, Jr., eds., *The Lincoln Assassination: The Evidence* (Urbana and Chicago: University of Illinois Press, 2009), 1319–1320 (hereafter *Evidence*).

23. Walton, 57; William A. Tidwell, with James O. Hall and David Winfred Gaddy, *Come Retribution: The Confederate Secret Service and the Assassination of Lincoln* (Jackson: University Press of Mississippi, 1988), 62, 87–90; Hall, *Surratt Family*, 9; Trindal, 54, 244; "Isaac D. Surratt Dead," *Baltimore Sun* (November 4, 1907), 4, col. 6; Anna Surratt, "Some Letters of Anna Surratt," ed. Alfred Isacsson, *Maryland Historical Magazine* 54 (September, 1959), 310–313.

24. Trindal, 65, 247; Anna Surratt, *op. cit.*; Weichmann, 14; George Alfred Townsend, "Interview with Dr. George Dyer Mudd," *Cincinnati Enquirer* (April 16, 1883).

Chapter 2

1. Trindal, 65; Kenneth J. Zanca, *The Catholics and Mrs. Mary Surratt* (Lanham, MD: University Press of America, 2008), 37.
2. Tidwell, Hall, and Gaddy, 9–10, 35.
3. John H. Surratt, "A Remarkable Lecture!," *Washington Evening Star*, December 7, 1870 (hereafter *Lecture*).
4. William A. Tidwell, *April '65: Confederate Covert Action in the American Civil War* (Kent, OH: Kent State University Press, 1995), 31–32.
5. Tidwell, Hall, and Gaddy, 62, 87.
6. Thomas A. Jones, *J. Wilkes Booth* (Chicago: Laird & Lee, 1893), 23–32.
7. Alfred Isacsson, "A Biography of John Surratt," PhD diss. (New York, 1957), 6.
8. Samuel Carter III, *The Riddle of Dr. Mudd* (New York: G.P. Putnam's Sons, 1974), 59.
9. L.C. Baker, *History of the United States Secret Service* (Philadelphia: L.C. Baker, 1867), 102; *Evidence*, 1084–1085; William A. DeGregorio, *The Complete Book of U.S. Presidents* (New York: Barricade, 1993), 218–219; James O. Hall, "A Line of Communication," unpublished note, J.O. Hall papers, *op. cit.*; Alecon Trubey Pierce, certified genealogist, "Report to W.A. Tidwell," May 12, 1999, copy in Hall Papers, *op. cit.*; Pierce to Tidwell, "John Callahan Addenda," May 19, 1999, copy in Hall Papers.
10. William Nelson Barker, "Consolidated Report of the Signal Corps, C.S.A. East Miss. for Quarter ending March 31st '64," National Archives (Clinton, MD: Surratt Society, J.O. Hall Research Center), copy in William A. Tidwell Papers.
11. Thomas Nelson Conrad, *The Rebel Scout* (Washington: National, 1904), 25.
12. Thomas Nelson Conrad, *A Confederate Spy* (New York: J.S. Ogilvie, 1892), 128.
13. *Washington Evening Star*, August 4, 1862, p. 3; James O. Hall, Note regarding T.N. Conrad, "Rev. T.N. Conrad arrested...." Conrad File, J.O. Hall Papers; Patricia L. Faust, ed., *Historical Times Illustrated Encyclopedia of the Civil War* (New York: Harper Collins, 1991), 795.
14. Terry Alford, manuscript on T.N. Conrad, Papers of J.O. Hall, 5; Walton, 61.
15. Trindal, 68–69; Weichmann, 19; Surratt House Museum, *op. cit.*
16. H.B. Ste. Marie to the Judge Advocate, Bureau of Military Justice, May 23, 1865, National Archives.
17. Weichmann, 16–18; *Evidence*, 112–113.
18. Lewis J. Wiechmann [*sic*] (Weichmann's name appears in a variety of spellings) to Henri B. Ste. Marie, Esq., April 23, 1863, *Evidence*, 503–506; J. Harrison Surratt to H.B. Ste. Marie, April 24, 1863, *Evidence*, 112–113.
19. Joseph George Jr., "H.B. Ste. Marie and His Role in the Arrest of John H. Surratt," *Lincoln Herald* 85, no. 4 (Winter 1983), 269–279.
20. Weichmann, 19–22.
21. M-599, Reel 7, frames 445–451.
22. Weichmann, 24.
23. Frederick Hatch, "The One That Got Away: The Story of John H. Surratt," *Journal of the Lincoln Assassination* 11, no. 1 (April 1997), 1–9; Walton, 62–63; Postmaster General's Journal 51, folio 33 53, folio 133, National Archives; Postmaster's Appointment Record for NJ, DE, MD, PA (1857–1874). Prince George's County Stamps and Licenses, M.H.R. accession No. 6166, folio 3, 4 (Annapolis, MD: Maryland Hall of Records); Charles Calvert to E.M. Stanton, letter recommending John H. Surratt, http://www.stampauctionnetwork.com/F/134/130.jpg.
24. Morison, Commager, and Leuchtenburg 1, 422–3; John H. Surratt to E.M. Stanton, letter asking for clerical appointment, October 17, 1863 (Washington, D.C.), original in private collection, copy in Frederick Hatch Papers.
25. Ben. Perley Poore, *The Conspiracy Trial for the Murder of the President*, 2 (Boston: J.E. Tilton, 1865), 150–158.
26. Ibid., pp. 160–165, 167.
27. Ibid. 2, pp. 300–306; Mark E. Neely Jr., *The Fate of Liberty* (New York: Oxford University Press, 1991), 53; Constitution of the United States of America, Article I, Section 9.
28. Poore, 2, pp. 381–384; Tidwell, Hall, and Gaddy, 338.

Chapter 3

1. James M. McPherson, *Battle Cry of Freedom* (New York: Oxford University Press, 1988), 6–8, 369, 855–859; Ralph Andreano, ed., *The Economic Impact of the American Civil War* (Cambridge, MA: Schenkman, 1962), 198.
2. Tidwell, *April '65*, 107–110; Allan Keller, "Canada and the Civil War," *Civil War Times Illustrated* 3, no. 7 (November 1964), 49–54; Robin W. Winks, *Canada and the United States: The Civil War Years* (Baltimore: Johns Hopkins University Press, 1960), 67, 131–132; McPherson, 389–390.
3. Wilfrid Bovey, "Confederate Agents in Canada during the American Civil War," *Canadian Historical Review* 2, no.1 (March 1921), 46–57.
4. Tidwell, Hall, and Gaddy, 171–177.
5. Winks, 141; Clayton Gray, *Conspiracy in Canada* (Montreal: L'Atelier, 1957), 31, 47–48.

6. James D. Horan, *Confederate Agent* (New York: Crown, 1954), 80–81; Winks, 272–273; William A. Tidwell, "Confederate Covert Action," Part II, manuscript in W.A. Tidwell Papers (Clinton MD: James O. Hall Research Center).
7. Horan, 86.
8. Tidwell, *April '65*, 127–129, 163.
9. William A. Tidwell, "Confederate Expenditures for Secret Service," *Civil War History* 37, no. 3 (September 1991), 219–231.
10. McPherson, 763–767; Larry E. Nelson, *Bullets, Ballots, and Rhetoric* (Tuscaloosa: University of Alabama Press, 1980), 64–72; *The War of the Rebellion: A Compilation of the Official Records of the Union and Confederate Armies*, Series III, p. 4 (Washington: Government Printing Office, 1899), 500–501 (hereafter OR); Tidwell, *April '65*, 133–135; Abraham Lincoln, *Speeches and Writings, 1859-1865* (New York: Literary Classics of the United States, 1989), 611–612; Tidwell, Hall, and Gaddy, 197–198.
11. Tidwell, *April '65*,107–159; Donald E. Markle, *Spies and Spymasters of the Civil War* (New York: Hippocrene, 1994), 192–215; Horan, xxi-xxii; "The Rebel Invasion," *Burlington (VT) Daily Times*, October 21, 1864, pp. 3, c. 4; "George Denison (Canadian Politician)" Wikipedia; J.P. Benjamin, letter to Jas. P. Holcombe, April 20 (1864), copy in J.O. Hall Papers; "Confederacy's Canadian Mission: Spies across the Border," (HistoryNet.com); "Conspiracy in Canada," Central Intelligence Agency Publications; Bovey, *op. cit.*; Arthur Loux, "Montreal Notes," copy in J.O. Hall Papers; "Thomas Dixon Davis," *Virginia Military Institute Alumni News* (March 1927); William A. Tidwell, letter to Hugh P. MacMillan, February 2 (1987), copy in J.O. Hall Papers; J. Wilkinson, *The Narrative of a Blockade Runner* (New York: Sheldon, 1877), 168–188; "St. Albans Raid History," Vermont Civil War (vermontcivilwar.org); Gray, 17–19, 23–25, 30–36, 37–45,47–49, 50–57, 61–73, 78; Winks, 67, 140–149, 264–268, 272–278, 284–336; James O. Hall to William A. Tidwell, "rough notes," n.d., W.A. Tidwell Papers (J.O. Hall Research Center).
12. Jacob Thompson, letter to J.P. Benjamin, December 3, 1864, in OR, Series I, 43, part 2, pp. 930-6; Nat Brandt, *The Man Who Tried to Burn New York* (Syracuse: Syracuse University Press, 1986), 77, 110; Michael V.V. Kauffman, *American Brutus* (New York: Random House, 2004), 150; *Burlington (VT) Daily Times*, col. 4, October 21, 1864, p. 3; Bovey, *op. cit.*
13. John W. Headley, *Confederate Operations in Canada and New York* (New York: Neale, 1906), 256–257, 262.
14. The St. Lawrence Hall Register, Montreal, Quebec Province, Canada, "A List of Suspicious and Prominent Names Compiled from the Period of 1 July 1864 through 30 April 1865," by Randall Haines for Mr. James O. Hall of McLean, Virginia; Papers of J.O. Hall; Tidwell, commentary on letter of H.H. Emmons to William H. Seward, April 28 (1865); William A. Tidwell Papers.
15. John H. Surratt, letter to Louis J. Weichmann, September 21, 1864, *Evidence*, 1229–1230.
16. McPherson, 600–601.

Chapter 4

1. James O. Hall, notes in file "541 H St. House, Equity No. 7," J.O. Hall Papers.
2. James O. Hall, "Mrs. Surratt," manuscript of a lecture given by Hall, undated, unpublished, J. O. Hall Papers; *Washington Evening Star*, col. 1, March 6, 1862, p. 3.
3. Hall, *Surratt Family*, 10; Harold Wang, "A Visit to the Surratt House Boardinghouse, Washington, D. C.," *Surratt Society News* 7, no. 8 (August 1982), 5–6; Zanca, 20; Weichmann, 26–28.
4. Hall, "Mrs. Surratt," *op. cit.*; Tidwell, *April '65*,144–145, 156–157, 236–237; Tidwell, Hall, and Gaddy, 14–21, 329–331, 333–334; Hall, *Surratt Family*, 10; John C. Brennan, "General Bradley T. Johnson's Plan to Abduct President Lincoln," *Chronicles of St. Mary's* 22, no. 11 (November 1974), no. 12 (December 1974).
5. Hall, "Mrs. Surratt," *op. cit.*; Carter, 74–75; *Evidence*, 948.
6. Tidwell, Hall, and Gaddy, 255–265; Hall, *Surratt Family*, 12; Hall, "Mrs. Surratt," *op. cit.*; David C. Keehn, *Knights of the Golden Circle* (Baton Rouge: Louisiana State University Press, 2013), 9, 30–31.
7. *Trial of John H Surratt in the Criminal Court for the District of Columbia* I (Washington: Government Printing Office, 1867), pp. 204–206 (hereafter *Trial*); Surratt, *Lecture, op. cit.*
8. Hall, *Surratt Family*, 12; Jones, 39–43; Weichmann, 31; *Trial*, 356–357.
9. *Trial*, 371–372; Poore I, 70–71. Weichmann, 32–34; Tidwell, Hall, and Gaddy, 338.
10. Francis Wilson, *John Wilkes Booth: Fact and Fiction of Lincoln's Assassination* (Boston: Houghton, Mifflin, 1929), 64.
11. Hanson Hiss, "John H. Surratt's Story: His Connection with the Plot to Abduct President Lincoln Told for the First Time," *Washington Post* (April 3, 1898).
12. Hall, "Mrs. Surratt," *op. cit.*; Richard Mitchell Smoot, *The Unwritten History of the Assassination of Abraham Lincoln* (Clinton, MA: W.J. Coulter, 1908), 7–9; *Evidence*, 841–843, 868; Rossiter Johnson, ed., *The Biographical Dictionary of America* (Boston: American Biographical Society, 1906), 397–398; Article on Frederick Stone. Kauffman 397–398; James E.T. Lange and Katherine DeWitt Jr., "The Gift of John Harrison Surratt, Jr.," *Surratt Courier* 20, no. 9 (September 1995), 5–7; *Statutes at Large* (1862), 589; Alfred Isacsson, "The Conspirator Who Was Not There," *Journal of the Lincoln Assassination* 24 (2010), 2–22; Hall, "J.H. Surratt, Jr.," chronology notes, J.O. Hall Papers; Land Records, District of Columbia, Equity Case #623, Docket 1810 (Prince George's County, MD), records; *Trial*, 373–374.
13. Betty J. Ownsbey, *Alias "Paine": Lewis Thornton Powell, the Mystery Man of the Lincoln Conspiracy* (Jefferson, NC: McFarland, 1993), 11–24, 35–39.
14. *Evidence*, 876, 1021–1022.
15. Tidwell, Hall, and Gaddy, 340–341; Poore I, 273; *Trial*, 429; Benjamin F. Butler Papers, Box 175, Fowle testimony (Library of Congress).
16. Hall, "The Lady in the Veil," *Maryland Independent* (June 25, 1975).
17. Unfiled papers and slips belonging in compiled Confederate Service Records, M-321, roll 9, and M-347, roll 67 (National Archives); Ed. Pitman, 133–135; Weichmann, 86.
18. Weichmann, 78, 85–86 ; Samuel Bland Arnold, *Memoirs of a Lincoln Conspirator*, ed. Michael W. Kauffman (Bowie, MD: Heritage, 1995), 134; *Trial*, 265–266; Hall, "The Lady in the Veil" (July 2, 1975).
19. Hall, "Mrs. Surratt," *op. cit.*; Weichmann, 85.
20. Poore I, 30–31, 88–89; Arnold, 24; Arthur F. Loux, *John Wilkes Booth: Day by Day* (Arthur F. Loux, 1990), 421–423; M-599, Reel 5, frames 49–57, National Archives; Gordon Samples, *Lust for Fame: The Stage Career of John*

Wilkes Booth (Jefferson, NC: McFarland, 1982), 223–224.
21. Arnold, 134; Loux, 422–423.
22. Weichmann, 88; Poore I, 115–116.
23. *Evidence*, 810–812, 1026; Hall, "Mrs. Surratt," *op. cit.*
24. Weichmann, 97–98; Frederick Hatch, "The Meeting at Gautier's Restaurant," *Journal of the Lincoln Assassination* 26 (2012), 2–9.
25. Arnold, 149–150; Kauffman, 184–185.
26. Samples, 176; Loux, 412–435; Weichmann, 119–120; *Evidence*, 172–173, 1224, 1329–30; Tidwell, Hall, and Gaddy, 65, 415; General List of Prisoners, M-598, Reel 85 (National Archives), 41; Kauffman, 395–396.
27. Weichmann, 120; Poore I, 381, 384–385.
28. Pamela Humphreys, "Daniel Henry Lawrence Gleason, 1841–1917," *Lincoln Herald* 113, no. 2 (Summer 2011), 108–114; D.H.L. Gleason, "Conspiracy Against Lincoln," *The Magazine of History* 13, no. 2 (February 1911), 59–65; *Evidence*, 594–596.
29. Hall, "The Lady in the Veil"; Hall, "Mrs. Surratt"; *Evidence*, 1318; M-347, Reel 194, "Unfiled papers…," *op. cit.*; *Trial*, 790–791.

Chapter 5

1. Loux, 434; Hall, "The Lady in the Veil," *op. cit.*; Surratt, "A Remarkable Lecture," *op. cit.*; Weichmann, 128.
2. Weichmann, 128; Hall, "Mrs. Surratt," *op. cit.*; Hall, Surratt Chronology, *op. cit*;. *Evidence*, 1221–1222; Samples, 224; St. Lawrence Hall Register, *op. cit.*
3. John F. Potter, U.S. Consulate General, Montreal, to Hon. W.H. Seward, April 24, 1865; James Mitchell and Jess Stein, ed., *The Random House Encyclopedia* (New York: Random House, 1977), 2296, 2338–2339; Alexandra Lee Levin, *"This Awful Drama": General Edwin Gray Lee, C.S.A., and His Family* (New York: Vantage, 1987), 135, 193; Edwin G. Lee, ""Canadian Diary,""; Microfilm Accession 1456, Southern Historical Collection (Chapel Hill, NC: University of North Carolina); Copied letter in manuscript book of unknown person (Richmond, VA: Confederate Museum), 30; Quoted in Levin, *op. cit.*, 152.
4. Loux, 436;Tidwell, Hall, and Gaddy, 5; U. S. Congress, "Impeachment of the President," House Report 7, 40th Congress, 1st Session (1867), 674.
5. Levin, 153; Michael Horigan, *Elmira: Death Camp of the North* (Mechanicsburg, PA: Stackpole, 2002), 1–2, 4, 15, 171, 173, 176; Lonnie R. Speer, *Portals to Hell: Military Prisons of the Civil War* (Mechanicsburg, PA: Stackpole, 1997), 241; Ausburn Towner, *Our County and Its People: A History of the Valley and County of Chemung from the Closing Years of the Eighteenth Century* (D. Mason, 1892), chapter 5; OR, Series II, vol. 7, pp. 152, 157, 424–427, 504–505, 560, 682–683, 891–892, 1003–1005, 1091–1095, 1134–1137, 1173–1174; James I. Robertson Jr., "The Scourge of Elmira," in *Civil War Prisons*, ed. William B. Hesseltine (Kent, OH: Kent State University Press, 1962), 80–97.
6. Weichmann, 130–131; Edwin M. Stanton to General John A. Dix, April 15, 1865, 4:10 A.M., in OR, Series I 46, part III, 781; Pitman, 45; Poore I, 420; Loux, 436.
7. Weichmann, 133–134; Poore I, 117; Pitman, 126.
8. Weichmann, 135–138; *Evidence*, 341–345; John F. Coyle, *Washington Post*, April 17 (1898), 6; Frederick Hatch, *Protecting President Lincoln* (Jefferson, NC: McFarland, 2011), 170–173.
9. Poore I, 85–87, 117–118, 121–122 II, 483; *Evidence*, 810, 1238–1239; *Trial*, 276–277, 280–281, 293; Frederick Hatch, "The Men Who Hanged Mary Surratt," *Journal of the Lincoln Assassination* 22 (2008), 2–20; Hall, "Mrs. Surratt," *op. cit.*; *Evidence*, 1239–1240; Weichmann, 84. Poore I, 12; *Washington Constitutional Union*, April 15, 1865; *Washington National Intelligencer*, April 15, 1865.
10. George S. Bryan, *The Great American Myth* (New York: Carrick & Evans, 1940), 178–227; Weichmann, 164–172; William P. Wood, War Department Archives (National Archives); Wood's report is undated; *Evidence*, 594–595.
11. Surratt, "A Remarkable Lecture," *op. cit.*; "Defends Mrs. Surratt," *Washington Post*, January 7, 1908; Roy Z. Chamlee Jr., *Lincoln's Assassins* (Jefferson, NC: McFarland, 1990), 75, 189. Weichmann to Col. H.L. Burnett, May 5, 1865, War Department Records, Judge Advocate General's Files; John T. Ford, "Behind the Curtain of a Conspiracy," *North American Review* 148, no. 389 (April 1889), 484–493.
12. John W. Clampitt, "The Trial of Mrs. Surratt," *North American Review* 131, no. 286 (September 1880), 223–240.
13. Kauffman, 233;. OR, Series I 46, part III, 937; Cottingham to Col. Burnett, May 14, 1865; Affidavit of J.W. Ridenour, December 1, 1865; Bureau of Military Justice Records (National Archives).
14. Poore I, 3–14; Edward Steers, Jr., and Harold Holzer, ed., *The Lincoln Assassination Conspirators* (Baton Rouge: Louisiana State University Press, 2009), 41–42, 96, 152–153.
15. Clampitt, *op. cit.*; Constitution of the United States of America, Article I, section 9; Frederick Hatch, *The Lincoln Assassination Conspiracy Trial and Its Legacy* (Jefferson, NC: McFarland, 2015), 105;United States Supreme Court, Ex parte Milligan, 71 U.S. (4 Wall.) 2 (1866); Theodore Roscoe, *The Web of Conspiracy* (Englewood Cliffs, NJ: Prentice Hall, 1959), 487; Weichmann, 277.
16. Steers and Holzer, 51–55, 152–153; Clampitt, *op. cit.*

Chapter 6

1. Surratt, "A Remarkable Lecture," *op. cit.*; *Trial* I, 725–728 II, 729–733; Scott Jenkins, "Confederate Spy Visits Elmira," *Chemung Historical Society* (March 1997) 42, no. 3, 4620–4621; Lee, ""Canadian Diary,""" *op. cit.*; *Brighman's Elmira City Directory* (Elmira, NY: Chemung County, NY, 1863).
2. Alfred Isacsson, *Travels, Arrest and Trial of John H Surratt* (Middletown, NY: Vestigium, 2003), 1–2; Weichmann, 177–179; *Evidence*, 485; A.C. Richards to Weichmann, April 29, 1898, in Weichmann, 177; Weichmann, 178–179; OR, Series I 46, part III, 847–848.
3. Alexandra Lee Levin, "Who Hid John H. Surratt, the Lincoln Conspiracy Case Figure?" *Maryland Historical Magazine* 60, no. 2 (June 1965), 175–184; Surratt, Lecture, *op. cit.*; *Montreal Gazette*, April 26, 1865, described Edwin G. Lee as "the Confederate officer of the highest grade in Canada."
4. Poore III, 116, 134, 138–139; Carman Cumming, *Devil's Game: The Civil War Intrigues of Charles A. Dunham* (Urbana: University of Illinois Press, 2004), 14, 18, 107, 130.
5. Weichmann, 218–221, 369; James A. McDevitt and Albert Daggett, "Tragic Memories," *Washington Evening Star*, April 14, 1894, p. 17; Levin, *"This Awful*

Drama," 154–155, 165–166; Surratt, *Lecture, op. cit.*; Levin, "Who Hid John H. Surratt?" *op. cit.*; *Trial,* 676–677, 857–858, 895–897, 902–905, 932; Lee, ""Canadian Diary,,"" *op. cit.*; Rev. Leo Sansoucy, Superior, Seminaire de Saint-Hyacinthe, to James O. Hall, June 23 (1966), J.O. Hall Papers; Marie Baboyant to James O. Hall, September 23 (1981), J.O. Hall Papers; Charles H. Blinn, "How I Lost One Hundred Thousand Dollars," *Overland Monthly* 59, no. 1 (January 1912), 21–23.

6. *Trial,* 906–908. Levin, "Who Hid John H. Surratt?" *op. cit.*; Levin, "*This Awful Drama,*" 168–169; John F. Potter, U.S. Consul General, Montreal, to Hon. W.H. Hunter, Acting Secretary of State, May 22, 1865; L'Abbe J.B.A. Allaire, *Dictionnaire Biographique du Clerge Canadien-Francais* (Montreal: Imprimerie de l'Ecole Catholique des sourds—Muets, 1910), 188, 194; Marie Baboyant to James O. Hall, September 23, 1981, J.O. Hall Papers.

7. *Trial,* 909–912; Lee, "*Canadian Diary,*" *op. cit.*; James O. Hall, notes, "John Surratt, Jr., in Canada: His relationship to E.G. Lee, etc.," J.O. Hall papers, *op. cit.*; Levin, "Who Hid John H. Surratt?," *op. cit.*; Ludwell H. Johnson, "Notes and Documents: Beverley Tucker's Canadian Mission, 1864–1865," *Journal of Southern History* 29, no. 1 (February 1963), 88–99; J.B. Jones, A Rebel War Clerk's Diary II (Philadelphia: J.B. Lippincott, 1866), 319–320.

8. Roswell Ripley (Wikipedia); Patricia L. Faust, ed., *Historical Times Illustrated Encyclopedia of the Civil War* (New York: Harper Perennial, 1991), 634–635; Levin, "Who Hid John H. Surratt?"; *Trial,* 461–463; Ezra J. Warner, *Generals in Gray* (Baton Rouge: Louisiana State University Press, 1959), 257; "Mr. Beverley Tucker," *New York Times,* July 16, 1867.

Chapter 7

1. Surratt, *Lecture, op. cit.*; Lee, "Canadian Diary," April 19, 1865; May 4, 1865; Sept. 5, 1865; Andrew C.A. Jampoler, *The Last Lincoln Conspirator* (Annapolis, MD: Naval Institute Press, 2008), 70–73; George H. Sharpe, "Report of George H. Sharpe relative to the Assassination of President Lincoln," in U.S. House of Representatives, 40th Congress, 2nd Session, Ex. Doc. No. 68 (December 13, 1867), 3.

2. *Trial,* 462–484; William Cornell Jewett in the *Free Online Encyclopedia*; Jampoler, 75.

3. *The Pursuit and Arrest of John H Surratt: Despatches from the Official Record of the Assassination of Abraham Lincoln* (Austin, TX: Civil War Library, 2000), 1; Nathaniel Hawthorne, *The Consular Letters, 1853–1855,* 19 (Columbus: Ohio State University Press, 1988), 15–16; Nathaniel Hawthorne, *Our Old Home: A Series of English Sketches* 5 (Columbus: Ohio State University Press, 1970), 6–7; Brenda Wineapple, *Hawthorne: A Life* (New York: Alfred A. Knopf, 2003), 296; Robert L. Gale, *A Nathaniel Hawthorne Encyclopedia* (New York: Greenwood, 1991), 503.

4. Mr.Wilding to Mr. Seward, No. 539, September 30, House of Representatives, 39th Congress, 2nd Session (Liverpool: United States Consulate, 1865), Ex. Doc. No. 9; Francis Russell, *Adams: An American Dynasty* (New York: American Heritage, 1976), 6–7, 260–272; Mr. Wilding to Mr. Seward, No. 544, October 10 (1865), *op. cit.*; Mr. Potter to Mr. Seward, No. 236, October 25, 1865, *op. cit.*; *Pursuit and Arrest,* 2–3; John Fox Potter, http://bioguide.congress.gov/scripts/biodisplay.pl?index=P000465.

5. Isacsson, *Travels,* 8–9; Surratt, *Lecture, op. cit.*

6. Morison, Commager, and Leuchtenburg, 468–469.

7. "Col. Caleb Ruse Dead," *New York Times,* March 13, 1905, p. 7; "George Alfred Trenholm," http://www.findagrave.com/eg:-bin/fg.cgi?page=gr&GRid=14733778; Wikipedia,"George Trenholm"; John D. Bennett, *The London Confederates* (Jefferson, NC: McFarland, 2008), 25–33; McPherson, 389–391.

8. Eli N. Evans, *Judah P. Benjamin: The Jewish Confederate* (New York: Free Press, 1988), 280; John B. Castleman, *Active Service* (Louisville, KY: Courier Journal Job Printing, 1917), 201–202; James D. Horan, *Confederate Agent: A Discovery in History* (New York: Crown, 1954), 293–298; Bennett, 170; Tidwell, *April '65,* 19–29, 201.

9. William A. Tidwell, "Confederate Expenditures for Secret Service," *Civil War History* 37, no. 3 (September 1991), 219–231; Tidwell, *April '65,* 128, 163; Tidwell, "Confederate Expenditures," *op. cit.* (the reference to "Captain Booth" is on page 224).

10. Isacsson, 8–9; Gray, 124; "A Vigne Descendant and Fulkerson Cousin Jacob Thompson," http://www.fulkerson.Org/thompson.html; William C. Davis, "The Conduct of 'Mr. Thompson,'" *Civil War Times Illustrated* 9, no. 2 (May 1970), 4–7, 43–47; Bennett, 156.

11. *American Leaders, 1789-1987: A Biographical Summary* (Washington: Congressional Quarterly, 1987), 85; Burke Davis, *The Long Surrender* (New York: Random House, 1985), 129–130, 163–167; Wikipedia, "John C. Breckinridge," http://en.wikipedia.org/wiki/John C. Breckinridge; Wikipedia, "John Slidell," http:en.wikipedia.orglwiki/John Slidell; Wikipedia, "James Murray Mason," http://en.wikipedia.org/wiki/James_Murray_Mason.

12. Charles S. Davis, *Colin J McRae: Confederate Financial Agent* (Tuscaloosa, AL: Confederate, 1961), 25, 30, 35–42, 50–51, 82–83.

13. Kenneth Coleman and Charles Stephen Gurr, ed., *Dictionary of Georgia Biography I* (Athens: University of Georgia Press, 1983), 136–138; James D. Bulloch, *The Secret Service of the Confederate States in Europe* (New York: Modern Library, 2001), 594–595; Hubert Leroy, "Ambrose Dudley Mann: Diplomat of the Lost Cause" (Confederate Historical Association of Belgium, n.d.); George H. Sharpe to William H. Seward, London, June 12, 1867, Department of State records.

14. Wikipedia, "Venerable English College, Rome," http://en.wikipedia.org/wiki/venerable_English_College%2C_Rome; Isacsson, *Travels,* 10.

Chapter 8

1. Edgar Holt, *Risorgimento* (London: Macmillan, 1970), 230–23l; Raffaele de Cesare, *The Last Days of Papal Rome* (Boston: Houghton, Mifflin, 1909), 30, 35–37; Braudel, 330; Wikipedia, "Italian Unification," http://en.wikipedia.org/wiki/Risorgimento.

2. Wikipedia, "Zouave," http://en.wikipedia.org/wiki/Zouave; Isacsson, *Travels,* 10–13.

3. Mr. Potter to Mr. Seward, No. 236, October 25 (Montreal: 1865); In "Message from the President of the United States, Transmitting a Report of the Secretary of State Relating to the Discovery and Arrest of John H. Surratt," U.S. Congress, House of Representatives, Ex. Doc. No. 9, 39th Congress, 2nd Session, and Mr. Seward to Mr. Speed, November 13 (1865); Awards for the Capture of Booth and Others, U.S. Congress, House of

Representatives, Ex. Doc. No. 90, 39th Congress, 1st Session, reproduced in Microcopy 619, reel 457, frame 0235, National Archives; James L. Swanson and Daniel R. Weinburg, *Lincoln's Assassins: Their Trial and Execution; An Illustrated History* (Santa Fe, NM: Arena, 2001), 50; Isacsson, *Travels*, 13; Testimony of E. M. Stanton before House Judiciary Committee, January 10, 1867.

4. Mr. King to Mr. Seward, No. 53, April 23 (Rome, 1866), in "Message from the President," *op. cit.*; George H. Holt, U.S. Consul at Quebec, to Frederick W. Seward, Assistant Secretary of State, January 23 (1868), in *Evidence*, 699–700; George, "H.B. Ste. Marie and His Role in the Arrest of John H. Surratt," *op. cit.*; *Trial*, 851, 990–991. Weichmann, *True History*, 23–25.

5. George, "H.B. Ste. Marie", *op. cit.*; "Message from the President," *op. cit.*; *American Leaders*, 335. Otto Eisenschiml, *In the Shadow of Lincoln's Death* (New York: Wilfred Funk, 1940), 248–251; *Washington Daily Morning Chronicle*, March 4, 1867; William Hanchett, "An Interview with William Hanchett," *Journal of the Lincoln Assassination* 3, No. 2 (August 1989), 18–21, 30–32; Wikipedia, "Transatlantic Telegraph Cable," http://en.wikipedia.org/wild/Transatlantic_telegraph_cable.

6. Isacsson, *Travels*, 13;"Mr. King to Mr. Seward, No. 59," July 14 (Rome, 1866), in "Message from the President"; "Mr. Seward to Mr. Stanton, August 7, 1866"; "Mr. King to Mr. Seward, No. 62, August 8, 1866"; General Charles King, "Rufus King: Soldier, Editor, and Statesman," *Wisconsin Magazine of History* 4, no. 4 (June 1921), 371–381.

7. Duane Koenig, "General Rufus King and the Capture of John H. Surratt," *Wisconsin Magazine of History* 25, no. 1 (September 1941), 43–50; "Mr. Seward to Mr. King," October 16, 1866, "Mr. King to Mr. Seward," November 2, 1866, and "Mr. King to Mr. Seward," November 3, 1866, in "Message from the President," *op. cit.*

8. Alfred Isacsson, "The Search for John Surratt's Military Records," *Surratt Courier* 15, no. 5 (May 1990), 4–5; "Lt. Col. Allet to the General, Minister of War," November 8 (1866), in "Message from the President," *op. cit.*; Isacsson, *Travels*, 21, 24; "Helping Surratt to Escape," *New York Daily Tribune*, February 21, 1881, p. 3; *Life, Trial and Adventures of John H Surratt, the Conspirator* (Philadelphia: Barclay, 1867).

9. "Mr. Marsh to Mr. Seward," November 18, 1866, King to Marsh, November 12, 1866, King to Marsh, November 13, 1866, King to Marsh, November 16, 1866, Marsh to Visconti Venosta, November 16, 1866, Marsh to Visconti Venosta, November 17, 1866, in "Message from the President," *op. cit.*; "John H. Surratt, His Arrest in the Ranks of the Papal Army—His Escape," *Washington Evening Star*, December 5, 1866, p. 1

10. Mr. King to Mr. Seward, no. 67, November 19, 1866, in "Message from the President," *op. cit.*; Jampoler, 112; Evan M. Duncan, Office of the Historian, Bureau of Public Affairs, U.S. Department of State, to Frederick Hatch, May 31 (2013), Frederick Hatch Papers. Frank Swan to Rufus King, November 18, 1866, in "Messages from the President," *op, cit.*

11. Ibid., "Mr. Swan to Mr. Seward, November 21 (1866)," "Mr. Winthrop to Mr. Seward, November 22, 1866," U.S. House of Representatives, 39th Congress, 2nd Session, Ex. Doc. No. 25; "Wm. Winthrop to R. C. Legh, Acting Secretary to Gov't," November 21 (1866), "R.C. Legh to W. Winthrop, No. 4598, Valletta, Malta, November 19, 1866," "R.C. Legh to W. Winthrop, No. 4608, Valletta, Malta, November 21, 1866"; Jampoler, 134.

12. Ibid., No. 25, "William Winthrop to Charles Hale," November 19, 1866, "Mr. King to Mr. Seward," No. 68, November 26 (Rome: 1866), "John Watson [Surratt] to Edward T. O'Connor," Ceroli, August 30, 1866.

13. Ed. George E. Baker, *The Works of William H Seward* 5 (Boston: Houghton, Mifflin, 1884), 474.

Chapter 9

1. *Pursuit and Arrest*, 51; Frank Freidel, ed., Harvard Guide to American History (Cambridge, MA: Belknap Press of Harvard University, 1974), 199; "Mr. Hale to Mr. Seward," No. 66, Alexandria, Egypt, November 27, 1866, in "Message from the President," No. 25, *op. cit.*; "John H. Surratt and the Conspiracy against the Government," *New York Times*, November 26, 1866, p. 5; "Arrest of John H. Surratt," *Washington Evening Star*, December 4, 1866, p. 2; *London Times*, December 6, 1866.

2. Louis J. Weichmann to Joseph Holt, December 5, 1866, Holt Papers 54, No. 7507–7508 (Library of Congress); "Mr. Hale to Mr. Seward," No. 70, December 8 (Alexandria, Egypt, 1866), *op. cit.*; George, "H.B. Ste. Marie and His Role", *op. cit.*; "Mr. King to Mr. Seward," No. 72, December 17 (Rome, 1866), "Mr. Hale to Mr. Seward," Telegram received at War Department, Washington, December 29, 1866, in "Message from the President," No. 25, *op. cit.*; Log Book of the U.S. Screw Sloop *Swatara*, National Archives (Washington, DC); Paul H. Silverstone, *Warships of the Civil War Navies* (Annapolis, MD: Naval Institute Press, 1989), 56; "John H. Surratt," Report No. 33, U.S. Congress, House of Representatives, 39th Congress, 2nd Session, March 2 (1867); "John Surratt's Capture," *New York Sun*, May 20, 1916.

3. "Surratt on the *Swatara*," *Washington Evening Star*, January 31, 1867, p. 2; "Surratt," *Washington Evening Star*, January 23 1867, p. 2; "Surratt," *Washington Evening Star*, January 30, 1867, p. 2; "Surratt," *Washington Evening Star*, February 11, 1867, p. 2; "Arrival of Surratt," *Washington Evening Star*, February 18, 1867, p. 2.

4. "The Surratt Case," *New York Times*, February 16, 1867, p. 5; "William H. Seward to D.S. Gooding, Marshal of the U.S. for the District of Columbia," February 18, 1867, in *Pursuit*, 73–74; "The Surratt Indictment," *Washington Evening Star*, February 5, 1867, p. 2; "Indictment of Surratt," *New York Times*, February 5, 1867, p. 5; Constitution of the United States of America, Amendment 1; *Cincinnati Commercial*, February 22, 1867; Henry Greenleaf Pearson, *The Life of John A. Andrew* (Boston: 1904), 302–303.

5. "Arraignment of Surratt," *Washington Evening Star*, February 23, 1867, p. 2; Jampoler, 162–165; "A Visit to Surratt," *New York Times*, April 8, 1867, p. 4; *Chicago Tribune*, June 24, 1867.

6. Wikipedia, "George P. Fisher," http://en.wikipedia.org/wiki/George_P_Fisher; "George Purnell Fisher," Dickinson College Archives and Special Collections, http://archives.dickinson.edu/people/george pumell fisher1817-1899; Carol E. Hoffecker, "Abraham Lincoln and Delaware," *Delaware History* 32, no. 3 (Fall/Winter 2008), 155–170; Wikipedia,"United States District Court for the District of Columbia," http:en.wikipedia.org/wiki/United States District Court_for_the_District_of_Columbia.

7. Chamlee, 517.

8. Weichmann, 355; Eisenschiml, *In the Shadow*, 267–269, 393–394; Wikipedia, "Edwards Pierrepont," http://en.wikipedia.org/wiki/Edwards_Pierrepont, and

"Albert G. Riddle," http://en.wikipedia.org/wiki/Albert_G_Riddle.

9. "Joseph Habersham Bradley," Find a Grave Memorial, http://www.findagrave.com/cgi_bin/fg.cgi?page & GRid:-46605697; Wikipedia, "Abraham Bradley, Jr.," http://en.wikipedia.org/wiki/ Abraham_Bradley_Jr. Chamlee, 219, and "Richard T. Merrick," http://en.wikipedia.org/wiki/Richard T Merrick; Grace Dunlop Ecker, *A Portrait of Old Georgetown* (Richmond, VA: 1951), 280; *American Leaders*, 233.

10. Joseph George Jr., "The Trials of John H. Surratt," *Maryland Historical Magazine* 99, no. 1 (Spring 2004), 17–49; *New York Herald*, February 24. 1867.

11. "The Surratt Trial," *Washington Evening Star*, June 10, 1867, p. 1; *Trial*, 51–117.

12. "Comparison of Testimony of Major Henry R. Rathbone," in Eisenschiml, *In The Shadow*, 282–283; Weichmann's testimony in *Trial*, 432–433; Weichmann, 32–35, 362; *Trial*, 131–135, 183–189, 206, 210–211, 308–314; Chamlee, 367–368, 427; John H. Surratt, "Sworn Statement," copy in D.R. Barbee Papers.

13. Chamlee, 513; *Trial*, 166–168, 183–189, 198–200, 205–213, 216–217, 220–225.

14. *Trial*, 232–235.

15. Ibid., 277–286, 289–293.

16. Ibid., 369–434.

Chapter 10

1. Edwin Haviland Miller, ed., *Walt Whitman: The Correspondence, 1842–1867* (New York: New York University Press, 1961), 314–315, 320, 333–334; Gay Wilson Allen, *The Solitary Singer* (Chicago: University of Chicago Press, 1967), 380.

2. *Trial*, 387–388, 400, 405–406, 455; *Philadelphia Inquirer*, July 29, 1867, p. 2; Weichmann, 12, 328, 362, 488.

3. *Trial*, 482–483, 559, 565–566, 569; Thomas A. Bogar, *Backstage at the Lincoln Assassination* (Washington, D.C.: Regenery History, 2013), 203.

4. *Trial*, 640, 714, 722, 725, 729.

5. Ibid., 781–782, 814–815, 820; Seward to Dr. McMillan, February 19, 1867, Department of State Archives.

6. *Trial*, 842–847, 848–853, 857–858, 893, 897–898, 941–947; "John H. Surratt," *New York World*, September 3 1867.

7. Ibid., 1081–1083, 1089–1091, 1102–1105, 1121.

8. Ibid., 1142, 1150–1151.

9. Ibid., 1156–1159, 1164–1165, 1179, 1218–1246.

10. Ibid., 1255, 1257, 1259, 1282, 1285, 1314–1364.

11. Ibid., 1369, 1371–1378, 1379; Chamlee, 526–528; "Judge Fisher Not Assaulted," *Washington Evening Star*, July 5, 1867, p. 3.

12. Miscellaneous Letters, Department of State Archives: Pierrepont to Seward, February 21, 1868, Riddle to Seward, September 25, 1868; George, "The Trials of John H. Surratt," *op. cit.*; James E.T. Lange and Katherine DeWitt Jr., "The Three Indictments of John Harrison Surratt, Jr.," *Surratt Courier* 17, no. 1 (January 1992), 6–7; Mark E. Neely Jr., ed., *The Abraham Lincoln Encyclopedia* (New York: Da Capo, 1982), 39; William Morris, ed., *The American Heritage Dictionary of the English Language* (Boston: Houghton Mifflin, 1969), 891; Henry Campbell Black, *Black's Law Dictionary*, 5th ed. (St. Paul, MN: West, 1979); *United States v. John H. Surratt*, Criminal Docket No. 5920, Decided November 6, 1868; Franklin H. Mackey, *Reports of Cases Argued and Adjudged in the Supreme Court of the District of Columbia* (Washington, D.C.: Law Reporter, 1889); District of Columbia Reports [17 Dist. Col.] 6, 306–309; "The Surratt Trial," *New York Times*, September 25 1868, p. 1. *Life and Extraordinary Adventures...*, 136. *New York Tribune*, August 12, 1867; *Baltimore American*, August 15, 1867; *New York World*, August 10, 1867; Edward C. Carrington to Attorney General James Speed, June 9, 1868, Department of Justice Archives; Morris, ed., 891; *Baltimore Sun*, August 10, 1867; Supreme Court of the District of Columbia, *United States v. John H. Surratt*, No. 5920, December term 1868).

Chapter 11

1. Wikipedia, "Alphonse de Lamartine"; *Washington National Intelligencer*, February 3, 1868; William Rose Benet, *Benet's Reader's Encyclopedia*, 3rd ed. (New York: Harper & Row, 1987), 546; "Book Review: Private Journal and Diary of John H. Surratt the Conspirator," Papers of James O. Hall; *Life and Extraordinary Adventures of John H. Surratt, the Conspirator: A Correct Account and Highly Interesting Narrative of His Doings and Adventures from Childhood to the Present Time* (Philadelphia: Barclay, 1867).

2. *Washington National Intelligencer*, November 13, 1865.

3. Copies of Confederate Company Muster Rolls, Dated March–December 1862, in papers of James O. Hall; Faust, ed., *Historical Times Illustrated Encyclopedia*, 695; http://freepages.genealogy.rootsweb.ancestry.com/prsjr/Omary/chapter/chap_12b.htm; P.H. Sheridan to Hon. E.M. Stanton, Sec. of War, Headquarters Division of the Gulf, New Orleans, October 18, 1865; War Department Records, National Archives, copy in J.O. Hall Papers; Chamlee, 556.

4. Laurie Verge, "What Happened to the Children?" *Surratt Society News* 9, no. 7 (July-August 1984), 4–5.

5. John H. Surratt to Major William Norris, Alderman Library, University of Virginia at Charlottesville; "The Remains of Mrs. Surratt," *New York Times*, February 9, 1869, p. 1; "The Removal of the Remains of Mrs. Surratt," *New York Times*, February 10, 1869, p. 1; "City Intelligence," *Washington Daily Chronicle*, February 10, 1869; "Interment of the Remains of Mrs. Surratt," *Washington Daily National Intelligencer*, February 10, 1869.

6. "Marriage of Miss Surratt," *Baltimore Sun*, June 18, 1869; Mary Tonry Walsh to James O. Hall, November 6, 1982, J.O. Hall Papers; "Washington Facts and Impressions," *Washington National News*, July 2, 1869; Ellen Hart, "Descendants of Mary Surratt," *Surratt Society News* 4, no. 3 (March, 1979); "The Surratt Family Tree," http://www.surratt.org/genealogy/su genl.html.

7. Surratt, *Lecture*; Arnold, *Memoirs*, 149–150; Loux, *John Wilkes Booth Day By Day*, 434; Lee, "Canadian Diary," April 6, May 4, August 11, August 18, September 5, September 16, 1865.

8. "John H. Surratt," *New York Times*, December 8, 1870; "John H. Surratt at the Cooper Institute," *New York Times*, December 10, 1870, p. 5; "Surratt in Baltimore," *Baltimore Sun*, December 30, 1870, p. 1.

9. Chamlee, 535–537; "Surratt in Washington," *Baltimore Sun*, December 31, 1870, p. 1, c. 5; David Rankin Barbee, "John Surratt's Ill-fated Lecture Tour," *Baltimore Sun*, December 25, 1932, magazine section; *New York Daily Tribune*, January 4, 1871.

10. "John Surratt," Abraham Lincoln's Assassination, Surratt House Museum, wysiwyg://6/http:/members.

aol.com/RVSNorton!Lincoln37.htn; Jane C. Sween, Librarian, Montgomery County Historical Society, to John C. Brennan, April 7, 1987, copy in J.O. Hall Papers; Isacsson, "Biography," 62; "The Rambler Finds Another Historic Spot," *Washington Sunday Star*, September 29, 1919, p. 2; Alexander Crosby Brown, *The Old Bay Line* (New York: Bonanza, 1940), 152; Jane C. Sween to John C. Brennan, March 22, 1987, copy in J.O. Hall Papers; James O. Hall to John C. Brennan, March 26, 1987, J.O. Hall Papers (Rockville, MD: baptismal records of St. Mary's Catholic Church), copied by J.C. Brennan, J.O. Hall Papers.

11. *New York Times*, February 15, 1893; OR, Series I 21, 111; OR, Series IV 2, 395; OR, Series IV 2, 841, 866; OR, Series I 32, Pt. 2, 551;OR, Series I 36, Pt. 2, 987; OR, Series I 47, Pt. 2, 1444; OR, Series I 47, Pt. 3, 687–688, 695; Bennett, 60; Col. John Moncure Robinson (1835–1893), Find a Grave Memorial, http://www.findagrave.com/cgibin/fg.cgi?page=gr&GRid=46829097; Brown, *The Old Bay Line*, 71.

12. Alexander Crosby Brown, "The Old Bay Line of the Chesapeake: A Sketch of a Hundred Years of Steamboat Operation," *William and Mary College Quarterly Historical Magazine* 18, no. 4 (October 1938), 389–405; Brown, *The Old Bay Line*, 71, 152–153; Morison, Commager, and Leuchtenburg I, 621; McPherson, 287; Eugenia Roush to James O. Hall, reply to Hall's letter of June 25, 1973, undated, papers of J.O. Hall.

13. Isacsson, *Travels, Arrests and Trial*, 33; Jampoler, 87; James Mitchell and Jess Stein, ed., *The Random House Encyclopedia* (New York: Random House, 1977), 1628–1629, 2594; "Interment Today of Remains of Isaac D. Surratt," *Washington Evening Star*, November 5, 1907, p. 17; Brown, "The Old Bay Line of the Chesapeake."

14. Western Union Telegraph Company of Baltimore City, received at S.W. corner of Calvert and Baltimore streets, J.Z. Jenkins to Professor Tonry, dated 1878, copy from Mrs. Mary T. Walsh, papers of J.O. Hall; *Martenet's Map of Prince George's County, Maryland* (Baltimore: Simon J. Martenet, 1861), 14.

15. "John H. Surratt—A Talk with a Once Famous Man Who Narrowly Escaped the Scaffold—A True Story of His Flight—He Would Have Returned Had He Thought His Mother Was in Danger," by "Pilgrim," Special Correspondent, *Philadelphia Times*, October 4, 1885; Hiss, *op. cit.*; Chamlee, 219; "John H. Surratt, Sole Survivor of Those Accused of Plotting to Kill Lincoln, Now a Well-to-Do Citizen of Baltimore" (from the *Brooklyn Eagle*), *Springfield (MA) Daily Republican*, October 21, 1901; "How the Plot Against Lincoln Was Formed," *New York Times*, February 7, 1909.

16. Brown, *The Old Bay Line*, 100; Wikipedia, "Baltimore Steam Packet Company," "Great Baltimore Fire of 1904," hnp://www.mdch.org/fire/text only.htrnl; Peter B. Petersen, *The Great Baltimore Fire* (Baltimore: Press of the Maryland Historical Society, 2004), xiv-xv, 14–39, 43–67, 83–93, 196, 199; Brown, *The Old Bay Line*, 103; "Baltimore Steam Packet Company," *Old Bay Line Magazine* 1, no. 9 (April 1911), 1–7; Robert H. Burgess, *This Was Chesapeake Bay* (Cambridge, MD: Cornell Maritime, 1963), 69–70; "Directory of Agencies," *Old Bay Line Magazine* 1, no. 1 (August 1910), iv.

17. *Baltimore Steam Packet Company, Norfolk, Va., Old Bay Line Records* (Baltimore, MA: Maryland Historical Society, 1906): "Memorandum," November 21; "Investigation of Freight Expenses at Norfolk, Va.," November 24, 1906; John R. Sherwood, President and General Manager, to Mr. J.H. Surratt, Auditor and FCA, January 25, 1908; John R. Sherwood to Mr. J.B. Kumsden, James E. Byrd, J.H. Surratt, Geo. G. Hobson, T.W. Jordan, H. M. Woods, J.B. Kimberly, A.H. Jones, July 29 (1909); John R. Sherwood to Key Compton, July 29 (1909); Key Compton to John R. Sherwood, July 30 (1909); John R. Sherwood to Key Compton, July 31 (1909); John R. Sherwood to Departments and Agents [named above], August 2, 1909; Baltimore Steam Packet Company, Accounting Department, Statement of the Earnings, Expenditures and Statistics During the Month of March, and Comparison with Same Period of Previous Year, May 1, 1910; J.S. Wilson Jr. & Company, Bankers, description of Railroad Equipment Bond, April 18, 1910; J.S. Wilson Jr. & Company, Proof Circular, Chesapeake Steamship Company, Equipment & Terminal First Mortgage 5 percent Gold Bonds (April 1910).

18. "Presentation of Medals of Honor," *Old Bay Line Magazine* 3, no. 2 (September 1912), 1–3.

19. John W. Starr, *Further Light on Lincoln's Last Day: A Study of the Attendant Circumstances* (Harrisburg, PA: J.W. Starr, 1930), chapter 27.

20. Alice Camalier Behrendt, notes on Anna Surratt, November 6, 1982, James O. Hall Papers. See also *Surratt Society News* 4, no. 2 (February 1979); "Surratt," *Baltimore Sun*, November 4, 1907, p. 4. "Isaac D. Surratt Dead," *Baltimore Sun*, November 4, 1907, p. 4, c. 6; Helen Jones Campbell, *Confederate Courier* (New York: St. Martin's, 1964), 289–291; "Death Ends Long Illness and Eventful Career," *Baltimore Sun*, April 22, 1916, p.1; "Lincoln Discussion Symposium, Mary Victorine Hunter Surratt," http://rogernorton.com/Lincoln DiscussionSymposium/archive/indexphp?thread_116.html; J. William Joynes, "The Missing Link in Lincoln's Assassination," *Baltimore News-American*, February 12, 1974.

Bibliography

Books

Allaire, L'Abbe S.B.A. *Dictionaire Biographique du Clerge Canadien Francais.* Montreal: Muets, 1910.
Allen, Gay Wilson. *The Solitary Singer.* Chicago: 1967.
Andreano, Ralph, ed. *Economic Impact of the American Civil War.* Cambridge, MA: Schenkman, 1962.
Arnold, Samuel Bland, and Michael W. Kauffman, ed. *Memoirs of a Lincoln Conspirator.* Bowie, MD: Heritage, 1995.
Atlas of Fifteen Miles around Washington Including the County of Prince George, Maryland. Philadelphia: G.M. Hopkins, 1878.
Atlas of Prince George County, Maryland, adapted from Simon J. Martinet's Map of Prince George's County, Maryland. Baltimore, 1861.
Baker, George E., ed. *The Works of William H. Seward.* Boston: Houghton, Mifflin, 1884.
Baker, L.C. *History of the United States Secret Service.* Philadelphia: L.C. Baker, 1867.
Benet, William Rose. *Benet's Reader's Encyclopedia.* New York: Harper and Row, 1987.
Bennett, John D. *The London Confederates.* Jefferson, NC: McFarland, 2008.
Black, Henry Campbell. *Black's Law Dictionary.* St. Paul, MN: West, 1979.
Brandt, Nat. *The Man Who Tried to Burn New York.* Syracuse: Syracuse University Press, 1986.
Braudel, Fernand. *A History of Civilizations.* New York: Penguin, 1994.
Brown, Alexander Crosby. *The Old Bay Line.* New York: Bonanza, 1940.
Bryan, George S. *The Great American Myth.* New York: Carrick & Evans, 1940.
Bulloch, James D. *The Secret Service of the Confederate States in Europe.* New York: Modern Library, 2001.
Burgess, Robert H. *This Was Chesapeake Bay.* Cambridge, MD: Cornell Maritime, 1963.
Campbell, Helen Jones. *Confederate Courier.* New York: St. Martin's, 1964.
Carter, Samuel, III. *The Riddle of Dr. Mudd.* New York: G.P. Putnam's Sons, 1974.
Castleman, John B. *Active Service.* Louisville, KY: Courier Job Printing, 1917.
Cesare, Raffaele de. *The Last Days of Papal Rome.* Boston: Houghton-Mifflin., 1909.
Chamlee, Roy Z., Jr. *Lincoln's Assassins.* Jefferson, NC: McFarland, 1990.
Coleman, Kenneth, and Charles Stephen Gurr, ed. *Dictionary of Georgia Biography.* Athens: University of Georgia Press, 1983.
Conrad, Thomas Nelson. *A Confederate Spy.* New York: J.S. Ogilvie, 1892.
_____. *The Rebel Scout.* Washington: National, 1904.
Cumming, Carman. *Devil's Game: The Civil War Intrigues of Charles A. Dunham.* Urbana: University of Illinois Press, 2004.
Davis, Burke. *The Long Surrender.* New York: Random House, 1985.
Davis, Charles S. *Colin J McRae: Confederate Financial Agent.* Tuscaloosa, AL: Confederate, 1961.
De Gregorio, William A. *The Complete Book of U.S. Presidents.* New York: Barricade, 1993.
Dictionaire Etymologique des Noms de Famile et Prenoms de France. Paris: Larousse, 1961.
Donald, David Herbert. *Lincoln.* London: Jonathan Cape, 1995.
Dubois, Marguerite Marie. *Larousse's French-English, English-French Dictionary.* New York: Washington Square, 1968.
Ecker, Grace Dunlop. *A Portrait of Old Georgetown.* Richmond, VA, 1951.
Edwards, William C., and Edward Steers, Jr. *The Lincoln Assassination: The Evidence.* Urbana and Chicago: University of Illinois Press, 2009.
Eisenschiml, Otto. *In The Shadow of Lincoln's Death.* New York: Wilfred Funk, 1940.
Evans, Eli N. *Judah P. Benjamin: The Jewish Confederate.* New York: Free Press, 1988.
Faust, Patricia L., ed. *Historical Times Illustrated Encyclopedia of the Civil War.* New York: HarperCollins, 1991.

Freidel, Frank, ed. *Harvard Guide to American History*. Cambridge, MA: Belknap Press of Harvard University, 1974.
Gale, Robert L. *A Nathaniel Hawthorne Encyclopedia*. New York: Greenwood, 1991.
Gray, Clayton. *Conspiracy in Canada*. Montreal: L'Atelier, 1957.
Hall, James O. *The Surratt Family and John Wilkes Booth*. Clinton, MD: Surratt Society, [1976].
Hatch, Frederick. *The Lincoln Assassination Conspiracy Trial and Its Legacy*. Jefferson, NC: McFarland, 2015.
_____. *Protecting President Lincoln*. Jefferson, NC: McFarland, 2011.
Hawthorne, Nathaniel. *The Consular Letters, 1853–1857*. Columbus: Ohio State University Press, 1988.
_____. *Our Old Home: A Series of English Sketches*. Columbus: Ohio State University Press, 1970.
Headley, John W. *Confederate Operations in Canada and New York*. New York: Neale, 1906.
Hesseltine, William, ed. *Civil War Prisons*. Kent, OH: Kent State University Press, 1962.
Hill, J.R. *The Oxford Illustrated History of the Royal Navy*. Oxford: Oxford University Press, 1995.
Holt, Edgar. *Risorgimento*. London: Macmillan, 1970.
Horan, James D. *Confederate Agent*. New York: Crown, 1954.
Horigan, Michael. *Elmira: Death Camp of the North*. Mechanicsburg, PA: Stackpole, 2002.
Isacsson, Alfred. *The Travels, Arrest and Trial of John H Surratt*. Middletown, NY: Vestigium, 2003.
Jampoler, Andrew C.A. *The Last Lincoln Conspirator*. Annapolis, MD: Naval Institute Press, 2008.
Johnson, Rossiter, ed. *The Biographical Dictionary of America*. Boston: American Biographical Society, 1906.
Jones, J.B. *A Rebel War Clerk's Diary*. Philadelphia: J.B. Lippincott, 1866.
Jones, Thomas A. *J. Wilkes Booth*. Chicago: Laird & Lee, 1893.
Kauffman, Michael W. *American Brutus*. New York: Random House, 2004.
Keehn, David C. *Knights of the Golden Circle*. Baton Rouge: Louisiana State University Press, 2013.
Laws Made and Passed by the General Assembly of the State of Maryland. Annapolis: E.S. Riley, 1854.
Levin, Alexandra Lee. *"This Awful Drama": General Edwin Gray Lee, C.S.A., and His Family*. New York: Vantage, 1987.
Lincoln, Abraham. *Speeches and Writings, 1859–1865*. New York: Library of America, 1989.
Loux, Arthur F. *John Wilkes Booth: Day By Day*. Arthur F. Loux, 1990.
Mackey, Franklin H. *Reports of Cases Argued and Adjudged in the Supreme Court of the District of Columbia*. Washington, D.C.: Law Reporter, 1889.
Markle, Donald E. *Spies and Spymasters of the Civil War*. New York: Hippocrene, 1994.
Martenet's Map of Prince George's County, Maryland. Baltimore: Simon J. Martenet, 1861.
McHale, Charles F. *Vox New College Spanish and English Dictionary*. Lincolnwood, IL: National, 1984.
McPherson, James M. *Battle Cry of Freedom*. New York: Oxford University Press, 1988.
Miller, Edwin Haviland. *Walt Whitman: The Correspondence*. New York: New York University Press, 1961.
Mitchell, James, and Jess Stein, ed. *The Random House Encyclopedia*. New York: Random House, 1977.
Morison, Samuel Eliot, Henry Steele Commager, and William E. Leuchtenburg. *The Growth of the American Republic*. New York: Oxford University Press, 1980.
Morris, William, ed. *The American Heritage Dictionary of the English Language*. Boston: Houghton Mifflin, 1969.
Neely, Mark E. Jr., ed. *The Abraham Lincoln Encyclopedia*. New York: Da Capo, 1982.
_____. *The Fate of Liberty*. New York: Oxford University Press, 1991.
Nelson, Larry E. *Bullets, Ballots, and Rhetoric*. Tuscaloosa: University of Alabama Press, 1980.
Nott, Charles C., and Archibald Hopkins. *Cases Decided in the Court of Claims at the December Term, 1873, and the Decisions of the Supreme Court in the Appealed Cases from October, 1873, to May, 1874*. Washington: W.H. & O.H. Morrison, 1874.
Ownsbey, Betty J. *"Alias Paine": Lewis Thornton Powell, the Mystery Man of the Lincoln Conspiracy*. Jefferson, NC: McFarland, 1993.
Pearson, Henry Greenleaf. *The Life of John A. Andrew*. Boston, 1904.
Peterson, Peter D. *The Great Baltimore Fire*. Baltimore: Press of the Maryland Historical Society, 2004.
Pitman, Benn. *The Assassination of President Lincoln and the Trial of the Conspirators*. Cincinnati and New York: Moore, Wilstach & Baldwin, 1865.
Poore, Ben Perley. *The Conspiracy Trial for the Murder of the President*. Boston: J.E. Tilton, 1865.
The Pursuit and Arrest of John H. Surratt. Austin, TX: Civil War Library, 2000.
Roscoe, Theodore. *The Web of Conspiracy*. Englewood Cliffs, NJ: Prentice-Hall, 1959.
Russell, Francis. *Adams: An American Dynasty*. New York: American Heritage, 1976.
Samples, Gordon. *Lust for Fame: The Stage Career of John Wilkes Booth*. Jefferson, NC: McFarland, 1982.
Silverstone, Paul H. *Warships of the Civil War Navies*. Annapolis, MD: Naval Institute Press, 1989.
Simpson, D.P. *Cassell's Latin Dictionary*. New York: Wiley, 1977.
Soanes, Catherine, and Sara Hawker. *Compact Oxford English Dictionary of Current English*. Oxford: Oxford University Press, 2005.
Speer, Lonnie R. *Portals to Hell: Military Prisons of the Civil War*. Mechanicsburg, PA: Stackpole, 1997.

Starr, John W. *Further Light on Lincoln's Last Day: A Study of the Attendant Circumstances.* Harrisburg, PA: J.W. Starr, 1930.
Steers, Edward, Jr., and Harold Holzer, ed. *The Lincoln Assassination Conspirators.* Baton Rouge: Louisiana State University Press, 2009.
Surratt, John H. *Life and Extraordinary Adventures of John H Surratt, the Conspirator.* Philadelphia: Barclay, 1867.
———, and George Purnell Fisher. *Trial of John H. Surratt in the Criminal Court of the District of Columbia, Hon. George P. Fisher Presiding.* Washington: G.P.O., 1867.
Swanson, James L., and Daniel R. Weinburg. *Lincoln's Assassins: Their Trial and Execution; An Illustrated History.* Santa Fe, NM: Arena, 2001.
Tidwell, William A. *April '65: Confederate Covert Action in the American Civil War.* Kent, OH: Kent State University Press, 1995.
———, with James O. Hall and David Winfred Gaddy. *Come Retribution.* Jackson: University Press of Mississippi, 1988.
Towner, Ausburn. *Our County and Its People: A History of the Valley and County of Chemung from the Closing Years of the Eighteenth Century.* D. Mason, 1892.
Trindal, Elizabeth S. *Mary Surrat: An American Tragedy.* Gretna, LA: Pelican, 1996.
United States. *War of the Rebellion: A Compilation of the Official Records of the Union and Confederate Armies.* [Correspondence, Orders, Etc., Relating to Prisoners of War and State from April 1, 1864 to December 31, 1864; Series 2, Vol. 7]. Washington, DC: [s.n.], 1899.
Walton, John M., Jr. *Historical and Architectural Archaeological Research at the Surratt Dwelling House-Tavern.* Clinton, MD: Contract Archaeology, 1973.
Warner, Ezra J. *Generals in Gray.* Baton Rouge: Louisiana State University Press, 1959.
Weichmann, Louis J., and Floyd E Risvold, ed. *A True History of the Assassination of Abraham Lincoln and of the Conspiracy of 1865.* New York: Alfred A. Knopf, 1975.
Wilkinson, J. *The Narrative of a Blockade Runner.* New York: Sheldon, 1877.
Wilson, Francis. *John Wilkes Booth: Fact and Fiction of Lincoln's Assassination.* Boston: Houghton, Mifflin, 1929.
Wineapple, Brenda. *Hawthorne: A Life.* New York: Alfred A. Knopf, 2003.
Winks, Robin W. *Canada and the United States: The Civil War Years.* Baltimore: Johns Hopkins University Press, 1960.
Zanca, Kenneth J. *The Catholics and Mrs. Mary Surratt.* Lanham, MD: University Press of America, 2008.

Articles

"Arraignment of Surratt." *Washington Evening Star*, February 23, 1867.
"Arrest of John H. Surratt." *Washington Evening Star*, December 4, 1866.
"Arrival of Surratt." *Washington Evening Star*, February 18, 1867.
"Baltimore Steam Packet Company." *Old Bay Line*, April 1911.
"Baltimore: The Convention City." *Old Bay Line*, June 1913.
Barbee, David Rankin. "Interview with Dr. Reginald I. Tonry, November 13, 1931." *Surratt Courier*, April 1987.
———. "John Surratt's Ill-fated Lecture Tour." *Baltimore Sun*, December 25, 1932.
Blinn, Charles H. "How I Lost One Hundred Thousand Dollars." *Overland Monthly*, January 1912.
Bovey, Wilfrid. "Confederate Agents in Canada During the American Civil War." *Canadian Historical Review*, March 1921.
Brennan, John C. "General Bradley T. Johnson's Plan to Abduct President Lincoln." *Chronicles of St. Mary's*, November and December 1974.
Brown, Alexander Crosby. "The Old Bay Line of the Chesapeake: A Sketch of a Hundred Years of Steamboat Operation." *William and Mary College Quarterly Historical Magazine*, October 1938.
"City Intelligence." *Washington Daily Chronicle*, February 10, 1869.
Clampitt, John W. "The Trial of Mrs. Surratt." *North American Review*, September 1880.
"Col. Caleb Huse Dead." *New York Times*, March 13, 1905.
Cox, Phillis. "The Surratts' Physician: A Story of His Own." *Surratt Society News*, May 1983.
Coyle, John F. *Washington Post*, April 17, 1898.
Davis, William C. "The Conduct of Mr. Thompson." *Civil War Times Illustrated*, May 1970.
"Death Ends Long illness and Eventful Career." *Baltimore Sun*, April 22, 1916.
"Defends Mrs. Surratt." *Washington Post*, January 7, 1908.
"Directory of Agencies." *Old Bay Line*, August 1910.
Ford, John T. "Behind the Curtain of a Conspiracy." *North American Review*, April 1889.
"From Whence Cometh Surratt?" *Surratt Society News*, November 1980.
George, Joseph, Jr. "H.B. Ste. Marie and His Role in the Arrest of John H. Surratt." *Lincoln Herald* 85, no. 4 (Winter 1983): 269–279.

_____. "The Trials of John H. Surratt." *Maryland Historical Magazine* 99, no. 1 (Spring 2004): 17–49.
_____. "'A True Childe of Sorrow' Two Letters of Mary E. Surratt." *Maryland Historical Magazine* 80, no. 4 (Winter 1985): 402–405.
Gleason, D.H.L. "Conspiracy Against Lincoln." *The Magazine of History*, February 1911.
Hall, James O. "The Lady in the Veil." *Maryland Independent*, June 25, 1975.
_____, with Norman and Laura Sarratt. "Some Surratt Background." *Surratt Courier*, October 1995.
Hanchett, William. "An Interview with William Hanchett." *Journal of the Lincoln Assassination*, August 1989.
Hart, Ellen. "Descendants of Mary Surratt." *Surratt Society News*, March 1979.
Hatch, Frederick. "The Meeting at Gautier's Restaurant." *Journal of the Lincoln Assassination* 26 (2012): 2–9.
_____. "The Men Who Hanged Mary Surratt." *Journal of the Lincoln Assassination* 22 (2008): 2–20.
_____. "The One That Got Away: The Story of John H. Surratt." *Journal of the Lincoln Assassination*, April 1997.
"Helping Surratt to Escape." *New York Daily Tribune*, February 21, 1881.
Hoffecker, Carol E. "Abraham Lincoln and Delaware." *Delaware History* 32, no. 3 (Fall/Winter 2008): 155–170.
"How the Plot Against Lincoln Was Formed." *New York Times*, February 7, 1909.
Humphreys, Pamela. "Daniel Henry Lawrence Gleason, 1841–1917." *Lincoln Herald* 113, no. 2 (Summer 2011): 108–114.
"Indictment of Surratt." *New York Times*, February 5, 1867.
"Interment of the Remains of Mrs. Surratt." *Washington Daily National Intelligencer*, February 10, 1869.
"Interment Today of Remains of Isaac D. Surratt." *Washington Evening Star*, November 5, 1907.
"Isaac D. Surratt Dead." *Baltimore Sun*, 4 November 1907.
Isacsson, Alfred. "The Conspirator Who Was Not There." *Journal of the Lincoln Assassination* 24 (2010): 2–22.
_____. "The Search for John Surratt's Military Records." *Surratt Courier*, May 1990.
Jenkins, Scott. "Confederate Spy visits Elmira." *Chemung Historical Society*, March 1997.
"John H. Surratt." *New York Times*, December 8, 1870.
"John H. Surratt." *New York World*, September 3, 1867.
"John H. Surratt and the Conspiracy Against the Government." *New York Times*, November 26, 1866.
"John H. Surratt at the Cooper Institute." *New York Times*, December 10, 1870.
"John H. Surratt, His Arrest in the Ranks of the Papal Army—His Escape," *Washington Evening Star*, December 5, 1899, p. 1.
"John H. Surratt, Sole Survivor of Those Accused of Plotting to Kill Lincoln, Now a Well-to-do Citizen of Baltimore," *Springfield [MA] Daily Republican*, October 21, 1901.
"John H. Surratt's Capture," *New York Sun*, May 20, 1866.
"John H. Surratt's Story—His Connection with the Plot to Abduct President Lincoln Told for the First Time," *Washington Post*, April 3, 1898.
Johnson, Ludwell H., "Notes and Documents—Beverley Tucker's Canadian Mission, 1864–1865," *Journal of Southern History*, Vol. 29, no. 1, February 1963, pp. 88–99.
"Judge Fisher Not Assaulted," *Washington Evening Star*, July 5, 1867, p. 3.
Keller, Allan, "Canada and the Civil War," *Civil War Times Illustrated*, Vol. 3, no. 7, November 1964, pp. 49–54.
King, General Charles, "Rufus King: Soldier, Editor, and Statesman," *Wisconsin Magazine of History*, Vol. 4, no. 4, June 1921, pp. 371–81.
Koenig, Duane, "General Rufus King and the Capture of John H. Surratt," *Wisconsin Magazine of History*, Vol. 25, no. 1, September 1941, pp. 43–50.
Lange, James E. T., and Katherine De Witt, "The Gift of John Harrison Surratt, Jr.," *Surratt Courier*, Vol. 20, no. 9, September 1995, pp. 5–7.
_____, "The Three Indictments of John Harrison Surratt, Jr.," *Surratt Courier*, vol. 17, no. 1, January 1992, pp. 6–7.
Leroy, Hubert, "Ambrose Dudley Mann—Diplomat of the Lost Cause," *Confederate Historical Association of Belgium*, no date.
Levin, Alexandra Lee, "Who Hid John H. Surratt, the Lincoln Conspiracy Case Figure?" *Maryland Historical Magazine*, Vol. 60, no. 2, June 1965, pp. 175–84.
"L.J. Weichmann Goes to Rest," *Anderson [IN] Herald*, June 6, 1902.
Mandell, David, "Shuey Versus United States," *Civil War Times*, Vol. 38, no. 6, December 1999, pp. 62–5.
"Marriage of Miss Annie Surratt," *Baltimore Sun*, June 18, 1869.
McDevitt, James A., and Albert Daggett, "Tragic Memories," *Washington Evening Star*, April 14, 1894, p. 17.
"The Missing Link," *The [Baltimore] News American*, February 12, 1974, pp. 1B–2B.
"Mr. Beverley Tucker," *New York Times*, July 16, 1867.
"New Post Office," *The Planter's Advocate and Southern Maryland Advertiser*, November 1, 1854, reprinted in *Surratt Society News*, Vol. 3, no. 4, April 1978, p. 1.
Oertly, Louise, "The Financial Page," *Surratt Courier*, Vol. 34, no. 6, June 2009, p. 4.
Pilgrim, "John H. Surratt—A Talk with a Once Famous Man Who Narrowly Escaped the Scaffold—A True

Story of His Flight—He Could Have Returned Had He Thought His Mother Was in Danger," *Philadelphia Times*, October 4, 1885.
"Presentation of Medals of Honor," *Old Bay Line Magazine*, Vol. 3, no. 2, September 1912, pp. 1–3.
"Rambler Finds Another Historic Spot," *Washington Sunday Star*, September 29, 1919, p. 2.
"The Rebel Invasion," *Burlington [VT] Dailey Times*, October 21, 1864, p. 3, c. 4.
"The Remains of Mrs. Surratt," *New York Times*, February 10, 1869, p. 1.
Rice, Allen Thorndike, ed., "New Facts About Mrs. Surratt," *North American Review*, Vol. 147, no. 380, July 1888, pp. 83–94.
Smith, Rick, "An Interesting Detail," *Surratt Courier*, Vol. 29, no. 10, October 2004, p. 3.
"Sudden Death of Surratt's Captor," *New York Times*, September 12, 1874, p. 7.
"Surratt," *Baltimore Sun*, November 4, 1907, p. 4.
"Surratt," *Washington Evening Star*, January 23, 1867, p. 2.
"Surratt," *Washington Evening Star*, January 30, 1867, p. 2.
"Surratt," *Washington Evening Star*, February 11, 1867, p. 2.
Surratt, Anna, "Some Letters of Anna Surratt," ed. by Afred Isacsson, *Maryland Historical Magazine*, Vol. 54, September 1959, pp. 310–13.
Surratt, Bernice, "A Little Extra on the Surratt Genealogy," *Surratt Courier*, Vol. 20, no. 12, December 1995, p. 3.
Surratt, John H., "A Remarkable Lecture!" *Washington Evening Star*, December 7, 1870.
"The Surratt Case," *New York Times*, February 16, 1867, p. 5.
"Surratt in Washington," *Baltimore Sun*, December 31, 1870, p. 1, c. 5.
"The Surratt Indictment," *Washington Evening Star*, February 5, 1867, p. 2.
"Surratt on the Swatara," *Washington Evening Star*, January 31, 1867, p. 2.
"The Surratt Trial," *New York Times*, September 25, 1868, p. 1.
"The Surratt Trial," *Washington Evening Star*, June 10, 1867, p. 1.
"Thomas Dixon Davis," *Virginia Military Institute Alumni News*, March 1927.
Tidwell, Williams A., "Confederate Expenditures for Secret Service," *Civil War History*, Vol. 37, no. 3, September 1991, pp. 219–31.
Tierney, Rev. John J., S.S., "St. Charles College: Foundation and Early Years," *Maryland Historical Magazine*, Vol. 43, no. 4, December 1948, pp. 294–311.
Townsend, George Alfred, "Interview with Dr. George Dyer Mudd," *Cincinnati Enquirer*, April 16, 1883.
"Townsend Interviews Weichmann," *New York Tribune*, May 20, 1867.
Turner, Thomas R., "Did Weichmann Turn State's Evidence to Save Himself?" *Lincoln Herald*, Vol. 81, no. 4, Winter 1979, pp. 265–7.
Verge, Laurie, "The Surratt Mill," *Surratt Society News*, Vol. 4, no. 1, January, 1979.
_____, "What Happened to the Children?" *Surratt Society News*, Vol. 9, no. 7, July–August 1984, pp. 4–5.
"A Visit to Surratt," *New York Times*, April 8, 1867, p. 4.
Walsh, Jim, "John Surratt: A Respected Deadbeat?" *Surratt Courier*, Vol. 14, no. 4, April 1989, pp. 1, 6–7.
Wang, Harold, "A Visit to the Surratt House Boardinghouse, Washington, D.C.," *Surratt Society News*, Vol. 7, no. 8, August 1982, pp. 5–6.
"Washington Facts and Impressions," *Washington National News*, July 2, 1869.
"With the Rambler," *Washington Evening Star*, October 13, 1912.
Zanca Kenneth J., "Was Mrs. Surratt Married in the Church?" *Surratt Courier*, Vol. 28, no. 1, January 2003, pp. 5–7.

Newspapers

Alexandria [VA] Gazette
Anderson [IN] Herald
Baltimore American
Baltimore Sun
Brooklyn Eagle
Burlington [VT] Daily Times
Chicago Tribune
Cincinnati Commercial
Cincinnati Enquirer
London Times
Montreal Gazette
New York Daily Tribune
New York Herald
New York Sun
New York Times
New York World
Philadelphia Inquirer
Philadelphia Times
Springfield [MA] Daily Republican
Washington Constitutional Union
Washington Daily Morning Chronicle
Washington Evening Star
Washington National Intelligencer
Washington National News
Washington Post

Documents

Alderman Library, University of Virginia at Charlottesville
Benjamin F. Butler Papers, Library of Congress
Bureau of Military Justice Records, National Archives
Central Intelligence Agency Publications
Compiled Confederate Service Records, Microcopy 321, and 347, National Archives
Constitution of the United States of America
Copied Letter in Manuscript Book of Unknown Person, Confederate Museum, Richmond, VA
David Rankin Barbee Papers, Lauinger Library, Georgetown University
D.C. Equity Case No. 559, Washington National Records Center, Suitland, MD
D.C. Land Records, Liber JAS 70: 301–304, and Liber JAS 70: 311, et seq., Washington National Records Center, Suitland, MD
Department of Justice Archives
Department of State Records
Frederick Hatch Papers, Waldorf, MD
General List of Prisoners, Microcopy 598, National Archives
Historical Documents Under the Jurisdiction of the Clerk of the Circuit court for Prince George's County, Upper Marlboro, MD
Investigation and Trial Papers Relating to the Assassination of Abraham Lincoln, Microcopy 599, National Archives
James O. Hall Papers, Surratt Society, James O. Hall Research Center, Clinton, MD
Joseph Holt Papers, Library of Congress
Judge Advocate General's Files, War Department Records
Lee, Edwin G., Canadian Diary, unpublished. Southern Historical Collection, University of North Carolina, Chapel Hill, Microfilm Accession 1456
Letters Received by the Adjutant General, Reward Claims, Microcopy 619, National Archives
Log Book of the U.S. Screw Sloop Swatara, National Archives
Maryland Historical Society, Baltimore, MD
Montgomery County, Maryland, Historical Society, Inc.
Office of the Historian, Bureau of Public Affairs, U.S. Department of State
Postmaster General's Journal, National Archives
Postmaster's Appointment Record for N.J., Del, Md., Pa., 1857–1874, National Archives
Prince George's County, Maryland, Records
Prince George's County Stamps and Licences (1851–1854), M.H.R., Accession Number 6164, folio 17, Maryland Hall of Records, Annapolis, MD
St. Mary's Catholic Church, Baptismal Records, Rockville, MD
U.S. Congress, "Impeachment of the President," House Report 7, 40th Congress, 1st Session, 1867
War Department Archives, National Archives
William A. Tidwell Papers, Surratt Society, James O. Hall Research Center, Clinton, MD

Pamphlets, Brochures, Dissertations

Isacsson, Alfred, "A Biography of John Surratt," a dissertation submitted to the faculty of the Graduate School of Arts and Sciences of Saint Bonaventure University, New York, 1957.
Martin, Thomas Michael, "The United States Government versus John Harrison Surratt: A Study in Attitudes," a thesis submitted to the faculty of Old Dominion University, in partial fulfillment of the requirements for the degree of Master of Arts History, Old Dominion University, August 1996.
Smoot, Richard Mitchell, "The Unwritten History of the Assassination of Abraham Lincoln" (Clinton, MA: W.J. Coulter, 1908).
"The Surratt House and the Saga of Mary Surratt," brochure of the Maryland National Capital Park and Planning Commission, no date.
Verge, Laurie, and Joan Caconas, "Surratt House Museum" (Greendale, IN: The Creative Company, 1997).
"We Lived Here, Too—Slavery in Prince George's County, Maryland, 1860–1864 (Clinton, MD: Surratt House Museum, no date).

Index

Academy for Young Ladies 6–7
Adams, Charles F. 102–105
Adams, John 105
Adams, John Quincy 105
Adams Express Co 42, 45
Aiken, Frederick A. 81
Alaska 28
Albany, NY 89, 92, 183
Alexandria, Egypt 126–132
Allens Fresh 15, 16
Allet, Lt. Col. 123
Almy, William C. 187–188
Anacostia, D.C. 69
Andersonville, GA, POW camp 67
Andrew, John A. 137
Andrews Air Force Base 6
Antonelli, Giacomo 121–122, 125
Arnold, Samuel B. 40–41, 50, 52–57, 63, 68, 174
Arsenal Prison 80, 83, 171
Ashley, James M. 145–146
Atkinson, Frank H. 86
Atlantic Cable 119
Atzerodt, George A. 15, 44–46, 50–52, 54–57, 63, 69–70, 83, 88, 114, 136, 146–147, 171, 174
Augur, Christopher C. 60, 91

Baker, Lafayette C. 15, 35
Baltimore, MD 14, 19, 29, 39, 46, 48, 52–53, 68, 85, 89, 94–95, 117, 153, 170–172, 175, 178, 180, 184–185
Bannon, John 109
Barker, William N. 16
Barnes, Joseph K. 142
Barry, David 60
Barton, William S. 5, 14
Bates, David H. 62
Bates, Edward 139
Bayne, John H. 7
Beckwith, Samuel 79
Benjamin, Judah P. 30, 48, 62–63, 65–66, 87, 90, 98–99, 108–109, 111, 151, 174, 183
Bermuda 35
Bigley, Daniel R.P. 91
Bill of Rights 82
Birkenhead, UK 101
Blinn, Charles 92
Blockade of the South 27–28, 34, 45, 50, 60, 65, 96, 107, 117

Bloyce, Julia A. 24
boats for conspirators 45–46
Booth, Edwin 33, 40, 50, 64
Booth, John Wilkes: accomplices 19, 40, 46–48, 52–53, 63, 68, 72, 77, 88, 93, 136, 146, 162; acting 33, 40–41, 53, 56, 58; actions 4, 14, 65, 69; Confederate involvement 48–49, 109; escape route 79; Gautier's Restaurant 55–57; Lincoln assassination 66–68, 73, 85; Lincoln kidnapping plot 40–46, 48–58, 60, 66–67, 77, 80, 151, 173; meets John Surratt 41–44, 173, 183; oil business 94; performs with brothers 33; reward for 114; "Sam Letter" 68; visits Canada 64; watches Lincoln 52; weapons 53, 69
Booth, Junius B., Jr. 33, 40
Booth, Junius B., Sr. 40
Booth, Mary Ann 50
Boston, MA 64
Boucher, Charles 93–94, 106, 158
Boutwell, George S. 48
Boyle, Sister Bernard 6
Bradley, Abraham 140
Bradley, Joseph H. 136–137, 140, 152, 164–165, 190
Bragg, Braxton 30
Brainard, E. 38
Branson family 46
Breckinridge, John C. 110, 179
Brennan, John C. 168
Brogdon, Henry F. 62
Bromwell, William J. 31
Brophy, John P. 78, 83–84, 152
Brown, John 12, 63
Browne, Daniel J. 38
Browner, James A. 45
Browning, Orville H. 165
Bruton, George D. 133–134
Bryantown, MD 16, 18–19, 23, 41
Buchanan, William J. 95–96
Bulloch, James 111
Burlington, VT 91–2
Burnett, Henry L. 13, 46, 78
Burr, Aaron 158–159

Callahan, John 16
Calvert Family 8, 13, 20, 70, 169

Campbell Hospital 57–58
Canada 14, 19, 27–37, 40, 42, 48, 62–3, 65, 80, 85–86, 100, 108–109, 117, 137, 157, 174, 182
Canandaigua, NY 87–88, 89
Canning, Matthew W. 52
Capston, James L. 109
"Captain Booth" 109
Carland, Louis J. 152–153, 156
Carlisle, J.M. 183
Carrington, Edward C. 137, 139, 159, 162, 164–167, 191
Carroll, Charles 11
Carroll, Joseph 86
Carroll Prison 78, 156
Cass, John 85, 87, 158
Castle Thunder Prison 117
Cawood, C.H. 16
Charles County, MD 5, 11, 15, 23, 40–41, 46, 59
Charleston, SC 28
Chesapeake Steamship Co. 187–188
Chester, Samuel K. 68
China 27
Churchill, Mr. 33
Ciphers 50
Civil War, American 14, 27, 46, 65, 67, 89, 114, 132, 161, 180
Civita Vecchia, Italy 111, 129, 132
Clampitt, John W. 78–79, 79, 84, 190
Clarvoe, John A. W. 91–92
Clay, Clement C. 29, 31, 96, 150
Clayton, John M. 138
Cleary, William W. 29–37, 66, 114
Cleaver, William E. 41–42, 144, 154–155, 159–160
Clinton, MD see Surrattsville
Cobourg, Ontario 87
Colfax, Schuyler 70
Come Retribution 14, 66
Compton, Key 187–8
Confederate Canada Mission 28–37, 80, 85, 89, 108–109, 174
Confederate Secret Service 14–26, 27–37, 45–46, 48–49, 63, 109, 120, 151, 190
Conrad, Thomass N. 17, 40
Conover, Sanford see Dunham, Charles A.
Conspiracy to Assassinate Lincoln 73, 159

207

Constitutional Union (newspaper) 16
Cooper, Robert H. 142, 144
Cooper Institute 175-176
Corse, J. B. 64
Cottingham, George 79
Cotton's Value for Economy 27, 107
Coyle, John F. 69
Cuba 28
Cutter, David K. 139, 165, 167

Davis, Jefferson 17, 29-30, 80, 96, 99, 108-114, 116, 120, 151, 190
Dean, Mary A. 38, 54, 146
Declaration of Independence 11, 46
Dent, Stoughton W. 15
detectives 63, 65, 73, 88-89, 91, 99
Dewson, George 109
Dix, John A. 68
Doster, William E. 17
Douglas, Stephen A. 12, 140
Draft, Military 36-37, 39, 51
Drake, James F. 38
Duffs Texas Partisan Corps 169
Dunham, Charles A. 90, 140, 145
Dunn, Charles C. 42
Dye, Joseph M. 142, 144, 154, 167
Dyer, Jeremiah 23

Eckert, Thomas T. 79
economic issue for war 27-28, 33
Eglen, Elzee 22
Egypt 27, 126-131
Eisenschiml, Otto 118-119
Elmira, NY 66, 69, 85-88, 160, 182-183, 191
Emery, M.G. 176
Emmitsburg, MD 172-173
Emmons, H.H. 35-36
England see United Kingdom
English College see Venerable English College
"English Gentlemen" help J. Surratt 126-127
Erlanger, Emile & Co. 110
Ewing, Thomas, Jr. 21-22
execution of conspiracy suspects 84

Ferguson, James P. 88
Fillmore, Millard 139
Finotti, Joseph M. 10-11
fires at Old Bay Line offices 185-186
Fisher, George P. 137-138, 150, 157, 162-165
Fitzpatrick, Honora 38, 52, 54, 146, 155, 171
Floyd, John B. 16
Ford, John T. 78
Ford's Theatre 54, 69, 73-74, 76, 142, 146
Fort Jefferson, FL 53
Fort Leslie J. McNair 80
Fort McHenry, MD 19, 117
Fortress Monroe, VA 16, 122, 134
Foster, Lafayette S. 70

Foster, Robert S. 78
Fowle, James H. 48
Foxhall 5-7
France 27-28, 107, 110-111
Fraser, Trenholm & Co. 107-108, 111
Fredericksburg, VA 15, 49

Gaddy, David W. 41
Gautier's Restaurant 55-57
Geary, Thomas 155
Georgetown College 16, 172
Gibson, Augustus A. 9, 38
Gifford, James G. 153-154, 156
Gilliat, John K., & Co. 108
Gleason, Daniel H.L. 60, 77-78
Goldsborough, Louis M. 131, 133
Gooding, David S. 134-135
Grant, Ulysses S. 66, 73, 79
Greek Fire 33
Greeley, Horace 31-32, 166
Greenhow, Rose O. 14
Grover, Leonard 154
Grover's Theatre see National Theatre
Gwynn, Andrew 20-23
Gwynn, Bennett F. 17, 71, 136

Habeas Corpus 24, 82
Haco, Dion 168
Hale, Charles 127, 130
Hale, Edward E. 131
Hale, John P. 69
Hale, Lucy L. 69
Halifax, Canada 28-29, 168
Hall, James O. 41, 48, 64, 168
Hanchett, William 118-119
Hancock, Winfield S. 82, 84
handkerchiefs, J. Surratt's 91-92, 100
Harbin, Thomas H. 15, 17, 41, 45, 57
Harpers Ferry, WV 12
Hartranft, John F. 83-84
Harvey, Richard 171
Hawthorne, Nathaniel 104
Hay, John M. 31
Headley, John W. 34
Heim, Jacob B. 46
Henry VIII, King 112
Herold, David E. 19, 54-57, 63, 66, 69-70, 79, 81, 83, 88-89, 114, 136, 140, 171, 174
Hess, Courtland V.R. 154
Hess, Dwight 154
Hines, Thomas H. 29-30, 108
His Lordship's Kindness 6-8
Hiss, Hanson 44, 182
Hoffman, William 66-67
Holcomb, James P. 30-31, 109
Holohan, Charles E 39
Holohan, Eliza J. 39, 60
Holohan, John T. 38, 58, 63, 88, 90-92, 174
Holohan, Mary C. 39
Holt, Joseph 35, 79, 81, 83-84, 106, 117, 119, 131, 176
Hook, E.P. 190
Hooker, J. Clinton 125

Howard, John 56
Howell, Augustus S. 48-50, 60, 153
Hoyle, Annie 8
Hunter, Mary V. see Surratt, Mary V.
Hunter, Robert M.T. 29
Hunter, William 106, 116
Hurst, William B. 187-188
Huse, Caleb 107

incendiarism 33
Ingraham, Timothy I. 60, 91
Intelligence Service, Union 15
Isacsson, Alfred 112, 123, 172

Jackson, Thomas J. "Stonewall" 65
Jarber, Rachel A. 8
Jeffers, William N. 131
Jenkins, Archibald 6
Jenkins, James A. 6
Jenkins, John Z. 6, 181
Jenkins, Mary E. see Surratt, Mary E.
Jenkins, Olivia 39
Jewett, William C 31, 99
Johnson, Andrew 51, 69, 81-83, 90, 100, 140, 165, 169, 171
Johnson, Bradley T. 40
Johnson, Reverdy 14, 82
Johnson Island 33
Jolivet, Charles C. 106, 109, 179
Jones, Avonia S. 56
Jones, Evan 5
Jones, John B. 96
Jones, Thomas A. 14-15, 42
Jones, William E. 179
Juchault de Lamariciere, Christopher L.L. 113
jury at J. Surratt trial 163-165

Kauffman, Michael W. 46
Kean, Charles 95
Keith, Alexander 29
Kelly, John F. 92
Kerby, William A. 7
Key, Francis S. 177
King, Rufus 116-117, 182
King George County, VA 16
Kings Creek 45
Knights of the Golden Circle 41
Knott, Joseph 72

Lake Champlain 92
Lake Ontario 87
Lamartine, Alphonse de 168
La Pierre, Pierre 93-99, 106, 190
Leaton, S.P. 64
Lee, Edwin G. 36, 62, 64-66, 85, 87-89, 93, 98, 102, 106, 109, 155-156, 160, 174, 183
Lee, John 144
Lee, "Light Horse Harry" 65
Lee, Robert E. 65-66, 88-89, 122, 162, 180
Leonardtown, MD 47
Letcher, John 14
Lincoln, Abraham: assassination 66, 73, 80, 135; box at theatre 76; death 75; debates Douglas 12, 140;

elected president 12; guards for 60; kidnap plot 40–48, 55–57, 60, 66, 77, 80, 151, 159, 173; last public speech 66; opposition 16, 32; peace offers 31–32; watched by Booth 52; wider conspiracy against 120
Lipman, Henry 123
Little Gleaning 8
Liverpool, UK 96, 101–102, 114
Lloyd, John M. 39, 54, 57, 68–72, 76–80, 147–149, 161–162
Lodge, J. Friend 188–189
London, UK 119–120
Londonderry, UK 100
Longfellow, Charles A. 60
Longfellow, Henry W. 60
Loring, William W. 179
Lovell, John 95

Maddox, James 157
Maim, Ambrose D. 95–96, 107, 111
Malta 126, 130–132
Manning, Thomas 56–57
Marlboro, MD 16–17, 72, 148
Marsh, George P. 124
Marshall, John 158–159
Martin, M. Edward 44–45
Martin, Mary 10–11
Martin, Patrick C. 29, 40
Martin, Winfred 10–11
Mason, James M. 28, 31, 107, 109–110
Matthias Point 15–16
Maught, Conrad F. 173
Maury, John W. 38
McCullough, John 58
McDevitt, James A. 88, 91–92
McDonald, William L. 29
McGill, John 153
McMillan, Lewis J. A. 97–106, 114, 120–121, 127, 153, 157–167
McPhail, James L. 45–46
McRae, Colin J. 31, 109–110
Menu, John B. 59
Merrick, Richard T. 136, 140, 158, 160, 162, 166–167, 190
Mexico 27, 67, 96, 108, 132, 139–140
USS *Michigan* 33
Miles, John T. 56
military commissions 24, 78–79, 80–83, 89, 119, 141, 145, 163, 166
Montgomery County, MD 178
Montreal, Canada 29–37, 40, 49, 63–66, 87, 89, 92–93, 116, 144, 150, 155, 157
Morehead, Charles S. 29
Mosby, John S. 46, 49, 55
Mudd, George D. 11
Mudd, Henry L. 22–23
Mudd, Samuel A. 11, 20–26, 41–42, 57, 80–81, 148–149, 152, 183

Nagle, Sarsfield B. 157
Naples, Italy 126
Napoleon I 107, 112
Nassau, Bahamas 28
National Hotel 52, 73

National Theatre 52, 154
Navy, U.S. 28
Navy Yard 42, 132–134
Navy Yard Bridge 55
Neale, Richard 6–7
Neale, Sarah 6–7
Neve, Frederick 112, 127, 129
New York City 33, 48–49, 59, 63–64, 68, 85, 119–120, 175, 185
Niagara Falls 29
Norfolk, VA 180, 185, 187
Norris, William 14–15, 170
Nota, Father 11
Nothey, John H. 69–71

O'Beirne, James R. 158
O'Laughlen, Michael 40, 50, 52–53, 63, 68, 174
Old Bay Line 178–180, 182, 184–191
Old Capitol Prison 17, 60, 77–78, 82
Old Northwest 32
Olin, Abram B. 139, 165, 167
Ontario Bank, Montreal 40, 90, 109
Oratory of the Holy Cross Roman Catholic Church (Liverpool) 104, 106, 109
Our American Cousin 154
Oxon Hill 10
Oxon Hundred 5

Papal Army 113, 116
Papal States 113
Paris, France 111, 187
Parr, David P. 46–48, 52
"Pasture and Gleaning" 7–9, 38
Payne, Lewis *see* Powell, Lewis T.
SS *Peruvian* 96, 98
Petersen House 75
Philadelphia, PA 91, 185
Pierce, Franklin 104
Pierre, Andre J., la 95
Pierrepont, Edwards 139, 157, 160–161
Piles, John V. 50–51
"Pilgrim," 181–182
Pius IX, Pope 112, 122
Point Lookout, MD 67
Pope's Creek 15–16
Port Tobacco, MD 15, 42, 45–46, 60
Porterfield, John 33, 64–65, 90, 92, 96, 100
Potomac River 14–19, 42, 45, 49, 55, 63
Potter, John F. 92–93, 106, 114
Powell, Lewis T. 46, 48, 50, 52, 54–57, 60, 63, 66, 72–73, 79, 81, 83–84, 88, 105–106, 114, 136, 146, 171, 174
presidential succession 69–70
Prince George's County, MD 5–8, 38, 42, 45, 69, 73, 136, 181
prisoner of war camps 50, 66, 85, 88, 183

Quebec, Canada 14, 29, 64, 95–96, 98, 116
Queen, William 40–41

Radical Republicans 165
Ramsay, George D. 171
Rathbone, Henry R. 142
Reading, Frank R. 16
reasonable doubt 161
Reeves, John J. 93
rewards 88–89, 102, 114–115, 117, 120, 157
Richards, Almarin C. 87, 91
Richmond, VA 15, 18, 29, 41–43, 45–46, 60–66, 68, 71, 85, 96, 98, 120, 126, 148, 150–151, 153, 174
Riddle, Albert G. 139–140
Ridenour, J.W. 80
Ripley, Riswell S. 96, 190
Risorgimento 113
Robinson, John M. 179
Roby, Andrew V. 20, 170
Roby, Edward 169
Robystown, MD *see* Surrattsville
Rochester, NY 87
Rockville, MD 172–173, 175, 178
Rome, Italy 106, 109, 111
Ross, H.M. 94
Rosser, Thomas L. 65
Rost, Pierre A. 107
Ruse, Caleb 110

St. Albans, VT 34–35, 89–92, 184
St. Charles College 11–12, 17
St. Lawrence Hall 29, 40, 64–65, 89, 92, 144
St. Marie, Henri B. 8–19, 116–132, 133–134, 137, 150, 157–158, 167, 182
St. Mary's Catholic Church, Alexandria, VA 6
St. Mary's County, MD 15
St. Matthew's Institute 18–19
St. Peter's Church, Washington, DC 7
St. Thomas Manor 11
"Sam Letter" 68
Sanders, George N. 29, 40, 65, 90, 114
Sarratt, Francis 5
Sarratt, Joseph 5
Sarratt, Kathrine 5
Schoepf, Gen. 16
Seaboard Air Line Railway 186
secret line 14, 42, 45
Seddon, James A. 30
Severens, Joe 16
Seward, Frederick W. 106
Seward, William H. 16, 28, 35, 69–70, 73, 85, 114, 116–119, 122, 127, 157
Sharp, Joshua W. 60, 87–89, 103, 106
Sharpe, George H. 98, 111
Sheridan, Philip H. 169
Sherwood, John R. 187, 191
shooting irons 54, 69–71, 76–77, 79, 147–148, 162
Sicotte, Louis W. 157–158
Simms, Mary 20–26
Simms, Milo 22–23, 26
Sisters of Charity 6–7
Slater, Rowan 49

Slater, Sarah A. 36, 49, 51–52, 60–64
slavery 6–8, 12, 17–24, 27–28, 31–32, 44, 70
Slidel, John 28, 31, 107, 109–111
Smith, Edmund K. 169
Smoot, Richard M. 45
Sons of Liberty 32
Spangler, Edman 57, 80–81
Speed, James 83, 114, 150
Stabler, Brooke 60, 146
Stanton, Edwin M.: assassination investigation headed by 74; intimidated witnesses 78; kidnap plot revealed 60; orders issued by 24, 35, 67–68, 88–89, 106, 115; rumored to be assassinated 73; Surratt recommended 20; testimony 116; trials, involvement in 21, 83
Starr, Ella 52
Stewart & Ufford 86
Stone, Elizabeth L. 13
Stone, Frederick 46
Stone, Thomas 46
Sulpician Society 11
Supreme Court of District of Columbia 139
Supreme Court, U.S. 82
Surratt, Elizabeth S. "Anna" 7, 10–12, 19, 38, 52, 59, 67, 81, 83, 98, 136, 138–139, 150, 168, 170–172, 181, 184, 189
Surratt, Ella K. 178
Surratt, Isaac D. 7, 10–11, 13, 150, 158, 169–170, 181, 184, 189
Surratt, John H., Jr.: aliases 36, 60, 62, 64, 66, 87–88, 90, 94, 97, 116, 120, 123, 126–127, 174; birth 7; books about 168; Confederate courier 14–26, 36, 48, 120, 142; death 191; description 12, 20, 64, 86, 89, 92–94, 137, 182–183, 188–189; detectives search for 63, 174; disguises 19, 96, 130; education 10–11; Elmira, NY, spy mission 66, 69, 85–86; employment sought 20, 42; escape 123–130; finances 45, 50, 62–63, 87, 90, 95, 98–99, 102–111, 134, 151, 168, 170, 174, 183; friend of Dr. Mudd 20–26; Gautier's Restaurant meeting 55–57; handkerchief 91–92, 100; health 36, 92–94, 133, 159; lectures 44, 173–177, 191; meets Booth 41–44, 173, 183; meets Weichmann 12; Old Bay Line employment 179–180, 182–183; passport 98; personality 11–12; postmaster 14, 19–20; reward offered 89, 114–115, 117; rumored to be assassin of Seward 73, 88; school teacher 172–173; service in Zouaves 113, 116, 123, 130, 159, 168, 175, 182; threatens to kill A. Johnson 100; trial 42–43, 47, 71–72, 81, 85–86, 99, 136–166, 183; transfers property 44, 51; voyage across Atlantic 98–112; weapons brought to tavern 54

Surratt, John H., Sr. 5–13, 17, 38, 44, 69
Surratt, John H., III 178, 184
Surratt, Leo J. 178, 184
Surratt, Mary Elizabeth (mother of J. Surratt, Jr.): birth and childhood 6–13; burial 171; conspiracy 44, 57, 68, 70–72, 76–77, 80, 84, 136, 174; description 17, 19, 81; education 6–7; execution 83–84, 120, 182; financial problems 168–169; petition for clemency 83; trial 44, 49, 78, 80–85, 119–120, 137–149, 166
Surratt, Mary Eugenia (daughter of J. Surratt, Jr.) 178
Surratt, Mary V. (daughter of J. Surratt, Jr.) 178
Surratt, Mary V. (wife of J. Surratt, Jr.) 178, 184, 191
Surratt, Susana S. 178
Surratt, William H. 178, 184, 189–190
Surratt Boarding House, Washington, DC 9, 16, 23–25, 38–39, 47, 78, 143, 146, 169, 174
Surratt family 5–13, 38, 189
Surratt Tavern 8–9, 14–18, 42, 47–48, 51, 54, 68, 79, 147, 169
Surrattsville, MD 10, 14–15, 17, 46–48, 51, 54, 68, 70–71, 79, 147, 170
Swan, Frank 126–127
USS *Swatara* 132–133, 182
Sweeny, Hugh B. 38

Taylor, G.T. 67
Taylor, Richmond 169
T.B., MD 54, 145, 147
Texas 108
Texas, MD 18, 117
Thomas' Inheritance 5
Thompson, Jacob 29–37, 40, 62, 64–66, 89–90, 96, 108–111, 114, 127, 150, 155, 174
Thompson, John C. 40–41
Tidwell, William A. 35, 41, 59
Tilly, Joseph F. du 93, 158
Tonry, Albert S. 172
Tonry, Catherine 172
Tonry, Charles S. 172
Tonry, Reginald 172, 189
Tonry, William P. 171–173, 175, 181, 189
Tonry, William S. 172, 189
Toronto, Canada 30, 87, 94–95
Townsend, Edward 114
Townshend, Jeremiah 8–9, 13
Treadway, Alfred 38
Treadway, William H. 38
Trenholm, George A. 107
Trent Affair 28, 107, 110
trial of conspiracy suspects (1865) 13, 21, 42–44, 46–47, 49, 68–69, 78, 80–83, 119–120, 137, 141, 145, 166
trial of John Surratt (1867) 43, 47, 71–72, 81, 85–86, 99, 136–166, 183
Tucker, Nathaniel B. 96, 99, 104, 114
Twain, Mark 176–177

Uniontown, D.C. 68
United Kingdom 27–28, 107, 111–112, 118

Venerable English College (Rome) 112, 114, 116
Venice Preserved 67
Villefranche, France 133
Vittorio Emanuele, King 113

Wadsworth, James S. 17
Waldron, E.Q.S. 17
Walker, Jonathan T. 38
Walker, N.S. 109
Wallace, James Watson *see* Dunham, Charles A.
Walter, Jacob A. 83–84, 171–172, 176
War of 1812 5
Ward, Annie 67
Washington, Lucius Q. 62
Washington, Melvina 22
Washington, D.C. 15, 17–18, 41, 63, 86, 175, 185
Watson, Roderick D. 58–59
Webster, Elizabeth A. 6, 181
Weed, Thurlow 122
Weichmann, Louis J.: confides in Gleason 60; description 60–61; detectives helped by 91–92, 131; early life 12; friendship with Surratts 18–26, 38, 42, 59, 63, 68; hearing problems 43, 69, 71, 76, 140; letter to "Clara" 59; meets John Surratt 12, 17; pro–Southern 18, 50, 153; questionable accounts 43, 71–78, 80, 119, 148–149, 156–157, 159, 174, 183; Surratt house boarder 38–39; teaching career 18, 116
Weighel, Samuel 5
Weir, B. & Co. 29
Westmoreland County, VA 16
White, J.A. 64
Whitman, Walt 150
Wiget, Bernardine 11, 84
Wilding, Henry J. 101–106
Wilks, Charles 28
Wilmington, NC 28
Wilson, Francis 43–44
Wilson, James F. 118
Wilson, Nathaniel 139
Winder, John H. 117
Winthrop, William 126–128, 130
Wise, Henry H. 11, 179
Wood, Mr. or Reverend *see* Powell, Lewis T.
Wood, William P. 77–78
Wylie, Andrew B. 82, 139, 165–167

Yancy, William L. 107
Yellow Fever Plot 35
Young, Bennett H. 34
Young, Miss 95

Zanca, Kenneth 14
Zechiah Swamp 41
Zouaves 113, 116, 123, 130–131, 175, 182–183

www.ingramcontent.com/pod-product-compliance
Ingram Content Group UK Ltd.
Pitfield, Milton Keynes, MK11 3LW, UK
UKHW050702160426
5217IPUK00038B/1836